From Tellers to Sellers

From Tellers to Sellers

Changing Employment
Relations in Banks

edited by Marino Regini,
Jim Kitay, and Martin Baethge

The MIT Press
Cambridge, Massachusetts
London, England

This book was set in Palatino by Asco Typesetters, Hong Kong.

Printed and bound in the United States of America.

Library of Congress Cataloging-in-Publication Data

From tellers to sellers : changing employment relations in banks /
  edited by Marino Regini, Jim Kitay, and Martin Baethge.
     p.   cm.
  Includes bibliographical references and index.
  ISBN 0-262-18193-2 (hardcover : alk. paper)
  1. Bank management. 2. Banks and banking—Personnel management.
3. Bank employees. 4. Banks and banking—Labor productivity.
I. Regini, Marino, 1943–   . II. Kitay, Jim. III. Baethge, Martin.
HG1615.F76   1999
332.1'068'3—dc21   99-25719
                                                           CIP

Contents

Preface   vii
Contributors   xi

I   **Introduction**   1

1   Managerial Strategies, Human Resource Practices, and Labor Relations in Banks: A Comparative View   3
    Martin Baethge, Jim Kitay, and Ida Regalia

II   **Country Studies**   31

2   Market Challenges and Changing Employment Relations in the U.S. Banking Industry   33
    Brent Keltner and David Finegold

3   Change in Tandem: Employment Relations in Australian Retail Banks   63
    Jim Kitay

4   Employment Relations in the New Zealand Banking Industry   95
    Erling Rasmussen and Andrea Jackson

5   Employment Relations in U.K. Banking   129
    John Storey, Adrian Wilkinson, Peter Cressey, and Tim Morris

6   Institutional Innovation and Market Challenges: Changing Employment Relations in the Italian Banking Sector   159
    Marino Regini, Simonetta Carpo, Asher Colombo, and Marco Trentini

7   French Banks: Between Deregulation and State Control   187
    Marnix Dressen (translation by Edgar Blaustein)

8   Employment Relations in the Spanish Banking Industry: Big
    Changes   223
    Faustino Miguélez, Carlos Prieto, and Cecilia Castaño

9   Corporate Strategy, Institutions, and Employment Relations in Dutch
    Banking   255
    Jelle Visser and Pieter-Jan Jongen

10 The End of Institutional Stability? The German Banking Industry in
    Transition   287
    Martin Baethge, Nestor D'Alessio, and Herbert Oberbeck

III Conclusions   317

11 Comparing Banks in Advanced Economies: The Role of Markets,
    Technology, and Institutions in Employment Relations   319
    Marino Regini

    Index   331

Preface

This book presents research findings on the changing nature of employment relations in the retail banking industry in nine OECD countries from the early 1980s to the late 1990s. Although changes have swept through most industries in these countries, few examples can match the profound transformation of retail banks from stolid, strictly regulated organizations epitomizing lifetime employment to highly competitive enterprises with fragmented career structures and a new focus on sales and performance. The changes to banking, as a major employer of labor, have significant implications for the job opportunities and workplace experiences of a significant proportion of the workforce in OECD and newly industrialized countries.

The chapters in this book are the outcome of intensive study of selected banks in Australia, France, Germany, Great Britain, Italy, the Netherlands, New Zealand, Spain, and the United States. As part of a wider project on industrial relations and human resources management practices, a network of researchers in each country used a common research framework to explore the changing industry context and competitive strategies in relation to a number of key employment relations practices. The research focused on changes in such human resources practices as skill formation and development, work organization, staffing arrangements and job security, and compensation. An additional key area was industrial relations policies and enterprise governance, including employee involvement practices as well as relationships between management and trade unions. Throughout the volume, this complex set of human resources management and industrial relations policies will be referred to as HR/IR practices.

The main objectives of the research were to explore the nature of the HR/IR practices in one industry in different countries and to examine the extent to which management strategies or institutional factors such as public policies and trade union activities influence the patterns of stability or change.

The chapters on the various countries are based on detailed research on employment relations practices in selected enterprises in each country. Scholars associated with an international study of changing industrial relations and human resource management in OECD and newly industrialized countries conducted the research on which the chapters are based. Initiated by researchers at the Massachusetts Institute of Technology, the project was conducted primarily within networks in the automobile, steel, telecommunications, and banking industries (Katz 1997; Kochan, Lansbury, and MacDuffie 1997; Verma, Kochan, and Lansbury 1995). These industry studies were borne out of a common framework first put to test in comparing developments in employment relations at the national, economy-wide level (Locke, Kochan, and Piore 1995).

A broad research agenda was set for the project as a whole (Kochan and Piore 1990; MIT Research Team 1991), with details worked out within the industry networks. Although the inspiration for the project arose from controversies surrounding works such as Kochan, Katz, and McKersie 1986 and Piore and Sabel 1984, the participants in the networks brought to bear a range of perspectives on the nature and sources of stability and change. The international networks focused on a specific set of industrial relations and human resources management practices as potential windows on the extent to which changes had occurred in enterprises in different countries, and sought to determine the relative influence of management strategies and institutional pressures.

In pursuing these issues, the research protocol called for the study of a small number of enterprises in each industry in each country. This approach, rather than a survey methodology, was considered to be most appropriate for gathering the detailed information necessary to understand the nature of changes taking place in workplace practices as well as the strategies and motivations of managements and unions. It was felt that strategies and motivations in particular would best be addressed in this manner and that this approach would also provide insight into the way the practices had developed over time. Indeed, if significant change or a "transformation" has occurred, it would be impossible to discuss this without placing the enterprise in historical perspective.

The banking industry network met on three occasions in 1994 and 1995, at which meetings a common framework of research questions and procedures were adopted. The researchers in each country were responsible for studying at least three—and preferably four or more—banks. The objective was not a survey of the field in each country, but rather an in-depth examination of enterprises selected to allow an assessment of which employment relations strategies were being applied and the reasons why these practices had been adopted. The primary research instrument was in-depth interviews conducted with managers, employees, and union and government officials, supplemented by documentary material. Details on the methods used in each country can be found in the individual chapters.

The chapters provide detailed analysis of the findings in the nine countries participating in the international banking network. Each chapter contains extensive material on the context of the banking industry, labor and product markets, competitive strategies, and the key HR/IR practices—work organization, skill formation, staffing arrangements and job security, and compensation—as well as industrial relations policies and enterprise governance.

The introductory chapter provides an overview of the main findings from the research and introduces the individual country studies that follow. In the concluding chapter, we assess the role of markets, technology, and institutions in employment relations and discuss the interpretive frameworks that help make sense of their change and variation across countries.

We wish to thank the Hans Boeckler Foundation, Düsseldorf (Germany) and IRES Lombardia (Italy) for hosting and supporting two meetings of the banking industry network, in Berlin and Milan respectively. We also wish to thank the University of Trento for providing resources to coordinate the research project.

References

Katz, H. (ed.). (1997). *Telecommunications: Restructuring Work and Employment Relations Worldwide*. Ithaca, NY: ILR Press.

Kochan, T. A., H. Katz, and R. McKersie. (1986). *The Transformation of American Industrial Relations*. New York: Basic Books.

Kochan, T. A., R. D. Lansbury, and J. P. MacDuffie (eds.). (1997). *After Lean Production: Evolving Employment Practices in the World Auto Industry*. Ithaca, NY: Cornell University Press.

Kochan, T. A., and M. Piore. (1990). "Proposal for Comparative Research on Industrial Relations and Human Resource Policy and Practice." Unpublished manuscript, Massachusetts Institute of Technology, Cambridge, MA.

Locke, R., T. Kochan, and M. Piore (eds.). (1995). *Employment Relations in a Changing World Economy*. Cambridge: MIT Press.

MIT Research Team. (1991). "Working Paper on Comparative Industrial Relations Project." Unpublished manuscript, Massachusetts Institute of Technology, Cambridge, MA.

Piore, M., and C. Sabel. (1984). *The Second Industrial Divide*. New York: Basic Books.

Verma, A., T. Kochan, and R. Lansbury (eds.). (1995). *Employment Relations in the Growing Asian Economies*. London: Routledge.

Contributors

Editors

Marino Regini is Professor at the Institute of Labour Studies, Faculty of Political Sciences, University of Milan, Italy.

Jim Kitay is Senior Lecturer in the Department of Industrial Relations, Faculty of Economics, University of Sydney, Australia.

Martin Baethge is Co-Director of SOFI and Professor at the Department of Sociology, University of Göttingen, Germany.

Other Contributors

Ida Regalia, University of Turin (Italy)

Brent Keltner, RAND (USA)

David Finegold, University of Southern California (USA)

Erling Rasmussen and **Andrea Jackson,** University of Auckland (New Zealand)

John Storey, Open University (UK)

Adrian Wilkinson, UMIST (UK)

Peter Cressey, University of Bath (UK)

Tim Morris, London Business School (UK)

Simonetta Carpo, Asher Colombo, and **Marco Trentini,** Ires Lombardia (Italy)

Marnix Dressen, Conservatoire National des Arts et Metiers, Paris (France)

Fausto Miguélez, Autonomous University of Barcelona (Spain)

Carlos Prieto and **Cecilia Castaño,** University of Madrid (Spain)

Jelle Visser and **Pieter-Jan Jongen,** University of Amsterdam (The Netherlands)

Nestor D'Alessio and **Herbert Oberbeck,** SOFI Göttingen (Germany)

I Introduction

1

Managerial Strategies, Human Resource Practices, and Labor Relations in Banks: A Comparative View

Martin Baethge, Jim Kitay, and Ida Regalia

It is evident from the national reports in this book that banks throughout the OECD are experiencing a profound transformation unleashed by deregulation, privatization, and technological change, that affects not only the way bank business is conducted but also traditional employment practices and systems of industrial relations. Twenty years ago, commercial and savings banks were highly bureaucratic organizations whose prevalent business activities were to take deposits, give credits, and organize the payment system within highly protected and compartmentalized national markets. Today, banks are transforming into more flexible organizations that offer a wide range of products, including deposits, credits, payment systems, insurance, credit cards, cash management, and pension and mutual funds. They are exposed to increasing levels of competition within deregulated international and national markets.

The Changing Industry Context

The adjustment process to the new rules of the game is not easy. Bailout mergers and the state's rescue of financially strapped institutions have accompanied the transformation of banking in several countries. These dramatic episodes, in addition to ordinary mergers and acquisitions, new business strategies for a more competitive environment, and the increasing use of technology, have placed traditional banking organization, employment practices, and industrial relations institutions under strain.

However, the presence of common elements in the transformation of the banking industries in OECD countries does not mean that national differences have ceased to exist. As the national reports show, the degree of concentration within the industry and the intensity of competition differ considerably from country to country. Furthermore, the national financial systems have distinctive organizational models and functions. Finally, the systems of industrial relations in which the banks are embedded continue to be different.

It has become commonplace in the banking literature to discuss the changes transforming banking either in terms of the "convergence" hypothesis, which stresses the common elements observed in the transformation process, or from the point of view of the "persistence" of distinctive national patterns. Both approaches have merit, although each runs the risk of oversimplification. Thus it would be wrong to think of convergence as a process that leads to "one best practice." As a reading of the national reports shows, the changes across countries bear considerable resemblance, though they do not suggest a convergence to a single model or best practice. The evidence suggests rather the existence of national patterns that are influencing the concrete way in which the adjustment processes take place. At the same time, given the transitional character of the transformation process, the identification of national patterns does not permit a definitive judgment about how they will shape the design of the banking industry in each case.

Deregulation, Competition, and Concentration

With the exception of Germany, where the deregulation process began as early as the late 1950s, the banking industries of the other countries remained highly regulated at the beginning of the 1970s. Banking was separated from the insurance and securities businesses, conducted by insurance companies and brokerage houses, respectively. Normally the central banks in each country defined the kind of business the different categories of banks were permitted to conduct. Cooperative and savings banks had a particular status within the banking systems. In countries like Australia, France, Italy, New Zealand, and Germany, public banks played an important role in allocating financial resources. In several countries, the entry of foreign banks was strictly regulated, and the opening of new branches by the domestic banks required the permission of the central bank. The interest rate ceilings and trading prices for different lines of business were controlled as well.

The consequence of the regulatory framework was a high degree of compartmentalization of the financial markets as well as a low level of competition. Every category of financial institution—commercial banks, savings banks, public banks, insurance companies, and brokerage houses —conducted its business in its own segment, and regulated prices generally assured their viability. Exceptions like the subsidies required for public banks running at a deficit only confirmed the rule. Being a banker or a broker was a comfortable job in the world of regulated financial markets.

High inflation, the abandonment of fixed foreign exchange rates, the adjustment of the national production systems to new price relations, and the increasing internationalization of the bank business in the 1970s as a result of the external shocks produced by the demise of the Bretton Woods monetary system and the two oil crises put the financial systems of the industrialized countries (and their banks) under strain. A growing volume of nonperforming assets resulting from the international debt crises and speculative financial transactions, along with the surge of new financial actors such as mutual funds, credit card companies, and quasi banks, which were not subjected to the constraints of bank regulations, affected banks' competitive position in the 1980s. In this new business context, the traditional regulation frameworks became obsolete, and financial deregulation accelerated in all the industrialized countries.

Taking into account national peculiarities, deregulation had two primary goals: first, the abolition of rules that gave competitive advantages to certain categories of financial companies to the detriment of others; second, the stimulation of competition among banks as well as between the banks and other financial actors. In this sense, the new rules were designed to strengthen banks' position, licensing them to conduct new business as well as forcing them to control their costs through more intense competition.

The national reports show that business diversification, greater competition, and cost reduction practices have occurred everywhere as a result of the deregulation process. Banks have expanded their activities to include securities, insurance, mutual funds, and credit cards. Savings banks transformed to full banks in Great Britain, Holland, Spain, and Australia. With the exception of Germany, where the public banks continue to have a strong market position, privatization of public banks took place in Australia, France, Italy, and New Zealand. The abolition of regulations concerning interest rates was another factor that increased competition.

Such abrupt changes as those deregulation produced necessarily affected the structures of national banking industries. The number of banks peaked between 1980 and 1985, followed by a decrease in all the countries investigated. Australia (−54%) and France (−43%) registered the sharpest drops, followed by Germany (−35%), the United States (−34%) and Great Britain (−30%); the decreases in Spain (−16%), Italy (−15%) and Holland (−13%) were relatively modest (table 1.1). An intensive process of mergers and acquisitions, which in several cases included state-supported bailout

Table 1.1
Changes in the number of banks and branches (1980/1995), assets concentration, and number of inhabitants per branch and ATM

Country	Number of banks			Number of branches (in thousands)			Assets concentration[2]		Inhabitants per branch 1995	Inhabitants per ATM/case 1991
	1980	1995	Changes in %[1]	1980	1995	Changes in %[1]	1980	1995		
United States	35,875	23,854	−34	58.3	69.6 (1994)	—	14	21	3,704	2,987
Germany[3]	5,335	3,487	−35	39.3	37.9	−5	—	28	1,850	5,840
France	1,033	593	−43	24.3 (1986)	25.5	−2	69	63	2,254	3,508
Italy	1,071	941	−12	12.2	23.9	—	42	45	2,389	4,995
Great Britain	796	560	−30	20.4	16.6 (1994)	−22	80	78	3,487	3,240
Australia	812	370	−54	6.3 (1987)	6.7	−6	80	79	2,626	—
The Netherlands	200	174	−13	6.6 (1981)	7.3 (1994)	−14	69	83	2,095	4,502
Spain	357	318	−11	25.8	36.0	—	58	62	1,097	—

Sources: Bank for International Settlements, Arthur D. Little, own calculations.
Notes: The table includes commercial, savings, and cooperative banks. Number of branches without credit cooperatives in the cases of the United States and Australia.
1. The changes are related to the peak level the banks have reached between 1980/1995.
2. Share of the ten largest banks by total bank assets.
3. Only West Germany.

mergers, led to this decline. Profitability problems and cost-cutting strategies as well as efforts to increase market share seem to be driving the mergers and acquisitions. A general tendency toward a higher degree of concentration within the national industries has resulted, and as the recent mega-mergers in the United States testify, the process has not yet come to an end (table 1.1).

Despite the common elements associated with deregulation in the various countries, national differences persist. Whereas banks in the United States must compete with financial actors that have penetrated their core markets, in some other countries banks remain at the center of the financial system. This is the case in Holland, where the banks have adopted a strategy of neutralization of outsiders through cooptation, or in Australia or Germany, where the banks retain control of their core markets.

The Critical Role of Technology

Since at least the 1960s, technology has changed the face of banking, and the industry today is unthinkable without technology. Information technology first attracted bankers because it enables administrative work to be performed more quickly and accurately. Later the development of databases of customers' relationships with the bank permitted the banks to develop cross-selling strategies and to expand their business activities. Banks offered a wider range of products and services following deregulation, and technology helped them handle the growing volume of transactions more efficiently.

Today, banks are trying to improve the internal application of technology as well as developing new delivery channels. As the national reports indicate, the standardization of products, the automation of procedures, the development of new credit-scoring programs, the organization of internal data transfers, and the centralization of processing tasks away from branches have priority in several of the banks investigated. At the same time, banks are vigorously pursuing alternative delivery channels such as the introduction of ATMs and home and telephone banking services.

However, technology confronts the banks with a range of problems with no clear solutions, two of which we mention here. First, there are growing pressures to keep costs to a minimum. Although technology helps to cut costs, it is itself a cost, and not all banks can afford to keep up with the technological race. Increasing technological costs affecting banks' viability are mentioned as one of the reasons for merger and acquisitions.

In some countries, like Italy and Germany, cooperative technological innovations have been introduced that minimize costs.

The second problem involves the mix between self-service and personal contact in branches. Technology contributes to higher productivity in banks and reduces the costs of a work-intensive industry. However, particularly in retail banking, the use of new technology can also damage the business, as when banks do not find the right balance between self-service and personal contact with clients. Despite the growing importance of ATMs and home and telephone banking as delivery channels, not only do clients continue to prefer branches and personal contact, but they also play a central role in the shift toward a sales focus for retail staff. Against this background, it can be a high-risk strategy for a bank to reduce its number of branches sharply, because this might lead to a loss of clients. Maintaining a large number of costly branches might be risky as well, however, if their profitability is not sustained.

There are no general criteria that enable individual banks to establish the most appropriate mix between personal contact in branches and self-service via other delivery channels. As the national reports suggest, banks in every country are trying to find their own solutions, shaped by their business strategies and the national peculiarities of their service cultures. The most widely used strategy for reducing the uncertainties associated with the restructuring process involves the segmentation of client markets. This includes making distinctions such as high net worth and mass sectors in personal banking, and large, medium, and small sectors in business banking. Branch structures and other delivery mechanisms are then devised to cater to different requirements according to such criteria as cost-effectiveness and developing market share. In essence, banks are seeking to channel less profitable mass market transactions into less costly electronic mechanisms, while reserving personal contact for developing new business or catering to the needs of their major personal and business customers.

A general tendency toward a reduction in the number of bank branches can be detected in the industrialized countries, although this is not homogeneous. The number of branches has decreased in all countries investigated with the exceptions of Italy, Spain, and the United States. Great Britain (−22%) and Holland (−14%) have experienced sharp reductions from peak levels, with Australia (−6%), Germany (−5%) and France (−2%) undergoing more modest reductions. At the same time, the Continental countries are showing an increasing trend toward self-service; the number of ATMs/cash dispensers there has grown noticeably in recent years (table 1.1).

Pressures on Employment Levels and Personnel Costs

Not surprisingly, increasing competition, profitability problems, mergers and acquisitions, and the massive use of technology have had consequences for employment levels and personnel costs.

With regard to employment levels, the banking industry in the industrialized countries seems to have fallen from its peak. Employment in banking has decreased in all countries. Even Germany, which was an exception until 1995, has recently experienced a slight reduction in bank employment. However, whereas Great Britain, Australia, and the United States have registered a significant decline in employment, the reduction has been less marked in France, Spain, and Italy (table 1.2). In contrast to the decrease in the number of banks, a process that started at the beginning of the 1980s, the drop in employment did not begin to accelerate until the end of the decade as a series of adjustment crises took place in banking.

Even though a reduction in personnel costs (as share of income) coincides with a decrease in the employment in all the countries investigated except Germany, it is nevertheless not easy to determine exactly which variables have effected the changes, as a comparison of the cases of France and Germany shows (table 1.2). Whereas personnel costs have decreased in Germany from 48 percent in 1980–82 to 39 percent in 1992–94 without a reduction (and in fact a gain) in employment, personnel costs in France decreased only from 47 percent to 44 percent in the same period despite a decrease in employment of 5 percent. To what extent business strategies, the use of technology, organizational structure, or the systems of industrial relations contribute to these differences is therefore difficult to establish. Even in the case of the United States, it would not be convincing to assert that the weakness in the U.S. system of industrial relations is the only reason it has the lowest personnel costs among the industrialized countries.

Patterns of Human Resource Management

The chapters in this book reveal that work in banks has undergone significant change over the last two decades. A number of changes appear to be common to most countries, though a range of variations can be identified both between and within countries. In all cases, the twin processes of deregulation and technological change have influenced work in banks and

Table 1.2
Employment and personnel costs

Country	Employment (in thousands)[1]		Changes (in %)[2]	Personnel costs[3] (in % of gross proceeds)	
	1980	1994		1980–82	1992–94
United States	1,900	1,891	−12.0	36	27
Germany[4]	533	658	—	48	39
France	399 (1985)	382	−5.0	47	44
Italy	277	332 (1995)	−0.3	46	44
Great Britain	324	368	−15.0	47	36
Australia	265 (1984)	311	−13.0	—	—
The Netherlands	113 (1984)	112	−6.0	42	38
Spain	252 (1981)	245 (1995)	−4.0	47	37

Source: Bank for International Settlements.
Notes:
1. Without credit cooperatives in the case of the United States. Includes all sectors of finance industry in the case of Australia.
2. Changes are related to the peak level of employment between 1980 and 1994.
3. Only commercial banks.
4. Only West Germany.

the ways banks are structured. A combination of organizational and institutional factors appear to influence how these processes affect banking in different countries and individual banks within countries.

Deregulation and the accompanying increase in competition have significantly affected the banking industry. Although deregulation has allowed banks greater flexibility in setting fees and interest rates, it has exerted a downward pressure on profit margins, particularly in corporate banking. In conjunction with a proliferation of vehicles for investment, banks have placed considerable emphasis on cost reduction. At the same time, banks have shifted away from a transaction-based organizational model toward a sales and service orientation. This shift has various facets, including a diversification of delivery channels for bank products; product market segmentation; and the redefinition of customer interaction away from processing transactions toward "sales opportunities". Both cost reduction and the sales culture have relied on the availability of computerization and telecommunications links. However, institutional arrangements, particularly labor regulations, as well as corporate history have affected the trajectories of different countries and of individual banks within countries.

Work Organization and Enterprise Structure

Among the changes to work organization and organizational structure that have taken place in most countries are the allocation of different market segments to different groups of employees, the removal of many processing tasks from branches and the specialization of large numbers of staff in either sales or processing, and the downgrading of branches and the proliferation of delivery systems. Additionally, branch operating hours have increased, and there is evidence as well of work intensification.

Perhaps the most noticeable change to retail banking has been the long-term transition of branches from largely autonomous sites that catered to the full range of banking needs of all but large, corporate clients to more tightly controlled sales outlets that are but one of a number of delivery channels. Branches, traditionally found in "High Street" locations, have long played a central part in the commercial and social fabric of communities. Virtually all banking business was conducted in the branch, including minor transactions, and customer records were held locally. Competition for customers was limited, and customer loyalty was strong, with employees in customers' "home" branch often knowing them by name. Branch managers enjoyed considerable discretion in their decision making, particularly in the area of lending, and occupied positions of influence within both the bank and the wider community.

The development of new technology for banking enabled a series of changes. One of the most significant involved data processing and record keeping, which could readily be automated. Rather than going into a back office and finding a paper copy of the customer's account, branch staff instead could now access records held in a central location. Front office staff could perform preliminary data entry during the transaction, and some banks took advantage of this opportunity to eliminate paperwork. The new technology also enabled data processing to be performed centrally. Rather than having branch employees perform a range of processing tasks through the day, processing work could be centralized in large offices, with all the advantages of high throughput and specialization—and all the liabilities of Taylorized production regimes. Most of the chapters in this book report a trend toward centralization of processing functions in the various countries, though in France and the United Kingdom the findings suggest that within this overall trend exist variations and even countertrends. Two banks in France have restructured some processing tasks out of centralized offices into regional centers and even branches. Chapter 5 refers to two competing models of processing in the United Kingdom, one highly centralized, the other retaining the branch as "a holistic area of work for the clerical and administrative staff in the bank." The U.K. researchers suggest that whether one model will emerge to the exclusion of the other remains uncertain. These findings indicate that technological change has enabled new organizational forms to develop, though the key determinant is not the technology itself, but the manner in which managements choose to use it.

The information storage and retrieval capabilities of new technology were also instrumental in the development of what has been variously referred to as a "sales culture" or "sales and service culture" in banking. With the possible exception of Spain, a shift toward an emphasis on sales can be found in every country discussed in the chapters of this book. Previously, banks operated on the basis of large volumes of transactions, most quite simple, taking place in branches. Bank staff were primarily required to process these transactions quickly, accurately, and honestly. Customers initiated transactions and could reasonably be expected to be aware of the narrow range of banking products available. Banks envisioned "service" in terms of a long-term relationship with customers, many of whom the staff knew personally, and above all, of keeping the queues moving during peak periods.

New technology, however, enabled a sales culture to develop, for with the new technology front office employees could have immediate access to a full range of financial information on any customer who entered the branch. Encounters with customers were redefined as "sales opportunities." Staff were provided with customer profiles to assist them in identifying the possibility of "cross selling" the rapidly growing and increasingly complex range of bank products, as well as scripted sales pitches designed to elicit the interest of customers, who could then be directed to other staff, who would engage in the more complex work of opening new accounts or lending. Branch employees came to be redefined as sales staff, and branches as sales outlets, with the dark wood paneling of the traditional bank branch replaced by brighter colors and lighting, and the branch itself relocated from its traditional High Street setting—which in many cases was declining in commercial importance—to shopping malls and increasingly "micro" branches located in supermarkets and other large retail outlets. In the Anglo-Saxon countries, banks sought to stay open for longer hours, particularly on weekends, when branches in suburban shopping malls might expect to conduct considerable business. The industry union was able to maintain some restrictions on hours of operation in Australia and New Zealand through penalty rates and outright limitations on operating hours. In Spain, collective agreements limit increased hours for lower-level staff, though managers' hours of work, as in most other countries, are becoming more unstructured. In France, legislative restrictions limit banks' operating hours.

New technology also enabled the diversification of delivery channels for banking services. Customers no longer had to enter a branch to conduct business. Simple transactions could be performed using electronic means such as ATMs and EFTPOS, significantly reducing the staff and property costs associated with branches and allowing customers the convenience of twenty-four-hour banking. It became unnecessary for branches to deal with customer inquiries, as telephone centers could be established to handle a high volume of calls. Customers were encouraged to change their behavior from entering branches to using the new, low-cost channels. Where they proved reluctant to do so voluntarily—particularly those who valued the opportunity to speak face to face with a bank employee—banks introduced fee structures with incentives to use the lowest-cost mode of delivery and penalties for transactions carried out in branches.

Various models of retail branches emerged, the common element of which, in most countries, was that the traditional, autonomous bank branch declined in number and was frequently downgraded in practice. Allied to this was the segmentation of the product market. Personalized service continued to be provided to "high value" personal and business customers, often with separate staff operating from their own offices. For the mass market, retail branches in the Anglo-Saxon countries have generally been downgraded, though there are exceptions to this trend, particularly in the United States, where the widest array of structures and practices can be found. The role of manager is often performed by lower-level staff than previously, and the prestigious job of lending is often circumscribed and even removed from the branch to telephone centers or mobile lenders. In Germany, one finds a range of branch types, from automated branches without staff to full-service branches. In Spain, however, the branch network has been expanding, and considerable discretion remains with the branch manager. Managers in Italy also retain discretion over lending, and their powers in the area of staffing have increased, contrary to trends in countries such as Australia, where most staffing decisions apart from opportunities for training occur at levels above the branch.

The trend toward downgrading branches has been taken to its logical conclusion in some countries with the establishment of direct banks. These banks operate without branches, using a full array of alternative delivery channels, the common element being lower costs and fewer restrictions on operating hours. These providers range from specialists in mass products such as mortgages to more general institutions. Examples can be found in Germany, the United States, Great Britain, and Australia.

Where processing has been removed from branches and centralized, specialization has increased concomitantly, with some staff concentrating on sales and transactions, others on processing. Chapter 7 mentions the Taylorization of many jobs, and deskilling of some positions is a common theme in the countries discussed in this book. This is a particular risk in processing centers, in which low-trust relations, conflict, and high staff turnover are likely. Job rotation does little to ameliorate these conditions, though staff at higher classifications in processing centers do have some amount of discretion, albeit limited. Many processing staff share a dislike for the new sales model, however, preferring the routine of the back office to the requirement to sell products, which many employees find intrusive and distasteful.

If the physical separation of front and back office work inherently entails greater specialization and a degree of deskilling has undoubtedly taken place in some banks in some positions, the situation in branches is nevertheless complex. In some cases, the demise of the branch employee with a full range of banking skills does, indeed, mean that jobs are narrower and more routine and require less skill. In other cases, however, branch staff are expected to be able to perform any front office task apart from substantial loans and more complex financial products. These employees must be familiar with a far wider range of products than in the past, in addition to possessing the traditional banking skills of performing quick and accurate transactions. Furthermore, although the sales culture may involve scripts and computerized customer profiles, it undoubtedly requires new skills. It is impossible to make confident generalizations in this area, for there are no clear patterns within the countries. Technology allows different forms of work organization to emerge, but management, affected in some cases by union pressure, seems to make the choice among the forms.

If no common trends can be identified in the skill requirements of banking jobs, the same cannot be said for work intensification. Back office work in central processing areas is subject to the efficiencies of large volumes of standardized work, and most banks set branch staffing levels using sophisticated computer models. Employees commonly view the results as chronic understaffing. (A possible exception to this pattern is Italy, where deregulation and privatization have proceeded more slowly than elsewhere.) In most other countries under study, executives with an eye to their share prices have sought to operate with leaner staffing profiles. Pressures on staff have also mounted with the introduction of sales targets for branches and individual employees. Computerization's information-sharing potential can be used not only for providing branch staff with financial records, but also for keeping management informed of the outcome of customer interactions. Tellers are expected to make referrals and customer service staff to sell products. Whereas branches once reported to higher levels of management in terms of months, they can now be monitored nearly in real time down to individual work positions. A common theme in this regard is that not only do employees have little input into the level at which their targets are set, but also targets are frequently moved—usually higher—before they can realistically be achieved.

Skill Formation

Training has always been an important focus of bank human resources practices. The changing nature of training practices is linked to changes in strategy generally and the decline of the generalist banker career path in particular. The twin emphases on cost reduction and a sales and service orientation have led to a greater targeting of training toward specific jobs rather than the development of employees who have expertise across the full range of banking skills. The fragmentation of internal labor markets has amplified this trend, with different groups of employees viewed as requiring a different quality and extent of training and education. However, the countries show considerable internal diversity in training and education of employees.

In broad terms, two models of skill formation can be identified, depending upon the extent to which industry or enterprise training is dominant in a particular country. Germany and the Netherlands fall into the former category, whereas the Anglo-Saxon countries, Italy, and Spain are in the latter. France appears to have experienced a long-term shift from the first group to the second.

Until recently, most German bank employees had undertaken an apprenticeship, cooperatively organized between employers, unions, and the government of two and a half to three years. Advanced training was available in specialized industry institutions controlled by employer associations. Greater numbers of university graduates recruitment and increased product market segmentation, however, have led to differing emphasis on training provisions within banks. Chapter 10 reports that some German banks foresee some downgrading in the training required for entry level standard retail positions, with the possibility that the system of vocational education might be downgraded in the medium to long term. In the Netherlands, banks customarily arranged industry training cooperatively, but more recently, bank training has been incorporated into public sector educational institutions. However, Dutch banks differ in the extent to which they rely on enterprise and job-specific training.

In most other countries, banks have catered for their own training needs beyond the generic skills public education provides. Furthermore, they have shown a reluctance to accept industry training standards, although common skills within the industry are clearly readily transportable between firms. Poaching is commonplace among specialist corporate bankers, and mobility is increasingly commonplace at lower levels, particularly among married women who move in and out of the workforce. Several countries report that the level of qualifications among staff has increased through a combination of slack labor markets and a general up-skilling of the population, with tertiary qualifications a prerequisite for recruitment to fast-track management career paths or for those seeking promotion through internal labor markets. However, the detail of skill formation practices differs within countries. This is evidenced dramatically in the American case studies, in which recruitment practices for management positions range from primarily drawing from the external labor market to primarily drawing from the internal labor market. As with work organization, this variety provides clear evidence that even where there are predominant industry trends, there can be considerable diversity due to employment strategy within a particular enterprise. The Australian cases show divergent training practices at lower levels, with one bank requiring a month-long training period for new staff, with systematic follow-up programs in the form of formal training courses and roving training specialists. Other banks, however, have shorter formal requirements and in practice may skimp on induction training to the point of tipping new staff into customer service positions with only a few days' preparation.

At lower levels, there is a growing trend toward identifying employees for rapid promotion; the bank will carefully design and monitor training for these employees, often with support for outside study, whereas other employees whose career horizons are more limited are left to fend for themselves beyond task- and product-based training and the development of sales skills. In France, training is a bank employee's right under the collective bargaining agreement, but management encourages only selected employees to seek training, and some get little or no opportunity to enhance their skills.

Staffing Arrangements and Job Security

In conjunction with new patterns of work organization, skill formation, and remuneration, changes to staffing arrangements and job security have led to a decline in the pervasive model of the rounded, career banker. Employees, particularly men, traditionally joined the bank through junior entry level positions in branches, learning the full range of retail banking skills as they ascended career ladders through customer service or lending, culminating for some in the relatively senior role of branch manager. With the exception of the expectation in some countries that married women would leave the industry at some point, banking promised most employees a secure lifetime career.

Despite widespread predictions of job losses due to automation, employment in banking has increased in most countries because of business growth. However, with the growing emphasis on cost reduction and the diversification of delivery channels, combined with greater economic uncertainty, including in some cases instability in the financial industry, employment levels in banks are declining, and along with them, levels of job security. Again, however, there are exceptions to this trend.

Australia, New Zealand, and Great Britain share a trend toward a segmentation of career horizons in banking, with lower-level staff in branches and processing centers experiencing reduced career advancement opportunities; the New Zealand situation is described as a "dual internal labor market." Promotion has become difficult from clerical positions in these countries because of a general decline in the availability of management positions due to delayering, the introduction of fast-track career paths for recruits with tertiary qualifications, and the proliferation of entry ports. Similarly, advancement to management is more likely for German employees who deal with high net worth rather than mass market customers. Most Spanish banks have not been hiring at all recently, but those who have taken on new recruits place them in junior positions, with only those with tertiary qualifications able to expect promotion. The one country that stands out to some extent from this general trend is Italy. Like those in the other countries, new recruits with qualifications have better promotional prospects in Italy. Although the link between seniority and advancement has decreased, this has been a slow process, and the long-established rights of experienced employees have been protected, effectively creating distinct career structures for different categories of employee. The most diverse range of recruitment and promotion practices can be found in the United States. Although many American banks rely increasingly on the external labor market for recruitment to management positions, some retain strong policies of promotion from within.

There has been considerable downsizing throughout the banking industry, but it has had varying effects on job security. All countries have resorted to voluntary redundancies, but some banks in the Anglo-Saxon countries have implemented forced retrenchments. Yet this practice varies as well, with one Australian bank seeking to restrict involuntary retrenchments to small pockets of employees, and one of the U.S. banks in chapter 2 trying to keep staffing levels constant through the business cycle by making use of a range of flexible practices. Banks in France, Spain, Italy, Germany, and the Netherlands have avoided involuntary layoffs through a combination of legislative restrictions and negotiated agreements with unions.

Banks employ a range of labor force adjustment mechanisms in addition to voluntary and involuntary redundancy. Most banks use sophisticated staffing models in conjunction with mechanisms such as variable working hours and part-time and casual employment. The Anglo-Saxon countries appear to make the most use of part-time and casual employment; among these, the United States again shows the greatest variation, with some large banks drawing almost 50 percent of their employees from among part-time and casual workers. Levels of part-time employment are lower on the Continent, with France, Italy, and Germany reporting levels around 10 percent of the workforce. The great majority of part-time employees in all countries are women, although in some countries part-time employment in banks is popular among both male and female university students.

Banks in the anglophone countries, France, and Spain have turned to outsourcing for noncore functions as well as some processing work. Outsourcing is also under consideration in the Netherlands. It is limited to some nonspecialized back office tasks in Italy, where it is regulated by contract and relatively unattractive.

The proportion of female employees in banks varies among the countries studied, with the lowest level reported in Italy, and top levels of about 60 percent in Australia and the United Kingdom. Although EEO policies are widespread, so too are low levels of women in senior management positions.

Compensation

Two conflicting aims appear to characterize current practices—and rhetoric—in the field of remuneration in banking: on one hand, the urgent need to reduce, or at least contain, the cost of labor within a context of increasing competition and decreasing profitability, and on the other, the necessity of compensating and adequately rewarding employees' performance and commitment within an uncertain context of continuous and challenging change.

Of course, such a dilemma—whether to resort to labor cost reduction because of external constraints or to develop compensation policies enhancing employees' responsibilities and commitment to the organization's goals—is not unique to the financial sector. In this case, however, determining the way to cope with this general dilemma seems to be particularly problematic for two principal reasons.

The first reason relates to the intrinsic features of an industry traditionally characterized not only as labor intensive but, even more, as labor dependent.[1] From a merely quantitative point of view, the presence of large numbers of well-paid staff in banks led to very high labor costs (which in the United Kingdom, for example, came to account for about two-thirds of total banking costs). From a more qualitative perspective, however, the crucial role played by human resources, rather than by fixed capital and technology, within the trust-based client relationship (Courpasson 1995) tended to prevent the development of generalized labor substitution policies. Therefore, banks face a structural dilemma involving the scope for change through extensive reductions in labor costs and fears of undermining the firm's main source of competitive advantage.

The second reason relates to specific traditions and institutions of labor regulation. With the exception of the United States, the compensation policies in banking of all the surveyed countries relied on centralized patterns of salary determination until approximately the mid-1980s. This applied even to the financial sector in the United Kingdom, where the consolidation of a national system of collective bargaining, contributing (as illustrated by Storey et al. in chapter 5 of this volume) to the coordination of the price of labor, represented a marked difference from other industries. Quite obviously, the specific features of such centralized policies varied across countries according to the different HR/IR national traditions, within which tendencies toward more homogeneous, industry-specific conditions of employment can be identified.

In Australia and New Zealand wage conditions traditionally were set by awards negotiated centrally by employers' associations and trade unions and handed down by tribunals, within a highly institutionalized system of compulsory public conciliation and arbitration, to which fringe benefits might be added in specific workplaces. In Europe compensation policies relied on strong traditions of sectorwide regulation through collective agreements. In many cases (e.g., the Netherlands, Germany, and Italy), such agreements used to define standard rather than minimum conditions. More generally, they set the impersonal and socially accepted criteria (based on seniority and essentially automatic progression through formalized classification systems) through which a smooth, gradual, and predictable pattern of salary differentiation could be assured.

Historically, the rationale for these centralized, formalized, and rather uniform compensation policies lay in the preferences of both the state and employers for strategies aimed at stabilizing the sectors, by taking the cost of labor out of competition, and at minimizing the risk of unions' interference in the organization and delivery of crucial and vulnerable services, by formally recognizing their role in collective bargaining at the central level (see chapter 5). However, the resulting patterns of compensation introduced considerable rigidity. As the banking industry became more competitive, the traditional compensation patterns added additional complexity to the dilemma between cost and commitment identified earlier in this section.

Thus recent trends in compensation policies can be described as attempts to move from the traditional models toward more contingent, individualized, and explicitly performance-related systems, while seeking to avoid diminishing labor's loyalty and commitment to the goals of production. This is why in most cases (the United Kingdom, Australia, New Zealand, Spain, Italy, Germany, and the Netherlands) changes to compensation in banking have tended to be less dramatic than expected in comparison with both current rhetoric and the experience of other industries.

The main exception to the industry trend is the United States, where in the absence of a collective wage agreement or any kind of coordination between banks in the area of wage setting, wide differences in compensation levels both between and within financial institutions have always been the rule. Furthermore, since the late 1980s, a significant increase in the use of incentive pay has supplemented the traditional differentiations based on detailed—and company-specific—job distinctions. Sales-based bonuses, either individually based (as for lenders in wholesale operations) or distributed—via managers—to branch offices, are the most widespread examples of incentives, whereas commissions have become increasingly common for crucial commercial jobs, such as investment advisors. As argued by Keltner and Finegold in chapter 2, however, this recent and accelerated move toward contingent pay schemes has not been uniform but appears inversely related to the strength of internal labor markets. Those banks with the weakest internal labor markets—therefore with the weakest structural motivating mechanisms—make the greatest use of contingent, performance-related schemes. This appears to confirm the motivational intention of these initiatives. The massive shift toward the use of part-time employees, many of whom work for an hourly wage rather than for salary and often do not qualify for nonsalary welfare and company benefits such as health insurance, pension, and vacation schemes, exacerbates variability in compensation.

In the other countries, banks increasingly seek a solution to the conflicting needs of cutting labor costs while motivating employees adequately through the adoption of new compensation patterns based on the reduction—if not the abolition—of general pay increases and the development instead of contingent payment mechanisms. The ways this trend is pursued vary across countries according to dimensions such as the extent to which variable (i.e., reversible or at-risk) remuneration schemes are diffused across and within banks, the proportion of variable remuneration in total compensation, the relative importance assigned to job and/or performance evaluation in determining compensation, the preference given to individually or collectively based incentives, the extent to which nonmonetary forms of compensation are employed, and the way change is introduced.

Contingent pay practices appear to be most widely diffused in the British banking industry, followed closely by that of New Zealand, and at some distance by those of the French and the Dutch. At the other extreme, banks in (West) Germany appear to have changed their remuneration policies the least, with the remainder (Australia, Spain, Italy) falling somewhat in between. Even in Great Britain, however, after the end of multiemployer bargaining in the late 1980s, the search for a new, business-oriented approach did not lead to a generalized shift to performance-related pay and individualized remuneration schemes. On the contrary, the outcome is described as being not too far removed from traditional salary-based patterns of compensation. The main difference with respect to the past is that the new practices became highly differentiated because of variations in union strength, industrial relations traditions, and corporate culture. At the same time, poaching of staff became widespread. In New Zealand, the dramatic general move to direct and decentralized bargaining favored the introduction of a variety of performance-related pay schemes but did not prevent unions from securing general pay raises. Ironically, a noticeable move toward increased pay flexibility appears to characterize the financial sector in the Netherlands, where the introduction of a variable incentive system, against a background of very moderate collective increases, has taken place with unions' support within the general framework of industry-wide collective agreements.

Conversely, in Germany, performance-linked compensation is still the exception, mainly confined to the remuneration of executives and credit officials in corporate finance, although plans to rearrange wage groups and gradually introduce performance-related payment schemes are being intensely debated between the social partners. Finally, more gradual introduction of variable pay schemes appears to characterize the compensation strategies in the remaining countries, where the new techniques are quite widespread among managerial staff and technical experts in the sales and customer service areas. Sometimes (e.g., in some Italian and Spanish organizations) the innovations are being experimented with first with new recruits to avoid affecting the commitment of more experienced staff. Temporarily, however, this gives rise to a dual, virtually contradictory system.

In quantitative terms, the incidence of variable pay is generally rather small, except for managerial staff and for positions with crucial responsibilities in sales and customer service fields. Even in these cases, however, the variable component seems to be most pronounced in the United States (where it may reach 25 percent of income) and in Great Britain. In France it is estimated to average about 7 percent of annual salary. Surprisingly, collective agreements in the Netherlands allow up to a rather high maximum of 15 percent variability for all staff.

The significance of variability in performance-related payment should not be overstated. In the Anglo-Saxon countries (Australia and New Zealand, and in some of the British organizations), pay and benefits are still mainly awarded according to job evaluation schemes, sometimes integrated with performance-related payment mechanisms. However, as illustrated by the Australian case, the shift to job evaluation, which rewards positions rather than performance, does represent a substantial reduction to seniority's traditional role. Furthermore, except for managerial staff and selected experts, collectively based incentives are often preferred to individualized schemes—and not only by unions. The case of one innovative British bank is instructive, for it makes no use of individual performance—

related pay, which is considered to be incompatible with the new, cooperative, teamwork-based organization of work. Similarly, collective performance premiums and profit-sharing schemes are often preferred to avoid reducing internal cohesion among staff.

Somewhat unexpectedly, given current cost constraints and banks' general preference for more flexible compensation patterns, the tradition of fringe benefits, a typical nonwage and rigid component of remuneration in the financial sector in many countries, has not been dismantled. In Australia and New Zealand, among other countries, although management has criticized fringe benefits and in some cases reduced them, they remain relevant because of their great popularity among staff. In Spain, these benefits (such as cheap home loans, life insurance, school loans, vacation homes, company stores, and the like) have recently been reinforced through collective agreements. However, it is possible that these instruments are being maintained to make it easier to promote the acceptance of more radical changes.

These developments highlight the problematic nature of changes to remuneration practices if they potentially threaten employees' commitment and consent to the organization's goals.

Turning to the ways in which the new compensation practices have been introduced, a distinction can be identified between innovations devised as part of a more general union avoidance or substitution strategy, as appears to be the case in some banks in New Zealand and the United Kingdom,[2] and policies implemented with at least some open and formalized support of the unions, through various information, consultation, or negotiation mechanisms. This latter model applies to most organizations in Australia and in continental Europe, especially in Germany, the Netherlands, and Italy. But some examples are found in the New Zealand and the United Kingdom as well, showing the importance of distinguishing between rhetoric and real practices.

Enterprise Governance and Industrial Relations

The preceding sections have mainly referred to industrial relations patterns and institutions as factors influencing or modifying—either as constraints or as resources—the ways banks could actually introduce changes responding to structural pressures. This, however, presents only a partial story, because over time the same pressures for change in turn influence and transform previous HR/IR models. We now turn our attention to these developments.

At a general level, current trends in banking appear similar to those taking place in each country's broader economy. Most significantly, these include recent moves toward a decentralization—and even a dismantling—of industrial relations and collective bargaining mechanisms and attempts to reduce or eliminate union influence over employment conditions (Traxler 1996). The impact of these changes varies considerably, however, according to the unions' strength and ability to organize industrial action in the various countries. Whenever the unions have been able to maintain their following among employees, the disruption to established practices has tended to be lower than in other industries.

The objective of some employers to be left almost unconstrained in their HR strategies appears most closely approximated in the United States, where the effective absence in banking of any tradition of collective pressure and organized action is a key determinant of the market dependency of employment conditions and their extreme variability. As Keltner and Finegold argue in chapter 2, however, an unintended consequence is often a low level of investment in skills training, which in turn makes it more difficult to develop high-skill employment strategies.

The picture is somewhat different in the United Kingdom. Again, British management's search for greater flexibility to confront increased market pressures put an end to the traditional multiemployer bargaining in banking. However, this did not put an end to collective bargaining itself, which generally continued at the company level—even if in an uncoordinated way—within a context of high union density, deteriorating corporate climate, and new threats of industrial unrest. Similarly, in New Zealand the shift from a conciliation and arbitration system to a free-market employment model in banking did not end collective bargaining. Although most HR managers would prefer a "union substitution model," as Rasmussen and Jackson argue in chapter 4, in practice banks appear to be reluctant to abandon traditional collective bargaining, mainly because staff increasingly support a reinvigorated, single union in a changing environment characterized by low trust, growing cynicism, and increased staff turnover. In Australia, the rather cautious move from a centralized awards-based system and the development of enterprise bargaining even offered opportunities for the union to gain recognition in the traditionally less organized area represented by smaller regional banks.

In continental Europe, with the partial exception of Spain, the increased decentralization of industrial relations coexists with the permanence of industry-wide collective agreements. This dual-level pattern is clearest in Germany, the Netherlands, and Italy, where strong unionism, in terms of affiliations and/or institutional recognition, makes it risky for banks to dismantle the traditional system. Change is rather sought for transforming the industry-wide agreements into broad framework accords and devolving an increasing range of issues to company level collective bargaining or codetermination. In France, the unions are weaker but institutionally supported, with commitment to unionism stronger among banking staff than in most other industries. Significantly, French employers' threat to withdraw unilaterally from industry-wide agreements if unions were unprepared to negotiate new, more "up to date", employment conditions had no practical consequences when negotiations were suspended in the early 1990s.

The decentralization of industrial relations appears instead to have gone farther in Spain than elsewhere on the Continent. In this case, a large number of militant and, by Spanish standards, exceptionally strong workplace unions have recently been playing a leading role at the company level. In contrast to those of other Spanish industries, banking unions in Spain directly perform the functions of *comité de empresa* (i.e., of works councils).[3] This arrangement, which is the result of agreements between the social partners, was meant to facilitate policy coherence and coordination over highly dispersed company structures. As well, the decentralization of industrial relations did not necessarily lead to a more disorganized system (Traxler 1996).

Turning to company level industrial relations and governance, a tendency toward the redefinition and redeployment of managerial competences and functions resulting from the overall decentralization process must be emphasized. The ways these changes are taking place in practice are highly variable and company specific but they have a common source in a double transformation. First, in structural terms, there is a general trend toward the growing importance of the human resources and training functions within a context where the traditional bureaucratic personnel departments are being downsized. Second, functions have been redefined, involving tighter centralization of control over human resources strategies and industrial relations, paralleled by an opposite trend toward the devolution of responsibilities for personnel management to line managers.

The extent of the changes to management structure and function tend to be inversely related to the importance of external rather than internal labor market mechanisms in the regulation of employment relations. Thus in the United States such changes are likely to be greater in the banks falling into the model Keltner and Finegold characterize in chapter 2 as a "high-end, value-added strategy", where investments in human resources are paramount, rather than in those relying on a price competition strategy, where external recruitment for skilled positions is usually the rule.

More generally, changes to the governance of the human resources function appear to anticipate broader changes in employment regulation. Furthermore, this seems to be an area in which employers can often introduce innovative practices with some freedom. In New Zealand, for instance, where an unexpected moderation in the use of contractual flexibility in the financial sector has been observed, personnel departments are undergoing radical changes involving the replacement of traditional staff with managers specializing in human resources management, employee relations, and training. Similarly, in the United Kingdom, where despite business-oriented rhetoric many traditional HR/IR practices show an unexpected persistence, investment in new personnel techniques is on the contrary considered among the greatest novelties. Similar considerations apply to the other countries. Everywhere, the experimental, tentative nature of innovations is evident.

Overall, changes in managerial functions and practices seem to have been devised as preconditions of or catalysts for deeper changes within a context of sensitive social relations at work, where abrupt modifications to traditional practices could have detrimental effects.

This point is most clearly described in chapter 5, where it is presented as a managerial dilemma: British banks, it is argued, cannot be too parsimonious to staff, because to do so would risk industrial action and recruitment problems, nor can they be too generous, because of tight margins for concessions. Although the "old 'deal' based on loyalty in exchange for security ruptured," banks continued to rely upon their employees' commitment, and through trial and error sought to devise ways to meet both market constraints and the exit/voice behavior (i.e., high turnover and conflict) from their employees (Hirschman 1970). From this perspective, the changes in the organization of personnel management are a starting point that anticipates more wide-ranging initiatives. However, strategies of direct employee involvement and motivation (to assuage exit threats) and of their representatives' consultation and participation in relevant aspects of the companies' decision making (to avoid disruptive voice and conflict) must complement changes to management practices. This leads us to our final issue, regarding the relationships between management, employees, and their representatives in workplaces.

Changes in the organization of banking services have not led simply to dismantling the traditional collective mechanisms of employment regulation in favor of automatic market regulation, let alone straightforward authoritarian imposition. On the contrary, the emerging patterns of labor governance often disclose new chances for employee involvement and various forms of unions' or works councils' participation. Again, this is most likely to apply to the extent that banking operations rely on employee commitment. Where this is not a primary consideration, as in much U.S. retail banking, it may be more convenient simply to resort to highly differentiated incentive payment systems complementing an essentially market-based regulation.

This is not, however, the prevailing model. Even in the United Kingdom and New Zealand, which have experienced the most dramatic changes in industrial relations, union and nonunion employee representation arrangements have been maintained and in some cases extended to new issues.[4] Especially in New Zealand, the necessity of coping with the deterioration of workplace climate after the restructuring of the 1980s and 1990s led to a massive reevaluation of direct employee involvement and communication policies in which the union is sometimes involved because of its considerable support among staff.

In countries that underwent less-dramatic transformations in their institutional IR framework, new opportunities for the development of more cooperative employment relations are even more evident. Australia and the Netherlands provide perhaps the best examples. In Australia, the decentralization of collective bargaining and the need for union cooperation with the restructuring of branch organization led on the one hand to establishing joint management-union committees and working parties on workplace issues that previously had been subject largely to management prerogative. On the other hand, new chances were provided for the organization and recognition of the union in smaller banks.

In the Netherlands, where a long tradition of both employee involvement (or *verkowerleg*) and collective codetermination through the works councils at the company level already existed, recent changes led to the elaboration of rules governing the methods and scope of internal communications, to sophisticated forms of direct participation, to consultation between management and the works councils, and to negotiation at the workplace. In Italy, a multiplicity of formal and informal opportunities (such as joint committees, temporary working groups, and ad hoc meetings) for discussion and consultation with unions and worker representatives has been spreading, complemented by a revitalization of company level negotiation. In France, new opportunities for *comités d'entreprise* developed along with greater recognition of the importance of training policies. In Spain, although programs of direct participation have increasingly

been used to gain worker commitment, the wider diffusion of joint committees signals the importance attributed—at least formally—to representative participation.[5]

The evidence in the national studies represented in subsequent chapters
therefore does not support a simplified interpretation of current tendencies
in terms of the fading away of collective bargaining and their progressive
replacement by market regulation. However, our data conversely do not
support an interpretation based simply on the preeminent role played by
traditional IR institutions. The case of the banking industry in Germany is
particularly significant in this respect. Considerable stability characterizes
German labor relations, based strongly on the central role played by
external unions and internal works councils. Nevertheless, new challenges
are putting the traditionally strong representative capacity of staff organizations under great stress. The new issue of determining employment
conditions in direct banking, where currently employees are not covered
by collective agreements, and over which the position of the parties
appears to be irreconcilable, points to a range of possible scenarios.
Although the popularity of direct banking is expected to remain relatively
limited, the symbolic effect of employment relations in this area might
have unanticipated wider implications leading to heightened uncertainty
in the industry.

Conclusion

At the risk of repeating arguments already raised in this introduction, a
first major conclusion to be drawn from the reports on the nine countries
contained in this volume is that the common elements present in the
transformation process of the banking industry in the OECD countries,
such as deregulation, increasing competition and concentration, massive
use of technology, and reduction of employment, do not suggest a convergence to a single model or "best practice." Differences persist not
only across countries but across enterprises in the same countries. As the
reports in chapters 2 through 10 show, distinctive institutional arrangements in the national regulation frameworks of the industry, employment
practices, and systems of industrial relations significantly influence the
differences observed.

However, the reports suggest the existence of other sources of diversity, a more systematic consideration of which should be part of a future
research agenda. In this sense, the structural character of the industry,
which embraces banks performing different functions within the different

national money economies and whose size and market position differ strongly across countries, should be more closely considered as a source of diversity in labor relations. Furthermore, different national service cultures, which in the case of the banking industry reflect different attitudes to money, saving, time, trust, and risk, presumably constitute another source of institutional diversity. In this context, the social acceptance across countries of such technological innovations as the call centers that are transforming the character of service relations deserve more attention in the future.

A second major conclusion to be drawn from the studies in this volume is that the social actors—management, employees, and unions—are moving within a business and social environment characterized by a high degree of uncertainty. In addition to the national patterns influencing the restructuring process, we also find that technological and organizational options, customer segmentation, new forms of work organization, and new incentive schemes represent not only opportunities but also risks for banks, and their responses to the available options in terms of business policies are not always clear-cut. All of these elements give the transformation process a strong experimental character that does not at present allow us to predict with any certainty the future design of national banking industries. In the middle of such a fluid process, the only generalization that seems valid is that the traditional world of banking is dead.

Notes

1. Within this perspective, the situation is very different not only from traditional large-scale, mass production manufacturing industries but also from most low-skilled, poorly qualified service sectors.

2. Of course, this also applies to financial sector organizations in the United States. But this is a different case, wherein employment relations developed independently from previously strong union traditions and influence.

3. For more on the topic, see Escobar 1995.

4. Note for instance the union involvement in the introduction of a highly innovative skills-based payment scheme in one New Zealand bank in chapter 4.

5. On the relationship between direct and representative participation according in the view of the social partners, see Regalia 1996b.

References

Courpasson, D. (1995). Éléments pour une sociologie de la relation commerciale: les paradoxes de la modernisation dans la banque. *Sociologie du Travail*, 37(1), 1–24.

Escobar, M. (1995). Spain: Works Councils or Unions? In J. Rogers and W. Streeck (eds.), *Works Councils: Consultation, Representation, and Cooperation in Industrial Relations*. Chicago: University of Chicago Press.

Hirschman, A. O. (1970). *Exit, Voice, and Loyalty: Responses in Decline in Firms, Organizations, and States*. Cambridge: Harvard University Press.

Regalia, I. (1996a). Relazioni di lavoro e costruzione sociale delle risorse umane nelle «regioni motore». In M. Regini (ed.), *La formazione delle risorse umane. Una sfida per le «regioni motore» d'Europa.* 237–66. Bologna, Italy: Il Mulino.

Regalia, I. (1996b). How the Social Partners View Direct Participation: A Comparative Study of 15 European Countries. *European Journal of Industrial Relations*, 2(2), 211–34.

Traxler, F. (1996). Collective Bargaining and Industrial Change: A Case of Disorganization? A Comparative Analysis of Eighteen OECD Countries. *European Sociological Review*, 12(3), 217–87.

II

Country Studies

2 Market Challenges and Changing Employment Relations in the U.S. Banking Industry

Brent Keltner and
David Finegold

Over the last two decades, the American banking industry has undergone a dramatic transformation. Traditionally one of the most stable and least concentrated industries in the United States, banking has been rocked by the combination of waves of deregulation, major technological change, and the entrance of new, innovative competitors in its core markets. Business headlines reflect the results of these trends, with weekly announcements of record-sized bank mergers and major restructuring initiatives. Indeed, the competitive pressures in banking are currently so strong that they have led some experts to speculate on whether banks in their present role as financial intermediaries will survive far into the next century (Bryan 1988). This chapter explores the changes underway in the U.S. banking sector, banks' strategic responses to this new competitive environment, and the impact of these strategic responses on employment relations in the sector.

Changes in the Institutional Environment

Two types of changes to the institutional structures governing the U.S. banking industry have led to increased competitive pressure. The first is change to the regulatory regime governing the financial services industry. Starting in the early 1980s, successive waves of legal deregulation allowed banks and other financial service firms both to expand the scope of their operations geographically and to expand the range of the products they offer. The second significant change in the institutional structure is a shift in American corporations' financial practices. Large and even some small and medium-sized business enterprises have increasingly moved away from relying on bank loans as their primary source of finance toward direct access to capital markets, which has increased competition among banks for the business of small and medium-sized business enterprises.

Deregulation

Entering the 1980s, the U.S. banking industry remained highly segmented. Legal regulation stemming from Depression era reform kept each type of financial service institution in strictly limited, geographically bounded market segments and prevented competition for many financial service products. The Glass-Steagal Act of 1933 legally separated investment banks from commercial banks, with each type of institution barred from undertaking activities performed by the other. Commercial banks were limited to taking deposits and providing credit to business enterprises. They were specifically prohibited from investment banking activities. Investment banks were limited to activities such as underwriting equities and debt and managing financial portfolios.

Savings and loans under Glass-Steagal were expected to funnel very stable, low-interest deposits to home owners for mortgages. They were explicitly prohibited from offering demand deposits. Insurance companies were left to provide insurance, and securities dealers offered stocks, bonds, and mutual funds. A fragmented regulatory regime mirrored barriers to competition among types of financial service firms, with a different body regulating each type of financial service firm. The Federal Reserve and several other federal agencies have overseen commercial banks and savings and loans. Brokerage houses and securities dealers have been in the domain of the Securities and Exchange Commission. State regulators have monitored insurance companies.

Over the course of the 1980s the financial services industry has gradually become more dynamic and competitive. Deregulation has taken place in several steps.[1] The first wave of financial deregulation involved a limited lifting of restriction on depository institutions' product offerings. The Depository Institutions Acts of 1980 and 1982 enabled banks to raise additional revenue by allowing them to expand the number of financial service products they offered to include simple investments. The acts lifted regulatory restrictions that had prevented commercial banks and savings and loans from offering interest rate returns on their checking and deposit accounts, providing a new vehicle to compete for additional customers. The acts also granted savings and loans the authority to make commercial and industrial loans.[2]

The second wave of financial deregulation involved a gradual relaxation of geographical restrictions on bank branching. Federal authorities were the first to move to ease limitations on interstate banking. A provision included in the Depository Institutions Act of 1982 allowed out-of-state banks to acquire troubled banking institutions. Following the federal government's lead, state governments also began to remove restriction on interstate branching. By 1984, more than half of the 50 states had amended laws to allow entry of out-of-state financial institutions. A decade later, every state but Alaska permitted interstate banking. Federal legislation in 1995 paved the way for the removal of all restrictions on interstate banking.

A third step in the erosion of barriers to competition in the financial service markets was the trend toward depository institutions' offering alternative investment products and nondepository institutions' offering traditional banking products. Nonbank financial institutions first began to compete for banking customers in the late 1970s by offering money market mutual funds. By the 1980s, finance companies, insurance dealers, and other nonbanking financial service companies had begun to enter the market for standard banking products. Business enterprises like Sears and Ford Motor Company set up their own financial companies to provide consumer credit, while other traditionally one-product companies like AT&T, USAA Insurance, and American Express expanded into deposit products, checking services, and credit cards. By the early 1990s, nonbanking financial service institutions had made significant inroads into markets for traditional banking products,[3] prompting legislators in many states to loosen restrictions on banks' ability to sell insurance and investment products.

A fourth and final step in the erosion of barriers to competition in the financial service market has been the growth in the number of company acquisitions involving mergers of commercial banks, investment banks, insurance companies, and brokerage houses. Among the more spectacular mergers was the acquisition of the investment banking house Salomon Brothers Inc. by the large insurance conglomerate the Travelers' Group. Combined with Salomon Brothers' earlier acquisition of a brokerage house, this merger produced a behemoth financial service group with product offerings across the spectrum of investment banking, brokerage services, and insurance products. Some leading commercial banks, including Bank of America, Nationsbank, and Bankers' Trust moved to acquire small investment banking houses to complement their line of commercial banking products. Others such as the Boston-based Fleet Financial Group merged with discount brokers in an attempt to make itself more attractive to affluent retail customers. In its 1997 legislative session, the U.S. Congress attempted but failed to produce legislation outlining a framework for integrated legal oversight of the financial service industry.

Relationships among Banks, Finance, and Industry

Whereas the blurring of lines between formerly distinct sectors of the financial services market affected both the personal and business segments of the commercial banking industry, the impact of the trend toward "financial disintermediation" has been mostly felt in the business end of the market. Disintermediation started with large corporate customers in the 1970s, as more and more large businesses turned to alternative sources of finance, most notably bond and commercial paper markets, to meet their short- and long-term financing needs. Through the 1980s, disintermediation ratcheted down to the midsized- and even some small-business enterprises (Sipple 1989; "A Survey of International Banking" 1994: 9). Between 1980 and 1991, the share of the total financing volume of American businesses banks financed dropped 38 percent to just 30 percent (Keltner 1994: 46).

The loss of large corporate customers to financial markets markedly increased the level of competition among banks for lending opportunities to small and medium-sized enterprises. From the perspective of the business customers themselves, this intensification of competition has been a mixed blessing. It has on the one hand driven prices on loans downward, as banks have tried to win market share by reducing their profit margins ("when to throw 'em bank" 1994: 81). It has, at the same time, decreased the stability of bank finance. Higher levels of competition have encouraged banks to adopt a more hands-off approach to lending. Revolving lines of credit have largely replaced longer-term, fixed interest rate loans as the primary means by which banks extend loans to their commercial customers. Revolving credit lines tend to be medium term in maturity (e.g., three years) and have variable interest rates adjusted according to money market conditions. This type of credit carries higher interest rate risk for customers because interest rates and, therefore, payments often go up just at the beginning of recessions. But they also offer flexibility in terms of when the credit can be drawn down and repaid (Vitols 1994).

Changes in Labor Market Regulation and Labor Supply

While changes in institutions regulating the structure of competition and changes in capital markets have been dramatic over the last decade, institutions regulating the labor market have changed very little. Institutional mechanisms to represent employee interests remain underdeveloped.

Table 2.1
Salary range in different employment positions, California banks, 1991

Employment position	1st quartile	Average	3rd quartile
Branch manager (>$50 mil)	$44,574	$57,592	$70,610
Branch manager ($20–$50 mil)	41,655	53,985	66,314
Branch manager (<$20 mil)	35,838	46,533	57,227
Commercial lender (VP)	40,174	52,102	64,030
Commercial lender (AVP)	30,784	39,375	47,967
Consumer credit officer	25,186	32,641	40,095
Investment adviser	18,524	23,463	28,402
New accounts	15,566	19,633	23,710
Teller	13,068	16,208	19,348

Source: Deloitte and Touche (1992), *California Banks Compensation Survey.*

Supports for vocational skill formation in the banking sector to smooth the transition from school-to-work work are also weak, with most entry-level employees coming to banks with poor job-related skills.

General Features of the Industrial Relations System

The industrial relations system in the U.S. banking industry is relatively weak and poorly coordinated. Less than 5% of the banking labor force is unionized and collective wage agreements play no role in wage determination.

Each bank is currently left to decide independently on its compensation policies and practices. This has resulted in large differences in the level of compensation received by employees doing the same job in different banks, with differences of up to 40–50 percent common even for banks operating in the same part of the country (see table 2.1).

Not only are there no collective bargaining arrangements, but there are no legal provisions for the establishment of the types of enterprise-based works councils common in Europe to give workers input into key corporate decisions, such as the introduction of new technology or organizational restructuring. Only a handful of states have laws that require 60 to 90 days' notification in the event of a mass dismissal, and even these states offer no legal recourse to financial compensation in the event of a worker's being laid off. The weakness of the industrial relations system gives American banks virtually unrestricted freedom in their hiring, firing, and staffing decisions.

Vocational and Educational Preparation

Just as there has been little cooperation among banks in the area of wage setting, banks have done little to coordinate in setting up training institutions. The result is that as in other sectors of the U.S. economy there are few mechanisms to prepare young persons for a career in banking. Entry level hires typically have scant knowledge of financial services and no previous experience working in a bank. In many cases they lack basic reading, writing, and arithmetic skills (Hargroves 1989; Lunt 1990). In higher-skill positions, new recruits have a more solid academic and theoretical training but lack practical work skills. Bank managers often complain that what new recruits learn at the university is too removed from the world of work. The poor vocational preparation of those leaving school puts the entire burden of training investment on banks.

   In recent years, large commercial banks have increasingly used college recruiting for front office positions. For some large commercial banks, college student recruits now account for as much as 60 percent of new hires in entry level, part-time positions. This shift toward hiring college students seems to be driven, however, not by a need for hiring skilled employees in branch offices but by the need for flexibility in staffing. College students are often hired on a part-time basis while they complete their studies. The relatively inert structure of employment in the American banking industry suggests that there is not a strong relationship between college recruiting and skill needs. The relative percentages of employees in low- and high-skill positions have remained constant in the United States between 1984 and 1993, as table 2.2 shows.

Table 2.2
Changes in occupational structure in U.S. commercial banks, 1984–1993

Occupational group	1984*	1987	1990	1993
Managerial and administrative workers	11.9%	11.8%	11.1%	11.3%
Professional, paraprofessional, and technical workers	13.4	15.5	16.4	15.4
Clerical and administrative support workers	70.0	68.5	68.1	68.4
Other	4.3	4.2	4.4	4.9
Industry total	100.0	100.0	100.0	100.0

Sources: Bureau of Labor Statistics, *Occupational Employment Statistics Survey*; authors' own calculations.
* Data before and after 1987 not strictly comparable; included in the 1984 data are a few stock savings banks.

Competitive Pressures from Markets and Technology

Along with deregulation and changes to bank-company relations, shifts in consumer demand and the availability of new forms of information technology are also increasing competitive pressures on U.S. banks.

Changing Patterns of Demand

In the retail banking segment, consumers have begun to use consumer credit products more intensively and to expand into investments and insurance. Bank loans for personal consumption expanded rapidly over the 1980s, as more individuals took on debt to finance their education, mortgages, and purchases of consumer durables. Meanwhile, between 1980 and 1992, deposits as a percentage of personal assets dropped by 10 percent, while investments in mutual funds, money market funds, and government bonds increased by 10 percent and holdings in life insurance by 6 percent.[4] Changes in patterns of consumption have also been evident in the shift toward higher levels of demand for international banking products. More retail consumers have turned to international financial markets to make investments, and an increasing number of small and medium-sized enterprises look to banks for financial help to expand into overseas markets ("America's little fellows surge ahead" 1993; Barrett 1995; Glasgall 1993).

The Growing Importance of Information Technology

Information technology has changed the character of competition in the banking sector in at least three ways. First, it has reduced barriers to entry. Advances in information and communication technology have made it easier for finance dealers, insurance companies, and other nonbanking institutions to offer consumers financial service products without needing to maintain a network of branch offices. Computer technology similarly has contributed to the rise of securitized forms of credit by making it easier for all investors to gather information about borrowers.

Second, information technology has helped banks and other financial service companies reduce costs by reducing the labor involved in formerly labor-intensive work processes. Productivity in bank office work such as check processing and data entry has increased dramatically through automation (Seaman 1992). Information technology has also allowed banks to increase the efficiency of the front office. American banks were quicker than their overseas counterparts to invest in on-line terminals for tellers and new accounts personnel.[5] On-line terminals have enabled branch employees to complete both routine and complicated customer requests with greater accuracy and speed.

A third way in which information technology has altered competitive dynamics is by allowing banks to shift toward nonbranch distribution channels for products and services. ATMs, point of sale (POS) terminals, automated telephone programs, and direct deposit services all allow customers to complete their basic banking transactions without contact with branch-based personnel. ATMs offer customers an alternative vehicle for completing routine transactions, such as deposits, withdrawals, and transfers, inside branch offices. Both POS terminals in retail outlets and direct deposit have also become increasingly important channels to customers for handling deposit and withdrawal needs (BAI 1993). The shift toward nonbranch distribution systems can be used both to increase customer convenience and to achieve cost savings by reducing labor costs.

Competitive Pressures and Market Strategies

In responding to this combination of institutional changes and market challenges, American banks have employed several different competitive strategies. To win market share in market segments for customers with fairly standard financial service needs, banks have relied on cost-efficient delivery and intensive price competition. In markets for midsized to large business customers with more complicated banking needs, banks have focused on cultivating financial service relationships. In market segments for affluent retail customers and small-business customers, an emerging mass customization strategy combines cost-efficient delivery with relationship management. In addition to these new and evolving market strategies, a final competitive response is the pursuit of mergers with or acquisitions of other commercial banks. The need to cut costs and raise capital to invest in technology has prompted a wave of consolidation among U.S. banks.

Price Competition

Through much of the 1980s banks' primary competitive response to new institutional and market conditions was to try to out-compete one another along the dimension of cost. In their retail operations, banks reacted to the deregulation of the market for deposit products in the early 1980s with an extremely high pace of innovation in standard banking products.

Frequent changes of fee schedules and interest rate returns and offers of special giveaways (e.g., air miles, prize drawings) were used to attract a steady stream of new customers away from competitors. Monthly or quarterly product campaigns were designed to attract price-conscious consumers with relatively unsophisticated banking needs.

In the wholesale banking segment, banks responded to the rise of alternative financial vehicles by engaging in acquisitive behavior. The availability of other financing options made large corporations increasingly price sensitive. Commercial banks began to employ individuals whose major or sole responsibility was to solicit new business by following up on referrals or simply cold calling potential customers. Efforts to win new customers revolved around promises of lower interest rates on loans and lower prices on related financial service products. Price competition between banks often became so intense that the margins earned on loans become razor thin ("When to throw 'em back" 1994).

The use of technology to shift consumers to nonbranch distribution strategies has acted as a critical support for strategies based on price competition. The first step away from branch-based delivery involved heavy investments in ATMs, POS terminals, and automated telephone programs. American banks were among the earliest to introduce automatic tellers as a substitute for completing routine transactions like deposits, withdrawals, and transfers inside branch offices.[6]

The second phase of the shift to nonbranch distribution channels involved an increase in the range of financial services that customers could complete outside the branch. By the early 1990s, many major American banks were allowing their customers to use both ATMs and telephone banking not just to check balances on their accounts but also to apply for lines of credit and open new deposit and investment accounts. The final phase of the shift to nonbranch distribution channels in retail banking has been the use of incentives, both positive and negative, to force customers out of the branches. Starting in the early 1990s, large commercial banks began to introduce ATM checking accounts, waiving all fees for customers that completed their basic banking transactions exclusively through ATMs. To discourage branch traffic further, some banks have turned to charging fees for branch transactions.[7]

Relationship Banking

In many market segments, intensive price competition has been an appropriate strategy to win market share in an increasingly competitive marketplace. Both large corporate customers and the low end of the retail banking market are very price sensitive and have little need for a close relationship with the bank. Between these highly price-competitive ends of the banking market, however, are a large number of customers who need and value a more intensive relationship with their bank. This is particularly true among small and medium-sized firms that view their bankers not just as a source of finance but also as advisers with perspective on their business.

By the beginning of the 1990s, banks had begun to rethink their approach to these financial services customers. Innovative banks increasingly began to use a "case manager" approach to deliver services to affluent clients (Keltner and Finegold 1996). By allowing a single, broadly skilled employee to attend to all the needs of individual customers, these banks could promise speed, convenience, and customization in service delivery (Davenport and Nohria 1994). The increased sophistication of banking consumers and growing complexity of the world of finance has raised opportunities for those banks that can add value to service delivery by leveraging information across product areas.

The move to relationship banking strategies has been most pronounced in the corporate middle-market lending segment. The shift to a relationship banking strategy has gone hand in hand with a shift to giving greater attention to middle-market companies. Middle-market businesses have a broad range of financial service needs, including credit products and investment and deposit products as well as possibly cash management and international banking services. The trend for both small and large commercial banks is to attempt to act as full-service banks for their business clients. By winning all of these types of business from a single small or medium-sized enterprise, banks can earn a healthy amount of revenue from each business client (Svare 1989). In the retail banking segment, some banks are taking advantage of loosening restrictions on involvement in insurance and investment markets to introduce an integrated service delivery strategy to win affluent banking customers' business. These institutions are broadly training their new account employees in investment, insurance, and consumer credit products.

Mass Customization

A final emerging market paradigm is a mass customization strategy that focuses on designing bundled packages of standard service products while also building on technology-based distribution to provide efficient service operations. This strategy seeks to combine the benefits of price competition and relationship management. It draws on direct contact to customers through broadly trained case managers that can identify product needs and cross sell customers across product families. It involves standardizing and limiting product development and the number of products offered to consumers to support the efficiency of service delivery. It also involves directing customers to automated forms of service delivery (e.g., ATMs, automated telephone programs) for routine service transactions to enhance the efficiency of service delivery.

The target group for the mass customization strategy is consumers that have product needs across a range of product families (e.g., deposits, credits, investments) but that cannot be cost effectively served using a more intensive relationship management strategy. These may include small business owners who need help managing both their private and business finances, retirees who must achieve the appropriate balance between liquidity and investment, and young professionals who need a strategy to pay off student loans while also beginning to invest for their children's education and their own retirement.

Mergers and Acquisitions

A final reaction to higher levels of competitive pressure has been a dramatic increase in the numbers of mergers and acquisitions. The number of commercial banks and savings and loans shrank by almost a third between 1984 and 1994 from approximately 18,000 to 12,500, and most experts predict continued rapid consolidation in the industry (table 2.3; "American Banking" 1995 and Hylton 1995.) Mergers have been particularly intense among the largest commercial banks, with most of the nation's largest

Table 2.3
Changes in number of banks and branch offices, 1984–1994

	1984	1987	1990	1994
Commercial banks				
Number of institutions	14,496	13,723	12,347	10,451
Number of branches	41,799	45,357	50,406	55,145
Federal savings banks				
Number of institutions	3,418	3,622	2,815	2,160
Number of branches	23,388	23,111	19,104	15,000

Source: FDIC, Historical Statistics on Banking, 1934–1994, vol. 1.

banks involved in some type of merger activity in the last two years. An important force driving the large numbers of mergers and acquisitions has been the need to reduce costs. Taking advantage of the end to geographic restrictions on branch banking, large banks have moved to cut costs by leveraging their administrative and business functions across a larger number of branch offices.

More recently, the need for higher levels of investment in information technology has reinforced the drive toward consolidation. The shift toward nonbranch distribution channels and demands for continued cost cutting in administrative areas has made high levels of investment in information technology (IT) an imperative. During the 1980s, American banks invested $60,000 per employee in IT. Though a very high figure when placed in internationally comparative perspective (McKinsey 1992: 9), the pace of technology investment continued to accelerate during the 1990s. Between 1988 and 1933, IT spending in the banking industry increased from just over $10 billion to just over $20 billion (*Economist*, 1994a: 28)

Changes and Variations in Employment Relations

The regulatory and competitive trends outlined in the previous section have strongly affected the way individual banks organize their human resources management. The industry-wide trend has been toward a reduction in investment in human resources. Pressures to reduce prices and save capital for investment in information technology have led banks to increase use of contingent employment, to keep training expenditures at a low level, and to increase the amount of external recruiting for high-skill positions. Pressures to win market share have encouraged banks to use compensation policies to provide incentives for their workers to focus on acquiring new business rather than cultivating existing customers. Some banks, however, have moved against this industry-wide trend. Those banks most interested in using relationship management strategies or pioneering mass customization strategies have prioritized training investment and employee stability.

This section uses four detailed case studies along with data collected at the industry level to explore trends and variations in how banks have responded in their employment practices to higher levels of competitive pressure. The case studies include one of the largest U.S. commercial banks (Bank A), a leading commercial bank with a strong international presence (Bank B), a small savings and loan (Bank C), and a small whole-

Table 2.4
Employment growth in U.S. finance industry, 1984–93

	1984	1987	1990	1993
Commercial banks	1,496.0	1,539.0	1,563.8	1,496.5
Federal savings banks	185.2	221.7	231.6	168.4

Source: Bureau of Labor Statistics, *Employment, Hours and Earnings*, 1909–94, vol. 2.

sale that is a subsidiary of a major Japanese bank (Bank D). The sample is intentionally biased toward banks that highlight the divergent human resources paradigms in the banking sector and do not always accord with national trends in the sector.

Staffing and Employment Security Policies

Between the early 1980s and early 1990s, overall employment levels in the banking sector remained very steady (table 2.4). Total employment rose slightly through the late 1980s only to decline by a similar amount during the early 1990s.[8] Data on total employment, however, fails to capture dramatic changes in staffing patterns. Over the course of the 1980s banks moved increasingly toward using a part-time labor force as a means of cutting costs. Part-time employees typically work for an hourly wage rather than a salary and do not qualify for health insurance, pension schemes, or vacation benefits, enabling banks to save on their total wage bill. According to one estimate, the number of full-time workers in the banking sector dropped by more than 25 percent between 1984 and 1991.[9]

All four of the banks in our sample have substantially increased the number of branch employees working on a part-time basis. One of the largest commercial banks Bank A has made the most dramatic moves in this direction. Part-time work in the bank was first introduced in 1987, and by 1992 all teller and new account employees, or about 60 percent of the branch labor force, were working on a part-time basis. The other large commercial bank and the small savings and loan (Banks B and C) have gradually moved toward making all teller positions part-time. Over the past five years, part-timers have gone from constituting less than 10 percent to about 30 percent of total branch employment in both banks.

The weakening of ties between employers and employees is also evident in reduced employment security. Banks used to offer some of the most secure jobs in the private sector. Once employed by a specific bank, an individual could reasonably expect to work with the same bank until retirement. Deregulation, fierce competition, and the accompanying waves of consolidation and downsizing, however, have put an end to this job security. Among the banks we interviewed, only the small savings and loan (Bank C) has used the promise of a high level of employment security as a tool of human resource management. This bank is conservative in its hiring practices. Rather than bringing on new employees during times with very high levels of business activity, it asks its existing employees to work harder. Conversely, when the business cycle turns downward, employees are expected to work together in cutting costs. Over the last ten years, the bank has not laid off a single employee. At least two of the other banks, on the other hand, use the lack of employee security to motivate the labor force toward higher levels of performance. Both Bank A and Bank D make it clear to employees that their job security is based on their performance, or in the jargon of the industry, they are "only as good as their last deal."

Work Organization

In the retail banking segment, American banks have traditionally had a high level of task segmentation (Keltner and Finegold 1996 and Hunter 1995). Tellers perform a limited range of tasks from taking payments and cashing checks to checking account balances. New accounts employees are responsible for selling deposit products, checking accounts, and credit cards. Consumer credit officers deal with loans for consumer durables and mortgages.

Over the last decade, however, the trend across the industry has been toward even more fragmentation. Consistent with the move toward non-branch distribution channels, many banks are moving important revenue-generating operations out of the branches. The trends in retail work organization in bank A are typical of the shifts taking place more broadly in the banking industry. When the bank first began to sell investment and insurance products in 1990, it gave little thought to using the branch as a focal point of distribution, because it did not expect enough demand for investment products to justify locating investment services in the branch offices.

The decision to locate investment services outside the branches was soon followed by a similar decision for consumer credit and small business banking. Through the 1980s, branch managers and branch-based consumer credit officers could grant loans of up to $50,000 for individual consumers or small-business owners without needing higher-level approval. Beginning in 1991 the bank began to strip branches of all credit authority. Under the current organization of work, branches take applications for credit cards and standard consumer loans, such as car loans, and send them on to a central office where they are evaluated. Nonstandard consumer loans are referred to a consumer credit officer outside the branch office. Cultivation of business with small enterprises similarly takes place in regional business offices.

The second large commercial bank (Bank B) and the small savings and long (Bank C) are increasingly moving in the opposite direction, toward integrated service delivery and using branches as a focal point for distribution. In Bank C, deposits, money market funds, consumer credit, and simple investment products are all being consolidated around the new accounts position. Tellers have also been cross trained for selling deposit and simple consumer credit products.

Bank B is redesigning work practices not only in its retail operations but also in services to small-business customers. Investment services to affluent clients are increasingly provided by branch-based financial advisors who can also sell consumer credit and deposit products. Lending to small business enterprises is also increasingly coordinated out of branch offices. As of this year, small-business lenders report directly to branch managers and develop their strategies for acquiring new customers in conjunction with branch operations. Each small-business lender is paired with a branch-based investment adviser to support the cross selling of credit, deposit, and investment products.

In the banking market for middle-market and larger corporate clients, integrated service delivery has always been the norm. To be responsive to larger business customers, banks need commercial lenders who know not just credit products but also investments and deposits, electronic banking and cash management services, and international banking products. In most banks, specialists who can handle complex requests support relationship managers, who are generalists. Differences in how banks organize middle-market lending stem mostly from their attitude toward generating business. Banks that place a heavy emphasis on customer acquisition as opposed to cultivating existing clients expect their relationship managers to spend large amounts of time finding new clients. They also tend to employ several individuals per lending group whose major or sole responsibility is to solicit new business. These individuals either follow up on referrals or simply cold call potential customers.

Table 2.5
Branch level training

Position	Length	Initial training Subjects covered	Ongoing training Subjects covered
Teller	5–10 days	• teller duties • basic product knowledge • referrals and service procedures	• sales skills • communication • skills • new accounts • product knowledge
New accounts	2–3 days	• bank-specific product and procedure orientation	• advanced new accounts • sales skills • computer skills
Consumer credit officer	5 days	• bank-specific product and procedure training	• advanced credit • computer skills
Management	1–2 days	• supervisory skills orientation	• communication skills • leadership skills

Source: Keltner, B. (1994), "Comparative Patterns of Adjustment in the U.S. and German Banking Industries: An Institutional Explanation," unpublished Ph.D. dissertation, Stanford University: 114.

Training, Skill Formation, and Career Ladders

In the retail banking segment, training as a rule is short and job specific (table 2.5).[10] Rather than training that focuses on broad and general skill formation, employees in retail banking operations are generally given just enough training to perform the job to which they will be assigned. Those hired into entry level teller positions generally receive five to ten days of classwork and on-the-job instruction to cover the basics of teller duties and product knowledge as well as service and referral procedures. For all positions above the entry level teller, initial training involves a very short orientation in product and technical knowledge. New accounts employees receive two to three days of orientation training, consumer credit officers five days. The tendency to keep training short and job specific is uniform across retail banking operations in all banks.

What primarily differentiates banks' retail training philosophies is the degree to which short training modules are integrated into coherent competency-based career ladders. Bank A makes little attempt to integrate training modules in different product areas to encourage broader skill formation. Because the bank keeps work so highly segmented, there is little need for cross training. The bank's employees can enroll in training in different product areas, but the bank does not actively encourage it.

The small savings and loan and second large commercial bank (Banks B and C) have taken a different approach to training, actively using modular training programs to create strong career paths. Bank C began a program nine years ago to ensure that all branch employees acquire over time a broad training in banking products and procedures. The training course involves eighteen modules of sequential training in subjects related to teller duties, new accounts, and supervision. All employees must complete the training program within eighteen to twenty-four months of being hired. As an incentive to encourage employees to move through the program more quickly, employees receive a salary increase after demonstrating mastery of the skills in each training module. They must first complete the course and then six months later pass a performance review.

Bank B has also used a modular training programs to encourage higher levels of skill formation but has done so in a much less structured manner. Rather than setting up a single uniform course of training to meet increased skill needs, this commercial bank has moved over the last three years to a "self-directed" training regime. Only branch managers have a required course of training. With the branches becoming a focal point for business development, bank executives have come to view formal training for branch managers as important. In other advanced branch positions, bank executives have tried to set out clearly the skills and competencies employees need to develop for advancement but have left employees to develop their own skills as they see fit.

In the commercial banking segment, training in all banks has focused on broad skill development. The training strategies banks have used to develop these skills, however, vary in important ways. The traditional approach to training commercial lenders has focused on MBA recruiting and long periods of initial training. Bank A follows this pattern. It hires new MBAs into a year-long training consisting of both classroom instruction and structured work experience. During the first three to four months of training, future commercial lenders study accounting, financial analysis techniques, product knowledge, and relationship management skills in a classroom setting. Over the next eight to nine months, they rotate through different lending groups to learn to put these skills into practice and to learn about the dynamics of lending in different market settings.

This broad-based initial training has the advantage of making it easier for the bank to move trainees immediately into a position as a commercial lender. It has the drawback, however, of making it much easier for competitors to poach the bank's employees away. Commercial lenders emerge from the training course with a clear and recognizable skill set but not enough experience with the company that trained them to have developed a strong attachment. The lack of coordination between banks in wage setting makes it relatively easy for other banks to lure these employees away by offering a wage premium. As a result, turnover among commercial lenders in this bank can run as high as 35–40 percent a year.

Reacting to the disadvantages of a heavy investment in initial training, some commercial banks are moving toward modular skill development. To fill commercial lending positions, Bank B recruits both retail bank employees and new college graduates into a training program for credit analysts. The training course lasts for four months and consists of classes in finance and accounting combined with project experience in lending groups. Following the completion of training, the trainees are essentially apprenticed to a commercial lender. While performing credit analysis for this commercial lender, they learn the other skills necessary to be a relationship manager. After several years of working for a commercial lender, they can begin to act as a relationship manager for small clients and then move on to larger clients.

In addition to differences in the structure of training programs, variation in the way banks approach the issue of skill formation can be found in how they approach selection and recruiting. The trend in the banking sector over the last decade has been toward more external recruiting of high-skill employees. An earlier study of the U.S. banking industry suggested that whereas 80 percent of branch managers are internally recruited, the figure for consumer credit officers is typically 50 percent and for investment advisors it may be as low as 20 percent (Keltner 1994a). Similarly, many banks recruit up to half their commercial lenders from competitors rather than looking to the ranks of their own employees.

External recruiting for high-skill positions is attractive because in a more cost-conscious environment it has allowed banks to save on training expenses. Of the three high-skill branch positions, only in the branch manager position can most skills be learned on the job. Both consumer credit officers and investment advisers demand considerable extra product and technical training, requiring a hefty training investment. Developing commercial lenders internally, as bank A does, is similarly very expensive. A one-year training course can cost a bank up to $75,000 per commercial lender.

Both Bank A and Bank D conform to the pattern of high levels of external recruiting. A few years ago, Bank A filled up to half its consumer credit officer and small-business lender positions through internal promotion. Now that both the consumer and small-business credit operations have moved outside the branch offices, nearly all new employees in these two positions are recruited externally. As the bank has moved into investment products, it has trained only a small number of its own investment advisors. Instead, it has hired large numbers of investment specialists from other financial institutions, particularly brokerage firms. The small wholesale bank (Bank D) is not averse to using external recruiting as a way of dramatically changing its employee mix. It has recruited many of its credit analysts and all of its commercial lenders from the external labor force.

A second approach to recruiting and selection is found in Banks B and C. As part of their commitments to competence-based career ladders, each bank has moved to increase the level of internal recruiting. Bank B now recruits branch managers almost exclusively from the ranks of new accounts employees, and new accounts employees come predominantly from the ranks of tellers. Of the individuals employed in the branch-based financial advisor position, 60 percent are recruited from within, a figure about three times the industry average, and 40 percent of the bank's small-business lenders are recruited internally from the new accounts and financial advisor positions.[11] In contrast to general industry practice, many of these individuals are promoted to wholesale operations without an undergraduate degree.

The small savings and loan (Bank C) has similarly moved to increase internal recruiting in most positions. Five years ago, it hired 50 percent of its teller and new accounts employees from the external labor market and promoted the other 50 percent from within. At present, the ratio is 70 percent to 30 percent in favor of internal promotion. In hiring for mortgage lenders, on the other hand, the bank has moved in the opposite direction. Where it once took about 50 percent of its employees from its own ranks, it now relies almost exclusively on external recruiting.

Levels and Structure of Compensation, Incentives

The number of levels of compensation in the U.S. banking industry is extremely large. Because there is no collective wage agreement to lump like jobs into pay bands, each job position is rewarded individually. Within each broad occupation, there are usually several levels of gradation. So for example, there are peak-time tellers, regular tellers, and merchant tellers, and commercial lenders move up a career ladder through the positions of lender, associate vice president, vice president, and senior vice president. Some banks use this wealth of job distinctions as a tool to segment work; others use it as an incentive to lengthen job tenure, with promotions continuing to be the primary means for individuals to increase their earnings.

With no new developments in the industrial relations system, the structure of compensation system has changed very little in the U.S. banking industry. What has changed dramatically, however, is the use of contingent pay schemes. Seven years ago banks had no contingent compensation, with all compensation coming in the form of salary. In an effort to motivate higher levels of performance, two types of types of incentive systems have become increasingly common. The first is the use of commissions rather than salaries. The use of commission-based pay began in mortgage lending in the late 1980s. In the course of a few years, commissions in many banks went from being a small percentage of mortgage lenders' pay to representing 100% of their compensation. Commission-based pay has also become an increasingly important means of motivating performance among investment advisors. As banks have moved to include investment and insurance products in their retail operations, many have hired independent brokers who work for a commission rather than a salary.

A second increasingly common incentive system involves sales-based bonuses. A decade ago most banks used nothing more than token prizes to encourage sales performance; for example, high-performing individuals could qualify to win a TV set. In the past several years, sales-based bonus pay has become increasingly important to both wholesale and retail operations. In retail banking, the typical bonus scheme revolves around branch offices rather than individual employees. Branches are given goals on asset growth, fee income, and sales of new products and are rewarded for exceeding these goals. Bonus money is normally given to the branch manager to distribute. For the average branch employee, bonuses account for 3–5 percent of total compensation (table 2.6), but branch managers suggest that particularly motivated branch employees can increase their base wages by as much as 10–15 percent. In wholesale operations, bonus schemes reward individual lenders for generating higher volumes of loans and increasing sales of related financial service products. Commercial lenders can earn thousands of dollars each year from performance-based bonuses accounting for 5–10 percent of their total compensation.

Table 2.6
Average salary and bonus compensation in California banks, 1992

Employment position	Average total Compensation	Average bonus
Branch manager (>$50 mil)	$71,724	$5,725
Branch manager ($20–$50 mil)	$62,180	$4,936
Branch manager (<$20 mil)	$50,596	$2,843
Commercial lender (VP)	$59,294	$4,604
Commercial lender (AVP)	$42,836	$2,239
Consumer credit officer	$41,805	$2,733
Investment adviser	$34,549	$1,475
New accounts	$19,825	$543
Teller	$15,703	$337

Source: Deloitte and Touche (1992), California Bank's Compensation Survey.

Although the industry-wide trend has been toward increased use of contingent pay, not all banks have moved uniformly in this direction. Evidence from our case studies suggests an inverse relationship between the strength of a bank's internal labor market and the use of incentive pay. The two Banks (A and D) that have the weakest internal labor markets are also the banks that make the most use of incentive pay. Bank A was a pioneer in using incentive-based pay to increase sales performance. Incentive pay as a percentage of total compensation has grown steadily to reach a point well above the industry average. In 1994, tellers received an average of 5 percent of their total compensation from incentives, whereas new accounts employees received an average of 15 percent from incentives. For branch managers, the figure was still higher, at 25 percent. Bank D makes heavy use of bonus pay to motivate higher levels of performance from its commercial lenders. Whereas the average commercial lender earns less than 10 percent of his or her total salary from bonus pay, in bank D the figure often runs as high as 20 percent of total income.

In Banks B and C, incentive pay has grown in importance but to a lesser extent. Bank B had no incentive pay systems outside of that for its mortgage operations throughout the 1980s. Five years ago incentive pay slowly began to creep into both its retail and its wholesale operations. Yet incentive pay still remains below the industry average. In most retail positions in Bank B, incentives account for less than 3 percent of total compensation. Even in the branch and small-business lender positions, incentive pay typically remains less than 5 percent of total salary. In Bank C, bonus pay stands at about the same level as the industry average. For

all branch employees except the branch manager, incentive pay is about
5 percent of total salary. For the branch manager, the figure is higher, at
13 percent. Mortgage lenders are again an exception to the overall thrust
of Bank C's human resources policies. As part of the shift toward higher
levels of external recruitment, mortgage lenders have been put on a pure
commission system for compensation.

Change in Business Governance

Employee involvement in business governance in the U.S. banking industry is weak to nonexistent. Because there are no company-based workers'
councils, employees typically have no formal input on decisions related to
hiring and firing, the organization of work, or the introduction of new
technology. Communication between management and workers tends
to take place sporadically and haphazardly. Most large banks have company newsletters that communicate changes in strategic policy and give
employees the opportunity to ask questions and receive answers from
executives. Most banks also encourage executives to meet with employees
informally to gather information about the workforce and changes in the
customer base. The most formalized type of employee involvement programs are suggestions programs that offer cash bonuses for money-saving
suggestions. In search of ways to provide quicker and more cost-effective
service, banks both large and small offer their workers a percentage of any
savings from labor-saving suggestions they make that are implemented.

Three of the four banks we studied exhibit this minimalist approach to
employee involvement. Bank C, by contrast, enlists employees to help
achieve its organizational and strategic goals. Over the past five years,
the bank has increased the use of employee involvement in product focus
groups directed by the marketing department and normally involving
both branch level employees and upper-level managers. The bank also
routinely enlists the help of employees to reduce costs. When pressed to
reduce costs in the early 1990s in response to the consolidation of the
regional banking market, the bank brought together a committee of
employees from all over the bank to develop ideas to bring down its
expense ratio.

Making Sense of Intrasectoral Variation in Employment Relations

Emerging competitive realities have generally had a negative effect on
employees, with the employment relationship weakening fairly uniformly

across the banking industry. All banks have reduced or abandoned altogether commitments to employment security in reaction to a large number of mergers and acquisitions and the accompanying waves of downsizing. The need to cut costs and improve convenience has similarly encouraged banks to increase the amount of contingent employment.

In other areas of human resources management, however, they show greater variation. The banks we profiled have taken very different approaches to training, recruiting and promotion, and compensation. Competitive forces strongly drive variation in these types of human resources policies.

A Low-Skill, "Commodization" Strategy

All banks have been forced by new market dynamics to cut costs and respond to consumer demands for increased levels of convenience, and many banks have made price and convenience the cornerstone of their competitive philosophies. Rather than trying to cultivate broad and long-term relationships with their customers, they have made generating a high volume of business transactions their primary strategic goal and used price and convenience to generate a continuous stream of new banking customers.

In its retail banking strategy, Bank A has been at the forefront of the shift toward transaction-based banking. It has gradually shifted toward a mass market retail strategy, looking to target low-margin customers with simple banking needs. It was among the first banks to invest heavily in ATM machines and one of the first to encourage customers to conduct much of their banking business, including opening new accounts, over the phone. It has pursued aggressive price competition and product innovation.

Bank D has pursued a similar strategy in its wholesale operations. After being acquired by a Japanese bank five years ago, the bank launched an aggressive strategy of expansion. It tried to acquire new business through promises of lower interest rates on loans and lower prices on related financial service products. In its mortgage lending operations, bank C has similarly shifted toward an emphasis on customer acquisition. Rather than generating new business through its existing customers, it has aggressively hired lenders with existing accounts.

In all cases, the shift toward a transaction-based banking paradigm has been linked with a decreased investment in human resources. The strategy is premised on attracting customers through promises of cheap and convenient service offerings rather than quality financial advising. In those business segments characterized by price competition, banks have shifted away from strong internal labor markets and minimized skill needs in many positions. For positions that require formal training, they have made heavy use of external recruiting. To encourage higher levels of job performance, they have increased the use of incentive pay.

Adding Value through Human Resource Investment

A different type of competitive strategy and different approach to human resource management can be found in the business segment for affluent retail clients and small-business enterprises. Both bank B and bank C have reacted to higher levels of competitive pressure by integrating high-quality service delivery into their overall banking strategies. Bank B has increasingly tried to use its branch distribution system to lock affluent retail and small business clients into long-term financial relationships. The shift toward a high-quality strategy began with a 1993 experiment to integrate investment services into branch delivery. The bank executives we spoke to stated that "they were not fully leveraging their branch-based distribution system to attract affluent clients." The experiment began in twenty-six selected branches in one U.S. state. After a very successful first year, the program was taken national in 1994.

A similar refocusing of business priorities has occurred in the wholesale segment. Over the past three years, Bank B's wholesale operations have been increasingly oriented toward the small-business and professional market. The bank is trying to move back to a "character lending" approach to its wholesale operations: an approach based on developing robust and long-term financial relationships. Strong working relationships are expected to make it easier to maximize the profits earned from each client by increasing the number of product cross sales. In shifting toward the relationship management strategy, bank executives have steered deliberately away from the middle market. Their feeling is that intense competition for middle-market clients makes it more difficult to develop strong working relationships with commercial enterprises in that market segment.

Bank C has also responded to higher levels of competitive pressure with an affluent relationship–management strategy. Rather than a new accounts position, they now have branch-based financial advisors who can cross sell deposit, consumer credit, and a range of simple investment products to retail customers. The bank has also increasingly prioritized cross selling existing customers to minimize the number of one-product accounts and correspondingly decreased the emphasis on acquiring new customers. In adopting the relationship management strategy, the bank's goal is both customer retention and the amount of revenues earned from each account.

An increased emphasis on human resources investment has accompanied the shift to an affluent, value-added strategy. Both Bank B and Bank C have used human resources policies to develop a more skilled and stable workforce. Task integration and an emphasis on broad skilling have replaced job segmentation to ensure that employees are capable of delivering high-quality advising to customers. To encourage higher levels of employee stability, each bank has created competence-based career ladders that link modular training programs and opportunities for upward mobility. As part of their commitment to higher levels of human resources investment, both banks have also increased the amount of internal promotion into high-skill positions.

Conclusions: Markets, Technology, and Institutions

Like the banking industries in other advanced industrial countries, the U.S. banking sector has undergone a dramatic amount of restructuring in the last decade. Deregulation and the entrance of new competitors have forced banks in all countries to reduce costs and increase responsiveness. The availability of new forms of information technology has forced banks to rethink their distribution systems and the way they organize work. Finally, mergers and acquisitions in the United States, like privatization in other advanced economies, has removed weak financial service firms and forced those that remain to increase efficiency.

In reacting to these common market trends, U.S. banks have adopted strategies with a number of distinctive elements. The first is the use of fairly intensive price competition and product innovation as a way of attracting new customers. The second is a very high level of investment in information technology. Investment by American banks in ATMs, POS terminals, and on-line terminals for teller and new accounts personnel has outpaced investment by banks in other countries. The third distinctive element is a low level of investment in human resources. American banks have not only abandoned any pretense of employment security but in comparison to their counterparts in other countries made greater use of contingent employment and invested considerably less in training of front line employees.

What best explains this distinctive pattern of reactions is the relative weakness of the institutional structure regulating the U.S. labor market. The weakness of employees' organizations has left banks almost completely unconstrained in their staffing and technology decision making. They find it relatively easy to hire and fire employees or to shift their labor force composition. Banks face no penalties for "dumping" workers and can undertake major layoffs or reorganizations with impunity. They also face few restrictions on employing part-time workers. At the same time, the lack of coordination on vocational training combined with the weakness of collective wage agreements makes it difficult to invest in skills training. Workers come to banks with poor vocational skills; if a bank tries to remedy these skill deficits through heavy investment in initial training, it leaves itself opening to poaching.

These aspects of the labor market environment make it relatively easier to pursue cost cutting and price competition and relatively more difficult to pursue a high-skill, relationship management banking strategy. But if favoring the low-skill outcome, the institutional structure because of its flexibility and openness is also conducive to heterogeneity in outcomes. Two of the banks we profiled have taken advantage of the weakness of employees' organizations to use more contingent employees and to raise investment in information technology and at the same time used human resources policies to create a skilled and more stable labor force in market segments for affluent customers. Each bank has combined broader job definitions, competence-based career ladders, and stronger internal recruiting to overcome institutional barriers to training investment. The openness of the institutional environment has made it possible for innovative companies to find strategies to improve investment in human resources.

Methodological Appendix

Bank A

With close to 100,000 employees and 2,000 branches in more than a dozen U.S. states, this bank is one of the largest in the United States. Through a series of mergers and acquisitions, the bank has evolved from a regional actor to one of the most important players in the banking system in the course of a few years. In its retail segment, the bank has implemented a mass market strategy, using both information technology and a large branch network to achieve wide penetration. The bank's wholesale strategy focuses on large corporate clients, particularly those with important overseas operations.

Interviews:
Branch manager
Commercial lender
Corporate manager of executive development
Corporate compensation manager

Bank B

Bank B is another leading U.S. commercial bank. In 1994, it had a total of 80,000 employees and 3,000 branches in seven different states. The bank has a significant international presence. In both the retail and wholesale segments, it has attempted to find new strategies to fit a new market environment rather than move out of traditional banking customer segments. It was the first large bank to use its branch-based distribution system to pursue a high value added strategy among retail customers. In its wholesale operations, whereas other banks its size have been busy moving into investment banking activities, Bank B has continued to focus on small and medium-sized business enterprises.

Interviews:
Division training and development manager
Corporate HR manager for retail banking
Corporate compensation manager
Commercial lender

Bank C

Bank C is a small savings and loan with 560 employees, 24 branches, and 7 loan offices. Its operations are confined to one major U.S. city. The bank's main products are loans on real estate for both housing and commercial properties. It makes no loans to commercial business. In its retail segment it has focused on traditional banking products up to and including simple investments.

Interviews:
Training manager
Branch manager
Manager, real estate lending
Regional manager of retail operations

Bank D

Bank D is a small wholesale bank wholly owned by a major Japanese bank. The bank has eight corporate lending offices throughout California and $1 billion in assets. The bank's lending activities are divided between three main divisions: the Pacific Rim, real estate, and corporate lending. In its corporate lending operations, the bank focuses on business enterprises with between $10 and $50 million in annual revenues.

Interviews:
Senior vice president, commercial lending
Human resources manager

Notes

1. For two excellent accounts of the historical roots of regulation and the causes of regulatory reform, see Rogers 1993 and Owens 1986.

2. As Sipple (1989: 55) points out, however, few thrifts have made use of these powers.

3. For a more detailed discussion on this point see Keltner 1995, pp. 47–48.

4. All data on private holdings are from U.S. Department of Commerce 1992, p. 506.

5. The gap in investment was particularly pronounced between German and American banks. In 1990, American banks had a combined total of 74 on-line terminals per 100 tellers or new accounts employees, whereas in Germany the combined total stood at 23 per 100 employees. See *Service Sector Productivity* 1992.

6. Investment in ATMs was particularly intense in the early 1980s, allowing the United States along with Japan to be the only OECD countries to reach a density level of 200 ATM machines per million inhabitants by 1983. See Broeker 1989 and Little 1994.

7. First Chicago's controversial move to impose a $3 service charge for visiting a teller was part of a general trend toward increased fees for branch services. See Mitchell and Melcher 1995 and Hannan 1994.

8. In the coming years, employment levels are expected to continue to drop with potentially hundreds of thousands of bank employees losing their jobs, see Holland 1995.

9. Data from McKinsey & Co. cited in "A Survey of International Banking," p. 28.

10. According to data from the Bureau of Labor Statistics, only 20 percent of tellers received any formal off-the-job training. The great majority of tellers receive both initial and upgrade training only on the job.

11. The bank recruits 20 percent of its small-business bankers directly from universities and trains them to be commercial lenders. It recruits the remaining 40 percent of lenders in wholesale operations from other banks. These individuals typically bring an industry expertise with them.

References

"American Banking: Roped Together." (1995). *The Economist*, October 28, 92.

"America's Little Fellows Surge Ahead." (1993). *The Economist*, July 3, 59–60.

Bank Administration Institute. (1993). *New Paradigms in Retail Banking*: The PDS Report on the Future of Retail Banking Delivery. New York: Bank Administration Institute.

Barrett, A. (1995). "It's a Small Business World." *Business Week*, April 17, 96–101.

Broeker, G. (1989). *Competition in Banking: Trends in Banking Structures and Regulation in OECD Countries*. Paris: OECD.

Bryan, L. (1988). *Breaking Up the Bank*. Homewood, IL: Dow Jones-Irwin.

Bureau of Labor Statistics. 1994. *Employment, Hours and Earnings, 1909–1994* (Washington, D.C.: U.S. Department of Labor).

Bureau of Labor Statistics. 1995. *Occupation Employment Statistics Survey* (Washington, D.C.: U.S. Department of Labor).

Davenport, T., and N. Nohria. (1994). "Case Management and the Integration of Labor." *Sloan Management Review* 35 (winter): 11–21.

Deloitte and Touche Consulting. 1992. *California Banks' Compensation Survey* (San Francisco: Deloitte and Touche Financial Services Group).

Federal Deposit Insurance Corporation. *Historical Statistics on Banking, 1934–1994*, Vol. 1 (Washington, D.C.: The Federal Deposit Insurance Company, Division of Research and Statistics).

Glasgall, W. (1993). "The Global Investor." *Business Week*, October 11, 54–59.

Hannan, T. (1994). "Recent Trends in Retail Fees and Services of Depository Institutions." *Federal Reserve Bulletin* (September): 771–81.

Hargroves, J. (1989). "The Basic Skills Crisis." *New England Economic Review*, September 1, 56–58.

Holland, K. (1995). "Blood on the Marble Floors." *Business Week*, February 27, 98–99.

Holland, K., and R. Melcher. (1995). "Why Banks Keep Bulking Up." *Business Week*, July 31, 66–67.

Hunter, L. (1995). "How Will Competition Change Human Resource Management in Retail Banking? A Strategic Perspective." Working Paper #95-04, Wharton Financial Institutions Center.

Hylton, R. (1995). "Merger Mania and Fat Profits Make the Big Banks Look Good." *Fortune*, August 7, 259–61.

Keltner, B. (1995). "Relationship Banking and Competitive Advantage: Evidence from the U.S. and Germany." *California Management Review* 37 (summer): 45–72.

Keltner, B. (1994). *Divergent Patterns of Adjustment in the U.S. and German Banking Industries: An Institutional Explanation*. Unpublished Ph.D. diss. Stanford University.

Keltner B., and D. Finegold. (1996). "Adding Value in Banking: Human Resource Innovations for Service Firms." *Sloan Management Review* (fall): 57–68.

Arthur D. Little. (1994). Hochleistungsorganisation Kreditinstitut: Mehr als Kursfristige Schlankheitskur." Wiesbaden.

Lunt, P. (1990). "Entry-Level Workers Get Extra Help." *ABA Banking Journal* (June): 37–39.

Service Sector Productivity. (1992). Washington, DC: McKinsey Global Institute.

Mitchell, R., and R. Melcher. (1995). "Thanks for Your Deposit. That'll Be $3." *Business Week,* May 15: 46.

Owens, J. (1986). "The Regulation and Deregulation of American Financial Institutions in the United States." In Andrew Cox (ed.), *The State, Finance, and Industry: A Comparative Analysis of Post-War Trends in Six Advanced Industrial Economies.* Worcester, U.K.: Billings and Sons, Ltd., 172–230.

Rogers, D. (1993). *The Future of American Banking.* New York: McGraw-Hill, Inc.

Seaman, D. (1992). "Branch Automation and Productivity." *Journal of Retail Banking* 14 (summer): 39–42.

Sipple, E. (1989). "When Change and Continuity Collide: Capitalizing on Strategic Gridlock in Financial Services." *California Management Review,* 31: 51–74.

"A Survey of International Banking." (1994). *The Economist,* April 30, 9.

Svare, J. (1989). "Forging Profitable Relationships: Competition is Keen For Middle Market Business." *Bank Administration,* 65: 14–24.

U.S. Department of Commerce. (1992). *Statistical Abstract of the United States: Flow of Funds Accounts—Assets and Liabilities of Households: 1980 to 1992.* Washington DC: U.S. Government Printing Office.

Vitols, S. (1994). "Banks and Industrial Finance in Germany and the U.S.: An Organizational Perspective on Long-Term Lending." Paper presented at conference, Institutions of Advanced Capitalism, March, Wissenschaftszentrum Berlin.

"When to throw 'em back." (1994). *The Economist,* March 12, 81.

3

Change in Tandem: Employment Relations in Australian Retail Banks

Jim Kitay

The Australian banking industry has undergone significant changes since the early 1980s. Competition has increased sharply as new banks have entered the market and a range of nonbanking institutions have encroached on markets that had long been protected. Restrictions on capital flows and credit have been eased to the point where Australia is now a full participant in the international financial system.

Once an industry in which lifetime job security was the norm, banks have embarked on extensive downsizing programs. Branches were traditionally the focus of retail banking, but alternative sources of delivery to customers are increasingly being used. Functions have been removed from branches and centralized, greater control over branch activities is exercised through performance targets, and a fundamental shift is taking place toward the introduction of a "sales culture". Although long career ladders remain, it has become harder to ascend them, because new entry ports have opened, formal qualifications are increasingly required for promotion to management, and organizational structures are flattened. More-specialized occupational structures are replacing the rounded "career banker."

Trade unionism has long been entrenched in Australian banking, and the Finance Sector Union continues to play a prominent role. Although the union is more willing than formerly to take industrial action over a range of issues, there is also a trend toward change by agreement between management and union.

Change in the industry has been rapid and profound, but interestingly, the range of changes in employment relations taking place in most banks is similar. Some differences have appeared among the major banks, but these have been matters of emphasis and detail rather than fundamental strategy. Although differences exist between large and small enterprises, the trend is toward more, rather than less, similarity in the industry.

Table 3.1
Number of financial institutions

Type of institution	1980	1995
Banks	19	43
Building societies and credit unions	765	321
Finance companies	117	103
Merchant banks	59	83
Mortgage originators	0	26
Funds managers	35	93

Source: Council for Financial Supervisors, Annual Report 1995, CANNEX, Campbell Inquiry, Interim Report, ASSIRT, reported in Westpac Banking Corporation (1996) Submission to Wallis Inquiry.

Changes in the Institutional Environment of the Banking Industry

Deregulation and Privatization

The Australian finance industry is more differentiated than that in some other countries. However, the trend is toward greater convergence, particularly between banking and insurance.

Retail banking serves households and small to medium-sized businesses. Customers are offered many variations on a small number of basic products such as savings, checking, and fixed-deposit accounts and credit cards, loans, and overdrafts. Some banks have affiliations with stock brokerage houses, and most offer insurance products and financial planning services.

As shown in table 3.1, in 1995 there were 43 banking groups in Australia (Prices Surveillance Authority 1995: 15). Four major domestic banks have dominated the market since the early 1980s—the ANZ (formerly Australian & New Zealand) Banking Group, Commonwealth Bank of Australia, National Australia Bank, and Westpac Banking Corporation. The majors are present in all states and territories. A small number of regionally based banks also compete in the retail market. Most of the remainder, particularly foreign-owned banks, restrict themselves to merchant banking activities.

Three main factors have contributed to the changes in the competitive environment and the way work is performed in banking: first and most far reaching, a reduction in state regulation; second, privatization of government-owned banks; and third, extensive technological change. The sharpest employment relations effects occurred in the early 1990s, triggered by a downturn in the business cycle, but changes began prior to that.

Government regulations concerning banks began to be eased in the early 1970s and accelerated after the election of a federal Labor government in 1983. New initiatives included floating the dollar, abolishing restrictions on capital flows and investment, removing ceilings on interest rates, and permitting foreign-owned banks to operate in all areas of the industry. As well, a number of domestic nonbanking financial institutions, such as building societies, were granted banking licenses.

Privatization also affected the industry. Originally, the federal government wholly owned one of the four major banks, the Commonwealth Bank. After absorbing the financially troubled State Bank of Victoria (SBV) in 1990, slightly under half of the Commonwealth Bank was sold, with the remainder privatized in 1996. Most of the state government banks have also been sold.

The privatization of the State Bank of New South Wales initiated a different aspect of deregulation. Although there has been some overlap in the activities of banks and insurance companies, there are restrictions on cross-ownership. However, in 1995 approval was given for the Colonial Mutual Insurance Company to purchase the State Bank of New South Wales. Furthermore, many of the bank branches of the restructured Colonial group now operate on a franchise basis.

Restrictions on bank ownership remain, and the Trade Practices Commission ruled in 1995 that further concentration would be limited. At present, individual or corporate shareholdings in banks are limited to 10 percent (Daugaard and Valentine 1993: 63). Conversely, banks are not large holders of equity in nonfinancial enterprises because the Reserve Bank requires that such investments "should not be substantial" (Martin Report 1991: 172).

Industrial Relations Developments

Deregulation has also affected Australia's industrial relations. General developments are considered here, with changes specific to the banking industry discussed below.

Since shortly before Australia became an independent federation in 1900, Australian industrial relations have featured public systems of compulsory conciliation and arbitration. Most Australian workplaces, whether unionized or not, are covered by awards handed down by the tribunals, the provisions of which apply to most employees below (and in many cases including) management level.

Although awards generally set minimum conditions that could be adjusted upward and the operation of the system was often quite flexible in practice, in the deregulatory climate of the 1980s the tribunals came to be seen as unduly centralized and inflexible. The banking industry was illustrative of this situation, in that the major banks were covered by one award negotiated at industry level between the employer association and the union.

A series of changes have led to the decentralization of Australian industrial relations. One of the most important was the development of an Accord between the leaderships of the Australian Council of Trade Unions (ACTU) and the Australian Labor Party in 1983. Although centralizing tendencies characterized the early years of the Accord, its focus shifted toward industry and enterprise levels in the late 1980s.

In another development, influenced by neoclassical economics, libertarian philosophy, and American human resources management concepts, Australian employers and employer associations began to seek decentralized mechanisms for setting terms and conditions of employment. Although no consensus on details emerged among unions, management, and governments, a broad constituency coalesced around arguments to the effect that more-flexible work arrangements and decentralized industrial relations institutions would enhance productivity.

Decentralization occurred through a series of decisions by the federal tribunal, the Australian Industrial Relations Commission (AIRC), beginning in the late 1980s with a focus on restructuring awards to improve work practices, increase training levels, and improve career structures. However, the pace of change was considered to be too slow, and in 1991 the AIRC announced a system in which "enterprise bargaining" between the parties was to be the primary model, with an arbitrated safety net available for workers unable to negotiate an agreement with their employer. Although post-Fordist models of production influence the rhetoric underlying enterprise bargaining (see Badham and Mathews 1989), the practice has been diverse, ranging from settlements reached largely at industry level to individual workplace agreements; and from simple cost-cutting approaches to initiatives in which the parties agreed to work toward a "learning organization."

The election of a conservative federal government in 1996 led to more radical changes to the institutional framework, with the introduction of legislation that permitted antiunion, individualizing initiatives on the part of employers.

A final institutional change has been a trend toward union amalgamations. A series of amalgamations in banking and insurance resulted in the formation of the Finance Sector Union (FSU),[1] with coverage of the entire industry.

Competitive Pressures from Markets and Technology

Competitive pressures in the banking industry have increased since deregulation. Foreign-owned banks had until 1984 been prohibited from providing retail services, but in that year sixteen foreign-owned banks were granted full licenses. As well, a number of domestic nonbanking financial institutions, such as building societies, subsequently became banks. Of the foreign banks, only Citibank has developed a significant retail operation, but some of the former building societies have achieved considerable success as regional banks. Table 3.2 shows that the percentage share of deposits held by banks has increased, but this can be attributed to some of the larger building societies' becoming banks, while the share held by other nonbank financial institutions has also grown. Within the banking sector, the major banks have maintained and even increased their dominance.

The boundaries between banks and other financial institutions began to erode in the 1980s. Most banks now offer insurance products, and insurance companies have entered the home loans market. Low-cost home loan providers that have not established branch networks have also appeared. Although such "mortgage managers" are not new in Australia, their

Table 3.2
Share of demand deposits

Banks and nonbanks		
	1981	1995
Banks	74.0%	79.6%
Building societies	22.7	8.4
Credit unions	3.3	8.2
Cash management trusts	—	3.8
Within banking sector		
	1980	1995
Major banks	68.8%	76.9%
Other banks	31.2	23.1

Source: Prices Surveillance Authority 1995, tables F1 and F3.

market share shot from 2.5 percent in the second quarter of 1994 to about 10 percent a year later, thanks in large part to interest rates typically 1 percent or more below those of banks (Sydney Morning-Herald, October 14 and 20, 1995; Australian Financial Review, November 1, 1995). The nonbank share of the mortgage market peaked at more than 20 percent in 1997 before sliding, as banks reduced their mortgage rates to more competitive levels, but at the cost of reducing the contribution of interest charges to banks' profitability (Sydney Morning-Herald, December 11, 1997).

Daugaard and Valentine (1993: 41) observed that prior to deregulation, "the demand for loans at the controlled rate almost always exceeded the supply, and banks were usually in the position of credit rationers." Deregulation increased the level of funds available to banks. However, a combination of the business cycle and growing competition between corporate lenders was an important factor in a "substantial increase in bad debts experienced in the late 1980's" (Moore 1992: 182), particularly in property development. By the early 1990s, doubts were being expressed about the continued viability of two of the four major banks, which have since returned to profitability.

The use of new technology has enabled banks to change the way in which they conduct business with their customers. Traditionally, Australian banks relied on extensive branch structures. The ratio of branches to population fell gradually from 80 per 100,000 in 1980 to 38 per 100,000 in 1994, the first year in which there was an absolute decline in branch numbers. This is a higher ratio than that of Canada, the United Kingdom, and the United States of America, but below that of much of Continental Europe. The major banks eliminated about 500 branches (9 percent) between 1992 and 1994, with further reductions regularly announced. Overall, branches appear to be operating more efficiently, with the real value of deposits per branch increasing by 56 percent between 1987 and 1994 (Prices Surveillance Authority 1995; ABS Cat. No. 3101.0; Reserve Bank 1996; Wallis et al. 1997).

Among the technological changes that enabled new methods of delivery were the introduction of ATMs in 1980 and EFTPOS in 1985. These have proliferated to more than 7,000 ATMS and 100,000 EFTPOS terminals serving a population of about 18 million (Prices Surveillance Authority 1995; Wallis et al. 1996). Telephone banking has increased rapidly in popularity, and home computer banking is gradually being introduced.

Technology has been instrumental in the development of new distributional channels, although the full capabilities of technology are only beginning to be realized. Computerization has also enabled the development of a sales culture by providing branch staff with information about customers to identify sales opportunities.

Competitive Strategies

A number of experienced managers asserted in interviews that prior to deregulation, banks did not really compete with one another. This is probably an exaggeration, but there was little attempt to seek market share aggressively or to cut costs.

Since the early 1980s, Australian banks have undertaken a range of initiatives designed to improve their competitive position. Interestingly, most retail banks have pursued most of the same strategies. This point was raised in interviews with senior managers, who agreed that there is little to distinguish among their strategic approaches. Given the high concentration of the Australian population in a small number of urban centers and the small number of retail banks in each state (the "big four" plus a few regional banks), it is not surprising that the banks watch each other closely and quickly copy new initiatives.

The structure of the Australian banking industry after the Second World War was very stable until the late 1970s. As the pressures for deregulation became greater in the 1980s, the major banks sought to position themselves for a more competitive environment through mergers and acquisitions. Two of Australia's current major banks, Westpac and the National Australia Bank, resulted from mergers in 1981 (Carew 1991).

When all the major banks returned to profitability in 1994, the regional banks became takeover targets, sparking a hunt for partners to make it more difficult for a larger bank to move in on their share register. For example, the New South Wales–based Advance Bank purchased the state-owned Bank of South Australia, but was itself subsequently taken over by another NSW-based regional, the St. George Bank.

Another strategy pursued by Australian banks has been internationalization. Though all four major banks have developed overseas activities, the National Australia Bank has internationalized most effectively. Since the mid-1980s, it has purchased banks in New Zealand, England, Scotland, Northern Ireland, and the United States. In mid-1995, only 56 percent of its assets were in Australia, with 27 percent in Europe, 15 percent in New Zealand, and 6 percent elsewhere (National Australia Bank 1995).

If mergers, acquisitions, and internationalization are primarily confined to Australia's largest or most profitable banks, other strategies appear to be common to nearly all banks. A key element in these strategies is undoubtedly the rise of shareholder power (see Useem 1993). The recent takeovers of regional banks, speculation about the possible takeover of a major bank, and the pressure to improve returns to shareholders have focused senior executives' attention on share prices, epitomized by a sign in the foyer of a major bank's training facility reading "The Real Bottom Line," with the previous day's closing share price prominently displayed.

The key indicator for market analysts for publicly listed banks is the noninterest cost/income ratio (table 3.3). The average cost/income ratio among the major banks has ranged between 60 and 67 percent during the 1990s, with the National Australia Bank consistently producing the lowest ratio, about 56 percent in 1996 (Prices Surveillance Authority 1995; National Australia Bank 1997), still well above the standard of less than 50 percent to which they aspire. Banks' competitive strategies have addressed both the cost and the income side of this ratio.

Perhaps the quickest way for banks to improve share prices is to cut noninterest costs. Westpac and the ANZ vigorously pursued this strategy after their financial losses in 1992, followed by the Commonwealth as it tried to absorb the State Bank of Victoria (SBV) and adapt to private ownership, while the National Australia Bank sought to maintain its lead in this area.

Although Australian banks have cut their costs, including personnel costs, no bank stands out as a cost leader, offering products at consistently lower prices than its competitors. Although banks constantly advertise their prices to the public, they do not view price leadership as a viable strategy, and they appear to have met the threat of the low-cost mortgage originators that tried to compete exclusively on price.

Similarly, although all banks have greatly expanded their range of products, managers also do not see product innovation as a viable competitive strategy. With both price and innovation, any advantage is likely to be temporary, as the lead time for matching competitors' initiatives is often only a matter of hours.

Australian banks instead base their competitive strategies on high-quality, convenient service to customers. In the major banks, this is articulated in terms of a shift from a "banking culture" in which money is processed or rationed to customers, to a "sales culture" or "sales and service culture."

The "service" component emphasizes easier access for customers to banking facilities, including extended business hours and the use of tech-

Table 3.3
Financial performance: Four major banks

Performance indicator	1995	1994	1993	1992	1991	1990
Noninterest expenses/ total operating income (%)	59.9	62.5	63.6	67.6	63.7	62.7
Net profit before tax/assets (%)	1.6	1.4	1.0	−0.1	0.7	0.9
Net profit after tax/equity (%)	15.3	13.7	6.9	−4.3	9.6	10.3
Net profit before tax/staff ($)	n.a.	37,226	24,653	−2209	14,481	18,698
Net profit before tax/branch ($)	n.a.	1,143,805	741,953	−67,366	465,973	707,042

Source: Prices Surveillance Authority 1995, table F8.

nology to reduce the need to visit branches. The "sales" component involves using technology to match customers with products, in conjunction with American-inspired sales techniques.

Banks are also seeking to segment the market and provide different levels of service. "High value" customers receive personalized attention, whereas less-affluent customers are guided into low-cost channels such as ATMs. Indeed, a Prices Surveillance Authority inquiry into bank fees and charges in 1995 revolved around a conflict between the banks' view that accounts with low balances and high levels of transactions were unprofitable, and accusations by welfare groups that the banks' fee structures sought to shift poorer customers to other banks or out of the banking system altogether.

Two points need to be made regarding competitive strategy. First, banks appear to have adopted broadly similar strategies. It is unclear whether any bank will be able to compete in terms of price leadership, or if a strategy other than sales and service will be adopted. Second, pressure from board and senior executive levels to reduce costs is interacting with the sales and service strategy to yield particular organizational forms and changes to jobs. The major banks in particular are seeking to rationalize their branch structures and increase customers' use of nonbranch banking. At the same time, many jobs are becoming more specialized, and task content is changing. Thus the sales and service strategy is being introduced in a way that seeks to reduce costs in the areas of staffing and property. The emphasis on cost reduction appears to have less to do with the price at which products are offered to the public than with decreasing the numerator of the cost/income ratio to enhance the price of shares.

Changes in the Labor Market

Banking has changed from an industry employing predominantly male, full-time employees to one that employs a majority of women, of whom a growing proportion work part-time. Since 1990 a small number of casual positions have been established.

The "big four" banks are among the largest enterprises in Australia. For example, even after a major downsizing program, the Commonwealth Bank employed more than 36,000 staff in 1995, down from more than 48,000 in 1991.[2]

Table 3.4 shows significant employment growth in banks through the 1980s.[3] There was a small drop between 1990 and 1992, and a sharp fall,

Table 3.4
Employment: Australian banking industry, 1984–1993

Year	Men			Women			Total		
	Full-time	Part-time	Total	Full-time	Part-time	Total	Full-time	Part-time	Total
1984	61.7	0.7	62.5	52.6	13.8	66.4	114.4	14.5	128.9
1985	67.2	0.5	67.7	54.7	15.8	70.5	122	16.2	138.2
1986	69.4	0.3	69.7	67.2	14.6	81.8	136.6	14.9	151.5
1987	69.9[1]	0.4	70.3	70.9	15.6	86.5	140.8	16	156.8
1988	68.3	0.5	68.8	68.4	15.5	83.9	136.7	16	152.7
1989	70.8	1.2	72	73.6	22.3	96	144.4	23.5	167.9
1990	71.2	0.8	72	75.1	20	95.1	146.3	20.8	167.1
1991	76.1	1.5	77.6	74.9	22.8	97.8	151.1	24.3	175.4
1992	65.4	0.7	66.1	73.6	26.3	99.9	139.1	27	166.1
1993	64.6	1.1	65.8	67.6	26.2	93.7	132.2	27.3	159.5

Source: Australian Bureau of Statistics, unpublished data.
Notes: Figures expressed are in thousands of employees.
1. The ABS data for this cell lists 79.9, which appears to be a typographical error.

nearly 4 percent of total employment, in 1993. Increasing business volumes generated the growth in the 1980s, which occurred despite warnings that technological change would lead to reduced employment. The decrease in 1991–93, more than 15,000 positions shed from of total of 175,000, resulted from major cost-cutting exercises in three of the four major banks during a recession. Staff reductions have continued through the 1990s.

The overall reduction in staff masks an increase in part-time positions. Slightly more than 12 percent of full-time jobs were lost between 1991 and 1993, matched by a nearly identical increase in part-time employment. The growth in part-time work has also continued through the 1990s. Casual employment is not currently a significant factor in banking.

Although a majority of bank employees are women, this is a relatively recent phenomenon. Data compiled by the Finance Sector Union[4] show that 59 percent of the workforce was male in 1975, falling to 54 percent in 1980. Different figures supplied by the Australian Bureau of Statistics show a steady increase in female employment, from 51.5 percent in 1984 to 54 percent in 1986, reaching nearly 59 percent of the workforce in 1993.[5] Much of the change can be attributed to the growth of part-time employment of women. Women constituted only a small majority of full-time employees in 1993, but were nearly 96 percent of the part-time

workforce. Nearly 28 percent of women worked part-time in 1993, compared with under 2 percent of men.

FSU data[6] show that the most noticeable change in age composition is
the decline in the proportion of employees under the age of 21, especially
women. The proportion of women over the age of 30, on the other hand,
has risen, reflecting the recruitment of married women to part-time positions in branches.

The level of educational qualifications in banking is not high compared
with that of the general working population.[7] Although the proportion of
finance industry employees with tertiary qualifications is nearly the same
as that in other industries, fewer finance sector employees obtain trade or
vocational qualifications. There is also a gender imbalance in qualifications
in finance, as the proportion of men with tertiary qualifications is considerably higher than that in other industries, but the proportion of tertiary
qualified women is considerably lower.

Change and Variation in Employment Practices

This section concentrates on the four main areas of human resources and
industrial relations practices: work organization, staffing arrangements,
skill formation, and compensation practices. The information is based on
materials gathered from two major domestic banks (bank A and bank B)
and one regional bank (bank C),[8] as well as from trade unions and industry sources. The focus is on branches rather than other retail functions.

Work Organization

Since the late 1980s, changes to work organization in the major banks
have been driven first by cost reduction and more recently by the development of a sales culture. The result has been a substantial change in
branch structure and division of labor. Superficially it appears that deskilling has occurred, but the reality is more complex. Branches in the
regional banks have undergone fewer changes to work tasks, but they
have led a move toward extended trading hours. Both large and small
banks are introducing new categories of lenders with nontraditional hours
of work whose sole responsibility is sales.

Prior to the establishment of new banks in the mid-1980s, branches
contained similar jobs and offered a similar range of services regardless of
location. New employees typically commenced with basic clerical duties.

Employees might spend some years in these back office positions before taking on the front office job of teller. Lending, supervisory, or more senior back office positions might follow, after which an employee could aspire to branch management.

Although banks developed elaborate standard procedures, branches traditionally enjoyed a degree of autonomy, particularly in three areas. First, they were relatively self-contained, performing most front and back office tasks in house. Second, the manager was a figure of considerable authority both inside the bank and to the outside world. The source of his authority (until recently bank managers were always men) was his role as a lender, a position of some influence in the wider community. Third, branches reported to more senior levels of the bank infrequently, typically only once a year.

Computerization opened up many possibilities. The technologies that were selected and the ways in which they were used should be understood in terms of the drive toward cost reduction and the sales culture. If work organization in banks is converging on a relatively narrow range of forms, this is due not to technological imperatives but to the ways banks have harnessed technology in the pursuit of particular strategies.

Computers, which were introduced in Australian banks in the 1960s, had three major effects on work organization. First, they increased the speed with which paperwork could be processed and allowed the elimination of steps in the processing chain. Second, they enabled rapid transfers of data to occur between branches and central areas of the bank. Third, they gave banks the ability to offer services outside branches, through ATMs, EFTPOS, and telephone and home banking.

From the mid-1970s, banks gradually took advantage of new technology by removing processing jobs from branches and centralizing them in large offices. This trend increased in the early 1990s. Although many processing tasks have never been highly skilled, the lower volumes in branches made it likely each employee would perform a range of activities. Centralized processing centers have a higher volume of throughput, and although job rotation has been introduced, there is less task variation on a daily basis than was the case in branches. Similarly, banks are establishing centralized telephone centers, seeking to divert questions about products or customer accounts away from branches. By removing processing, basic enquiries, and simple transactions from branches, the major banks are seeking to reduce the need for branches and reconstitute those that remain as sales outlets, while reorganizing the tasks that were removed along Taylorist lines.

The lending role has also been reduced in branches, which has eliminated one of the key functions of traditional branch management and downgraded that job. In the future, branches will continue to employ a "manager," but he or she will perform the tasks of, and in most cases be paid as, a customer service supervisor.

As well, new lending positions have been created. Many former branch managers became "business bankers," removed from branches and given a portfolio of high net worth individuals and small to medium-sized businesses. For standard retail products such as mortgages, mobile lenders, who typically are not based in branches and do not work "normal" banking hours, have been appointed.

What of the jobs that remain in branches? In traditional branches, the core of the teller's job is to perform basic customer transactions. The task range varies among banks, and even within banks. Bank B distinguishes between tellers, who deal with basic transactions only, and customer service officers, who deal with procedures such as opening accounts. In bank A, one generic customer service officer classification performs all customer service tasks except lending.

In the new-style branches in both bank A and bank B, tellers' tasks are restricted to basic transactions. The intention is to keep the queues for basic transactions moving, and therefore more complex activities such as opening new accounts are passed on to another officer, usually classified at a higher level.

It would be a mistake, however, to consider the reduction of tasks in isolation from the shift toward a sales culture. An additional responsibility has been added to the teller's role, that of cross selling. Tellers are being encouraged not simply to process transactions but to identify opportunities for making sales of additional bank products, for which the customers are then referred to other employees. Referral targets are set and monitored, with "league tables" of individual and branch output displayed on notice boards in staff lunchrooms. Tellers are also required to have knowledge about a wider range of products. Determining whether these changes constitute up-skilling or deskilling is not simple.

Turning to the regional banks, when bank C converted from a building society to a bank, it had small branches that did not offer a full range of services and managers whose duties and salaries were those of supervisors. The major banks are currently trying to look more like the smaller banks by adopting a similar branch setup. The smaller banks like bank C also have a strong ethic of customer service, which again the larger banks are seeking to emulate.

Bank C differs somewhat from bank B in that it has never distinguished between tellers and inquiries staff, nor has it given the same emphasis to stripping out functions from the branches. If anything, functions are being added to the branches as the former building societies take on more of the mainstream activities of traditional banks. The philosophy is that any branch employee—including managers—should deal with all retail transactions and inquiries except lending. (Unlike in the major banks, the lending function in Bank C was not formally attached to branches, although lenders often have offices in branches).

Managers in bank C asserted in interviews that their technology is more sophisticated and better integrated than that of the major banks. Thus customer service staff perform a range of processing functions on-line. Although it has centralized some operations and established telephone inquiries centers, bank C does not have the large, centralized processing centers typical of the major banks.

Banks use complex staffing formulas for branches based on the frequency and type of transactions that occur there. To reduce costs, these models have been used to cut staffing levels. Although new technology makes work in branches easier, interviews with experienced branch staff suggest that this does not compensate for declining staff levels combined with the increase in product knowledge required. The overall effect has been an increase in work intensity, particularly in bank B.

Although banks were once permitted to open on Saturday morning, this permission was removed from the award in 1963. Building societies, however, never lost this right, and the banks that were formerly building societies have sought to extend business hours further into the weekend. The objective, as expressed by management, is eventually to move to seven-day trading in branches. The larger banks have followed this lead, regaining the right to open for weekend trading through negotiation with the union.

Staffing Arrangements and Employment Security

Until recently, Australian banks used recruitment and natural attrition to adjust employment levels, but they now employ a wider range of methods, including retraining, redeployment, part-time and casual labor, and voluntary and involuntary redundancy. There has been some outsourcing of ancillary staff, and contract staff are now sometimes used to cover short-term requirements. Internal labor markets have also eroded. Career paths are now more differentiated, with varying horizons.

Internal Labor Markets

Until the introduction of computers, banks filled positions beyond entry level from within and effectively offered lifetime employment. Each year, banks recruited large numbers of those leaving school, aged 16–18, most of whom began by performing base grade processing tasks. This was their first step on a long career path, from customer service jobs to supervision or lending, then into management. Prior to deregulation, the path to branch management was slow. It was rare for managers to be appointed before the age of 35, and often not until an employee was over 40 did he join the ranks of bank managers. Movement between branches and other areas of the bank, such as personnel, was common.

The careers of men and women in banking typically differed. For many years women were expected to leave the bank after marriage. Banks had large numbers of young, single women serving in lower-level clerical positions. Unmarried women who remained in the bank seldom rose above premanagement positions. After the marriage ban was dropped, many more women remained with their banks. Women now commonly continue working for some time after marriage but resign when their first child is born, returning to the industry later on a part-time basis.

All banks have EEO policies and wish to increase the number of women in management. However, progress in this area has been slow. Table 3.5 shows the changing distribution of men and women among all bank employees.

In the regional banks, the majority of branch managers are women, but recall that these are not true managerial positions. At the time the interviews were conducted, bank C had significant numbers of women in management roles in a range of functional areas, but most of the line managers above branch level were men. In banks A and B, about 5 percent of executives were women in 1995 and 15 percent of managers. Although

Table 3.5
Gender distribution of staff by grade, 1987–1995 (two major banks)

	1987		1995	
	Male	Female	Male	Female
Senior managers	98.9%	1.1%	94.6%	5.4%
Managers	94.8	5.2	84.6	15.4
Supervisors	69.3	30.7	53.1	46.9
Clerical officers	28.2	71.8	18.2	81.8

Sources: Bodi et al. 1992; ANZ Banking Group (1995); National Australia Bank (1995).

many managers experience considerable pressure and spend long hours at work, interviews reveal that this applies particularly to married women as they seek to balance work and domestic responsibilities, especially if they have children.

Although internal promotion remains the favored form of filling positions above entry level, it was at one point the only method. This exclusivity began to erode after computers were introduced, because technical expertise was generally recruited externally. After deregulation, the new banks found that the quickest way to staff many positions in institutional banking was to poach employees from the established banks. Staff now move regularly among banks at all levels, though this accounts for a minority of staff turnover. Banks now also recruit externally in specialist functions such as industrial relations and personnel. In the banks that were studied, few of the most senior managers in these areas were career bankers.

Banks now offer a number of career paths with different entry ports. Senior managers believe that these paths require different skills and knowledge and increasingly look to recruit specifically for different types of work. As a result, there is less horizontal movement within banks than previously. There is also less prospect for vertical mobility. Many processing jobs are routine and provide little opportunity for advancement, and the proportion of genuine management jobs in branches is declining. Thus many staff must adjust their aspirations to the likelihood that management positions may be out of reach.

To cope efficiently with daily variations in demand, banks have increased the number of part-time staff. Most part-time staff are women, often women over 30 from the local area. Although part-time staff in theory have an equal opportunity for career advancement, in practice it is difficult for them to advance to senior supervisory positions and beyond. This is due to limited access to training, the belief that managerial jobs are difficult to separate into discrete tasks, such that different people could perform segments of managerial work, and a perception on the part of senior management that employees who are serious about promotion will work full time.

Although movement from customer service work to management is possible, it is much more difficult than in the past, for three reasons. First, organizational restructuring has left fewer management positions available. Second, the major banks require a postsecondary qualification for promotion to management. Third, access to fast-track career programs is more difficult for those who enter the industry through the traditional path of a junior clerical position straight from school than for graduate recruits.

Labor Market Adjustment

Over the past decade Australian banks have sought to adjust their staffing levels by increasing the use of part-time staff, thereby gaining greater flexibility in hours of work, as well as by shedding labor.

Part-time work has allowed more staffing flexibility in branches, and casual employment has generally been introduced to reduce numbers of permanent relief staff. Bank B calls on an employment agency to provide casual relief staff. Restrictions on the level of part-time staffing have gradually been removed by collective agreement. Part-time staff receive full pro rata terms and conditions of employment, whereas casuals receive a salary loading in lieu of entitlements.

Banks have also increased the flexibility of working hours. Most have negotiated a change from calculating standard working hours on the basis of hours worked per day in a weekly cycle to a 152-hour, four-week cycle. Ordinary hours of work have been extended, and banks are moving toward weekend and evening operations. Working hours for mobile lenders are being relaxed considerably.

Although the industry had a de facto policy of lifetime employment for career staff, the FSU became concerned about possible staff reductions in the 1970s, when banks began to introduce technological and organizational changes. The FSU's approach has been to negotiate redundancy agreements far in excess of the basic conditions required by the Industrial Relations Commission rather than oppose staff reductions outright, although the union has been highly critical of the extent of downsizing.

Despite the speed with which the major banks have reduced staff numbers, most of the losses were through attrition or voluntary redundancy. There has always been a considerable amount of labor turnover at the lower levels of banks, particularly among younger staff, whereas generous severance packages enticed more-senior staff to resign.

Executives in the banks under study here were aware of the problems that downsizing could create. In particular, they were concerned that a sales culture cannot operate successfully if staff fear for their jobs. Interviews with branch and processing center staff revealed that fear of redundancy was not a major concern for employees, but also indicated that many lower-level staff felt little attachment to their bank and that many employees decidedly lacked enthusiasm for the sales culture that banks are seeking to introduce. Furthermore, complaints of understaffing and pressure to work unpaid overtime were common. Creating structures that allow numerical flexibility without losing staff loyalty and performance is among the most significant challenges confronting bank management in the late 1990s.

Skill Formation

Banks traditionally placed considerable emphasis on procedures training to ensure that transactions were carried out properly. This task focus remains, but banks are turning their attention in training to product knowledge and sales skills. Most training is provided internally, but banks are now looking externally as well. The most significant initiative in this area is the requirement for postsecondary qualifications for promotion to management in the major banks.

Until the 1970s, banks provided different training for men and women. The major banks offered formal training for men at each stage of their careers prior to management. Women primarily received on-the-job training covering basic clerical duties. This changed with the removal of formal career barriers for female employees, after which men and women received similar training. However, the growth in part-time employment has created another impediment for women, because many part-time staff are unable to take advantage of training opportunities (Junor et al. 1993). Banks have sought to overcome these problems by various means, such as videotaping staff meetings, making computer-assisted learning available, and offering training sessions at different times of the day.

Training practices vary between banks and may not even be consistent within the same organization. When the study was conducted, bank A required five days of induction training for branch staff: bank B required two weeks for tellers and four days for customer service officers. Both received additional on-the-job training in branches. However, an experienced HR manager in bank A reported that new recruits are often shown training videos in a continuous sitting over two days, then thrust behind the counter to deal with customers. Supervisors anxious to meet staffing needs in the branch may fail to schedule adequate time for training, or resources such as computers may not be available when needed. Many recruits, however, are given sufficient time to attend an introductory course in which they learn basic banking skills, and then are placed in a branch with experienced supervisors and staff who are able to provide a more gradual introduction to the industry.

At the time of our study, bank C was recognized as an industry leader in training. It gave all new staff a three-week introductory course before placing them in a branch, where they were treated as trainees for a week before moving to the branch to which they were assigned. After several weeks they were removed from their branch to undergo further formal training in more advanced topics. This bank offered a range of short courses, including personal development and negotiation skills. In addition, all branch staff received a morning or afternoon of training every month focusing on product knowledge and bank procedures. These sessions were run by full-time trainers who were former branch managers. Interviews with staff in bank C revealed that they viewed their training very positively, although a number reported that at times they were unable to attend scheduled training because of inadequate relief staff to cover for their absence.

The major banks are developing competency-based training, although there is considerable debate as to what competencies mean and how they should be measured. Competencies are being developed on an enterprise basis, as is the entire area of training. This means that competencies are being defined by each enterprise rather than a common set of competencies defined for the entire industry. Senior training specialists expressed little enthusiasm for industry standards.

Most banks have low formal entry requirements: only 10 or 11 years of formal education, although at present most recruits from school have completed a full 12 years of study. There was no evidence of skills short-falls in the industry, apart from occasional shortages in the more technical areas of institutional banking, which involve small numbers of highly paid staff.

Compensation

The changes to compensation arrangements in banking form part of the shift away from lifetime employment. Prior to 1987, the main industry award included an incremental salary scale to age 34. Men and women had separate scales, with fewer steps and lower rates of pay for women. Women performing work usually performed by men began to be paid men's rates in the 1960s, and the separate women's salary structure was abolished in 1975 (Hill 1982). Promotion to supervisor and manager was based on merit. Compensation for accountants and managers was based on the number of employees in a branch.

This salary structure made sense in terms of the traditional career path for men. As a general rule, older male employees were in more-responsible positions than younger men, and young men were often in positions junior to women but would expect to match or pass them quickly. This began to change in the 1960s, and the traditional career structure began to break down in the 1970s. As a result, employees of different ages were often performing the same jobs but receiving different rates of pay. As well, with growing competition in the industry, management sought to develop ways to encourage greater productivity from staff.

Influenced by compensation practices in the United Kingdom, the private banks and the FSU in 1987 replaced the scale based on age and years of service with job evaluation. Job evaluation was carried out in the major banks by joint management-union committees. The parties also agreed to introduce performance-related pay. In banks A and B, salaries were determined according to a combination of job evaluation (which placed employees into a salary band) and an annual performance review (which placed individuals into a performance category, with different rates of pay within each band).

Total average weekly earnings for nonmanagerial employees in banking have remained slightly above the average for all industries but below those for manufacturing industries such as steel and automobiles (Kitay 1997).[9] Table 3.6 delineates wage differentials within one bank shortly after the new salary structure was introduced. By 1994 the total compensation for the managing director of Westpac was approximately $1.8 million,[10] whereas the base rate salary for the lowest adult clerical grade was slightly more than $21,000, a ratio of 85 to 1.

Table 3.6
The new salary structure in 1988: Data for a major bank

Grade	Appraisal base	Outstanding
Clerical Officer 1	100	120
Clerical Officer 2	104	126
Clerical Officer 3	111	135
Clerical Officer 4	118	143
Supervisor 1	134	164
Supervisor 2	145	178
Supervisor 3	160	197
Manager 1	175	211
Top-Graded Manager	252	308

Source: Bodi et al. 1992.

After the 1987 changes in the salary scale, the major banks began setting their salaries at an enterprise rather than an industry level. However, other terms and conditions under the award remained the same until the early 1990s, and apart from lags in timing the variations among banks have generally been minor.

Bank C does not operate an experience-related salary scale, nor has it embraced job evaluation for staff below branch manager level. Because the award does not apply to branch managers in the regional banks, and because these managers are effectively supervisors, awards and industrial agreements apply to a lower proportion of staff in the regional banks than in the major banks.

In bank C, jobs were grouped into a few broad classifications. Branch staff began on the base salary rate for their grade, then moved to a level above the award minimum after a few months of satisfactory performance. In locations where it is difficult to attract staff, a market loading was also paid. Effectively there were no standard salaries for branch staff above the base rate, and few people were on the base rate. Performance appraisals had no bearing on remuneration levels.

One of the attractions of the banking industry is nonsalary benefits, such as low-interest housing loans and insurance policies. As tax changes have increased the cost of these benefits, banks have been restricting their range and level. Bank B sought to eliminate a subsidy to an internal health insurance scheme, resulting in industrial unrest.

Banks have experimented with a range of incentive schemes (see Wright and the Australian Centre for Industrial Relation Research and Teaching 1994), including bonuses, profit sharing, gain sharing and share ownership schemes. These typically involve a small proportion of income: for example, 5 percent annually for managers in one recent scheme in bank B. Arrangements for mobile lenders often involve much higher levels of incentive payments.

Enterprise Governance and Industrial Relations

Two related developments suggest that a number of banks are attempting to develop a strategic orientation toward their human resources practices. First, these banks are seeking to develop human resources strategies that are consistent with their competitive strategies. Second, managements are seeking to change their relationship with the union in ways they believe will complement their business and human resources strategies. At the same time, the Finance Sector Union has developed a strategic approach to the industry. In some cases, this has resulted in cautious steps toward a more consultative relationship between the banks and the union, but in bank B, management believes that its relationship with the union was previously too close.

Bank C was not undergoing the degree of change typical of the major banks, so the role of the human resources function is less clearly articulated. As well, this bank was, at the time of our study, still in the early stages of developing a relationship with the FSU and lacked the high levels of union membership that have led to a reassessment of the union's role in the major banks.

The role of HR and IR staff in major banks appears to be changing. Under the industry awards that prevailed until the late 1980s, these banks had large, centralized personnel departments. In bank B, both management and union officials asserted that most organizational initiatives that affected staff traditionally required the approval of the personnel department, but that this was now much less likely to occur. Recently, there have been initiatives to downsize the head office HR function and give business units responsibility for their own personnel and industrial relations policy.

In bank A, senior HR and IR specialists reported in interviews that they were involved in the overall direction of the bank through participation in key committees. HR and IR policy remained centralized through the mid-1990s, though recently the bank initiated a process of decentralization through the establishment of site agreements.

In bank C, the HR department was a small unit whose staff saw themselves in a consultative role. Responsibility for HR activities such as recruitment was devolved to line management, and many personnel and training staff were located within the retail bank rather than the HR function. Industrial relations remained centralized at the head office, although cautious steps were being taken toward direct contact between line managers and the union. The relationship between bank C and the FSU was relatively recent and still developing.

The role of the FSU in enterprise governance has been changing. The changes predate enterprise bargaining, and although they are still relatively modest, the rate of change is accelerating. The FSU enjoyed a high level of membership in the major banks for many years, in the vicinity of 60–70 percent in the private sector and higher in the publicly owned Commonwealth Bank (which was still about 80 percent unionized in 1998). Although it has an extensive delegate structure, union authority is centralized. The FSU is not militant but is sophisticated and proactive, and its willingness to undertake industrial action has grown over the past 20 years.

Hill (1986) describes a situation in the early to mid-1980s in which managements resisted union attempts to influence workplace change and the FSU complained of managements' failure to consult with them. However, the banks asserted that initiatives such as technological change were business decisions and commercially confidential. The situation in the Commonwealth Bank was different. The bank had an enterprise union (which merged with the FSU in 1994) and regularly consulted with the union on a range of issues.

The regional banks brought their building society traditions with them when they obtained banking licenses. Like those of the major banks, these traditions included paternalistic employment relations, but a low level (in most cases 20 percent or less) of union membership.

The agreement to introduce job evaluation in place of seniority salary structures also established joint management-union committees to oversee the new arrangements. The conjunction of enterprise bargaining and the recession of the early 1990s brought about more far reaching changes. All the major banks saw a need for organizational restructuring and sought the FSU's cooperation.

The FSU had suffered sharp membership declines during the recession, which compounded its difficulties in recruiting the growing number of part-time staff. The union made a strategic decision to encourage actively a rapid return to prosperity in the industry and cooperate with the financially troubled banks that were downsizing. Both sides approached enterprise bargaining with a cautious but positive outlook.

Under enterprise bargaining the employers sought individual agreements with the union rather than operating as a single industry level bargaining unit under the umbrella of the Australian Bankers' Association. This led to the abolition of the ABA's industrial relations function in 1992.

Additional mechanisms for employee involvement were established through enterprise bargaining. For example, bank A's enterprise bargaining agreement (EBA) established a joint consultative committee to serve as a high-level forum for a range of business and industrial issues. The bank also recognized the difficulties the union confronted in maintaining membership levels with the growing proportion of part-time staff and agreed to provide recruitment opportunities. A senior union official described the relationship between bank A and the FSU as one of "cautious respect," whereas the bank's IR executives indicated they considered a positive relationship with the union to be consistent with the firm's business objectives. Bank A declined to take advantage of antiunion provisions in the industrial relations legislation despite pressure from the conservative federal government to do so.

A somewhat different story unfolded at bank B. Although the bank's relations with the union had traditionally been consultative, by the early 1990s senior executives decided that rapid organizational change was necessary for the bank to become more cost effective. The bank made use of the individualizing provisions of the new industrial relations legislation, but with only modest acceptance among the senior employees to whom individual contracts were offered and little attrition in union membership. Although consultation with the FSU continued, it occurred at a later stage than previously, and conflict occurred over a range of issues.

More generally, the FSU's preparedness to cooperate with the banks did not eliminate its willingness to undertake industrial action on issues such as wages. Industrial action occurred in three of the four major banks during 1996.

Although awards covered building societies, union density was low in those firms that took out banking licenses. Bank C had union membership levels of around 20 percent, and the FSU sought to use enterprise bargaining as a means of establishing its legitimacy with the bank's employees and management. The first agreement included a union-management consultative committee to oversee a trial of extended trading hours, which both parties considered to be a success. However, the bank was reluctant to provide additional avenues for union involvement, such as the recognition of delegates. The union reported that membership was growing in bank C, with a postmerger level around 50 percent.

Intrasectoral Variations

What is striking about the four major Australian banks is the similarity among them. Although the ANZ and National Australia Bank have adopted a more internationalist strategy than Westpac and the Commonwealth, in other respects their approach to the retail market is similar. All are seeking to minimize costs, but none has established itself as a price leader. All are introducing a sales culture emphasizing ease of access through multiple distribution channels and extended hours of operation. All are rationalizing and reorganizing their branch networks to centralize processing functions, narrow but deepen customer service jobs, and reduce the role of branch managers. Careers are being segmented, and access to the training necessary for elevation to management is more readily available to some career paths than others. Similarly, the skill base is being segmented, with the broad acquisition of skills for generalist banking careers replaced by more-specialized skills for specific roles. Although there are generic skills in the industry that are easily transferred, there are no common standards of skill or competency at industry level. Similar systems of compensation at the major banks with minor variations have remained broadly the same since their establishment.

One difference among the four major banks is that those that experienced financial difficulties directly (in the case of Westpac and the ANZ) or indirectly (in the case of the Commonwealth's takeover of the State Bank of Victoria) undertook rapid downsizing programs in the early 1990s, whereas National Australia Bank, which had remained prosperous throughout, did not. However, these initiatives were part of wider efforts to bring the other banks' cost/income ratios closer to National Australia Bank's, which itself was continuing to reduce costs and began cutting staff levels in the late 1990s.

The major banks continue to have high levels (more than 50 percent) of union membership and have sought union agreement to the programs of change they are undertaking. They are slowly introducing higher levels of employee involvement, albeit from a very low level, and management prerogative remains strong and banking culture paternalistic. Whether it is possible to develop a "learning organization" in an institution like a major bank, as one of the EBAs proposes, will be watched with interest.

Another difference can be found in the difference between the current industrial relations approach of bank B and that of the other major banks. In essence, bank B is trying to reduce the union's influence, while the others are seeking more consultative arrangements. This can be attributed largely to bank B's shift toward a more commercial basis of operations and management's belief that the previous level of union influence would slow the change process. It remains to be seen whether the relationship between bank B and the FSU stabilizes at a similar level to that of the other banks.

The clearest intrasectoral differences exist between the major banks and bank C. The main source of change in bank C was that it was floated on the share market and became subject to the same market pressures as other private enterprises, leading to an emphasis on cost reduction and return to shareholders. However, as a former building society, it had established a reputation for excellent customer service and ease of access, which it sought to build upon. One can attribute the strong emphasis on training, in which it was recognized as an industry leader to management's wish to maintain its client-friendly reputation. Access and quality of service also underlay the bank's heavy investment in technology, in which it was an industry leader.

The range of tasks performed in bank C increased after it became a bank in the mid-1980s, but unlike that of the major banks, its customer service staff continued to perform all functions apart from lending, a major reason for its continued heavy investment in training. The bank installed ATMs and established a telephone inquiry center, but it also employed new technology to support the wide-ranging roles of branch staff.

Bank C also differed from the major banks in its industrial relations practices. The level of union membership was low, and management only had to begin dealing with an active union in the early 1990s.[11]

Bank C was not party to the new salary arrangements introduced in the major banks in 1987. It did not apply job evaluation to non-managerial jobs, nor did it base compensation on performance appraisal. Several factors may account for this. First, its personnel section was small, and the resources necessary to introduce and maintain job evaluation were not available within the bank. Second, its emphasis on training may have reduced the need to use performance appraisal as a mechanism to encourage particular behaviors. Indeed, interviews with branch staff indicate a very high orientation toward good customer service. Third, because there was less differentiation among staff than in the larger banks, the need to distinguish among jobs was less pressing.

Bank C was also a leader in increasing access for customers through extended branch trading hours, although other banks have been quick to negotiate similar arrangements with the FSU. Bank C was able to do this because of the existing award provisions and the relatively weak position of the FSU in the bank.

Source of Change and Diversity

Assessing the relative importance of institutional and market forces in explaining changes to industrial relations and human resource management practices in Australian banking is like unscrambling an egg. Both have had an influence, and their effects have interacted over time.

The key change has been institutional, in the sense that many restrictions on the finance industry have been removed. However, this in turn increased the role of market forces in shaping policies concerning employment. The underlying pressures to improve value to shareholders are perhaps the primary market force (Useem 1993); responses to these pressures involve a simultaneous attack on costs and improvement in access and levels of service. Even here, disentangling the different influences is difficult. For example, part of the motivation behind branch reorganization in the major banks is to improve service in order to gain market share and increase income, but reorganization is being conducted in a way that will minimize costs. Not only are ATMs easy to access, they are also cheaper to operate than branches staffed with a full complement of employees.

Althou·3h market pressures have been a key influence on cost reduction, institutions—particularly industrial relations institutions—have played an important role in how the changes have been introduced and their substance. The industrial relations history of the industry prior to deregulation was that of a high level of unionization and centralized negotiations between the parties. Decentralization has occurred slowly, the banks have watched each other closely, and the union has been able to place constraints on what they do.

With declining employment levels, major banks could possibly have proceeded with their organizational change programs without union acquiescence during the 1990s. Several factors constrained this approach. First, the decentralization of the wider industrial relations framework made it possible to negotiate enterprise level changes in a way that would have been difficult before. Second, the union made a strategic decision to accept the need for organizational change and has adopted a generally cooperative approach. Third, had the banks taken on the union in a dispute, it is likely that they would have won, but the battle could well have been bitter. This is compounded by the fact that one of the major banks was in a stronger financial position than the others, and management could have accommodated the union while its competitors were engaged in industrial conflict.

Although all banks are trying to cut costs and improve quality and ease of access, they are not doing so in precisely the same way. The differences that appear in organizational design and employment practices in the large and small banks suggest that an element of strategic choice operates. It is not essential, for example, to reduce the task range of customer service staff in the major banks, because the task range has been growing in bank C. Similarly, the high level of training provided to staff in bank C suggests that although all banks say that they are trying to improve service quality, some banks emphasize this more than others.

Even though market forces have undoubtedly been the primary reason for the rapid staff reductions in three of the major banks, the fact that this has occurred with very few involuntary retrenchments is evidence of the influence of institutions, particularly the role of trade unions operating within a framework of industrial tribunals. Quite simply, large Australian employers cannot just do as they please. Within the framework of market pressures and institutional constraints, however, there are opportunities for strategic choices. It is interesting that the major banks have generally made the same choices, but this is perhaps not surprising in a market with the size and structure of Australia's. The differences between the large and small banks, however, attest to the scope for choice that exists.

Appendix: Research Methods

The primary source of information for this chapter was semistructured interviews conducted with employees ranging from senior executives to junior staff in branches, departments, and back office areas in three domestic banks. Forty-five interviews were conducted in bank A, sixty-two in bank B and twenty-one in bank C. Thirty additional interviews were conducted in overseas divisions of an Australian bank and Australian and overseas divisions of an international bank. Nineteen interviews were conducted with officials from the Finance Sector Union and two with employer association officials. Considerable documentary material was examined in the three domestic banks and the Finance Sector Union. Several staff training sessions were attended in bank C.

Notes

The author wishes to thank Malcolm Rimmer for his contribution to this research. The financial support of the Australian Research Council is gratefully acknowledged.

1. The unions that formed the FSU were known by various names but will be referred to as the FSU throughout.

2. The figures are taken from Commonwealth Bank Equal Employment Opportunity Reports.

3. The large jump between 1984 and 1986 is artificially inflated by a number of financial institutions' taking out banking licenses. Reliable employment statistics for the banking sector are unavailable after 1993.

4. The data are from Australian Bank Employees' Union/Commonwealth Bank Officers' Association, Reports on Age and Sex Statistics for the Australian Banking Industry, 1980, 1985, 1990.

5. Data from individual banks through 1995 show that the trend of feminization is continuing.

6. The FSU data are based on banks' replies to union surveys.

7. Estimates were obtained from the 1991 census for the finance sector, which is more inclusive than banking, and compared with the wider workforce excluding this sector. The author thanks Ian Watson for providing these data.

8. Bank C was taken over by another bank after field work was completed. The data offered here refer to the premerger period.

9. Below senior levels, remuneration in Australian banks is not particularly high.

10. This figure was widely reported in the business press at the time.

11. Prior to becoming a bank, bank C was covered by a state rather than federal award and dealt with a different, less proactive union.

References

[ABS] Australian Bureau of Statistics, *Australian Demographic Statistics*, Cat. No. 3101.0, ABS on-line service: Gopher://gopher.statistics.gov.au/

ANZ Banking Group. (1995). Affirmative Action Report, Melbourne.

Badham, R., and J. Mathews. (1989). "The New Production Systems Debate." *Labour & Industry*, 2(2): 194–246.

Bodi, A., H. de Cieri, R. Gough, and M. Rimmer. (1992). "Award Restructuring in Banking." Unpublished report, National Key Centre in Industrial Relations, Monash University, Melbourne, Australia.

Carew, E. (1991). *Fast Money 3: The Financial Markets in Australia*. Sydney, Australia: Allen & Unwin.

Commonwealth Bank of Australia. (1995). *Annual Report*. Sydney: Commonwealth Bank of Australia.

Daugaard, D., and T. Valentine. (1993). "The Banks." In M. Lewis and R. Wallace (eds.), *The Australian Financial System*. Melbourne, Australia: Longman Cheshire, 39–82.

Hill, John. (1986). "Barriers to Industrial Democracy in the Australian Private Banks." In E. Davis and R. Lansbury (eds.), *Democracy and Control in the Workplace*. Melbourne, Australia: Longman Cheshire, 146–162.

Hill, John. (1982). *From Subservience to Strike*. St. Lucia, Australia: University of Queensland Press.

Junor, Anne, K. Barlow, and M. Patterson. (1993). *Service Productivity: Part-Time Women Workers and the Finance Sector Workplace*. Equal Pay Research Series no. 5, Department of Industrial Relations. Canberra: Australian Government Printing Service.

Kitay, J. (1997). "Changing Patterns of Employment Relations: Theoretical and Methodological Framework for Six Australian Industry Studies." In J. Kitay and R. Lansbury (eds.), *Changing Employment Relations in Australia*. Melbourne, Australia: Oxford University Press, 1–43.

[Martin Report] Parliament of the Commonwealth of Australia, House of Representatives Standing Committee on Finance and Public Administration. (1991). *A Pocket Full of Change*. Canberra: Australian Government Printing Service.

Moore, David. (1992). *Financial Markets and Institutions.* 3d ed., Sydney: Serendip.

[NAB] National Australia Bank. (1997). 1997 Annual Report. Melbourne: National Australia Bank.

[NAB] National Australia Bank. (1995). "Group Results & Dividend Announcements for the Half Year Ended 31 March 1995." NAB World Wide Web Site.

[NAB] National Australia Bank. (1995). *Affirmative Action Report.* Melbourne.

Prices Surveillance Authority. (1995). *Inquiry into Fees and Charges Imposed on Retail Accounts by Banks and Other Financial Institutions on EFTPOS Transactions.* Report no. 65. Canberra: Australian Government Printing Service.

Reserve Bank of Australia. (1996). "Bank Branch Trends in Australia and Overseas." *Reserve Bank of Australia Bulletin,* November, 1–6.

Useem, Michael. (1993). *Executive Defense: Shareholder Power & Corporate Reorganization.* Cambridge: Harvard University Press.

Wallis, S., et al. (1996). Financial System Inquiry Discussion Paper. Canberra: Australian Government Printing Service.

Wallis, S., et al. (1997). Financial System Inquiry Final Report. Canberra: Australian Government Printing Service.

Westpac Banking Corporation. (1996). Submission to Wallis Inquiry, Australian Treasury web site: http://www.treasury.gov. au/

Wright, C., and the Australian Centre for Industrial Relation Research and Teaching. (1994). *Incentive Payment Systems in Australia.* Industrial Relations Research Series no. 9, Department of Industrial Relations. Canberra: Australian Government Printing Service.

4

Employment Relations in the New Zealand Banking Industry

Erling Rasmussen and
Andrea Jackson

The Employment Relations Context

Deregulation and Legislative Reforms

Since 1984, New Zealand has experienced more economic deregulation and legislative reforms than any other OECD country (Campbell-Hunt, Harper, and Hamilton 1993; OECD 1993: 9). This has had a significant impact on the operation of the New Zealand labor market (Rasmussen et al. 1996a).

Like other sectors, the finance sector underwent a process of deregulation after 1984. Economic deregulation had a strong impact on banks as new market opportunities suddenly became available. The deregulation of the banking industry, which was intertwined with economic deregulation in general, bolstered this impact. (Carew 1987: 170–80). The banking sector reforms were wide ranging, with the most crucial areas being

- dismantling of specific rules for business and lending activities.
- allowance of new entrants to registered bank status.
- abolition of restrictions on foreign ownership.
- privatization of government stakes in banks.

Prior to the banking deregulation strict rules governed what lending activities banks could get involved in and how much they could charge. Banking status was restricted to a limited number of banks, allowing the four trading banks and the Post Office Bank to dominate the market, although the trustee savings banks had an extensive network.[1] The new entry requirements under deregulation reduced the boundaries between banking, insurance, and building societies, as discussed below. This led to an influx of new banks, with the number increasing to a peak of 23 registered banks in 1991. Currently, there are 17 banks (KPMG 1995: 4).

Overseas ownership has always been a feature of New Zealand banking, with only one of the four trading banks being wholly New Zealand owned (Nicholl and King 1985: 165).[2] Overseas ownership has become more pronounced in the 1990s, with hardly any banks lacking the influence of foreign owners (*Yearbook* 1995: 585). Three of New Zealand's four largest banks are now Australian owned, the most notable being the Bank of New Zealand (BNZ), which the National Australia Bank purchased in 1992. Only Taranaki TSB, a small regional bank, is a New Zealand–owned bank.

Besides its regulatory influence, the government has had a strong presence in the banking sector through its ownership of various types of banks. The government formerly owned the largest bank (BNZ) and had a strong retail presence through the many outlets of the Post Office Bank. It also owned two so-called development banks: the Rural Bank and DFC Finance. Over the last decade, government stakes in banks have been privatized.

Labor Market Deregulation: Trends and Issues

Economic deregulation and the shift in the employment relations model have exerted strong influences on the labor market. An overview is presented here of major changes in labor market trends, the social welfare approach, and training and skills development. The main emphasis is on changes to the employment relations legislative framework and the associated changes to bargaining.

The driving force behind the post-1984 reforms was dissatisfaction with New Zealand's economic performance in the previous decades (James 1986; Myers 1996: 4). Britain's entry to the European Community, the oil crises of the 1970s, the fall in agriculture product prices, and the inability to reform the economy under Prime Minister Robert Muldoon (1975–84) all intensified this dissatisfaction. Low economic growth continued in 1986–92 as large-scale economic restructuring, including an anti-inflationary fiscal and monetary policy stance, started to bite.

The lack of economic growth corresponded with sharply rising unemployment in the 1980s. The unemployment rate accelerated from 3.6 percent in 1987 to 11.1 percent in 1992, with the subsequent decline being of similarly staggering proportions: from 11.1 percent in March 1992 to 5.9 percent in September 1995. The latter coincided with high economic growth: 5.2 percent in 1993, 6.3 percent in 1994, and 3.2 percent in 1995. The fall in unemployment led to skills shortages in certain industries and occupations, despite demographic trends favoring New Zealand, with no decline in the cohorts of young people expected before 2010. Part-time employment[3] has increased more sharply than full-time employment since the late 1970s. However, both full-time and part-time employment have grown strongly in the post-1992 period (Whatman 1994: 359). Self-employment has also risen strongly: 9.7 percent in 1987–93 period (Rasmussen, Deeks, and Street 1996).

The social welfare system has undergone radical changes, with alterations to: entitlements, benefit levels, and delivery mechanisms. In particular, the so-called December 1990 package reduced the level and availability of welfare benefits (Boston and Dalziel 1992). Generally, this had only an indirect and short-term effect on the banking industry, because the strong economic upswing from early 1993 onward led to a surge in business activity. However, one aspect of the changes has opened significant business opportunities for banks, namely, the changes in pensions and superannuation, which has coincided with an increased public awareness of the funding difficulties surrounding pension entitlements.

Training and skills development have become very topical in New Zealand in the 1990s. Worries over the reduction in training efforts caused by economic restructuring prompted the recent focus on training (Rasmussen et al. 1996b: 464). The increased level of unemployment became associated with the notion that the New Zealand workforce had a low level of educational qualifications compared to those of other OECD countries (Elkin and Inkson 1995: 155 ff).

This perception of inferior education led to a total reworking of the industry training framework with the Industry Training Act 1992 (Myers 1996; Rasmussen et al. 1996). Under the act, new industry training organizations (ITOs) would provide the administrative interface with industry and would deliver on the industry's chosen training objectives (Deeks, Parker and Ryan 1994: 426). The act placed industry training within a new national qualifications framework by linking industry training to a national, standards-based qualifications system developed under the auspice of the New Zealand Qualifications Authority (NZQA).

Although the transition from the old system is far from finished, it appears to have increased awareness and training efforts among employers (*National Business Review*, September 15, 1995: 21). Nevertheless, doubts have been raised about the effectiveness of the industry training approach. The government's promotion of an employer-driven skills development strategy has been questioned because it is based on the assumption that employers generally invest sufficiently in training and skill development (Janes 1997; Myers 1996).

The training and eduction approach in banking is discussed in the section on "Skills, Training, and Careers."

The Shift in Employment Relations Models

New Zealand has become known for two diametrically opposed employment relations models (Rasmussen and Boxall 1995: 79). The first model, the conciliation and arbitration model instituted by the Industrial Conciliation and Arbitration Act of 1894, reigned in 1894–90. The second model, a free-market employment contracts model based on the Employment Contracts Act of 1991, established direct and decentralized bargaining as the norm.

The Industrial Conciliation and Arbitration Act of 1894 was a regulatory model with a large dose of state interventionism. It was promoted as a way of overcoming "wasteful" industrial conflicts and securing better and fairer outcomes (Deeks, Parker, and Ryan 1994: 45). Instead of free collective bargaining, the arbitration system offered conciliation as a way of solving conflicts. If this failed, compulsory arbitration would produce a ruling binding the disputing parties (Holt 1986). Through the setting of minimum working conditions, the arbitration model had a strong impact on the overall level of pay and conditions. These minimums were applied widely through "blanket coverage" provisions in awards, which meant that all employers within a stipulated industry or occupation would be covered whether or not individual employers had signed the agreement (Deeks and Boxall 1989: 87).

Despite many legislative interventions, the basic features of the arbitration system remained essentially unchanged for nearly a century. The long duration of the system produced a number of distinguishing features: A legalistic and adversarial approach dominated employment relations; the support of union activity through the arbitration system resulted in many and often weak unions; collective bargaining was restricted to a number of narrowly defined issues ("industrial matters"); and minimum employment conditions were stipulated through the awards or through a network of supportive legislation (holidays, minimum wages, leave entitlements, etc.). However, individual employment contracts were under a different (common law) jurisdiction, and they gave employees little protection against unfair dismissals or unsatisfactory bargaining outcomes (Deeks, Parker, and Ryan 1994; Holt 1986; Rasmussen et al. 1996a: 147–48; Walsh 1993; Walsh and Fougere 1987).

The arbitration system's inability to implement fast and flexible wage adjustments was always its weak point. This became a crucial factor in its demise as the New Zealand economy became more integrated into the world economy (Boxall 1990; Walsh 1993). The Fourth Labour Government (1984–90) introduced the Labour Relations Act of 1987, but this more permissive legislative framework fell short of producing the expected strong shift away from the award system, and employers applied more pressure on the government to increase labor market flexibility (Boxall 1995; Harbridge and McCaw 1991; Walsh 1989, 1992, 1993).

The Employment Contracts Act of 1991 (ECA) shifted away from the collectivist traditions of the past by promoting the rights of individual employees and employers over collective rights (Grills 1994; Wailes 1994). The act facilitated a fundamental shift in the locus of employment relations: from predominantly industry or occupational level toward the individual organization or workplace. This prompted a sharp fall in union membership, from around 40 percent in 1990 to around 20 percent in 1996 (Crawford, Harbridge, and Hince 1997). Likewise, collective employment coverage altered sharply: It fell to less than half its 1990 level in just three years, and collective employment contracts began to be negotiated mainly at an enterprise level (Harbridge and Howard 1994; Hince and Harbridge 1994; Contract 1992–97, vol. 16). In the first post-ECA years, employees suffered degeneration in their employment conditions, with the main effects being felt in the secondary labor market (Harbridge and Street 1995; McLaughlin and Rasmussen 1998). Although changes to employment conditions have slowed since 1993, employees have had difficulty in reversing the setbacks suffered during 1991–93 (Rasmussen and Deeks 1997).

On the other hand, the ECA has provided employees in the primary labor market with more leverage, and this has influenced employment relations practices. The act covers all employees, whether on collective or individual employment contracts and in both the public and private sectors (Grills 1994; Walsh 1993). A more militant pursuit of employee rights has prompted a sharp increase in cases taken to the employment institutions since 1991. Managers have become, therefore, more careful regarding substantive and procedural fairness in dealing with their staff (Rasmussen 1996b).

An Overview of Bargaining Patterns in the Banking Industry
Increased competitive pressure and the legislative changes encouraged banks to seek further flexibility and cost savings, the drive being particularly

urgent during the 1987–92 economic recession. Nevertheless, the legacies of the arbitration system influenced the thinking of managers, unions and employees significantly.

Compared to most other awards at that time, it was a key difference that the bank officers' award did not contain "a blanket coverage provision."[4] Instead it was expressed as a "cited parties only" agreement (i.e., it covered only employers who had signed the agreement). The union had to persuade each individual employer to sign the award.

In the mid-1980s, the Bank Officers' Union attempted to have a blanket coverage provision inserted in its award, but the four registered banks resisted. Furthermore, the union was unsuccessful in covering wholesale banks through the award. The union obtained, after considerable pressure, collective coverage of the major new retail banks. However, this coverage was in the form of collective enterprise agreements (i.e., not part of the general award).

Thus collective coverage was considerably fragmented before the ECA came into force in 1991:

• The four major banks were under the banks officers' award negotiated with the Bank Officers' Union and subsequently with Finsec (the Financial Sector Union).

• The ten regional trust banks were registered as Trust Bank (New Zealand) Limited. They were covered by one award, which was negotiated by the Clerical Workers Union.

• One retail bank had an award negotiated with Finsec.

• Two retail banks had registered agreements: One was negotiated with Finsec, the other with the Post Office Union.

• Four retail banks had no collective coverage. However, three of these— former trustee savings banks—were rather small.

• The ten wholesale banks had no collective coverage and generally had few unionized employees.

The leaders of the Bank Officers' Union started to change their strategy in 1988–90 when it became a less attractive option for the union to have an all-inclusive award. Following deregulation and the share market crash, it became obvious that certain banks were financially exposed. Individual banks' profitability could fluctuate considerably and maybe even turn negative. The inability to gain a standard set of bargaining outcomes, which could have made the most profitable banks trendsetters on pay settlement, left the union with the prospect of the lowest common denominator dictating improvements. To avoid the dominant award's minimum conditions being dictated by the low profitability of one of the major banks, union leaders came to regard enterprise agreements as a less threatening option. With the arrival of the ECA, an industry-wide settlement became virtually impossible.

The bargaining strategy change coincided with changing union structures. The dominant player in the banking industry had been the Bank Officers' Union, though two other unions, the Post Office Union and the Clerical Workers Union, covered a number of employees. Additionally, the Insurance Union organized workers among insurance companies. In 1990, the Bank Officers' Union and the Insurance Union amalgamated to form the current Finsec. The Clerical Workers Union folded quickly after the ECA, and Finsec began organizing clerical and bank employees in the Trust Bank. At the Postbank, Finsec and the Post Office Union—later the Communication and Energy Workers Union (CEWU)—covered most employees. From 1995 onward, Finsec became the only union at the Postbank after the CEWU disintegrated because of financial difficulty. Thus, Finsec is currently the sole union representing banking employees.

Following the ECA, the bargaining and collective coverage structure fragmented further, with enterprise agreements becoming common. One bank is totally without collective coverage, and most banks have expanded their application of individual employment contracts to managerial staff.

Although collective coverage at the enterprise or business until level is still the norm in the banking industry, the current bargaining arrangements are quite clearly sitting uncomfortably with the banks' business and employment relations strategies:

Without exception the banks spoken to indicated their ideal of dealing directly with their own employees rather than through unions. Most went on to indicate their preference for individual contracts with their employees. They saw enterprise based unions covering only the employees of their particular bank as a positive step towards that goal. (Barlow 1990: 21).

Competitive Pressures: Market and Technology

Following deregulation, the granting of new banking licenses led to an influx of new banks (appendix 3), existing financial institutions expanded their branch networks, and the new overseas competitors tried to carve out market shares. This produced substantial excess capacity, and the competition within the sector resulted in New Zealand financial retailers' having the lowest interest rate margins of any OECD country (*New Zealand Herald*, August 9, 1994: 1 and May 4, 1995: 10). The competitive market gave rise to three trends—market withdrawal, mergers or takeovers, and downsizing of market presence—that have cut the number of registered banks. First, the withdrawal from the retail market started shortly after the 1987 share market crash, with six banks relinquishing their bank licenses during 1989–94 (Flux 1994: 17).

The dominant trend since the early 1990s has been toward fewer registered banks as a result of mergers or takeovers. For example, there were six fewer registered banks in 1993–94 (KPMG 1995: 7) than before. The merger of ten trustee banks, announced in July 1986, created Trust Bank. This left ASB[5] on its own as a significant bank in the Auckland region, whereas Taranaki Savings Bank is now the only regional bank left. Subsequent to the merger between Trust Bank and Westpac in 1996–97, deregulation has produced only two new players with significant market presence—ASB and Countrywide Bank—compared to the pre-1987 situation of four registered banks.

Interestingly, non banking organizations have had remarkably little success. Insurance companies have generally kept out of retail banking. NZI Bank and National Mutual Bank relinquished their bank licenses (see above), and the proposed 1989 merger of ANZ and National Mutual Life Association stalled on the opposition of the Australian Treasurer. However, the AMP insurance company established a telephone banking subsidiary, Ergo, in 1995, and this proved a successful venture. The foray of building societies into retail banking has been unspectacular, except for that of Countrywide Bank, which was the first building society to apply for a banking license. Specialized lending firms such as mortgage brokers have secured only a modest market share, probably because of the tight profit margins involved (Riordan 1996: 42).

Third, branch networks have also been significantly rationalized as ownership structures have changed. This has affected all the banks, though there are differences among the various organizations due to varying financial exposure and the size of their existing branch networks. Thus, banks with extensive branch networks, like ANZ and BNZ, were faced with more extensive adjustments than others (Parker 1995).

Technology: Driving Market and Organizational Changes
New Zealand banks were not especially early in introducing electronic banking because of the small market. The first ATMs were introduced in

1979, and all major banks offered an ATM service by 1982 (*Yearbook* 1995: 586).

New technology has facilitated the main organizational changes in banking. Technology made it possible to standardize laborious clerical work, leading to the split between front and back office. Technology also provided access to a wider range of information, allowing the targeting of niche markets and combining information about individual customers. This made cross selling possible, providing the foundation for the dominant sales culture of the 1990s.

Although new technology has reduced costs and enabled banks to offer a wider range of services, it was and still is a controversial area. The resulting adjustments in staff composition have lowered costs, but the investment in new technology has made it difficult for banks to reduce operating expenses (KPMG 1995: 10). The banks have also had difficulty in recruiting staff required to implement and maintain the new technology, resulting in an upward pressure on remuneration. The cost side and the small market have made collaboration around new technology an obvious choice (see ATMs owned versus ATMs accessible in table 4.1). A prime example is the Databank collaboration. The BNZ originally established Databank in the 1960s, but it became a joint venture for check clearance and for developing electronic banking among the trading banks in the 1970s (Carew 1987: 49). According to Flux (1994: 31), the joint venture project was unique in the world, and it worked surprisingly well in the 1970s and 1980s.

New technology collaboration appears to have become less advantageous over the last decade, however, with the falling cost of new tech-

Table 4.1
Automatic teller machines

Bank	ATMs owned				ATMs accessible			
	1993	1994	1995	1996	1993	1994	1995	1996
ANZ	183	254	286	306	1,010	948	1,033	1,094
ASB	232	253	259	275	n.a.	892	1,065	n.a.
BNZ	118	120	136	167	868	1,234	1,246	1,500
Countrywide	76	76	82	74	n.a.	n.a.	n.a.	n.a.
National Bank	156	188	204	205	n.a.	628	1,197	1,259
Trust Bank	280	294	303		523	880	1,193	
Westpac	100	109	148	440	n.a.	n.a.	n.a.	1,147
Sector total	1,163	1,315	1,439	1,489	n.a.	n.a.	n.a.	

Sources: KPMG 1995: 16–17, KPMG 1996: 28–29, KPMG 1997: 30–31.

nology and the integration of New Zealand banks into overseas-owned banking groups. Additionally, Databank developed into something of a white elephant due to management and technological problems, and a wave of redunancies took place when the banks abandoned the Databank project Integrated Banking Information System (IBIS) in 1990 (Interdata 1991: 47). It has been suggested that banks would try to introduce new electronic services to differentiate themselves from competitors (Flux 1994). However, there will probably be more of an uneasy balance between in-house projects and collaboration. For example, the six major banks announced a new joint venture around EFTPOS provision in early 1995 (KPMG 1995: 11).

Competitive Pressures: Strategic Responses

The traditional competitive strategy of absorbing competitors has already affected New Zealand banking, leaving limited scope for buying smaller or regional banks. Future takeovers or mergers are bound to reshape the whole industry because they will involve some of the major banks. The overseas ownership of most banks has foreclosed overseas expansion, another traditional strategy.

Apart from the takeover strategy, there is a paradox when one tries to evaluate the banks' market strategies in the face of a fast changing, competitive environment. On the one hand, there has been a lot of talk about product differentiation and strategies to "stand out of the pack." Thus, an array of new products has been introduced along with an emphasis on sales and service. On the other hand, the range of products offered by individual banks shows great similarities, and it is often difficult to differentiate the various banks' strategic approaches.

The main strategic responses of New Zealand banks, all driven or facilitated by technological changes, are as follows:

• focus on cost reductions
• split between front and back office
• promotion of a sales culture
• shift away from a paternalistic employment relations culture (discussed in a later section)
• emerging split between business and retail banking

Banks' financial exposure subsequent to the share market crash initially prompted the focus on cost reductions. The initial expansion of the branch network also proved a costly and mistaken strategy because of the high level of competition, the small population, and low geographic density (Harris 1994).

In the 1990s, senior executives have constantly reinforced the message of cost cutting to staff. This has coincided with increased focus on measures of efficiency such as the operating expenses/operating income ratio and the income per employee. The cost reductions have mainly come through trimming staff levels and rationalizing the branch network. Revenue has mainly been increased through a focus on sales (discussed below). Additional costs associated with the sales strategy, however, such as product development, advertising, staff training, and refurbishing branches, restricted the initial profitability of this strategy.

Cost-cutting considerations have also driven the recent growth in telephone banking, Internet services, and EFTPOS facilities. This growth is also, however, a way of restricting or preempting the market presence of new competitors (for example, mortgage brokers).

The split between the administrative and sales functions (or the so-called split between front and back office) attempted to streamline most of the processing and administration occurring in the back office. Processing centers have tended to be centralized in Auckland, Wellington, or Christchurch, and are becoming increasingly automated and distinct from the branch network. The strategy has reduced branch staff and increased their productivity (e.g., Flux 1994: 42–43). It has also allowed the employment of less-skilled people on a part-time or casual basis.

However, the split between back and front office has enhanced the duality in the internal labor market; back office staff are faced with repetitive work, low status and limited career prospects. Low career prospects have given rise to high staff turnover and the repetitive work to numerous complaints about occupational overuse syndrome (OOS). The split has also raised a gender and ethnicity issue, because most of the back office staff are female and predominantly of non-European origin.

There has been a conscious promotion of a sales culture within all banks as a way of increasing income. In the 1990s, banks have begun to offer a more differentiated product mix, such as a wider range of accounts, new types of mortgages, various kinds of insurance, investment products, and credit cards tailored to particular organizations. Cross selling—selling new, additional products during customer contact—has been promoted heavily, and banks have surveyed their customers to estimate how many products each customer has bought. In a tight market, selling to existing customers as opposed to winning new customers has been regarded as the most likely way to generate further income. This defensive approach explains why few banks or bank services "stand out of the pack," because keeping existing customers by offering the same level of convenience and products as competitors has been a priority.

No doubt the sales culture has lifted the service level considerably. It is, however, difficult to pinpoint any bank consistently doing this better than its competitors. The sales culture has been controversial among bank staff (Jackson and Rasmussen 1995), and there is still a way to go before adequate service levels are reached. High staff turnover rates in recent years have influenced the slowness in embedding a sales culture. Cross selling and relationship banking have a distinctly human element, and banks have had difficulty in getting it right.

A split is emerging between business and retail banking. Business banking has been the big moneymaker for banks in the 1990s. This has made it the top area for career purposes, and remuneration in it is far higher. Business banking has increasingly become a separate area from retail banking, with banks targeting businesses and high-income individuals as profitable areas (Pepper 1997). Competition has increased in business banking, however, since banks with no retail platform can compete with established banks because of their lower cost structure.

Change and Variations in Employment Relations in Banking

The strategic responses discussed in the previous section have interacted to produce a massive upheaval in traditional banking. A noteworthy shift has occurred in employment relations culture (explored in detail in later sections). Bureaucratic organizational structures and paternalistic cultures have historically characterized financial service institutions (Austrin 1991). The deregulation of the finance markets after 1984 and the ensuing competition, however, highlighted the inefficiencies of banks' bureaucratic organizational structure. The shift from a paternalistic banking culture to financial retailing has been so pronounced that most banks appear to have adopted the same employment relations strategies (see table 4.2). Although the next sections highlight differences among banks, they are less pronounced than the similarities.

Changes in Employment Relations Practices

Since our research started in 1993, we have interviewed all major banks in New Zealand. During this period, several banks have been integrated into

Table 4.2
The change in employment relations culture

Characteristics	Banking	Financial retailing
Framework	regulated	deregulated
Culture	regulated autonomy, service, dependent employees	control: limited autonomy, sales, independent employees
Organizational structure	hierarchical, relatively autonomous branches	decentralized, sales and administrative functions split
Recruitment	school leavers single point entry	graduates and professionals, multipoint entry
Training	generalist process based specialist position enterprise specific	specialized process and sales based multiskilled positions enterprise specific
Dual internal labor market	gender–males/females seniority	gender–full-time/part-time skills, banking area
Career progression	available	limited, compartmentalized

Source: Jackson 1995, 40.

other banks through mergers. The major banks—banks B, D, E, F, and I— have all become multipurpose banks. Thus previous strategic market positions in business banking (bank I), rural banking (bank F) or branch presence (banks B and D) have become less prevalent. Three banks— banks A, C, and J—have attempted to become national multipurpose banks but have yet to attain this status. Finally, bank H had a niche market status which it is currently attempting to develop further.

Staffing and Employment Security Policies
Employment in banks and the financial sector generally grew significantly in the 1980s (see appendix 1). Employment increased in the financial sector by 23 percent in 1981–86 and by 7 percent in 1986–91. In the banking industry alone, employment rose by 15 percent in 1986–91. Since restructuring started, banking employment has fallen from 1988–89 onward (see table 4.3 and 4.A.3). Staff numbers declined by around 13 percent in the four years to December 1994, influenced by large scale redundancies at the BNZ.

Predictions of large-scale redundancies, more part-time staff, and flatter organizational structures have been around for some time (e.g., "Responding to Change" 1988: 7; Stoopin 1989). Seen in this light, the actual em-

Table 4.3
New Zealand banking industry: Employment, 1989–96

Bank	1989	1990	1991	1992	1993	1994	1995	1996
ANZ	4,035	4,270	4,238	4,221	6,359[1]	6,351	6,202	5,839
ASB		1,898	1,809	1,848	1,938	2,075	2,268	2,377
BNZ	9,006[2]	7,670	6,051	5,720	5,810	5,772	5,860	5,622
Countrywide	598[2]	797	819	1,019	1,106	1,199	1,275	1,403
National Bank	3,708	3,495	3,541	3,805	3,627	3,785	3,785	3,539
Trust Bank		2,940	2,884	3,329	3,449	3,303	3,449	
Westpac	3,837	3,742	3,821	3,931	3,510	3,457	3,635	6,712[3]
Postbank	2,868	2,831	3,027	2,638				
Total[4]	30,046	28,603	28,379	27,819	26,051	26,207	26,934	26,030

Sources: KPMG 1990–97; Flux 1994.
Notes:
1. The 1993 figure for Postbank (2,421) is added to the 1993 ANZ figure (3,938 employees).
2. The 1989 figures for BNZ and Countrywide Bank are from Flux 1994: 28.
3. Trust Bank was acquired by Westpac in May 1996.
4. The total line includes other banks besides the eight for which specific statistics have been provided.

ployment changes look less draconian overall. Some of the managers interviewed stated that the banks could have taken a much tougher line. The HR director of bank B stressed that, contrary to union claims in the 1996 negotiations, the bank's overall employment had been stable for several years.

Nevertheless, the employment changes during 1989–96 had a traumatic impact on employees. They came after a steady rise in employee numbers in the 1980s and were associated with reduced job security, since the overall figures hide an alteration in employee patterns with new types of employees joining banks in the 1990s.

Besides the changes in employment levels, bank employment has shown three other key trends: the increased use of part-timers and casuals, the growing number of female staff, and the significant staff turnover among good employees of long tenure.

The use of part-time and casual employees gathered pace from the mid-1980s with the split between back and front office and with attempts to match work flow with front office staff numbers (Flux 1994: 34). Part-time employees constituted around 25 percent across the industry in 1994 (see table 4.A.4).[6] Finsec argued that, given the cost benefits for employers of using casual employees and temporary and contract staff, this would become a dominant employment feature (*Finsec News*, October 1994). This has yet to happen, however, and banks appear to have become more willing to employ casual workers as permanent part-time staff, both because of cost considerations and because many managers believe that casuals are less-desirable employees (Snelders 1997).

The majority of bank employees have been women since the 1970s (Brocklesby 1984). This gender distribution has become more pronounced in the 1990s with career structures being less biased against women and with part-time employment rising as a share of full-time employment. Women outnumber men by at least a 20 : 1 ratio among part-time staff (tables 4.A.1 and 4.A.2). Whereas the paternalistic culture severely limited women's opportunities for career progression (Game and Pringle 1983), explicit gender discrimination is less pronounced in the banks' current recruitment and promotion policies. For example, banks F and I use assessment centers, whereas bank H uses an outside consultant in its recruiting. However, the move toward more separated function areas and a higher proportion of part-time staff has foreclosed career opportunities for most women employed by banks.

Several HR managers appeared less concerned with the career blockages for general staff and more worried that so few women were rising to management positions. All banks have a policy of encouraging more young women to pursue a management career. In banks F and I, this has included changes to recruitment, pinpointing talented women on staff, pursuing more flexible training programs, and updating parental leave policies. Bank D undertook a comprehensive review of its diversity policy.

However, the long hours that most managers are currently working make it difficult for women (and men) to balance work and family life, and most banks restrict job sharing to nonmanagerial staff.

Staff turnover in banks has traditionally been high, largely because of turnover among young employees. During 1993–95, several managers noted that a larger proportion of the recent turnover had been among good performers with considerable tenure. Bank I's HR executive also expressed concern about the high turnover among part-time staff (around 30 percent in late 1995), and the turnover among permanent part-time staff with long tenure was viewed as detrimental to the bank's service quality. Turnover changes prompted banks to keep a closer eye on this issue; some banks were active in recruiting other banks' employees, and remuneration was revised somewhat in the Auckland market. The banks overcame most of their retainment problems from 1996 onward.

Organizations have historically offered employment security to solicit employee commitment and as an incentive for employees to train (Perrow

1986). However, employers argued that they could no longer guarantee either employee security or a career ladder in an increasingly competitive environment. For many employees, this withdrawal of employment security and promotional opportunities came as a huge shock. Bank employees were used to job security, and many had chosen banking for that reason. Additionally, flatter organizational structures left many employees with few career options. A significant number of employees left, voluntarily or otherwise, the industry altogether.

In comparison to other private sector organizations, banks do not have a reputation of being bad employers. As the industry has reconstituted its workforce, banks have generally tried to support people through redundancy options, outplacement support, or allowing transfer to other function areas (mainly back office positions), although different banks have different reputations. At one end of the spectrum, bank C promoted itself to its employees as being one of the most supportive employers in the industry; at the other end, bank I had a reputation for being tougher— "effective" was the term used by the HR executive—in adjusting its workforce composition.

Work Organization and Working Time

It can be argued that the wide-ranging changes in work organization have substituted one Taylorist approach for another. In the past, clerical workers and bankers involved in administrative and routine tasks used to make up the bulk of staff, performing narrowly defined and repetitive tasks. This was also the area of banking where mainly women and young people were employed and where staff turnover was high. On the other hand, people pursuing a traditional banking career benefited from job rotation, job enlargement, and performing less-defined tasks. Although the opportunity to work in different function areas clearly broke the Taylorist approach, this was less available for most people working in the branch network. Moving from branch to branch often meant progressing slowly through a number of jobs that seldom added much more responsibility or new experience.

New technology has clearly changed the nature of data entry and analysis, information transfer, and administrative tasks. Nevertheless, the split between front and back office, the branch's declining importance, and the emerging split between business and retail banking have all contributed to developing another Taylorist approach. This is clearly the case with work in the back office (as discussed above). Although front office staff benefit from customer contact, it is often at a very superficial level and involves a restricted range of skills. Initial training is often limited to "induction courses" of up to a week. Subsequent training has a clear sales focus. There is little job rotation within most branches and hardly any between the front and back office and the various function areas. Though banks have started to discuss and implement team-based approaches, there has been very little workplace reform in banking.

Working-time flexibility has been a key bargaining objective for banks from the late 1980s onward. The Shop Trading Hours Act of 1990 and the ECA were expected to result in an extension of operating hours, but this has yet to happen. Though most banks now have much more contractual working time flexibility,[7] it is remarkable how little banks have taken advantage of it, in part because of the costs associated with longer branch opening hours, as Finsec has managed to preserve penal rates in most collective employment contracts. Instead the banks have turned to nonbranch banking—ATMs, EFTPOS, telephone banking—to make services available to customers outside normal banking hours. One bank has tested supermaket banking, and another obtained an agreement to trade through the post offices.

Skills, Training, and Careers

Banks have had a strong tradition of training and skills development. Like public sector organizations, banks have been a supplier of skilled people to other private organizations. A number of training and education programs were developed under the auspice of the Bankers' Institute, an employer-funded organisation overseeing education programs in banking, in the 1970s and 1980s. This is still the educational basis for banks, but the role of training has changed dramatically. Historically, career progression was based on the attainment of a wide variety of skills by moving within one bank (Brocklesby 1984). Banks have moved away from this pattern of generalist training (Evans, Abel, and Holdsworth 1992: 26). Several HR managers acknowledged a growing tendency to hire new staff to bring in new skills and attributes. This tendency was explained as an expediency measure partly to increase the speed of attitudinal change and partly to obtain skills in short supply in the banking industry.

Nevertheless, an increased need for multiskilled staff because of flatter organizational structures and the increase in product lines resulted in significant expenditure on staff training in the 1990s. Generally, banks have targeted two areas. First, front office staff training has focused on improving two main areas of selling techniques: presentation skills and cross-selling techniques. Presentation skills involve not only physical appearance but also emotional displays, for example, appearing happy for the customer. Beyond this general trend, the selection of particular training programs has been rather random. The HR staff in bank C favored a particular training provider, but they were overruled when an operations manager opted for an American program. In bank D, the new CEO favored and implemented a particular program.

Second, management training has become more formalized and sophisticated. Several banks are using programs developed by their overseas owners, whereas others have adapted state-of-the-art programs internally. Support for postgraduate studies at New Zealand or overseas business schools has also grown. Line managers in particular have been targeted for training as flatter organizational structures have upgraded their role.

Industry training is a contentious issue in the banking industry. Although the training and education programs in place under the Bankers' Institute have the hallmarks of industry training, they are short of constituting an integrated process. The Bankers' Institute obtained ITO status (see earlier discussion of labor market deregulation) but an ITO training process, including an integration of off-the-job and on-the-job assessments into the national qualifications framework, was never finalized. The institute had developed detailed descriptions for various job positions, but the banks did not give their support to an ITO-led industry training process (Janes 1997). Several HR managers attacked the ITO training process as bureaucratic, a waste of resources, and at odds with the banks' current training strategies. Apparently, only one bank favored an industry approach.

It is unclear whether current training and education efforts are meeting the need for more-flexible and multiskilled staff. Insufficient maintenance of skill levels was a factor in the 1993–95 skills shortages, with the pool of redundant bank employees evaporating fast as the upswing gathered pace (Jackson and Rasmussen 1995: 10). Most banks felt the pinch of skills shortages, especially in business banking and computing. Subsequently, banks have focused more on training and skills development, with better internal training programs for front office staff and managers. Employers tend to argue, therefore, that the quality and quantity of training within the sector has been maintained if not improved. Employees are complaining, however, about lack of training availability and a tendency to provide employees with a limited set of skills (Edwards 1993). The union points to the increased use of part-time staff, who invariably receive less training than those who are full-time.

Remuneration Practices

The central theme of the new HR strategies is improving employee performance (Austrin 1991). In the back office, performance tends to be measured in terms of the speed and accuracy of processing, and in the front office, in terms of sales outcomes. Employees are now under considerable pressure to maintain or improve their respective levels of performance. Unsurprisingly, we found that this had negative consequences for employee satisfaction. Increased performance pressure is common for all banks, but there are significant differences among various banks and particular employee groups.

The focus on employee performance has led to the implementation of a variety of performance-based pay systems. This is often seen as a logical extension of the general remuneration basis that is provided by a "Hay Point" system in most banks. Hay Points stipulate a rough guideline for the size and relative position of a particular job. However, the system tends to reward the position rather than the performance, and the performance pay schemes are therefore targeted to reward extraordinary performance. The introduction of performance-based pay systems has been associated with two other important trends: a preference for total remuneration packages and an aversion to across-the-board pay increases.

The preference for total remuneration packages is a common private sector phenomenon, with consultants recommending since the late 1980s that organizations "cash up" their employee benefits, trading off non-salary benefits for salary. This suited bank managers under pressure to bring down costs. However, the cash-up strategy has proven costly, as employees traded off benefits and job security for "market remuneration." Bank E acknowledged this trade-off explicitly whereas banks B and C stressed the importance of the local market, in particular Auckland, as a factor influencing employer "generosity."

The aversion to across-the-board pay increases is prevalent among HR managers. Ideally, performance and productivity should drive raises. The reality is, though, that Finsec has obtained general wage raises in every bargaining round. Finsec's ability to secure general pay raises has grown during the 1990s, and it forcefully demanded cost-of-living increases during 1994–96 negotiations, a period when a tighter labor market forced the banks to "meet the market" and to provide "incentives," as they were euphemistically labeled, to recruit and retain particular types of employees. In Auckland, the cash up of benefits actually went into reverse during 1993–96, which may be one of the reasons why banks A, B, and E started to review their performance pay systems in 1996.

The banks have been reluctant to develop more sophisticated forms of remuneration such as gain sharing, profit sharing, team-based pay or share option schemes. Two banks have a type of profit-sharing scheme, and another bank has a bonus system that links bonuses to overall profitability. At bank H, both overall profitability and team and individual performance influence the total bonus payout. Banks' main innovative form of remuneration is skills-based pay, which Finsec has championed as a better form of remuneration than the various performance pay systems. One bank has introduced a form of this that appears to be a mixture of broad banding (of pay scales) and paying for competencies. Although it is too early to evaluate this particular skills-based pay system, it appears to have had some teething problems, with HR managers from other banks feeling that it was too costly and complicated.

Firm Governance and Employment Relations: Variations on a Theme

The banks' employment relations strategies appear to lack internal consistency in the 1990s. On the one hand, banks have been moderate in their use of the increased contractual flexibility under the ECA and, on the other hand, they have pursued a radical shift in employee attitudes through advancing the culture of financial retailing.

The introduction of the ECA in 1991 increased the contractual flexibility available to employers. At the time, most banks were undergoing a phase of dramatic rationalization, but they were generally restrained in their quest for change, and many continued to roll over their existing contracts without imposing draconian changes on employees. The pre-1991 award can still be traced in bank B's collective employment contract. Bank A's HR executive explicitly lamented the banks' reluctance to break out of traditional collective bargaining. Banks have followed a traditional HR strategy: They have a cautious relationship with the union (see below), have implemented performance management measures and remuneration changes slowly, and have yet to devolve key management functions. Banks have not been involved in workplace reform, and no bank has interest representation similar to European works councils (Rasmussen 1997).

As mentioned above, employees in the primary labor market have achieved more leverage through the jurisdiction developed at the employment institutions. HR managers have slowly adjusted to this change and have shown a clear preference for out-of-court settlements or mediation. Managers have found it difficult to interpret the procedural requirements being established by the employment institutions, which have produced outcome uncertainties, and even "winning" can be associated with considerable costs. It also appears difficult for line managers to get the procedural side of staff matters right despite the training and information material available.[8] Nevertheless, banks B, D, F, and I have all started to defend their personal grievance cases more vigorously. Similarly, bank C has become more alert to the problem after a couple of rather costly grievance settlements.

Banks and the Union: An Uneasy Relationship

Although the ECA "promotes individualism over collectivism" (Harbridge 1993: 47), Finsec has remained the primary bargaining agent for most bank staff (as discussed above). It is the only union in the industry, and it runs a highly efficient, low-budget organization. A couple of individual banks have made unsuccessful attempts to sideline the union through direct arrangements with staff. Several collective actions have provided further credence to the union's bargaining position. The union has pursued a closer relationship with the banks and has actually achieved it in some cases (for example, through joint presentation of bargaining outcomes and involvement in developing skill-based pay systems). Thus, Finsec has consolidated its bargaining position among the banks in the 1990s.

However, Finsec is by no means in an unassailable position. The decline in the industry's staff numbers and the rise in numbers of temporary employees are both undermining Finsec's position. The union's membership has dropped because of the sector's downsizing. Union sources suggest that union membership rates have remained high, at more than 60 percent of the targeted staff group in most banks. This figure exaggerates union membership in the industry, which is probably around 40 percent.[9] The reduction in union density is also caused by management staff being outside collective arrangements and by one bank having very few union members. Interestingly, management sources have pointed to a decline in union membership in some banks since 1994, but it has been impossible to verify this.

Further attempts to roll back Finsec's bargaining coverage are likely. HR managers are often under pressure from other managers to "get tough." There appears to be a continuum of employer strategies toward the union. Most HR managers advocate an accommodation with the union though they philosophically favor a "union substitution model." Several managers indicated that the union interfered with the direct relationship between employers and employees, and they voiced apprehension against "third-party intervention." The union substitution strategy has several problems, however. The union has considerable support among bank staff, with many employees turning to the union for support and information during the restructuring process. The substitution strategy assumes that the union is a third party to the employment relationship. Although this may be correct to a certain extent, the argument appears to hold little sway with employees, probably because the union organization is small and most negotiation teams include only one full-time official, with the rest being staff representatives. Full-time officials are also keen to show that Finsec is "member driven," with extensive consultation, opinion surveys, and information flow. On several occasions, member militancy has forced the union to become more aggressive in its bargaining approach.

Belman (1992) argued that low-trust organizations tend to be characterized by conflict that ultimately has a negative impact on organizational performance. This argument could be applied to the banking industry, as employees have openly put much more pressure on their employers since 1993. Stop-work meetings, spontaneous disruptions, warnings about strikes, and short strikes have become more common (e.g., *New Zealand Herald*, March 8, 1995: 2, *Dominion*, December 13, 1995). In particular, the use of strike action has become part of the bargaining agenda, with at least seven short strikes being staged at various banks over the last six years. For example, a 1996 strike at the ANZ Bank was disruptive and demonstrated an uncharacteristic militancy among staff. The likelihood of a strike's success is also higher since the tendency to centralize processing has made banks more vulnerable to potential strike action.

Employee Trust and Commitment

The restructuring of the banking industry has resulted in a low-trust employment relationship and reduced levels of organizational commitment that have made employment relations more difficult. (Jackson 1995). This section focuses on organizational cynicism and decreased job satisfaction.

Organizational cynicism is the result of unrealistically high expectations concerning the outcome of change (Kanter and Mirvis 1989). The employee expectations associated with a paternalistic culture ill fitted the labor market pressures of the 1990s. Employee job satisfaction suffered during the restructuring process, which was clearly conveyed to management through staff surveys, increased staff turnover, and less-harmonious employment relations.

Management often heralded the shift to a sales culture as a great opportunity for employees who, for example, wanted autonomy and responsibility. These expectations were unrealistically high, and new opportunities have failed to materialize for most employees. Instead, career paths have been compressed, with significantly fewer possibilities for career progression. When organizational cynicism does develop, it is a serious impediment to organizational change as employees tend to become more wary of change and change agents (Wanous, Reichers, and Austin 1994). Overcoming organizational cynicism and job dissatisfaction and establishing a new employer-employee relationship have therefore become a major task for HR staff. Progress in this area is regarded as a key to better service quality, reduced turnover rates, less-conflictual employment relations, and a decreased focus on remuneration issues. Besides improving the quality of the recruitment process, banks now have a much better chance of staff's accepting changes because the pace of restructuring has slowed and new employees with different attitudes have been employed. Additionally, banks are putting much effort and money into making staff accept work reorganization or structural changes. For example, bank D spent several million dollars on an extensive consultation process when it wanted to change the role of branch and line managers in 1995. It was a qualitatively different process from that employed when previous changes were implemented: more use of staff feedback, detailed communication, and (apparently) a better reception by the staff involved.

Most banks reevaluated their communication policy and practices during the 1993–96 period. The focus on communication follows the traditional argument by Kanter and Mirvis (1989) that employee cynicism can be avoided only if communication is adequate and realistic. Some consultants have advised banks that to achieve greater effectiveness, they need to adjust their communication—language, issues, and presentation style and format—to coincide with employee interests. Organizational communication, according to these consultants, should avoid raising employee expectations beyond the achievable and should focus on employees' work situation. For example, bank I reassessed its staff surveys, and this prompted it to update its communication effort. It found that line managers did not function adequately in the communication process. The uncertainty many line managers faced made them disinclined to participate positively and fully in the communication process. Several banks have attempted to integrate their line managers better in the communication process (through focus groups, feedback surveys, seminars, and communication training). It is still too early to evaluate whether the emphasis on organizational communication is paying off, but banks are certainly putting considerable effort and resources into improving their effectiveness in this area.

There is still a long way to go before the distrust among employees is overcome. It has already taken more time to overcome this distrust than most managers expected during our initial interviews in 1993–94. We are cautious, therefore, about the current positive assessment by many HR managers.

Change and Diversity: Driving Forces and Outcomes

As mentioned, the banks have responded fairly similarly to enhanced competition. Some differences between the banks, however, have led to different employment relations strategies. Many employees appreciate these differences, and the banks' reputations vary quite a lot. We found individual banks' market situation, changes in senior management, and bargaining strategy could explain some of the variations.

A bank's market situation involves factors such as financial exposure, the size of the branch network, strength or weakness in a particular banking area (e.g., business banking, mortgages), and the relationship to overseas owners. Financial exposure tends to dictate the extent and speed of employment relations changes. This was the case, for example, with the early 1990s restructuring at the BNZ. It was bound to create adverse reactions when nearly a third of all employees were made redundant in a matter of just over two years (see table 4.3). The mergers and takeovers in the early 1990s, when some banks clearly had to rationalize their branch network, generated similar pressure.

Although it is difficult to pinpoint the exact influence of overseas ownership it is clear that the relationship of employment relations to overseas owners varies considerably. Although the banks like to profile their employment relations strategies as independently determined, this is certainly less so in some banks. Bank D's HR manager actually saw this as a positive process because it gave the bank access to up-to-date human resources management techniques and training programs. Compared to other function areas, we generally found less pressure in this one to "toe the line." Managers in banks A, F, and I explained this as an effect of recent employment relations reforms in New Zealand that made some practices of the overseas owner look old-fashioned.

Traditionally, personnel departments were staffed with bankers working for a short period in the department as part of their general training.

This has changed in the 1990s, and specialist managers—in human resources, employee relations, and training—have been employed in senior positions. This has had a distinct differentiating impact on employment relations strategies. It has provided new inputs and experiences unavailable through the traditional recruitment strategy. This must be considered a positive development in a period with adjustments to new market conditions but, on the other hand, one that also provokes conflict. The new managers often have had too little "understanding" of banking: They are without knowledge of organizational history, of banking procedures and products, and of attitudes among bank staff. This has led to clashes with other senior managers, in particular, managing directors, who have long-term experience in banking. As a result, turnover of senior staff in human resources departments has been high. This has further resulted in too many new approaches being implemented and never really finished.

Bargaining strategies have varied as the banks' market situation and new HR managers have influenced them. Other influences also come into play, such as the relationship with the union and the extent of collective bargaining. Managers often explain a preference for individual employment contracts by asserting that they lead to a simpler, less conflictual approach to employment relations. They also point to greater scope for rewarding individual performance and tailoring the employment package to each individual. Managerial prerogative is seldom mentioned, though this is obviously what the "third-party intervention" curtails. Several banks have had a volatile relationship with the union, though some banks are more inclined to use the union as part of their employment relations or communication strategy. Nevertheless, most banks work reluctantly with the union, and although information is shared, it is often done begrudgingly and with considerable delays.

Conclusion

The extensive economic deregulation and legislative reforms over the last decade have dramatically changed the environment of the banking industry and dismantled restrictions on business and lending activities, opened up the market for new entrants, and privatized government stakeholdings. Additionally, new technology has facilitated organizational changes and the proliferation of new services.

Immediately after deregulation, the banking industry had considerable overcapacity, and a process of industry rationalization has been underway since the late 1980s. Though internationalization is not a possible strategic response, numerous players have exited, and mergers and takeovers have frequently occurred. There is only one New Zealand–owned bank left, and this is a very small regional bank. Adjusting institutional arrangements and market presence is an ongoing process.

Banks' strategic responses to these developments constitute a paradox: Most banks talk about the need to "stand out of the pack" and to compete on service differentiation, but the product and service strategies of the various banks often show little differentiation. The banks' identical, market-driven strategies have included a stronger focus on cost reductions, a split between front and back office, promotion of a sales culture, and increased differentiation between business and retail banking. Variations on these strategies could largely be explained by the individual bank's market situation, bargaining strategy, and changes in senior management. In light of the changes in government regulations, in ownership structures, and in the bargaining framework, one can expect more strategic diversity, and thereby more employment relations diversity, in the future.

However, the shift in the overall employment relations framework has influenced employment relations in banking significantly. This process has included decentralization of bargaining, introduction of new HR ideas, and banks' negotiating directly with their employees. The last of these has made Finsec's relationship with the various banks tenuous, but Finsec has bucked the general decline in union density. Finsec is the only union in the industry, and it has kept collective bargaining intact in nearly all banks. This has limited fluctuations in individual banks' employment relations approach in the 1990s despite the alteration or disappearance of many traditional institutional arrangements.

Though banks have been relatively moderate in their pursuit of bargaining concessions and labor market flexibility, they have implemented a radical shift from a paternalistic banking culture to a financial retailing culture. This has had significant effects on job security, work organization, the training and development approach, and career opportunities. As banks have benefited from a more buoyant economy, they have increased their attention to people management with more consultative processes and better communication and training options. This change was also precipitated by increased employee militancy, increased staff turnover, and service quality problems. Thus, employee commitment and trust have been damaged considerably, and it will take time before many of the banks reestablish a suitable employer-employee relationship.

Methodology

The evidence for this paper was mainly drawn from interviews and secondary sources. Interviews normally last from one to two hours and have been conducted periodically since August 1993. The interviews covered a total of nine financial sector organizations of which two were insurance companies. We have interviewed twenty-one managers—human resources managers, employee relations managers, or training managers—and some of them more than once. We have tested employee opinions and attitudes in various ways: employee interviews, informal discussions with employees, discussions with consultants working in the industry, and discussions with union leaders, organizers, and representatives. Finally, we have had access to confidential staff surveys.

Appendix: Employment Trends

Table 4.A.1
Banking (811)

Year	F-T Men	F-T Women	F-T Total	P-T Men	P-T Women	P-T Total
1986	8,856	13,413	22,269	144	2,148	2,292
1991	9,195	15,615	24,810	135	3,279	3,414

Source: Dept. of Statistic (NZ). Census, 1986, 1991.

Table 4.A.2
Financial institutions (81)

Year	F-T Men	F-T Women	F-T Total	P-T Men	P-T Women	P-T Total
1981	13,383	16,185	29,568	195	846	1,041
1986	14,346	19,911	34,257	375	3,036	3,411
1991	14,991	20,700	35,691	444	4,086	4,530

Source: Dept. of Statistic (NZ). Census, 1981, 1986 & 1991

Table 4.A.3
Banking (811)

	Full-time equivalent employees (FTEs)					
Year	0–5 FTEs	6–9 FTEs	10–49 FTEs	50–99 FTEs	100+ FTEs	Total
1986	1,157	1,744	11,631	2,028	4,978	21,538
1987	1,328	1,936	14,239	2,518	6,898	26,919
1988	1,375	2,050	14,258	3,012	6,898	27,593
1989	1,309	2,312	14,325	2,999	5,986	26,931
1990	1,575	2,501	14,201	2,614	5,888	26,779
1991	1,896	2,794	12,968	2,676	6,164	26,498
1992	1,909	3,322	11,996	2,681	6,733	26,641
1993	2,115	3,577	11,331	1,717	6,109	24,849
1994	2,086	3,509	11,039	1,961	5,319	23,913
1995	2,145	3,225	10,804	2,203	5,751	24,128
1996	1,753	3,006	10,937	2,220	6,487	24,403

Source: Statistics NZ: "INFOS-Business Pattern" (BUDA.SA8ASA + P).
Note: Size groups (ie 0–5 FTEs, etc.) are based on pay units, not on enterprises (as in table 4).

Table 4.A.4
Banking (811), grouped by size of full-time equivalent employees (FTEs)

Year	FTEs	Enterprises	Part-timers	Full-timers	FTEs
1994	Size: 0–5	3	0	1	1
	Size: 6–9	—	—	—	—
	Size: 10–49	—	—	—	—
	Size: 50–99	1	9	81	86
	Size: 100+	20	4,948	21,792	24,266
	Total	24	4,957	21,874	24,353
1995	Size: 0–5	2	0	0	0
	Size: 6–9	1	0	9	9
	Size: 10–49	1	2	10	11
	Size: 50–99	1	12	86	92
	Size: 100+	18	5,253	21,825	24,452
	Total	23	5,267	21,930	24,564

Source: Business Activity Statistics 1994: 37; 1995: 37 (Statistics NZ). Column 3 presents the number of enterprises; column 4, 5, & 6 present employee numbers.

Notes

1. Prior to 1987, the four multipurpose banks were called "trading banks," with the trustee savings banks being legally separated from trading banks and restricted principally to servicing the personal savings and investment needs of individuals (Bankers' Association 1993: 37)

2. There was a 75 percent limit on foreign ownership of merchant banks before deregulation, but the major banks were exempted from this limit because they preceded this legislation.

3. New Zealand statistics stipulate part-time employment as 30 or fewer hours per week.

4. The blanket coverage provision implied that an agreement would automatically be applied across a particular industry or occupation.

5. ASB was originally scheduled to be part of Trust Bank (Carey 1987: 44) but this did not occur.

6. An alteration of the statistical definition of part-time from on average 20 hours per week to on average 30 hours per week partly influenced the jump in part-timers between 1981 and 1986.

7. Contractual changes to working-time arrangements are important, but banks' ability to recruit employees for special positions—for example, mobile mortgage managers—outside the collective coverage has rendered these changes less crucial.

8. It was explained to us that work pressure and a preference for informal solutions often lead to a less efficient approach among line managers.

9. There has not been an official record of union membership since 1991, but surveys conducted by the Industrial Relations Centre at Victoria University found that union density in the finance and business services was 25 percent in 1994 (Harbridge, Hince, and Honeybone 1995: 167). However, this figure includes many small organizations where there is no union presence.

References

Armitage, C., and R. Dunbar. (1993). "Labour Market Adjustment under the Employment Contracts Act." *New Zealand Journal of Industrial Relations*, 18(1): 94–112.

Austrin, T. (1991). "Flexibility, Surveillance and Hype in New Zealand Financial Retailing." *Work, Employment and Society: A Journal of the British Sociological Association*, 5(2): 201–21.

Bankers' Association. (1993). *Getting it Right: A Guide to Banking.* Wellington, New Zealand: Bankers' Association.

Barlow, J. G. (1990). "Deregulation and the Labour Relations Act 1987: A Case Study of Bargaining in New Zealand Banking." Unpublished diploma thesis, Victoria University, Wellington, New Zealand.

Belman, D. (1992). "Unions, the Quality of Labor Relations, and Firm Performance." In L. Mishel and P. Voos (eds.), *Unions and Economic Competitiveness.* New York: M. E. Sharpe Inc., 41–108.

Boston, J., and P. Dalziel (eds.). (1992). *The Decent Society?* Auckland, New Zealand: Oxford University Press.

Boxall, P. (1995). "Management Strategy and Employment Relations in New Zealand: An Analysis of Contemporary Patterns and Outcomes." *International Employment Relations Review*, 1(1): 27–37.

Boxall, P. (1990). "Towards the Wagner Framework: Change in New Zealand Industrial Relations." *Journal of Industrial Relations*, 32(4): 523–43.

Brocklesby, J. (1984). "Technological Change and the Labour Process—Towards an Analysis of Computerisation in New Zealand Trading Banks." *New Zealand Journal of Industrial Relations*, 9(3): 195–210.

Campbell-Hunt, C., D. Harper, and R. Hamilton. (1993). *Islands of Excellence: A Study of Management in New Zealand*. Wellington, New Zealand: New Zealand Institute of Economic Research.

Carew, E. (1987). *New Zealand's Money Revolution*. Wellington, New Zealand: Allen & Unwin.

Contract. (1992–97). Vols. 1–20. Department of Labour, Wellington, New Zealand.

Deeks, J., and P. Boxall. (1989). *Labour Relations in New Zealand*. Auckland: Longman Paul.

Deeks, J., J. Parker, and R. Ryan. (1994). *Labour and Employment Relations in New Zealand*. Auckland, New Zealand: Longman Paul.

Edwards, D. (1993). "Training Courses: A Luxury Banks Can No Longer Afford?" *New Zealand Banker*, 6(1): 13–15.

Elkin, G., and K. Inkson. (1995). "Employee Development." In P. Boxall (ed.), *The Challenge of Human Resource Management*. Auckland, New Zealand: Longman Paul, 150–177.

Evans, T., D. Abel, and R. Holdsworth. (1992). "Training in the New Labour Market: A Management Issue." *New Zealand Banker*, 5(2): 25–27.

FinSec News, No. 1–44, April 1990–October 1997.

Flux, A. (1994). "From Tellers to Sellers." Research Monograph no. 6, Victoria University, Wellington, New Zealand.

Game, A., and R. Pringle. (1983). *Gender at Work*. Sydney, Australia: George Allen & Unwin.

Gilson, C., and Wagar, T. (1996). "In Pursuit of Individual Contracts: Australia and New Zealand Employers Compared." In R. Fells and T. Todd (eds.), *Current Research in Industrial Relations*. Perth: AIRAANZ, 167–174.

In R. Fells and T. Todd (eds.), *Current Research in Industrial Relations*. Perth, Australia: Association of Industrial Relations Academics of Australia and New Zealand, 167–174.

Grills, W. (1994). "The Impact of the Employment Contracts Act on Labour Law: Implications for Unions." *New Zealand Journal of Industrial Relations*, 19(1): 85–101.

Harbridge, R. (1993). "Bargaining and the Employment Contracts Act: An Overview." In R. Harbridge (ed.), *Employment Contracts: New Zealand Experiences*. Wellington, New Zealand: Victoria University Press, 31–53.

Harbridge, R., and A. Honeybone. (1995). "Trade Unions under the Employment Contracts Act: Will Slimming be Fatal?" In P. Boxall (ed.), *The Challenge of Human Resource Management*. Auckland, New Zealand: Longman Paul, 231–249.

Harbridge, R., and N. Howard. (1994). "The Impact of the Employment Contracts Act on Collective Bargaining Structures and Outcomes and Union Membership after Two Years." In D. Mortimer and P. Leece (eds.), *Employment Relations: Theory and Practice.* Sydney, Australia: University of Western Sydney, 59–75.

Harbridge, R., and S. McCaw. (1991). "The Employment Contracts Act 1991: New Bargaining Arrangements in New Zealand." *Asia Pacific Human Resource Management*, 29(4): 5–26.

Harbridge, R., K. Hince, and A. Honeybone. (1995). "Unions and Union Membership in New Zealand: Annual Review for 1994." *New Zealand Journal of Industrial Relations* 20(2): 163–70.

Harbridge, R., and M. Street. (1995). "Labour Market Adjustment and Women in the Service Industry: A Survey," *New Zealand Journal of Industrial Relations* 20(1): 23–34.

Harris, P. (1994). *Cut Jobs Cut Profits: The Cost: Income Ratio.* Wellington, New Zealand.: FinSec.

Hince, K., and R. Harbridge. (1994). "The Employment Contracts Act: An Interim Assessment." *New Zealand Journal of Industrial Relations*, 19(3): 235–55.

Holt, J. (1986). *Compulsory Arbitration in New Zealand: The First Forty Years.* Auckland, New Zealand: Auckland University Press.

Interdata. (1991). *Interdata Financial Handbook 1991*, Sydney, Australia.

Jackson, A. (1995). "Trust and Employee Relations in Financial Retailing." Master's thesis, Auckland University, Auckland, New Zealand.

Jackson, A., and E. Rasmussen. (1995). "Transition, Commitment and Disillusionment: Employment Relations in New Zealand Financial Retailing in the 1990s." Paper presented at the International Industrial Relations Association 10th World Congress, Washington, DC, May 31–June 4.

James, C. (1986). *The Quiet Revolution.* Wellington, New Zealand: Allen & Unwin.

Janes, N. (1997). "The Road to International Competitiveness: Industry Training in New Zealand." Master's thesis, Auckland University, Auckland, New Zealand.

Kanter, D., and P. Mirvis. (1989). *The Cynical Americans: Living and Working in an Age of Discontent and Disillusion.* San Francisco: Jossey-Bass Publishers.

[KPMG] (1990–97). "Survey of New Zealand Financial Institutions." Report, KPMG Peat Marwick, Auckland, New Zealand.

McLaughlin, C., and E. Rasmussen. (1998). " 'Freedom of Choice' and 'Flexibility' in the Retail Sector?" In R. Harbridge et al. (eds.), *Current Research in Industrial Relations.* Wellington, New Zealand: Association of Industrial Relations Academics of Australia and New Zealand, 244–250.

Myers, B. A. (1996). "Industry Training in New Zealand in the 1990s." Research essay, Department of Management and Employment Relations, University of Auckland, Auckland, New Zealand.

Nicholl, P., and M. F. King. (1985). "Financial Institutions and Markets in New Zealand." In M. T. Skully (ed.), *Financial Institutions and Markets in the Southwest Pacific.* London: Macmillan, 160–244.

[OECD] Organization for Economic Cooperation and Development. (1993). *OECD Economic Survey: New Zealand 1993.* Paris: OECD.

Parker, S. (1995). "Why the ANZ Chose a Kiwi Change Manager." *Management* (April): 78–83.

Pepper, C. (1997). "Strategic Human Resource Issues Facing Business/Commercial Banking Operations." MBA thesis, University of Auckland, Auckland, New Zealand.

Perrow, C. (1986). *Complex Organizations: A critical Essay.* 3d ed. New York: McGraw-Hill.

Rasmussen, E. (1997). "Workplace Reform and Employee Participation in New Zealand." In R. Markey and J. Monat (eds.), *Innovation and Employee Participation through Works Councils.* Aldershot, UK: Avebury, 389–411.

Rasmussen, E. (1996a). "Workplace Transformation under the Employment Contracts Act." In R. Fells and T. Todd (eds), *Current Research in Industrial Relations.* Perth, Australia: Association of Industrial Relations Academics of Australia and New Zealand, 454–462.

Rasmussen, E. (1996b). "New Zealand Employment Relations—Settling Down or ...?" *International Employment Relations Association,* 2(2): 59–73.

Rasmussen, E., and P. Boxall. (1995). "Workforce Governance." In P. Boxall (ed.), *The Challenge of Human Resource Management.* Auckland, New Zealand: Longman Paul, 53–88.

Rasmussen, E., and J. Deeks. (1997). "Contested Outcomes: Assessing the Impacts of the Employment Contracts Act." *California Western International Law Journal,* 28(1): 275–96.

Rasmussen, E., P. Boxall, N. Haworth, S. Hughes, M. Powell, T. Maloney, and M. Wilson. (1996a). "Industrial Relations and Labour Market Reforms in New Zealand." In Pacific Economic Cooperation Council, *Human Resources Development Outlook 1995–1996.* Melbourne, Australia: Monash University.

Rasmussen, E., J. Deeks, and M. Street. (1996). "The Entrepreneurial Worker: Changes to Work and Contractual Relationships." In J. Gibson (ed.), *Accord or Discord?* Hamilton, New Zealand: University of Waikato, 335–356.

Rasmussen, E., N. Wailes, and N. Haworth. (1996). "Where Are We and How Did We Get There? Skills Shortages and Industry Training in New Zealand." In R. Fells and T. Todd (eds.), *Current Research in Industrial Relations.* Perth, Australia: Association of Industrial Relations Academics of Australia and New Zealand, 463–472.

"Responding to Change." (1988). *New Zealand Banker,* 1(4): 6–7,

Riordan, D. (1996). "Mortgage Managers Undercut the Banks." *The Independent,* February 9, 42.

Snelders, B. (1997). "Executive Leasing: Work & Career in Times of Change." Master's thesis, University of Auckland, Auckland, New Zealand.

Stoopin, G. W. (1989). "People—The Challenge for the 1990s." *New Zealand Banker,* 2(2): 3.

Wailes, N. (1994). "The Case against Specialist Jurisdiction for Labour Law: The Philosophical Assumptions of a Common Law for Labour Relations." *New Zealand Journal of Industrial Relations,* 19(1): 1–15.

Walsh, P. (1993). "The State and Industrial Relations in New Zealand." In B. Roper and C. Rudd (eds.), *State and Economy in New Zealand.* Auckland, New Zealand: Oxford University Press, 172–191.

Walsh, P. (1992). "The E'mployment Contracts Act." In J. Boston and P. Dalziel (eds.), *The Decent Society*. Auckland, New Zealand: Oxford University Press, 59–76.

Walsh, P. (1989). "A Family Fight? Industrial Relations Reform under the Fourth Labour Government." In B. Easton (ed.), *The Making of Rogernomics*. Auckland, New Zealand: Auckland University Press, 140–170.

Walsh, P., and G. Fougere. (1987). "The Unintended Consequences of the Arbitration System." *New Zealand Journal of Industrial Relations*, 12(3): 187–98.

Wanous, J., A. Reichers, and J. Austin. (1994). "Organisational Cynicism: An Initial Study." In D. P. Moore (ed.) *Best Papers Proceedings Academy of Management*. Columbia, S.C.: The Academy, 269–273.

Whatman, R. (1994). "Non-standard work in New Zealand: What we know." In P. S. Morrison (ed.), *Labour, Employment and Work in New Zealand*. Wellington, New Zealand: Victoria University, 356–366.

Whatman, R., C. Armitage, and R. Dunbar. (1994). "Labor Market Adjustment under the Employment Contracts Act." *New Zealand Journal of Industrial Relations*, 19(1): 53–73.

5

Employment Relations in U.K. Banking

John Storey, Adrian Wilkinson, Peter Cressey, and Tim Morris

Until very recently, the U.K. banking industry and its employment management practices had, in a number of ways, been out of step with much of the wider U.K. economy. For most of the postwar period the industry enjoyed steady growth and high profitability. It was an industry that was cartelized and regulated. Its industrial relations were orderly, peaceful, and centralized. The banks offered lifetime employment, structured careers, and paternalistic, welfare-oriented personnel policies. During the last few years, however, there have been ample signs of fundamental change. Competition has become fierce. New players have entered the financial services arena. New technology presages a future in which software and hardware companies in computing and telecoms will become both direct competitors and architects of a radical new reshaping of the industry. New targets and performance measures seem to have become critical: Rate of return on equity rather than market share has become the order of the day. New tensions are seen as responsible for undermining the conventional practices. In the 1990s, the banks are not preserving employment security; still less are they adding to the employment stocks as they did throughout the previous decades. On the contrary, they have been shedding labor in a significant manner. Branch closures and other forms of restructuring have had an adverse impact on career opportunities. Contingent pay has replaced automatic pay increases. The paternalistic welfare cultures are being displaced, and new competitive, sales-oriented policies and values are being installed. Full-time, secure careers are perceived as giving way to part-time, less-secure contracts. In this chapter we describe and analyze these and related developments.

The chapter is organized in three main sections. We first identify trends within the banking industry in general, discussing shifts in the institutional regulation of banking and changing market and technological pressures. In the second section, we examine how industry level developments

are affecting specific banks and provide some case examples, along with
industry-wide data, to illustrate how changes in the banking sector have
affected key aspects of employment relations. In the third and final section
we examine reasons for the variation in employment practices.

The Context of Employment Relations

Changes in the Institutional Environment

The U.K. banking sector, when viewed in the round, embraces a range of
different institutions that perform varied (competing and noncompeting)
functions. When viewed in traditional terms, the main institutions include
the clearing banks, merchant banks, building societies, foreign banks,
finance houses, and government savings institutions. In recent years the
boundaries and demarcations between types of institutions have, however, been massively eroded. There are approximately 400 foreign-owned
banks operating in the City of London. They have tended to concentrate
on commercial lending, trade finance, and money market participation.
Some of the U.S.- and European-owned banks are also active in the capital
markets. In this chapter, we concentrate on the core banking institutions,
that is, the commercial banks that undertake a mix of personal retailing
services and commercial lending. These banks also control the national
check-clearing system. When so defined, the British banking industry
employed a total of 500,000 people in 1990.

There is considerable concentration in the banking sector. The four
largest clearing banks (Barclays, Lloyds/TSB, Midlands, and National
Westminster) account for more than half the total U.K. banking employment, that is, more than 250,000 people. These "Big Four" have extensive
branch networks throughout the United Kingdom. Table 5.1 shows
branch numbers for the clearing banks.

This network of branches is an important element in the banks' business
strategies and their calculations of strengths and weaknesses. Their presence in the High Street offers many competitive advantages, but at the

Table 5.1
Number of branch locations for the clearing banks in the United Kingdom

Year	1960	1968	1976	1981	1986	1991	1994
Number	10,886	12,315	11,659	10,993	10,436	8,912	8,005

Source: Annual Abstract of Banking Statistics, London.

same time the branch structure is an expensive overhead. New forms of competition—most notably, for example, home-based telephone banking as offered by new entrants such as First Direct—render the branches a liability, according to some observers. In the 1960s, the banks grew by expanding their branch networks and bringing in new customers. But all the main banks have now reversed this policy and have commenced branch closure programs. Uncertainty about the role of the branch carries critical implications for employment policies, and we return to this issue below.

The banks have also faced significant competition from other players. Building societies in the United Kingdom traditionally took consumer deposits solely for the purpose of house purchase. Until recently they had been prevented by regulative controls from becoming banks in the full sense. Subsequent deregulative measures have relaxed these barriers significantly. One important consequence has been the conversion of a number of building societies into banks with PLC status. A major objective in such conversions is to escape the limitations on raising money from wholesale deposits. At the moment, the Building Societies Commission tightly regulates the societies and limits their wholesale borrowings to 30 percent of their total funds. Even without full-blown conversion, the building societies are now major competitors to the banks. Many now operate what are, in effect, interest-bearing current accounts. The larger building societies, when measured by total deposits, rank among the world's 100 largest banks (Arthur Andersen 1986: 200).

Banks therefore see the building societies (and ex–building societies) as a major threat. Their marketing expertise has been shown to be impressive, and they have cost/income ratios superior to those of the banks. Competition from building societies has put pressure on banks' profit margins. Banks are being forced to respond by cost reduction strategies while also trying to counterattack by offering more-effective customer service. The market environment for all the British banks is fierce because of a tight economic situation, an intense squeeze on profit margins, increased competition, and the need to make considerable provisions for bad debts. This is undoubtedly the main current factor generating the pressure for job cuts in the short term for all the major banks. It is hardly surprising that the banks have chosen to concentrate on staffing levels given the fact that labor continues to represent around two-thirds of total costs despite the progress to date in increasing labor productivity and the growth in capital intensity within the banks.

Information Technology

Information and communications technologies (ICTs) helped to ease the processing of the phenomenal increases in business volumes (through back office automation, automatic teller machines, etc.) during the period when overall staff numbers continued to expand. Just as importantly, the new ICTs themselves facilitated the development of new, technically based products and services that the banks have to various degrees begun to market to customers (such as home banking, EFTPOS, smart cards, and debit cards). In general, the phasing in of technological change has been incremental, and it has affected different groups at different times. Formerly, technical innovation was concerned primarily with process development, mainly the automation of labor-intensive back office administrative and clerical work; current patterns of innovation retain some of this emphasis, but are now increasingly concerned with transforming the scope and nature of the portfolio of "products" and services being offered to the customer and with refashioning the manner in which these are delivered. In fact, management of both the process- and product-related forms of innovation encompasses an important human dimension in terms of the manner in which staff are used, redeployed, or rendered surplus to requirements.

New product innovations have been at least partly responsible for revolutionizing the role of the branch banking structure (Burton 1990; Howcroft and Lavis 1986). Some new methods of service delivery based on interactive communication, such as office banking, home banking, or telephone banking services, presuppose no local branch structure whatsoever. The expanding ATM network has absorbed much of the increased business that would otherwise have taken place over the branch counter and has moved increasingly into locations removed from the branch itself. Simultaneously, banks are using branch information technology to facilitate increased distinctions between tiers of service outlet and to forge greater de facto integration between the branches that remain. For instance, "satelliting" and clustering involves the concentration of back office facilities at one major urban branch and hitherto independent nearby branches being relegated to the status of subbranches offering counter services only. Moreover, the predominant functions performed by the remaining branches are being reconstituted: Essentially, many are evolving from processing centers into "finance shops" (Wilson 1992). The location of the remaining processing work varies, and is discussed below.

There is considerable debate over the consequences of these information technology changes for the future pattern of skill requirements in the present fast-changing environment. Rajan (1987) has suggested skill requirements are likely to polarize, whereas commentators such as Burton (1990) question this, arguing that as a consequence of the interaction of increasing competition and the greater sophistication of information technology, bank employees are arguably becoming more skilled and spending less time on data processing tasks. (Burton 1990: 585)

Perhaps this apparent contradiction is not as perplexing as it first appears. Rather, it can be explained in terms of the fact that the major banks are broadly pursuing one or the other of two main different strategies of labor utilization, depending on their preferred form of branch segmentation. These may have implications for branch, work, and career structures that are to some extent incompatible. The two broad patterns of bank staff reorganization are important because they have differing implications for career structure and division of labor. They involve either the devolution of much processing to branch level or the removal of processing work to separate regional centers. It is too soon to say which of these two will win out, if indeed they do not continue to coexist for a long period in different banks. It is worth reflecting on the implications of the two models.

Under the first option, the bank retains as much of the remaining processing work as possible at branch level, with the overall aim of trying to minimize response times. Lloyds Bank has historically preferred to pursue this policy. Notwithstanding this, it is also extensively refashioning branch layouts to resemble shops. The branch remains a holistic area of work for the clerical and administrative staff in the bank. Thereby, staff retain their traditional generalist character and task repertoire—combining tasks comprising administration, customer contact, and selling—to a larger extent than would be found under the alternative scenario.

Under the regional processing center option, the branch becomes mainly a financial retail outlet. Former back office space is converted to part of the shop front, open to customer access. This enables a greater segmentation of labor, with the tasks of clerical staff in both the branches and the regional processing centers becoming more compartmentalized and restricted. Greater use of part-time female labor in the processing centers becomes possible, with these staff having fewer promotion prospects than the majority of other bank staff.

The present generations of new technology currently being introduced in the High Street banks have great potential labor-displacing effects that may finally now be realized in practice. For more than a decade, the banking unions have warned of technology-driven job losses in banking (BIFU 1982, 1985; CBU 1984), only to be largely disproven because of employment generated through the increased use of staff in marketing new products and services. In the current situation, however, banks are explicitly seeing technology as a means of improving marketing while simultaneously allowing the reduction of staffing levels. Many of the technological changes now in progress are not occurring within the branch structure itself (and thereby directly affecting branch bank staff) but actually bypass the branch altogether. A gradual detachment of historic branch functions and their fragmentation in the wider external economy is evident in development such as EFTPOS and home banking.

However, technology has been a double-edged sword: It has also helped new entrants cut a swathe into the banks' retail markets. Nonbank businesses have won over consumer lending and money market mutual funds, though not to the same extent in Europe as in America. Retailers in Britain offer their own charge cards. Some, such as Marks and Spencer, finance their own consumer loans. The General Motors credit card has been launched also in the United Kingdom. In sum, information technology might be regarded as much of a threat as an opportunity to the banks. Changes in technology have carried significant implications for human resources management and industrial relations in the banks.

Market Strategies

As we have noted, branch reorganization is occurring because of both local and national policy decisions within the banks. Market segmentation has been a significant trend, in particular the separating of corporate and personal customers. Since the mid-1980s, banks have been abandoning the notion that the traditional High Street branch can cope adequately with the needs of both these sets of customers. In each region a few specialized corporate banking centers have been created to concentrate expertise. This carries implications, of course, for the traditional concept of the all-purpose, rounded banker. Reorganization also has an impact on received status patterns, job security, and working relationships. Recruitment, training, and career progression are all subject to alteration. It should not be assumed, however, that these will be entirely malleable.

Banks are also increasingly adopting a retail management model in redesigning their branch networks. Consultants experienced in supermarkets and other similar retail outlets have been engaged to redirect branch managers and their staffs in new role behaviors. Banks are also refurbishing branches to release more space for selling products such as insurance and unit trusts to customers across a desk rather than through a security screen. Open plan designs, a relatively novel feature in U.K. banking, require reducing back office operations to provide additional space and to free staff time so they can talk to customers.

Following some spectacular loss-making ventures (such as Midland Bank's acquisition of Crocker's in the United States, the onset of recession, and the losses incurred as a result of overexposure to debt-laden Third World countries, the heady brew came off the boil by the start of the 1990s. Furthermore, as market boundaries eroded and new players began to encroach on traditional banking territory, banks felt increased pressure.

Overall, the market context can be seen as one of massive change. New delivery channels and new entrants have begun to transform the industry. Banks' strategic responses have included branch closures, staff cuts, mergers, and acquisitions. Further consolidation seems likely, and we can also expect to see strategic alliances and joint ventures with High Street retailers, telecoms, and computer companies.

Change and Variation in Employment Relations

When viewed from a cross-sectoral of cross-national perspective, the common, shared features of the industrial relations and human resources practices of British banks seem all too easy to trace (Storey 1995a). Banks have been changing their personnel policies and approaches. The array of management-led initiatives found in many other sectors can be seen reflected here (Storey 1992). Flexible working, culture change programs, performance-related pay, new appraisal systems, and new and increased forms of direct employee communications—these and other components of the new management are very much in evidence in the banks today. Old-style personnel policies and practices designed for a previous era of steady growth in a benign environment are coming under increasing challenge (Hendry and Pettigrew 1987). Cressey and Scott (1992) contrast the old model of banking (paternalistic, cautious, staff as cost, loyalty, bureaucratic) with a new model (technocratic, performance oriented, staff as resource, sales oriented). This indicates the direction in which banks wish to move rather than their actual operation, but it provides a clear indication that what was appropriate in a predictable and stable environment is no longer suitable in the current climate. There is increasing recognition that the traditional approach to managing staff, which emphasized staff as a cost because of their association with the money transmission system, is outmoded (Morris 1986).

Chief executives have urged a shift toward responsive, performance-oriented, market-driven cultures. This in turn has suggested the need for a shift in behavior and attitudes. Loyalty, caution, conformity, and accuracy in every detail were qualities highly prized under the old regime. Under the new, the personnel were expected to be performance driven, competitive, sales oriented, and not averse to risk.

However, when the focus is adjusted to examine the detailed practices of particular banks, the variety and even unique singularity of their circumstances and behavior becomes especially evident (Storey et al. 1997). To further the analysis in this chapter, four banks are selected for special attention. They broadly reflect a cross section of retail banking in Britain, though because of their histories, size, cultures, and current situations, each is in many regards unique. Table 5.2 provides a summary overview of the four banks.

This part of the chapter presents the main findings about current changes in the industry and in each of the four cases. The description is structured around the five main themes used throughout this book. Table 5.3 provides a summary.

Recruitment and Staffing

In the 1980s employment in the British banking industry as a whole increased fairly steadily from 349, 700 to 503,900, a rise of 44 percent. The number of employees rose sharply by almost one-quarter in the years 1987–90 alone. But since its peak in 1990, employment has been in decline (see table 5.4).

Between 1980 and 1991 the numbers of women in the banks increased disproportionately: Their numbers increased by 32 percent during this period against only a 20 percent rise for men. The greatest increase of all was the 84 percent growth between 1980 and 1991 in the numbers of part-time women workers from 29,800 to 54,800. Until 1991, this did not represent a massive shift in the percentage of women working part-time as a proportion of all women employed in the banks, a percentage that remained virtually static between 1980 and 1990 at around 15–16 percent. However, later employment data suggest that the profile has begun to change rapidly—by 1991, part-time women as a proportion of all women had risen to 21 percent—as part-time female employees continue to grow

Table 5.2
The four banks compared (1996)

Criteria	Midland	Co-op	Abbey National	Lloyds
Market position	Long period of slippage; acquired by HSBC	Stuck between Big Four and building societies; now profitable	Profitable	Profitable
Number of branches	1,500	100	676	1,799
Total number of employees (1996)	42,700	4,000	20,000	40,600 (Lloyds/ TSB 62,900)
Part-time	8,500	1,500	4,000	16,000
% Female of total employees	70%	60–70%	78%	N/A
Image/culture	Legacy of decline leading to takeover	"Ethical bank"; links with co-op movement	Remnants of "mutual" past but new focus: adding "shareholder value"	From paternalist to "hard" human resources management
Market share (current accounts)	15%	2.5%	2.5%	18%
TU recognition	BIFU (90% density)	BIFU (75–80% density)	No	BIFU and staff association

numerically. (Our impression is that this trend has continued, but we have found it difficult to secure official data to confirm it.)

Women form the greater proportion of bank employees: they constituted 57 percent of the total in 1980, and this had risen to 62 percent by 1990. Yet this numerical preponderance is definitely not reflected in a proportionate distribution of the genders in the different grades of banking work. Women in banking are overrepresented in the lower clerical and secretarial grades of jobs at the expense of higher-level managerial positions, they make up almost 100 percent of part-time clerical workers, they stay in banking for a shorter time on average than males, and they tend to be promoted more slowly than men.

The new proposals for job cuts undoubtedly represent a sea change in employers' attitudes. Downsizing is clearly the major issue in British

Table 5.3
Comparison of HR strategies

HR/IR Element	Midland	Co-op	Abbey National	Lloyds
(1) Recruitment and staffing	Staff numbers reduced. Part-timers increased. Entry level shifted.	Marginal staff reductions over-all, but branches staff reduced.	No significant reductions.	Reduction of 20,000 since 1989.
(2) Work organization	Organization + Methods. Flexible working expectations.	Branch management dismantled. Central processing: Taylorization.	Divisionalization. Separate businesses.	Branch structure under threat.
(3) Skill formation	Graduate level Advanced Development Programme (2 yr. foundation). General level entry Management Development Programme.	Job profiles displaced job descriptions. "Training tracks."	Competency based. Job profiles.	Becoming increasingly multitiered. • Fast track • General • Part-time.
(4) Compensation	No performance-related pay. Job evaluation. Management pay individualized. Grade max/min?	Profit share. Performance management approach for all staff.	Performance-related pay scheme.	Performance-related pay. No minimum pay increase.
(5) Enterprise governance/IR	BIFU (sole rights). No staff association. No TU recognition in international banking divisions. TU recognition in First Direct. Negotiations confined to pay issues.	BIFU. Staff council includes reps who are not union reps. BIFU boycott.	Staff association only.	BIFU/Lloyds Group Union bargaining rights.

Table 5.4
Employment, gender, and mode of working in the British banking and bill discounting industry, 1980–1995

Year	All males[1]	All females	Part-time females	Total employees
1980	151.4	198.4	29.8	349.7
1981	152.9	202.9	30.2	355.8
1982	156.1	207.2	27.6	363.3
1983	154.8	208.2	30.8	363.0
1984	165.7	217.1	38.4	382.8
1985	172.1	223.5	42.8	395.6
1986	185.0	211.7	44.8	396.7
1987	191.6	217.1	47.6	408.7
1988	200.8	226.5	51.1	427.3
1989	189.9	293.3	47.4	483.3
1990	190.1[2]	313.6[2]	51.8[2]	503.9[2]
1991	181.5	261.6	54.8	443.1
1992	168.6	245.2	53.1	413.8
1993	162.7	233.8	52.1	396.5
1994	156.3	226.3	53.5	382.6
1995[3]	152.5	224.1	55.3	376.6

Sources: Employment Gazette, table 1.4, various issues, 1981–91; *Employment Trends,* various issues, 1992–1996.
Notes: All employment figures are in thousands.
1. The table does not present separate figures for part-time male employment. In some cases data is unavailable, and such data as are available from official sources demonstrate a suspiciously wide variation and are thus insufficiently reliable. However, male part-time employment in banking can be reliably said to be negligible: Estimates vary between 0.5 percent and 5 percent of total male employment.
2. The Abbey National became a bank in July 1989 and is thus included in the figures from 1990 onward. Its 1991 employment figures were unavailable at the time of writing. In 1990 it employed on average 12,659 staff: 3,889 of these were male and 8,770 were female, of whom 3,886 of the women worked part-time.
3. From 1996 the industrial classification changed, rendering post-1996 data noncomparable with this data series.

banks at the moment. Certainly the banking unions now believe so. The Banking Insurance and Finance Union (BIFU) is now devoting considerable attention to alerting its members about the latest proposals, and easily the largest number of inquiries from union members to BIFU representatives interviewed during the course of out research concerned the topic of job security.

Recruitment of school leavers into banking has dropped from an average intake of 35,000 a year just a decade ago to 5,500 in 1996. Recruitment for the banking industry is becoming increasingly segmented. Traditionally, the retail banks have been characterised by secure, jobs-for-life employment policies for career staff. (A regular amount of labor turnover has, however, always been experienced among clerical, mainly female staff). Recruitment of career staff was tiered, with school-leaving age groups and university graduates entering under differentiated schemes. The general pattern was one of full-time employment with long-term prospects. This pattern has altered dramatically.

Reflections of these trends, although with significant variations, can be seen in our four cases. For example, Midland Bank has increased its proportion of part-time staff to match service demand patterns. Clerical recruitment to the Midland Bank is either into the branch banking system, where the emphasis is on competencies required for customer service, or into the operations centers, where the emphasis is on ability to perform repetitive keyboard tasks accurately. The Cooperative Bank has reduced the number of branch staff dramatically. A branch that formerly would have typically had around forty staff now has only about eight. In consequence, whereas ten years ago the branches directly employed some 2,500 staff, they now employ only 600, as work is now allocated to paper factories: for example, the regional processing centers and the accounts management center the latter employing more than 600 staff and operating 7 days a week, 18 hours a day, having centralized much of the paperwork.

At Lloyds Bank (now Lloyds/TSB), overall staff numbers fell by 20,000 (one-quarter of the original total) between 1989 and 1994. The bulk of the reductions have occurred in the U.K. retail banking division. This reduction continued in 1994–95 with a 3 percent further loss in head count, so that staff numbers have fallen to around 70 percent of their 1989 peak. The career structure in Lloyds/TSB is under severe threat primarily because of closure of bank branches. Recruitment has followed the trend away from single-tier toward multiple-tier recruitment. This signals the end of a generalist clerical intake and together with branch closures reduces promotion opportunities across the broad clerical/branch structure.

Work Organization

Work organization shows a broad pattern of change that is common to each of the banks. First, nonselling activity has increasingly been moved away from the branches into central or regional processing centers. These processing centers have Taylorized, factory-like patterns of work organization. The distinction between their work and that of the branch outlets has become sharply marked. Second, within the branches the staff are increasingly being directed to focus on the sale of products and, to a lesser extent, on customer service. With the evolution of satellite branches, the position of branch manager is increasingly less tied to a specific branch location: One manager may now be expected to be responsible for a cluster of branches. Third, separate distribution channels have been created. Most notable here are the telephone-based banking services that operate quite independently of the branch network.

The Midland Bank was a pioneer in establishing a major new 24-hour telephone banking business, First Direct. For its part, the Coop has introduced a change that encourages customers to phone their accounts management center directly. Any calls made to the branches are rerouted to these centers. The other banks, to varying degrees, have followed suit. The staff operating in these telephone-based businesses have a pattern of working hours and working arrangements quite distinct and separate from those of the rest of the bank. A parallel innovation has been the direct postal account systems, which again operate independently.

The general trend in work organization has been toward fragmentation. Separate divisions and businesses have been set up, and staff are increasingly allocated to one or another of these profit centers, with very little opportunity to migrate between them. To a considerable extent the diverse channels specialize in different and distinct products. Given the potentiality of information technology systems to deliver customer-specific information and profiles, this fragmentation of effort may be challenged in the future for marketing reasons.

For many banks, Midland in particular, the reorganization of branch functions has led to a massive program of branch remodeling so that the High Street locations may be used as sites for selling financial services and offering financial advice. The same processes are at work in Lloyds/TSB, where existing staff are required to retrain and reskill as financial salespeople, assuming at the same time an outgoing commercial attitude and belief in the new "performance culture." Many staff have felt profoundly unhappy with the pace and direction of such moves and the changes that they imply for the characteristics, skills, and orientation of bank employees.

The branch structure largely sets the framework for the possibility of staff promotion. Any tampering with this means knock-on effects on the career structure and grades, as we discussed earlier; previously, organizational considerations always moderated the changes that technology bequeathed. Hence satellite banks, regional processing centers, and the separation of back and front office functions were largely held in abeyance because of the effect they would have on the branch structure, and through that, the staff itself. Recently it has become striking that the redundancies have borne most heavily on management because of the introduction of these changes to the branch network. Prior to the merger with Lloyds, the TSB reorganized 1,800 branches into geographical groups of eight to ten, with the creation of a new post of senior manager. At the same time, they were transferring back office paper processing to a set of new service centers, a move the Midland Bank began more than two years previously. In sum, this reduces managerial responsibilities and the need for some senior grades of management. With this in mind, the bank has reduced the thirteen managerial grades to five and reviewed each manager accordingly. Lloyds had a similar plan that reallocated managerial posts. In the TSB, the result was the voluntary loss of 2,000 managers and the formation of a group of nonallocated managers. All of the new senior managers have been given individual contracts, effectively derecognizing them in union terms.

With the introduction of new types of product and service, the human dimension revolves around the redeployment of some clerical and administrative staff as (essentially) sales personnel or "personal bankers"/financial consultants. The nature of changes to jobs places a greater stress on interpersonal contact with the customer. This is supported by an enhanced flow of readily available data on the financial profile of individual customers through branch information technologies as well as the use of laptop computers to assess instantly the financial implications of products and services. This type of work requires a new skills profile and, moreover, a transformed cultural outlook.

Variations can be seen in the degree and timing of these changes. Midland moved first to centralize and break its structure into separate businesses. Barclays centralized later but to a greater degree, however, to obtain maximum scale economies. Its restructuring into market-based business units has been affected by the need to diminish the influence of its traditional regional structure by a centralization of power. National

Westminster, by contrast, has yet to centralize its operations or to achieve comparable work flexibility, having been deflected by other strategic problems. From its position of relative strength, in terms of performance, Lloyds has also been slower on centralization and work reorganization but in 1997 embarked on a radical plan to reduce its head count and change jobs, while rationalizing its branch network following its merger with TSB.

Training, Skill Formation, and Careers

The changes to the staffing patterns described above have had a critical impact on skill formation policies. In crude terms, the fundamental shift has been from the uniform standard career for a nominal rounded banker to a greater emphasis on specific recruitment for specialized roles such as telesales or data processing. In consequence, the traditional skill formation system has changed dramatically.

The traditional rounded banker who was rotated through a wide range of general banking functions to gain the necessary experience for a managerial position is now seen as an inappropriate model. Entry now occurs on multiple tiers. Management and technical services are becoming ever more professionalized, with such positions being filled by promising graduates on rigorous accelerated promotion schemes or (increasingly) by specialists from outside the industry. This is already a long-established feature in the banks' computer sections. Extended hours and lunchtime opening, not to mention twilight data-inputting jobs for those banks that regionally concentrate back office work, have meant a larger number of part-time, almost exclusively female employees in the main U.K. banks. The growth in agency staff employed in banking has also been of a significant order: in 1996, more than 4,000 staff were supplied by just one agency alone.

At Midland Bank, for example, there has been very little standard clerical-level entry for the past eight years. Approximately 100 graduates per year are recruited to the Advanced Development Program (ADP), which takes all entrants to first-level management (i.e., supervisory level or equivalent), usually by age 26. During the two years of the program these graduates attend an initial ten-week group training course followed by a period in the retail network. Subsequent career progression is centrally monitored. The move toward telephone banking has also meant a dilution of banking skills and training levels. First Direct (the telephone banking arm of the Midland Bank) does not require retail bank experience in its new recruits nor does it follow the training practices of its parent organization.

The Cooperative Bank, like many others nowadays, claims to pay much greater attention to management development. It says it is now more proactive, systematic, and integrated in its approach to this issue. Given the parallel growth of the processing centers the union has expressed concern about an increasing divide between career and noncareer staff. Clerical staff training has increasingly placed emphasis on the specific areas of customer service and sales training. Training user groups (TUGs) have been given prominence, whereas the Training Department has been relegated to a consultancy role. The TUGs are required to produce "job profiles," which sketchout competencies in place of simple job descriptions. There is an aspiration also to identify "training tracks" which reveal the cumulative and inter-linked path of training events and experiences.

Abbey National also claims to have given increased attention to skill formation for all levels of staff. It has been a leader in competency-based training and also in job profiling. It made a key change in its training in 1988 from a traditional, individual-based job-related series of courses to an attempt to devise a model that would link business objectives with available or potential competencies. A management development unit operates a company-wide program designed to identify staff suitable for appointment to the management, senior management, and executive tiers. In addition, a standardized program is also operated for the development of graduate management trainees, whose careers are managed for the first two years of service.

Broadly similar initiatives in skill formation are also found in our fourth case, Lloyds Bank. Lloyds has shifted toward multitiered recruitment and placed a particular training and development emphasis on highfliers through the use of management development programs. On the other hand, basic processing functions have been targeted for computer-based skills enhancement in the areas of product knowledge and services. In addition, bank staff have been sent on customer service courses, including those of the "learning to smile" variety.

For nonmanagerial staffs, one of the most significant recent developments in training has been the wide-scale introduction of computer-based training (CBT), which is seen as necessary and cost effective given the need to train thousands of staff in hundreds of branches simultaneously on the introduction of new products and new systems applications. TSB has used CBT and interactive video extensively, for example, to standard-

ize learning materials. The Chartered Institute of Banking has also produced computer-assisted learning (CAL) courses for its banking certificate
examinations.

In the United Kingdom the banks in general have arguably been at the
forefront of the move toward competency-based management development. National Westminster and Abbey National, for example, have both
been prominent. Abbey has made a thorough, systematic review of
required competencies for most main jobs. At the same time, to allow
matching of person to post, it has also conducted a wide-ranging competency profiling of managerial staffs. Both sets of data are held in computer
files and are used for filling vacancies and for developmental purposes. In
these and other ways, human resources and personnel management practices in the banking sector could potentially be regarded as at the forefront of sophisticated practice. There is thus a paradox here. Whereas in
some measure HR and personnel in banking can be regarded as rather traditional in character when compared with those same functions in certain
other industries, in other regards, especially in relation to investment in
personnel techniques and technologies, the banks might claim to be at the
forefront of modern practice.

Recent trends point toward increased rather than reduced segmentation
in recruitment and promotion patterns among banks. Increasingly, entry
occurs at a number of different levels. Activities in the managerial grades
are becoming more specialized as tasks become increasingly complex. The
banks became ostensibly committed to equal opportunities policies in the
1970s, and the separate female pay structure was discarded. The expectation that women would resign upon getting married was also abandoned.
Despite these measures, women continue to predominate in the lower
clerical grades and to be underrepresented in supervisory and managerial
ranks. The banks, along with other large employers, have launched various equal opportunities policies in response to this situation in recent
years. Each of the main banks has appointed an equal opportunities manager, and a string of policy initiatives have resulted. Such measures have
come about, in part, from external pressure from bodies such as the Equal
Opportunities Commission. But also of importance in stimulating more
far-reaching action was the tight labor market conditions experienced in
the late 1980s and well-publicized warnings about scarcity of the sort of
qualified young recruits that the banks had traditionally used. In the
event, recessionary conditions took the edge off the dire warnings. But
prior to the onset of recession around 1990, the banks, along with the
building societies, were announcing, virtually daily, new initiatives such

as child care facilities and more-favorable schemes to encourage women to return after maternity leave.

The banks are placing heavy stress on new occupational requirements for the ability to sell financial products and services to customers. The emphasis on mainstream clerical careers in banking is thus likely to change as the shift away from administration toward more aggressive marketing of financial products gathers pace. This area is of course intimately related too to the development of performance-related payment systems. Our research indicates that there is considerable resistance among the banks' lower- and middle-managerial staffs aged in their forties and above to the idea of the bank administrator as a salesperson first and foremost. BIFU officials relate that many personnel with a traditional administrative outlook of twenty-odd years standing find it "almost demeaning" to now be asked to go out and sell to customers with whom they may have built up long-established trust relationships. Both managers and unions agree that this issue, combined with the promotions blockage (see below), is creating considerable friction among branch staff of middle age and above.

Although there is certainly no universal trend toward job enlargement in the clerical grades, significant variability can be detected among the High Street banks according to their chosen technical and organizational strategies. In some banks, the development of new, higher-grade front office jobs with specialized titles such as "financial planning consultant" or "personal banker" are restricting some of the opportunities for extensive customer contact among clerical staff. Moreover, in many banks the early automation of back office processing originally led to the centralization of tasks and mainframe equipment, often in regional processing centers, to benefit from economies of scale. Nowadays the banks diverge significantly regarding their policy toward such a strategy of regional concentration. This has important consequences for employment patterns and work organization. Some banks, notably the Midland, Lloyds/TSB, and Cooperative banks, have developed and are expanding the tendency to remove much back office branch administrative work to district or regional centers. In such offices, these banks are employing mainly part-time women workers on repetitive data-inputting tasks (such as keying in information from vouchers, etc.). Working hours normally consist of evening shifts, so that the same day's branch work can be processed. On the other hand, automation based upon mini- and microcomputer links makes feasible the decentralization of technology's center of gravity and the mechanization of much manual processing work within the branches; however, our specific case studies suggest this has not been the option chosen.

Compensation

In the face of heightened competition from new and old players alike, the banks' typical strategic reaction in the compensation policy area has been to move away from the traditional incremental and grade system and toward some form of contingent pay. The largest of the Big Four (Nat West) shifted markedly to outright performance-related pay in 1988. To what extent have our four banks followed suit and with what consequences? They have introduced performance-related pay widely and made it a more substantial element of the remuneration package. In Lloyds, a conflict over new gradings and the performance-related pay issue resulted in a vote for strike action. There it is proposed that pay progression will depend on gaining "good" or "excellent" performance ratings; this could mean that staff with low ratings receive no pay increases at all. The former TSB had planned to determine what (if any) increase an individual received using the appraisal system (performance management system). This was to be supplemented by a new bonus system—the Network Incentive Scheme—under which the performance of each branch would be assessed biannually, with each area assessed once a year. Payments of up to 15 percent of salary would have been forthcoming if both the branch and area performance merited it.

The long-standing system of rewards in banks had been an incremental ladder, with automatic annual increases assured between the ages of 16 and 31. In addition, all staff had come to expect a general raise to meet increases in cost-of-living expenses. Since 1988, when National Westminster Bank led the way into performance-related pay, all the main clearing banks have sought to break away from this traditional pattern. Hence, for example, Lloyds in 1992–93 paid no cost-of-living increase, but its performance-based system added on average some 3.4 percent to the pay bill. Profit sharing added a further 4.1 percent.

Abbey National still awards pay and benefits mainly according to job using the Hay job evaluation scheme. Each grade has an associated salary band. The salary scales and benchmark pay levels are reassessed annually in conjunction with the staff association. In addition to the salary scales, an individual performance–related pay scheme was introduced some five to six years ago. The scheme awards payments ranging from 0 to approximately 6 percent of salary based on personal performance review and subsequent rating. There are some exceptions: the Treasury Services division has an annual profit-sharing bonus based solely on its own business unit profits.

Managers at the Cooperative Bank also talk in terms of redesigning their compensation policies in line with business objectives. The principles of this are familiar: to move away from automatic annual increases in pay; to introduce some element of profit sharing; and to freeze salaries for those staff operating below an acceptable performance level. Perhaps the most interesting element in the context of this particular case was the introduction of profit sharing, for some regarded this as incompatible with the ethos of the cooperative movement in the late 1980s. The significance of the initiative has to be seen therefore in this light. One senior manager expressed the perceived need for this shift: "Unless we get their minds linked with profit we aren't going to get anywhere with the corporate plan." Supplementary to this is a performance management approach (PMA) introduced in 1993 and covering all staff. The PMA pays individuals according to a formula that reviews achievement against targets. A final element of the Cooperative's new remuneration policy was to persuade staff to "accept pay which the bank can afford"—and this meant paying less than the other clearing banks, reflecting Cooperative's less significant role in the marketplace as well as its position in terms of profitability.

In today's climate, the most distinctive feature of Midland Bank's compensation policy is the absence of a performance-related element in the salary structure. The bank takes the view that individual performance-related pay (PRP) is incompatible with teamwork. Midland negotiates with the union BIFU on the total wages budget but it does not negotiate on how this will be distributed. It introduced a new appraisal system in 1993, and this forms the basis of a revised pay system for clerical staff. The system is designed to encourage teamwork rather than individual performance evaluation and reward. The new appraisal system fits individuals to grade by concentrating on core skills. Rate for the grade is normally achieved after four years in post. A team award based, for example, on the performance of a processing center is also paid. Management pay is supposedly based on individual performance and is non-negotiable. Ratings are on a five-point scale, with the midpoint being equal to the external market.

Prior to the merger, Lloyds Bank went over to a form of PRP. Introduced first for management, it now affects all levels after the recent announcements ending annual increases as of right and implementing pay increases only for those staff 'performing' above average. The bank introduced a profit-sharing scheme for all of its employees in 1994. Together with the continuing redundancies, it pointed to a lean and mean approach that resulted in a drop in employee morale. The recent joint bank dispute undertaken in collaboration with Lloyds Group Union and an increasing preparedness to take industrial action are all signs of the changes in staff attitudes that the bank policies have provoked.

In summary, compensation policies across the four banks indicate a broad similarity at the rhetorical level but some interesting variation in the detail. Each of the banks urges a more 'business-oriented' approach to pay policy, but in practice they have been cautious about moving too far from the traditional salary-based patterns.

Enterprise Governance and Industrial Relations

Industrial relations institutions in banking were traditionally rather distinctive compared to those elsewhere in the United Kingdom, but it is arguable that there has been some convergence on the banking model in the last fifteen years. The banking sector's institutional distinctiveness was based on the long-standing existence of staff associations acting as rival employee representative bodies to the national union and operating outside the mainstream trade union structures. In addition, the banks' refusal to recognize the national union for many years meant that the typical U.K. pattern of workplace bargaining was never established and that local, unofficial disputes were rare. Pay determination was highly centralized, compared to the remainder of industries in the United Kingdom.

However, in the 1980s the banks started to decentralize pay determination to division or business unit levels. Coming from the other direction, other U.K. employers sought to establish more-orderly bargaining by centralizing pay negotiations, also at the company-wide or business unit level. Some, notably foreign firms setting up on greenfield sites, pursued no-strike agreements and other forms of dispute settlement similar to the banks' long-standing arbitration arrangements.

More generally, conservative governments introduced a web of statutory controls to which the whole union movement was subject. These tightly regulated the conduct and scope of industrial action and union governance. One consequence was a reduction in local unofficial action and much greater control over union finances and policy making. In effect, the rest of the British union movement became more like the banking unions in terms of internal organization and control over local activism.

The industrial relations system in the banks has contributed greatly to their stability as organizations. Disputes were few and far between, and there was little staff movement or poaching between banks. Industrial relations in banks since 1988, however, have been more fraught, as disputes over the extension of opening hours in particular exemplify, and now appear to be entering a very tense phase owing to a new trend on management's part toward unilateralism in collective bargaining on a broad spectrum of issues. Staff trust in management appears to be at a low ebb, producing the seeds for a future conflicts. There is evidence that extremely tough market conditions are essentially dictating a new, hard-nosed approach to industrial relations on management's part. Recent relations between bank managements and the unions and staff associations have deteriorated as accumulated staff grievances have led them both to threaten and to undertake disruptive action.

The breakup of the employers' federations left a vacuum that the return to bargaining between trade unions and individual banks has only partly filled to date. Industrial relations in banking have been edging uncertainly toward a new status quo in recent years. What some negotiators described to us as the "straightjacket" of multiemployer bargaining under the federations, in which no individual bank could determine pay or many other conditions for its own staff, has disappeared. Yet it appears to us that informal but no less real constraints on individual banks' freedom of action continue to exist. As one personnel manager said, all the banks are still "fishing in the same pond" for staff: Institutions cannot (indefinitely) afford to be abnormally parsimonious to staff, for this well lead to industrial relations and recruitment problems; equally, they cannot afford to be too generous because of the pressure on their own cost margins. So little has yet changed dramatically, despite an initial honeymoon period when unions could exploit the decentralization of bargaining slightly. Greater fragmentation has occurred in two areas, though: Each bank now follows its own policy on job evaluation systems (the federations formerly ran a central evaluation mechanism for clerical jobs) and on performance- or incentive-based pay packages. The latter are likely to be a particularly important source of diversity as the weight accorded to this aspect of salary grows.

A number of banks have recently been making agreements or impositions that change the landscape of industrial relations. Midland, TSB, and Nat West all have concluded agreements that include significant changes. The TSB negotiated with BIFU a new agreement involving 2,000 redundancies at managerial level and 1,000 from other grades. These reductions were achieved by natural wastage and a freeze on recruitment. The agreement also uprates the payments for those taking redundancy.

Three of the banks recognize a trade union for collective bargaining purposes but the fourth (Abbey National) does not. Abbey National recognizes an in-house staff association though senior managers are excluded. Staff association membership has remained relatively stable around 50 percent and is concentrated in the branch network. There is a company level forum known as the Joint Consultative and Negotiating Committee (JCNC) where company executives meet elected officials of the staff association, which is not, however, seen as wielding any significant power.

BIFU has maintained membership in the Coop Bank at a high level of 90 percent. Union members are worried, however, about the encroachment of personal contracts and the consequent removal of collective bargaining rights. A further indication of unions on the defensive is the ending of the "seconded representative" (union convenor) posts. There are still lay office representatives in each branch and in each department of the large offices, a total of 100 such reps. The bank wanted a "senior representative" tier, with one such representative for each of the 10 regions. These would be entitled to spend 20 percent of their time on trade union business. Although devolving decisions to the regions, management are known to want to see the senior representatives do the negotiating rather than full-time BIFU officials.

Midland, like the Coop, gives sole recognition to BIFU for bargaining and consultation. It opted to remove recognition from the other union, MSF, several years ago to reduce the problem of competitive bargaining, having failed to get the two unions to sit round the same table. Midland negotiates on base pay for each clerical grade and for technical staff, such as computer staff, but does not bargain over bonus payments or managerial salaries. As with other banks, the Midland's strategy is to negotiate over pay and conditions, including holidays, but not over work organization, staff deployment, or organizational change.

Lloyds Bank recognizes both BIFU and Lloyds Group Union, with the latter representing more staff than the former. As with all banks, the unions have tended to include all grades in the branch network in the union. This is now beginning to be questioned especially since performance-related pay was introduced for senior staff.

The banks have taken steps to engage in more direct communication with their employees. As job security and careers progression have been eroded there has been a perceived need for increased cooperation and commitment to compensate. Hence, the banks have invested in video communications, more professional staff newspapers, attitude surveys, and other employee involvement measures. In a new departure, chief executives have begun to communicate directly in bulletin form with every individual staff member when potential conflict arises. Thus at the Coop Bank the chief executive intervened personally in 1991 when a pay freeze had been announced and BIFU had called a ballot, visiting various parts of the bank warning that industrial action would mean a breach of contract. BIFU lost the subsequent ballot.

Discussion, Explanation, and Conclusions

In this final section we first summarize and highlight key similarities and differences we found between the four cases, then make some observations about the possible sources of these patterns.

The traditional model of employment regulation has undergone extensive dismantling; of that there can be little doubt. But a new model has yet to take its place. There remains uncertainty, for example, about the branches' future role and, by extension, the appropriate desirable role for branch managers and staff. Are these to be merely sales outlets or are they to be 'reempowered' so as to offer a broad and customer-focused range of services? Nor is it only a matter of organization structure that the existence of a coherent new model to replace the old seems questionable. The instability in the marketplace (with new players, significant merger and acquisition activity, forging of strategic alliances, and products and services reappearing in different guises, not least in the shape of telephone banking) is carried through into employment policies. Thus at one point, branch staff are being prepared for narrow, measurable roles; at another, corrective steps are taken to leave open the option of a wider, more rounded role set. Commensurately, performance-related pay is emphasized when the former mindset is in the ascendant and deemphasized when the latter policy holds sway.

Job losses, combined with the intimately related issue of branch restructuring, are having a knock-on effect on the key stabilizing pillar of the industry: its career structure. This factor, above all, threatens to create the most industrial relations instability as the existing staff expectations about promotions are confounded. Although there were threats to the career structure in the 1980s, they tended to bear overwhelmingly on the overlapping categories of women, part-time employees, and limited numbers of back office workers, segments of the workforce that were either weak, perceived as lacking career motivation, or defined as routine areas that could benefit from restructuring. The changes inaugurated in the recent period—the segmented recruitment, the growth of divisions/ specialisms, the development of new skills, and the closure of promotion opportunities because of branch disappearances—mean the banks will be unable to offer the security and steady promotion that the quiescent and homogenous workforce has grown to expect.

What Do the Four Cases Have in Common?

All four banks have followed the general trend toward cost reduction strategies. These have been manifested in branch closures, the automation of routine money transactions, and the reorganization of branches so that back office activity is removed to new, factory-like paper processing centers. Each of the banks studied has also heavily used the rhetoric of "customer focus," "customer service," and "quality." Each perceives itself as being, in varying ways, "innovative" in terms of products and in the expansion of new distribution channels (ATMs, telephone centers, direct mail services and the like) with a planned future of twenty-four-hour service based on intelligent voice recognition technology. Despite these innovations, the branches continue to be the dominant channel for delivery of services. Of particular note also is the reorganization of career structures.

The emerging interface among technology, new products, new distribution channels, and a changing marketplace is shaping many of the banks' corporate strategies. Along the way, a number of these banks have displayed errors in commercial judgment (especially so, arguably, in the international sphere) and possibly also in the recruitment rush and boom of the late 1980s.

Worthy of special note is the increasing impact of new technology. Prior to 1989, technology might have been viewed as relatively benign in that it seemed to aid staff in dealing with an increasing volume of transactions. Since 1989, technology has combined with recession and a new, fiercely competitive marketplace with many new players to create what some see as a virtual crisis in terms of job losses.

In What Way Do Their Employment Practices Differ?

Despite the similarities, there are also some notable points of contrast among the banks. The largest number of staff reductions have occurred in the traditional clearing banks, which had the largest branch networks. The experience of our two large clearers (Midland and Lloyds Bank) finds

reflection in the experience of the two other big players, National Westminster and Barclays. The Abbey National and the Cooperative have, by
contrast, had relatively few staff losses.

In terms of changes to work organization, the broad themes of flexibility, a shift to central processing, and a move to separate "businesses" in
place of unified bank structures find echo across our cases. But the particular point of emphasis differs in each case. These banks are still finding
their way in work (re)organization: There is, as yet, uncertainty about
appropriate organizational arrangements for the new era.

The ambiguity of work organization programs influences skill formation policies. The buzz words "competencies," "job profiling," and "open
learning" are widely found, but in practice, the four banks studied continue
to experiment with many different forms of training and development.
Graduate entrants still tend to find some general management development provision, but the banks vary in the extent to which specialist training for specialist careers kicks in at an early stage.

Clear contrasts exist in the area of compensation policies. Performance-
related pay can be seen as the theme in Lloyds and Abbey and more
recently in the Cooperative Bank, whereas the Midland Bank has so far
not introduced a performance-related pay scheme.

This variety of approach continues also in the area of industrial relations
and enterprise governance. Midland and the Coop give sole bargaining
rights to the national bank union, BIFU, and have no staff associations.
Abbey National recognizes no trade union, but it does have a staff association, albeit one that carries little weight or influence.

Final Comment

A key driver of change for each of the banks has been the need to cut
operating costs in the face of competition from the new players. Banks
and building societies have substantially different cost-to-income ratios.
Banks therefore have a direct interest both in taking over building societies and at the same time closing their own branch networks. What we
are witnessing is a move towards general financial services providers. Two
employment consequences are immediately apparent: First, the banking
branch network will continue to suffer losses in number of employees; and
second, there may, in future, be a move away from specialist recruitment
for each type of institution toward a more general sales staff function and
the consequent dilution of the traditional bank/clerical role. New information technologies have offered banks the scope to introduce new types of

product, such as debit cards, and new forms of product delivery, such as telephone banking, and personal computer and Internet banking. All of these bring further into question the value of extensive branch networks as a source of competitive advantage. New technologies have also provided innovatory methods of processing financial information that have led to organizational changes, such as the centralization of check processing away from the bank branches. These changes have substantially reduced employment levels in the sector in the last five years, mainly via the closing and rationalization of branch systems, changed skill requirements, and diminished career opportunities.

Into this new competitive environment has emerged a new set of managerial philosophies with regard to employment and staff representation, rupturing the old deal based on loyalty in exchange for security. In recent years indeed the literal starting point for discussions between the bank employers and unions has been the banks' unveiling of their planned job reduction program for the coming year. This has presented BIFU and other representative bodies for staff starkly with a very new agenda. Information technology, though undoubtedly a further factor, is perhaps best seen as but part of this overall new reality. In seeking to trace the initial movers in this chain of events our own studies point up the significance of state deregulation. The previously regulated order led to close relationships between the banks and the government's financial institutions. This placed an emphasis on commercial and organizational stability. Collaboration over interest rates, money transmission, and operating standards used to be the norm; competition occurred only in the location of branches, and efforts to attract new customers or grow market shares were heavily circumscribed. This picture has now changed substantially. The terrain on which competition can occur has been opened out dramatically. In consequence, we are witnessing variations in the severity of job reductions as the traditional large clearing banks seek to bring their costs in line with those of the slimmer new players. The significance of innovative policies in areas such as contingent pay has also been seen to vary: The outcomes of such policies remain uncertain, and so it is perhaps less than surprising that the banks differ on this front, whereas they have tended to follow each other much more closely in matters such as widening their product range and urging their staff to adopt more-commercial and market-oriented behavior patterns.

The national system of bargaining previously in place actually offered the banks a number of strategic advantages. It allowed them to continue to coordinate the price of labor, thereby taking it out of competition; it minimized the risk of union-led disruption by formalizing the arbitration arrangements; it ensured the survival of the staff associations, which could claim as much credit for the bargained outcomes as the national union; and it minimized the risk of union influence in areas of managerial prerogative over work organization and technical innovation. Employer coordination broke down in the early 1980s because of differences in profit performance and, more fundamentally, the opportunities new product and process technologies presented for altering the nature of competition among firms. National bargaining was abandoned as the employers shifted the focus of their strategies from stability to cost control, establishing company level negotiating arrangements to carry this out. Greater company differentiation in grading structures and work organization has emerged.

Despite the differences evident among the U.K. banks in their employment policies, from an international perspective the broad, common features are perhaps most striking. Here the most notable feature is the shift, in the past 10 years, from a long-standing model of stable personnel management practices to a more aggressive, cost-driven set of measures already of a sufficient breadth and scale to upturn the traditional model. In particular, the banks seem to have been willing to sacrifice loyalty and commitment in the face of radically changing market conditions. Whether the newly emerging policies and practices are sustainable over the longer term remains a question that is hard to answer at this time of rapid change. The focus of future research could profitably be upon closer attention to the logics key decision makers use when opting for particular employment initiatives, and the extent to which, and the way in which, they evaluate the range of feedback data from these innovations.

References

Arthur Andersen. (1986). *The Decade of Change: Banking in Europe—The Next Ten Years.* London: Arthur Andersen & Co.

[BIFU] Banking Insurance and Finance Union. (1982, 1989). *New Technology in Banking, Insurance and Finance.* London: BIFU.

[BIFU] Banking Insurance and Finance Union. (1985). *Jobs for the Girls? The Impact of Automation on Women's Jobs in the Finance Industry.* London: BIFU.

Burton, D. (1990). "Competition in the U.K. Retail Financial Services Industry." *Service Industries Journal* 10(3): 571–89.

[CBU] Clearing Bank Union. (1984). *New Technology and Developments.* Winchester, U.K.: CBU.

Cressey, P., and P. Scott. (1992). "Employment, Technology and Industrial Relations in Clearing Banks—Is the Honeymoon Over?" *New Technology, Work and Employment*, 7(2): 83–94.

Hendry, C., and A. Pettigrew. (1987). "Banking on HRM to Respond to Change." Personnel Management (November).

Howcroft, J. B., and J. Lavis. (1986). "A Strategic Perspective on Delivery Systems in U.K. Retail Banking." *Service Industries Journal*, 6(2): 144–58.

Morris, T. (1986). *Innovations in Banking, Business Strategies and Employee Relations*. London: Croom Helm.

Rajan, A. (1987). "New Technology and Career Progression in Financial Institutions." *Service Industries Journal*, 7(1).

Storey, J. (1995a). "Employment Policies and Practices in U.K. Clearing Banks: An Overview." *Human Resource Management Journal*, 5(4): 24–43.

Storey, J. (1995b). "Human Resource Management: Still Marching in or Marching out?" In J. Storey (ed.), *Human Resource Management: A Critical Text*. London: Routledge, 3–32.

Storey, J. (1992). *Developments in the Management of Human Resources*. Oxford: Blackwell.

Storey, J., P. Cressey, T. Morris, and A. Wilkinson. (1997). "Changing Patterns of Employment Relations in U.K. Banking." *Personnel Review*, 26(1/2): 24–42.

Wilson, A. M. (1992). "The Adoption of a Retail-Oriented Marketing Mix for Bank Branch Operations." *Service Industries Journal*, 12(3): 404–13.

6

Institutional Innovation and Market Challenges: Changing Employment Relations in the Italian Banking Sector

Marino Regini, Simonetta Carpo, Asher Colombo, and Marco Trentini

The Context of Labor Relations in the Banking Sector and Its Changes

Preface

The Italian banking system is passing through a period of profound institutional change. At the level of individual banks, however, changes in both human resources management and industrial relations are coming about relatively gradually. One may hypothesize that they are conditioned both by the characteristics of the industrial relations system and by the fact that transition to a market system is taking place rather slowly.

Changes in the Institutional Context

Deregulation and Privatization in the Banking Sector

In Italy, state intervention in the banking sector has assumed three forms: the definition of rules, control over individual banks, and the direct exercise of banking activity through the publicly owned banks.

Since the second half of the 1980s, changes have taken place in all three of these areas. First, deregulation of the sector has gotten under way.[1] The aim of the 1993 banking law, which is based on such principles as the despecialization of banking activity and freedom of branch installation, was less to stabilize the sector—which was the aim of the 1936 law (Lombardini 1986)—than to increase the competition among, and the efficiency of, the different banks.

Changes have also taken place in the principles regulating the control public authorities and the Bank of Italy in particular exercise over banks. There is a tendency to increase the decision-making and operational autonomy of individual banks and to restrict the regulators' discretion.

Finally, starting in the 1990s, the publicly owned banks have been undergoing a process of privatization. Whereas at the beginning of the 1990s the public banks managed around 70 percent of total deposits, by 1997 their share had fallen to around 50 percent. The privatizations have been undertaken for various reasons ranging from redefinition of the state's role in the economy to reorganization of the banking sector following transition to a market system.

Relationships between Banks and Firms

As regards relationships between banks and firms, Italy apparently does not correspond to either of the two major models identified in the literature: that is, the Anglo-Saxon and German models (Bianco and Trento 1995). By way of summary, the distinctive features of the Italian economic system are the following: the separation of bank and firm, the prevalence of either family or public ownership of firms, and the limited development of the financial market.

Two phenomena, among others, explain these features: first, the banking law of 1936, which mandated the separation of banks and firms; second, the peculiarities of the Italian industrial development, namely, a productive structure with the strong presence of small, family-owned firms, the importance of family capital in large firms as well, and the role of the state in the economy, which has largely taken the form of a direct intervention via the publicly owned enterprises.

A further characteristic of Italy is the dualism of its credit market, whereby large banks operate mainly with large firms and small banks mainly with small firms (Vaciago 1987). Activity by banks, however, is restricted to the financing of firms,[2] whereas their powers of control and guidance over the firms are rather limited.

However, the new banking law, which enjoins the despecialization of activity and envisages banks' purchase of shares in firms and vice versa,[3] should lay the foundation for change in the relations between them. At the moment, though, it is not possible to predict future developments with any reliability, as the legislative changes are too recent.

Tendencies toward Greater Labor Market Flexibility

In the banking sector, industry level bargaining, the personnel policies adopted by banks,[4] and the limited competition among banks until the early 1990s have exacerbated the traditional rigidities of the Italian labor market. These various factors have given rise to marked uniformity among banks in such areas as job classification, working hours, part-time work, and pay levels. Bank employees, moreover, at least until very recently, enjoyed privileges like job security and higher salaries than those in other industries, which helped confer particularly high socioeconomic status on employment in a bank.

Since the second half of the 1980s, however, both the general process of deregulation of the Italian labor market and changes in the banking sector have redefined the rules disciplining the employment relationship. At least according to the employers' representatives we interviewed, the national contract of 1994 represented a turning point. Its most innovative aspects concerned job classifications, the working hours in branches located in tourist resorts or in shopping centers, and the increase in the maximum percentage of the workforce that can work on a part-time basis (from 7 percent to 10 percent of the total workforce).

As we show in more detail later, the search for greater flexibility in the employment relationship in its various dimensions continues to be at the center of negotiations between the employers' associations and the trade unions.

The Training System
The distinctive feature of the training system in Italy is the sharp distinction between school and the firm. The Italian school system provides a general education, and the skilling of the workforce begins after work entry, with training provided by the firm.

This distinction also characterizes the banking sector (Trentini 1994). There do not exist in Italy, therefore, public training institutions that give specific preparation for bank work. But there are, on the one hand, training schools traditionally run by individual banks and, on the other, upper secondary schools—the *istituti tecnici*—and university faculties (economics, banking) that provide basic training that may prove useful for employees in the banking sector. And in fact, banks' recruiting policy tends to favor diploma holders from these schools or graduates from these faculties.

The training the employers' organizations (ABI, Assicredito, Acri, Federcasse) provide also takes the form of courses attended by personnel already in employment. However, mention should be made of an initiative by ABI (Associazione Bancaria Italiana) that, in collaboration with some large banks and training firms, is in the process of setting up a school of postgraduate specialization in banking.

Training, therefore, is mostly provided by the individual banks themselves.

Regulation of Industrial Relations

The Italian banking system exhibits a number of distinctive features as regards the regulation of industrial relations. Already in the 1970s, the national collective agreements, which defined both the levels of bargaining and the issues that could be negotiated at the various levels, precisely regulated relationships between the parties. Three types of relationship have been defined (Izzi 1991; Pelaggi 1995):

• Collective bargaining at the national industry level.

• Company-level bargaining, which was introduced in 1970 and concerns the subjects that the national contract devolves to this level (the specification of provisions in the national contract regarding job classification, performance related-bonuses, environmental and safety conditions, and training). Consultation and negotiation are envisaged in the cases of corporate reorganization, mergers, and the outsourcing of some activities.

• Information to unions at the company level, like that provided in the formal meetings held twice a year (since 1973) to address issues such as workloads, the working environment, etc., and yearly (since 1980) to discuss data on personnel management (employment trends, hirings, training, mobility, etc.).

This precise regulation is an anomaly within the Italian industrial relations system, which is otherwise characterized by low institutionalization (Cella 1989; Locke 1995; Regalia and Regini 1995). Regarding relationships between the parties in particular, until the agreement the government, employers' organizations, and unions signed in July 1993, there was no coordination between national-level and company-level bargaining.

Increased Competitiveness, Technological Innovation, and Market Strategies of Italian Banks

The Italian banking system has developed in a market with a high degree of fragmentation and low competition, limited mobility of customers among banks, and a product demand that tends to favor relatively traditional products like bank deposits and state bonds.

Also, the Italian banking sector presents a low degree of internationalization. On the one hand, foreign banks still have a limited presence in

Italy, even after the liberalization introduced by EU banking directives. The specific characteristics of the Italian market—its fragmentation and the limited amount of mobility by customers among banks—make it particularly difficult for foreign banks to enter Italy. On the other hand, the presence of Italian banks abroad may also be considered marginal.

As a consequence of these market features, the Italian banks, at least when compared with their counterparts in the leading industrialized countries, exhibit a number of weaknesses: their medium to small size, their relatively narrow range of products, and their limited product innovation (Forestieri and Onado 1989; Pietrabissa 1994).

However, in recent years, the Italian market too has been characterized by an impetus to change. First of all, the reform of the banking law as discussed above has begun to reduce fragmentation (Pietrabissa 1994). Moreover, the market entry of new actors, like insurance companies and finance companies offering services like factoring, investment funds, and leasing, has also increased competition. The relationships between banks and these other financial operators may differ according to the strategic choices made by individual banks. According to the 1993 banking law, in fact, Italian banks can opt to continue to operate as specialized banks, to become universal banks, or to set up multifunctional groups. Finally, the financial culture of both households and firms has developed, generating demands for new products and services.

As our interviewees confirmed, changes in the market have primarily been responsible for the process of company reorganization in which many Italian banks are currently engaged. Technology, on the other hand, is seen merely as a means by which such organizational change can be achieved. Italian banks on average make less use of information technology than their counterparts in other industrialized countries (Pietrabissa 1994), although during the early 1990s their investments in such technology have increased quite considerably. New technologies are introduced for various purposes, ranging from company reorganization, to enhancing the information system, to product innovation (on this see below).

Changes in the market, therefore, are inducing the Italian banking sector to abandon the sluggishness that characterized its past activities. The fact that individual banks operated in a fragmented and largely uncompetitive market guaranteed them a certain degree of profitability without their having to pursue particularly high levels of operational efficiency or adopt aggressive commercial strategies. Indeed despite high costs, at least until the early 1990s, Italian banks were able to achieve high profitability thanks to a spread between active and passive rates broader than that in other EU countries and to the fact that limited competition enabled them to transfer their high costs onto prices (Desario 1995).

Today, however, Italian banks are reorganizing and redefining their strategies to augment both their market orientation and their efficiency. The main strategies adopted for this purpose: increasing their size as a result of concentration; extending their outlet network; product innovation; and cost cutting.

The process of concentration got underway in the second half of the 1980s. (There were 1,109 banks in 1987 and 937 in 1996.) Following these mergers, in 1997 the first seven banking groups were capturing a 50 percent share of the assets market. (At the beginning of the 1990s, their share was 30 percent.)

Extending the branch network is one of the most important strategies Italian banks have currently adopted (Storer and Mazzini 1995). The number of branches, in fact, has grown quite considerably, from 15,365 in 1987 to 24,406 in 1996. In many cases these outlets are small (four to five employees). Only in the second half of the 1990s has use of other distributive channels like telephone banking and home banking grown significantly. However, experiments are currently underway in this sector.

As far as the supply of services is concerned, only a relatively small number of Italian banks can be regarded as standing at the forefront of product innovation in terms of supply of services. Nevertheless, the majority of Italian banks are concentrating on a strategy of diversification of their products to acquire competitive advantages.

In the 1990s, the Italian banks have given increasing importance to the family segment. Among the new services offered to this market segment are assets management and a new type of cash card.

Finally, all banks are committed to containing their costs, which became an especially acute problem in 1994, when a profitability crisis hit many banks due not only to temporary factors, like the difficulties of numerous firms in the industrial sector, but also to structural ones.[5] Added to the traditionally high cost of labor in the banking sector were the considerable investments made in new outlets and the effects of increased competition. Italian banks pursue two main strategies to cut their costs: reducing staffing levels or restricting hiring, and increasing efficiency by means of company reorganization, both of which are discussed in sections below.

Changes in Employment Relations: General Trends and Differences among the Cases Studied

Human Resources Management

Recruitment and Redundancy Management Policies and Their Impact on Employment

At a time when the Italian banks are committed to increasing their efficiency, one factor they must seek to adjust is labor, not least because, on the basis of the available data, the cost of labor in the Italian banking sector is among the highest in Europe (Pietrabissa 1994; Prosperetti and Durante 1993, 1994, 1995) and does not seem to be offset by improved productivity.

Until the second half of the 1980s, Italian banks based their recruitment policies on indiscriminate hiring according to numerical forecasts. They therefore failed to take account of the professional characteristics of the personnel the organization was taking on. Only at the beginning of the 1990s were hirings reduced in quantitative terms and their focus sharpened in qualitative ones (i.e., they responded to specific needs). As mentioned above, the need to contain personnel costs mandated this change in recruitment policies, which was simultaneously made possible by the greater productivity consequent on technological innovation, and by the more accurate monitoring of operational needs permitted by the new management instruments employed (e.g., by management control techniques).

In the case of the savings banks, the recent deregulation of the employment relationship, which has modified the recruitment criteria, has favored this process. The savings banks had been obliged to recruit by public examination. In general, however, even in the banks in which employment relations were already being regulated by rules of private industry, the introduction of not only numerical but also qualitative manpower planning has led to more-finely-tuned personnel policies.

Despite these ongoing changes, the logic of the internal labor market (see note 4) still largely predominates. Nevertheless, our study shows a growing willingness among banks to recruit personnel with previous experience gained in areas other than banking (banks B, D) or graduates with special-track degrees or MAs, who are assigned to higher-ranking positions than the traditional entry jobs or placed on more-accelerated career paths conditional on completion of specific training programs (as discussed below). A study conducted by Assicredito (Scalfi 1995) shows a slight increase in the average age of new recruits and confirms this tendency, a finding that suggests that more-experienced personnel are now being hired.

Since the second half of the 1980s, employment growth in the banking sector has slackened. Indeed, although employment has increased overall, rising from 274, 889 employees in 1980 to 326, 947 in 1996, the rate of increase has been rather uneven. Moreover, as a consequence of company reorganization, a number of large banks have encountered problems of overstaffing (as discussed below).

Our case studies[6] confirm this sectoral trend. Between the end of the 1980s and the middle of the 1990s, in fact, some of the large banks studied (banks A, B, and F) significantly reduced their staffing levels: Employment in bank A fell by 7 percent after 1989, in bank F by 6 percent in the period 1983–92, and in bank B, indeed, by 14 percent from the end of the 1980s onward. Since the banking sector does not have social shock absorbers, redundancies have been managed mainly by a partial freeze on labor turnover (banks A and F) or by means of voluntary exit (bank B). Significantly, in parallel with these staffing cutbacks, the three banks have pursued a policy of geographical expansion and a buildup in their retail services that the increased productivity consequent on technological and organizational innovation has made possible. As regards the savings banks (banks C, D, and G), regardless of size, occupation has been more stable.

The employment relationship displays marked uniformity as regards such matters as job classification, working hours, part-time work, and pay levels and structure. In the Italian banking sector, in fact, the predominant type of employment relationship is the job for life. Limited but increasing use is made of nontraditional forms of employment, namely

• Part-time work, which was introduced in the banking sector in 1984. Its regulation was updated by the national contract of 1994.

• training and work contracts, introduced in 1984 and revised several times since to favor the labor market entry of young people aged 15 to 29. This type of contract has a maximum duration of twenty-four months, after which the job may be confirmed or otherwise (in 98 percent of cases the young person, is taken on permanently). The advantages the firm derives from the scheme are mainly tax concessions and the possibility of hiring selected individuals rather than hiring on a numerical basis.

In 1994, 52 percent of new entrants to the banking industry were hired on a full-time, permanent basis, the remaining 48 percent with training and work contracts (28 percent), temporary contracts (19 percent), and part-time contracts (1 percent) (Scalfi 1995).

However, the particularly marked impetus toward greater flexibility in the employment relationship since the early 1990s has not yet had evident repercussions on employment structure in the banks studied. The employment relationship is still substantially the same in all the cases examined: More than 90 percent of personnel are employed on a full-time permanent basis. Women account for 92 percent of part-time personnel (up from 88.9 percent in 1990; Scalfi 1995). Part-time employment is still granted mainly at the request of the employee concerned and it is not considered an instrument for increasing the flexibility of working time.

In the banking sector (excluding the savings banks) women accounted for 26.2 percent of total employment in 1994.[7] During the early 1990s, therefore, employment of women increased slightly (from 23.4 percent in 1990). A further increase is expected in the future, because for a number of years the proportion of female recruits has been around 40 percent of the total.

The slow rate of employment growth mentioned above is also reflected in the high average age of bank employees: 47 years for managerial personnel and 37 for nonmanagerial personnel (for women, 42 and 35, respectively). The largest age cohort (70 percent) is between ages 30 and 50, whereas only 16 percent of all bank employees are younger than 30.

Organization of Work
The changed market conditions that characterized the Italian banking sector between the end of the 1980s and the beginning of the 1990s and the deregulation of the sector laid the basis for a process of corporate reorganization that has affected all the banks studied. The patterns of transformation in the organization of work in the seven banks studied are significantly uniform, independent of size, corporate form, type of ownership, or reference market. Differences among individual cases are therefore to be discerned mainly in the stage reached by innovation, rather than in the formula adopted.

As frequently mentioned, the primary objective of the banks studied is greater competitiveness. Reorganization has begun and has been mainly undertaken in bank branches. The main changes consist of (1) "lean" structures, (2) expansion of commercial activity, and (3) greater autonomy.

1. Operational structures have been streamlined by the centralization of back office activities in service centers or *filiali capogruppo* (head branch

offices) and in some cases (bank C, D) by the limited outsourcing of non-specialized back office activities.[8] The separation between administrative and commercial activities and the automation of many of the most routine banking operations have enabled front office workers to establish closer commercial relationships with customers.

2. Pursuit of the second objective, expansion of branches' commercial activity, has centered on enhancing "customer orientation" of old professional figures (*operatore unico*, or multitask teller) and new ones (commercial and financial operators).

3. As regards bank branches' greater autonomy, the spread of management-by-objectives systems has been of crucial importance in increasing the branch managers' autonomy. Although the margins of strictly operational autonomy (e.g., in the granting of credit) have not been substantially altered in recent years, branch managers nevertheless have greater discretionality in personnel management.

Training and Career Development Programs

As we have seen, the banking sector in Italy is also characterized by scant linkage between the vocational training system and the world of business. Some of the banks' training needs cannot be met by the general educational system (upper secondary schools and universities), which provide only basic preparation. For this reason, since the 1970s, the banking sector has developed a tradition of in-company training through the creation by many large banks of company training schools.

The training system in the banking sector consists of activities established by collective agreement as well as training organized at the discretion of individual banks. However, the training organized at the banks' discretion has become the most important component in the training supply from both a quantitative and a qualitative point of view.

Of course, the requirement of a personnel policy more focused on qualitative skilling needs affects the characteristics of the training provided for newly hired personnel as well and, as a consequence, it also affects their career paths. Basic initial training is a well-established tradition in the sector, and it is usually provided at company training centers.[9]

Because, as we said above, hirings are now made on the basis of less-generic criteria than in the past, initial training has also been cut back in terms of quantity and transformed in terms of quality. Whereas, for example, toward the end of the 1970s the training given to newly hired personnel might have lasted for a number of months, today its average duration is a few weeks (usually four). The separation of training in the conventional sense (introduction and socialization to the company, behavioral and commercial training) from instruction in technical-procedural aspects has made this reduction possible. The former type of training involves daylong courses with the temporary suspension of working activities; the latter frequently takes the form of on-the-job training and self-training (sometimes with the assistance of a tutor, as in the case of banks C and E) using specially prepared software packages. The implementation of technical instruction is often delegated to bank branches (banks A, B, and F), whereas commercial, behavioral, and managerial training is usually provided at the headquarters.

This distinction between instruction in banking procedures and training in the wider sense highlights the substantial investments that all the banks studied have made in an innovative training system. Not only, in fact, have investments in training increased considerably, but the contents of courses have also been radically revised. In all the banks considered, the range of courses offered has expanded substantially since the mid-1980s. Above all, traditional courses on banking subjects (foreign commodities, securities and the stock exchange, credit, etc.) are now flanked by a wide range of courses on market orientation, commercial operations, communication, customer orientation, and service quality. Moreover, numerous courses for managers—unknown only a few years ago—are now offered.

As frequently pointed out, career paths develop mainly according to the logic of the internal labor market. New recruits, both secondary school diploma holders and university graduates, are therefore usually hired to fill clerical positions.

Besides classroom instruction, the training of newly hired personnel involves their rotation among different jobs, although usually in the same branch. The banks studied displayed two principal patterns of job assignments. In the majority of cases (banks A, B, C, D, G), the new recruit's first contact with work takes place in the front office. S/he then rotates among progressively more specialized jobs. In other cases (banks E, F), on-the-job training instead begins with administrative tasks in the back office, so that the new recruit may learn all the principal procedures until s/he achieves the position, on completion of the training path, of *operatore unico di sportello* (multitask teller).

Somewhat different, however, is the career path marked out for the so-called high-potential recruits certain banks envisage (banks B, D, and F). These are university graduates with brief but relevant experience or graduates possessing MAs. Their career paths are significantly more rapid

Table 6.1
Job structure in Italian banks (excluding savings and cooperative banks)

Year	Management	Middle management	Senior employees	Junior employees	Other
1979	14.0%	—	38.6%	40.1%	7.6%
1984	15.3	—	48.8	29.3	6.6
1989	16.9	5.9%	52.0	20.6	4.7
1992	16.8	8.6	49.7	21.2	3.7
1994	16.9	10.3	50.5	19.2	3.1
1996	16.8	12.0	52.4	16.3	2.4

Source: Assicredito.

than those set out for the majority of new recruits, with arrival in positions of responsibility (*funzionariato,* or executive level) within four to six years.

The practices of the banks analyzed revealed the progressive uncoupling of career paths from automatic advancement by virtue of seniority. Our case studies therefore evidence innovations (though limited) in personnel management policies. Industry level data corroborate these findings. In the banking sector as a whole, in fact, in the last fifteen years, the structure of job rankings has changed substantially. An upgrading is evident, partly as an effect of collective agreements (see table 6.1).

From the point of view of educational qualifications too, a predominant clerical component with medium to high qualifications characterizes the banking sector. The largest component in the composition of banking personnel by educational qualification (in 1996) consists of those with a secondary school diploma (64.7 percent); university graduates account for 18.5 percent; and employees with degrees lower than a secondary school diploma make up 15.8 percent. Those with some other level of educational attainment account for only about 1 percent of all employees.

Finally job structure differs according to the size of the bank (Prosperetti and Durante, 1994). The large banks, compared with small ones, have a larger proportion of managerial and clerical personnel with higher-level qualifications.

Pay and Incentives
Traditionally, the Italian banking sector has been characterized by high pay scales (above the European average; see table 6.2), minor pay differentials, close control over pay dynamics by the trade unions, and the limited use of incentives, especially those paid unilaterally by manage-

Table 6.2
Pay levels in banks in 1994

Position	Net pay	Gross pay	Labor cost
Front office employee	32.9	45.3	64.2
Back office employee	31.7	43.3	61.4
Middle manager at bottom of scale	53.2	79.8	115.0
Middle manager at top of scale	89.4	147.1	212.5
Manager at bottom of scale	107.7	181.2	259.7

Source: Assicredito.
Note: Figures are in millions of lire.

ment. On the other hand, already in the 1980s the union had included recognition by the national collective contract of management's right to pay individual incentives to highly skilled employees according to transparent criteria (the sole example of this in Italy). The national industry contract of 1990 introduced pay incentives tied to productivity into the banking sector, and such incentives were subsequently confirmed on renewal of the contract in 1994. Also stipulated on the latter occasion was the possibility of negotiating at the company level a bonus to be linked to specific indicators of labor productivity and of overall corporate performance (Prosperetti and Durante 1995). In all cases, however, the introduction of some pay incentives is considered to be motivational in purpose rather than as the outright flexibilization of pay, especially as far as nonmanagerial personnel are concerned.

Firm Governance and Labor Relations in Banks

Representation of Interests and Trade Union Relations
Since the Second World War, a plurality of actors on both sides of the industry has characterized the Italian banking sector.

The employers' associations have organized themselves by replicating the distinctions among the various types of banks. Assicredito comprises most of the ordinary banks, Acri the savings banks, and Federcasse the rural savings banks, that is, the small local banks. Collective bargaining, which has traditionally been conducted at separate tables, reflects this division.

The banking system has recently seen the simplification of employers' representation. By mid-1997, in fact, the merger between Assicredito (the employers' organization) and ABI (the banks' trade association) was complete, as already envisaged in previous negotiations. Still unaffected by the process are Acri (which, however, has also expressed its intention to join ABI) and Federcasse.

The plurality of associations is also observed on the labor side, but for different reasons that have to do in part with the unions' postwar history and in part with the "sheltered" nature of the sector, which has favored behaviour designed to maintain and strengthen the positional advantages enjoyed by different groups of employees similarly to the public sector (Baglioni 1991). Five unions have the largest memberships. The confederal unions are active in the banking sector, with three organizations accounting for almost 60 percent of all union members.[10] Among these three organizations (and in contrast to what happens in most other industries) FIBA-CISL slightly predominates, followed by FISAC-CGIL and the UIB-UIL. Besides the confederal unions, "autonomous" unions have a strong and forceful presence in the banking sector. Two of these—FABI and FALCRI—have relatively large memberships. FABI is the largest union among the employees of the ordinary banks, whereas FALCRI, an independent "company union," is joint leader with FIBA in the savings banks.

Trade unions organize principally auxiliary personnel, clerical and supervisory staff; middle and top management, on the other hand, have their own organizations. The autonomous unions in the banking sector are not the recent phenomenon that they are in the school system or the civil service, nor do they compete with the confederal unions for monopoly of labor representation. They were created after the Second World War, with a certain amount of support from the confederal unions, and they are an entirely specific feature of a system of union relations in a sector that is anomalous in various respects.

Besides the plurality of actors, the second feature of labor relations in banks is the high level of unionization. However, according to some analysts (Regalia 1990), strong unionization has not always translated into greater bargaining power, on account especially of the already mentioned fragmentation of representation and of the competition among the unions themselves. The trade unions in the banking sector have frequently encountered the problem of mediating among divergent positions.

A third feature of the sector's labor relations is the primacy of industry level over company level bargaining. As a consequence of this hierarchization of industrial relations, the actors involved have given greatest symbolic and strategic importance to negotiations over renewal of the industry contracts. Accordingly, the unions have traditionally mounted highly visible industrial action,[11] and the employers have often adopted an intransigent posture (Carrieri and Provasi 1984).

Changes in the banking sector, however, have progressively offset the primacy of the national industry level. This process has been fostered by the unions' previous rootedness in the workplace (the workplace representative body, RSA, is present at practically all sites), which stemmed from the recognition and legitimation afforded by the employers' associations, unlike their counterparts in other industries, at least since the early 1970s. This factor proved crucial when, in the 1980s, the banks began, first timidly and then with greater determination, to introduce significant technological and organizational changes.

Thus the banks have simultaneously created, expanded, or reorganized industrial relations departments internally to their personnel departments, sometimes formally separating the functions of the former from those of the latter. In many of the banks in which we conducted our case studies, management on the one hand and union representatives on the other point to the proliferation of areas and opportunities for discussion, both formal and informal, as one of the major novelties in the industrial relations system. And they emphasise in particular the high number of collective agreements reached at the company level.

Flanking these formal agreements are a wide range of informal understandings. These are agreements between management and union representatives that are not transformed into written documents or formalized rules, but that both sides nevertheless regard as binding.

Recent Trends in the System of Labor Relations

Two main trends have emerged recently in the banking sector. First, the importance of the company level in the industrial relations system has increased, which has in turn increased the number of negotiating sites, extended the range of issues addressed, and accentuated the participative and consensual character of relations at this level. Second, collective bargaining themes at both the national and the company level have been renewed.

Two processes have enhanced the company level of industrial relations. The first process is legislative innovation that, following implementation by the Italian legislators of European Union directives, has encouraged the extension of bargaining powers in the workplace.[12] Numerous decisions have been delegated to company level collective bargaining, some concerning issues already subject to this level of bargaining—like job classification and working hours—and some concerning new issues, like the handling of redundancies and consequences of restructuring, mergers, and takeovers. The second process instead derives from ongoing changes within the banking sector, especially from the organizational innovations that the banks have been forced to introduce to cope with the changes in the institutional context and in the market discussed in the beginning of the chapter.

Organizational changes have become the most important issues collective bargaining addresses. At the top of the agenda is labor flexibility in its numerical, functional, and to a lesser extent, wage dimensions.

Numerical flexibility is becoming increasingly important in national bargaining. The overstaffing consequent on restructuring and privatization and especially on mergers has been a major problem at the company level as well. In these cases, banks (such as banks A, B, D, and E in our study) have had widespread recourse to company agreements aimed at finding "soft," negotiated solutions. The instruments used, in the absence of social-shock absorbers like those in the industrial sector, have therefore been principally a freeze on labor turnover, geographical mobility thanks to the opening of new branches, and incentives to voluntary redundancies and early retirement (as discussed above).

In 1994, the visible crisis of international competitiveness and profitability, brought on by high labor costs with respect to productivity and the already mentioned manpower surplus, gave increasing urgency to the question of redundant personnel in Italian banks. In the subsequent two years, following agreement on renewal of the contract and an agreement mediated by the Ministry of Labour, various strategies were tested for dealing with the problem: for example, voluntary redundancies, internal mobility, reductions in overtime and new hirings, abandonment of company bonuses, transformation of the employment relationship from subordinate to independent for certain occupational categories (e.g., financial promoters), and the setting up of a joint committee to devise measures to deal with the manplower surplus.

However, by early 1997, the banking system placed the problem of 30,000 redundant personnel—a little more than 9 percent of the total workforce in the sector—on the political agenda. The employers' association proposal was to persuade the government to introduce social-shock absorbers, in particular early retirements, from which banks have been traditionally excluded. At first the government, worried about the extra costs for the state, and the unions, which favored alternative measures like retraining, part-time work, solidarity contracts, and in any case were determined not to restrict bargaining to surplus manpower and labor costs alone, both resisted the proposal.

In June 1997, the social partners signed a preliminary agreement that addressed the issue of manpower surpluses by setting up a national fund created by the banks concerned that would support the mobility of redundant personnel and the early retirement of those closer to pensionable age. However, negotiations over definition of the technical aspects of this fund were postponed to collective bargaining. A final agreement was signed in February 1998.

Reforming the pay system by giving it greater flexibility has been at the center of wide-ranging debate among practitioners and scholars for some time (Di Monaco 1993). However, as discussed above, changes in this area are still largely to come. Whereas the unions seem generally to favor the introduction of forms of wage flexibility tied to well-established and universal criteria of performance assessment, managements seem reluctant to involve or even inform the unions, preferring instead individual and discretionary incentives. On the other hand, in the industry contracts signed in the 1980s, the unions had already recognized the legitimacy of merit-based incentives in exchange for information about them from the management, without which the unions oppose these forms of incentive, for both political reasons (incentives would thus be an area entirely outside their control) and organizational reasons (they would induce competition among employees to the detriment of cooperation).

Forms of Employee Representatives' Consultation and of Direct Employee Involvement

Collective bargaining is not the only instrument by which the unions participate in firms' decisions. There has been a recent tendency to set up bodies in which workers' representatives are consulted on all the crucial issues of organizational change. These bodies, varyingly called mixed committees or joint committees, were present in four of the banks studied (B, C, D, and E). The issues usually discussed were safety, transfers, promotions, training, equal opportunities, and sometimes service quality. Regarding these last two issues, some banks (C, D, and F) had carried out surveys of their employees. As already noted, these bodies are consultative in nature, but several attempts have been made to render their decisions binding. Also, informal meetings are commonly held that do not give rise to agreements but at which management provides the union representatives with information on several issues.

The style of industrial relations that predominates at the local level of individual banks is, to summarize, quite different from that prevalent at the center of the system, namely the national industry level. Whereas the latter has been called contractual and formalistic because of the rigidity and formality of relationships involved and also because of the ritual nature of relations between the parties, the former is more flexible, informal, and pragmatic. The actors at the company level also meet outside the arenas established by contract or law, often at ad hoc meetings called to deal with specific problems as they arise. At these informal meetings, the dominant attitude is that of problem solving.

The company level of industrial relations, then, is emerging as the most appropriate arena for confronting processes of reorganization and restructuring, deemed a crucial juncture in this phase. Nevertheless, the primacy of the national level still persists, and it will not diminish in the foreseeable future, partly because of an explicit strategy by the unions, which believe it important to preserve instruments that prevent the excessive differentation of employment conditions in the industry. Also, much company level collective bargaining has a national relevance, both because many banks are large, nation wide companies and because in some cases national collective contracts incorporate solutions already developed in company level agreements.

The adoption by managements of a consultative and participatory posture vis-à-vis the workers' representatives provides them with an alternative to direct employee involvement. In this area, compared with those of other countries, the Italian banks seem largely unreceptive to innovation. In all the banks studied, direct employee participation policies have never been a strategic component of managerial action.

The most widespread forms of employee involvement are those of a more traditional character. Workplace briefings are very common in some banks, especially in the larger-sized ones and the administrative headquarters, whereas in the branches these meetings are convened chiefly at the discretion of the individual manager. There are also internal communications, like letters from the director to the employees (banks A and F), company newsletters (banks A, E, and F), and meetings provided for by the contract at which employees are brought up to date on corporate policy. In the event of privatization, some banks have offered shares to their employees, but employees have seen these policies, precisely because of their timing, more as instrumental to the banks' occasional interests than as a long-term mechanism to motivate participation. Finally, banks offer various kinds of benefits, like free holidays to employees in branches that have met targets in commercial campaigns, or other rewards, more symbolic in nature, distributed at company conventions.

Making Sense of Variations in Employment Relations

As we noted earlier in the chapter, the human resources/industrial relations policies adopted by the various banks studied have only rather slight differences. Two factors in particular account for this near uniformity. The first factor is the primacy of the central-national level in industrial relations, which has led to the predominance of uniform rules applying to all banks. On the one hand, changes in the institutional context (deregulation and transition to a market system) have given rise to a generalized process of organizational change in the Italian banks; on the other, the features of the industrial relations system have imposed constraints on banks' choice of human resources management and industrial relations policies. The second factor concerns passage to a full market system, which for all banks is proceeding rather gradually. Moreover, the fact that several banks have achieved satisfactory economic results without pursuing a high level of operational efficiency has meant that many have not felt it necessary to undertake radical organizational change.

Against this background, our case studies show that the differences among human resources/industrial relations policies in Italian banks are connected to ownership (public or private), recent corporate history, and size (large or small) of the banks. Ownership and corporate history affect the bank's degree of dynamism, whereas size conditions the type of reorganization undertaken.

The most innovative banks are the privately owned ones (banks A, E, and F, which have recently been privatized) especially if they have a relatively turbulent corporate history, like bank E. This bank was established at the end of the 1980s following the merger of two regional banks. The management found that it had to reorganize the company completely, because a new entity had been created. (In fact, the two banks had similar features, so that one did not merely absorb the other). The objective was to establish coherence between the new corporate strategies (aggressive commercial policies focused mainly on the quality of services) on the one hand and organizational change (creation of a lean structure) and a new management style on the other.

In banks A and F, privatization has accentuated the impetus toward a more entrepreneurially oriented management in which the emphasis is on results (in terms of profitability, productivity, and commercial targets), with all the consequences that this brings for personnel policies as well. Moreover, these two companies have also oriented their strategy to the retail market and no longer solely to the traditional corporate segment by means of appropriate organizational change that has affected not only the branches but the headquarters as well.

If we focus on human resources management policies, these three banks differ from the more traditional ones mainly in the dynamism with which they have undertaken reform of a personnel policy still geared to the internal labor market. This becomes plain when one considers areas such as recruitment, career paths, and training, as we showed earlier in the chapter.

The three banks in our study that can be considered traditional (banks B, D, and G) are a different matter. In bank B, such factors as under-capitalization, management according to a public logic, and relatively high management turnover in the last ten to fifteen years have had negative repercussions on the company's dynamism. Thus, as regards personnel, despite the changes introduced, the policy of strong workforce expansion pursued in the 1980s still affects the company. Not only is the problem of overstaffing especially severe, but the bank has an occupational structure in which the average age of the workforce is particularly high, which according to the union representatives interviewed has had various harmful consequences. First, it has kept the cost of labor high, given the linkage between seniority and career advancement; second, it has restricted the career prospects of younger employees; third, it is among the factors that increase the employees' resistance to change.

Bank D has concentrated on product innovation rather than on change in personnel management policies. Conversely, one of the main factors in bank G's competitive success has been technological innovation. This company made substantial investment fifteen years ago in ATMs, new means of payment (an area in which it is the national leader), cash cards, and home banking. Also, it expanded its data processing center, which enables the bank to offer data processing services to other, small-sized banks as well.

A further variable differentiating among the banks studied is, as said, their size. For example, the overstaffing problems concern mainly all the large banks. Moreover, below the threshold of 1,000 employees, banks have a tendency to outsource not only services like security, cleaning, and catering, but also training and in some case (bank C) the information system.

Turning to industrial relations, the common patterns the case studies reveal consist principally in the enhancement of company level relationships and in the transition to a more participatory model of industrial relations, as we discussed in an earlier section. In this case, the variables that help explain the differences among the various banks studied are ownership and corporate history.

In the two recently privatized banks (A and F), the management aims by means of in-company negotiation to avert conflict with the union, which is seen as a potential obstacle to reorganization. However, to emphasize the distinction of roles, apart from institutional occasions like the renewal of the industry contract or the meetings stipulated by the contract, informal discussions predominate.

The publicly owned banks (B, C, D, and G) instead tend toward greater institutionalization of relationships among the parties, which takes concrete form in joint committees or in the frequent signing of collective agreements. The case of bank D is emblematic, since in this bank there tends to prevail a model of industrial relations typical, at least in Italy, of the publicly owned enterprises and based on comanagement of several issues (although the company management states that it wants to increase its discretionality).

Finally, the dynamism in the field of industrial relations displayed by bank E, which takes concrete form in frequent meetings on a wide range of issues, is due mostly to contingent factors, that is, to the fact that the the bank's activism (e.g., in the purchase of other small banks) means that emergencies are constantly on the agenda. Moreover, because this bank is firmly committed to company reorganization, it has also taken pains to establish an ongoing relationship of consultation and cooperation with the unions.

Market and Institutions as Factors of Change

The change in employment relations that we have described in the previous sections has occurred as a response to market pressures and technological innovation that are common to all advanced economies, as well as to processes of institutional regulation and deregulation that are instead specific to Italy and to its banking sector in particular. The findings presented above show that (1) it is often difficult to distinguish the respective influence of these two sets of factors on change in unequivocal ways; (2) each set of factors has a few clear-cut implications on employment relations, along with others that are far more ambiguous; (3) the two sets of factors sometimes reinforce each other's effects, but more often act as mutual constraints; and (4) as a consequence, the overall direction of change in employment relations is rather clear but by no means uniform.

Overall, it is safe to conclude that the two sets of factors have played a complex role in recent change in human resources management and industrial relations in banks. Usually, the need to respond to increased market competition and to the challenge and opportunities offered by technological innovation are translated into strong pressures to change. These pressures, however, are filtered through existing institutions (operating economy-wide or specific to the banking sector) that often retard or cushion their effects on employment relations; but in some cases they may be accompanied by processes of institutional transformation that reinforce these same effects.

As discussed in a previous section, the regulatory regime typical of the Italian financial sector is probably responsible for the rather limited variation in the features of employment relations observed among the seven cases studies. Several institutions play a role in engendering this near uniformity. First, the banking law, as well as the various laws regulating the Italian labor market, set rules and constraints that the banking sector—because of its high visibility, the heavy presence of public companies, and the controls by the Central Bank—cannot as easily circumvent as can the industrial sector (Regini 1997). Hence derives a far lower variation in common standards than is possible in the latter sector. Second, the decreasing but still unchallenged primacy of national industry collective bargaining over decentralized negotiation means that several aspects of human resources management and labor relations are uniformly regulated. Finally, the predominance of publicly owned or controlled banks (in spite of the recent privatization process) has given them a sort of informal pattern-setting role in employment relations, which largely accounts for both their relative uniformity and their rather limited innovation.

In fact, the relatively slow pace and the nondramatic character of change is perhaps even more noteworthy, in a comparative dimension, than the limited intrasectoral variation. More than to the retarding effect of existing institutions, this rather striking feature is due to the sluggishness of the processes of privatization and deregulation, as well as to the relative weakness with which market pressures to face increased competition have manifested themselves in banks. The Italian banking sector has long been a sheltered industry, with an oligopolistic structure and a traditional division of the market among types of bank, facing little if any foreign competition, and without any serious challenge from an underdeveloped financial market. Under these conditions, Italian banks have shown rather low cost consciousness. Moreover, the coalition of interests against change has been powerful. Top managers whose performance was scarcely evaluated in terms of bank profitability as they were placed in charge by political parties, employees enjoying wage privileges well above the average of the Italian economy, rather bureaucratized unions with a high membership rate and a high level of recognition: All these actors have, at least implicitly, conspired against major transformations in employment relations as required by the rapidly changing markets and technology.

Still, change is taking place, in both the context of employment relations in banks and their features (as we have documented throughout the chapter). As a conclusion to our analysis, then, we may look more specifically at how market pressures, technological innovation, and institutional processes are affecting human resources practices and industrial relations.

In the areas of work organization, of training and career patterns, and of pay structure, the interplay between the factors at work has largely conformed to the pattern described above. Namely, the need to respond to increased competition, and the challenge of technological innovation, have been translated into strong pressures to transform employment relations. These pressures from market and technology, however, have been mediated by institutions that tend to retard the potential effects of the former. Moreover, market pressures themselves have been weaker and have arrived later than in other advanced economies.

Consider work organization first. Here the need to achieve greater competitiveness has had a rather powerful and uniform impact. The imperatives (or the slogans) to transform branches into "lean" organizations with greater autonomy and a more central role of commercial activities have led most of them to introduce some externalization of back office activities, an automatization of routine front office functions, a greater orientation to customers—hence a focus on sales roles—and a decentralization of human resources management. Yet, externalization and decentralization processes have been limited, and the client orientation has not deeply affected job assignments for tellers beyond a generic request for greater functional flexibility, which rarely includes consulting activities. It is clear in this case how institutional regulation has slowed the pace and scope of change. The primacy of industry level collective bargaining and the presence of strong trade unions have limited banks' recourse to decentralization of human resources management. The strict regulation of outsourcing has made externalization of a wide set of activities less convenient to banks. And so on.

As to training and career patterns, traditional rules in these areas can especially be seen as the sediment of past collective bargaining and industrial relations. A given amount of initial training was to be provided to all employees following certain procedures, and seniority was the basic principle to follow for determining both pay levels and career advancement. Here, too, recent changes have been prompted by the need to introduce market signals among bank employees as well as to invest more selectively in the human capital of the crucial occupational roles. For these reasons all banks try to introduce greater discretionality as regards the amount and standards of training, aiming at a better matching of their human resources to the types of skill they need. And for the same reasons, they try to supplement the seniority principle with other criteria based on merit. But here too the legacy of the past is such that these processes are slower than in other advanced economies. Change, however, is also more incremental and cautious than in the Italian industrial sector, where institutional constraints are also present, which leads one to conclude that besides the retarding role of institutions, the market pressures in the banking sector have shown a lesser urgency until recently.

Not dissimilar is the conclusion to draw on pay structure. As we have seen, banks are increasingly allowing for incentives to play a greater role in the composition of pay, although these still account for a very minor percentage of it. But they must be framed and presented as just motivational mechanisms, not as introducing a principle of wage flexibility. This Italian banks cannot do unless they decide openly to break the unwritten rules of labor relations and to engage in outright confrontation with the unions. In fact, the Italian system of industrial relations negatively sanctions wage flexibility. Since the early 1980s, this system has focused on allowing a high degree of functional and working-time flexibility and on consensually managing redundancies as an implicit trade-off for avoiding unilateral numerical and wage flexibility.

This brings us to the issue of recruitment and employment security policies. In these areas, market pressures and organizational innovation have converged with, instead of clashing against, processes of institutional change in making transformation of these policies possible. As far as hirings are concerned, the main change under way is from procedures of aggregate recruitment on the basis of quantitative manpower planning to selective hiring based on specific needs. It is easy to see how each of the factors mentioned above has helped this process to develop. Increasing market competition has highlighted the need to contain labor costs through selective recruitment. This has in turn been facilitated by the widespread introduction of management control techniques. And in the large subsector of the savings banks, a crucial factor has been the partial deregulation of the work contract achieved by eliminating the obligation for these banks to hire through public competition procedures.

The recent slowdown of employment growth has inevitably diminished employment security, once a distinctive trait of the banking sector, in the absence of the institutional shock absorbers (the wages guarantee fund) widely used in industry. For this reason, several banks have had to implement previously unknown policies of redundancy management, mostly based on early retirement and incentives to voluntary resignation. However, in this case, too, institutional processes have helped to transform the long-held view of a right to employment security into one of "monitored consensual mobility." The recent banking laws, in fact, by deregulating the possibilities for each bank to open new branches, have led to a rapid territorial expansion by most banks. The number of outlets dramatically increased in the early 1990s (as discussed above), and this process has smoothed or at least postponed, if not offset, the problem of labor shedding.

Finally, changes in the actors and the levels at which industrial relations are conducted have been equally noticeable, if less dramatic than in other advanced economies. The Italian banking sector has not been immune to the seemingly universal trend toward decentralization; but this conclusion also needs several qualifications. First, the decreasing (though by all means still crucial) importance of the national industry level of collective bargaining and the corresponding rise in prominence of in-company bargaining, have been a consequence of both market pressures to flexibility—an issue more aptly negotiated at the latter level—and institutional innovation. The tripartite agreement of 1993, in fact, as well as some laws implementing EU directives, have delegated several subjects to the company level of collective bargaining. Second, trends to decentralization have meant a greater involvement of workplace representatives, rather than an increase in employees' direct participation, which remains rather low in comparison with most other countries covered in this volume.

Hence, although the importance of market pressures, technological innovation, and institutions in transforming employment relations in Italian banks has been empirically confirmed, the relative role played by each of these factors, and especially the interaction among them, has varied depending on the human resources and industrial relations practices considered. Such a conclusion defies most simplistic assumptions often held about the innovative role of market and technology and the conservative one supposedly played by institutional processes.

Acknowledgments

The research on which this chapter is based was funded by the Italian National Research Council and the Italian Ministry for university and research.

Notes

1. The most recent legislation, consists of the law of 1990, which provided for the transformation of the publicly owned banks into joint-stock companies; the decree of 1992, which enacted the the II EU banking directive; and the banking and credit law of September 1993. One consequence of the last law mentioned has been to reduce the differentiation among types of commercial banks, that is, among the publicly owned commercial banks, the banks considered of national interest (the state holding IRI was the majority shareholder until recently), the ordinary banks, the savings banks, the cooperative societies, and the branches of foreign banks.

2. Despite the separation between banks and firms imposed by the banking law of 1936, commercial banks have also financed firms, in essentially three ways:

• A number of large banks have created sections dealing in long-term credit.
• Small to medium-sized banks have set up regional consortia.
• All banks have granted short-term credit that is automatically renewed on expiration.

3. However, the banking law states that share holding cannot exceed 15 percent, to prevent the excessive involvement of banks in firms' risks, or firms' control of banks.

4. Traditionally, in fact, the Italian banks have adopted personnel policies oriented toward the internal labor market (Gasparini 1982). The main components of these policies are

• the hiring mainly of staff with medium to high levels of schooling (usually upper secondary school leavers, to a lesser extent graduates for the lower positions);
• gradual and very prolonged internal career advancement, for which seniority counts most;
• job security.

5. As regards the larger banks, special mention should be made of the crisis that has hit the Banco di Napoli and the Banco di Sicilia.

6. The seven case studies on which this paper is based have been conducted by M. Trentini (banks A, B, C, and G), S. Carpo (banks D and F) and A. Colombo (bank E), under the direction of M. Regini. Bank A is a large bank (in 1995, 15,230 employees and 647 branches) that was privatized in 1993 in the form of public company. Bank B is also a large bank (in 1995, 20,775 employees and 609 branches). Its privatization process has so far taken the form of the bank's transformation into a joint-stock company in 1992, although it is still publicly owned. Bank C is a medium to small savings bank (in 1995, 959 employees and 72 branches) that was transformed into a joint-stock company, in 1992. Bank D is a large savings bank (in 1995, 14,505 employees and 612 branches) that in 1991 changed its legal status and became a joint-stock company. Bank E is a medium to large private bank (in 1995, 8,885 employees and 586 branches) created in 1988 by the merger of two smaller banks. Bank F is a large bank (in 1995, 19,329 employees and 940 branches) that was privatized in 1993 in the form of public company. Bank G is a medium-sized savings bank (in 1995, 4,762 employees and 345 branches) that has been transformed into a joint-stock company.

7. The figures cited here have been kindly provided by Assicredito.

8. It should be pointed out that outsourcing is contractually regulated and is subject to rules that make it a relatively unattractive commercial proposition.

9. Only the small banks almost entirely outsourced their personnel training. In other cases training was provided using internal resources, and outside consultants were only used to a limited extent for nonbanking themes (mainly for management training).

10. The confederal unions are the most representative organizations at the national level, not only in the banking sector. Data presented here are based on estimates for 1995.

11. Indeed, the negotiators on both the unions' and the employers' side declare that they cannot remember the signing of a collective contract that has not been attended by strikes, in contrast to other traditionally "hot" sectors like engineering workers.

12. For instance, with regard to the problem of redundancies, a law has been enacted that obliges the bank to communicate the reasons for the redundancies to the union representatives in writing and to suggest possible alternative solutions. Also, the extension to the banking sector of instruments previously only available in other sectors, like solidarity contracts and the safety delegate, has augmented the role of the company level of industrial relations.

References

Baglioni M. (1991). "La vertenza negoziale nel settore del credito." In Cesos (ed.), *Rapporto sulle relazioni sindacali in Italia 1989/90*. Rome: Edizioni Lavoro, 175–187.

Carrieri M., and G. Provasi. (1984). "La vertenza dei bancari." In Cesos (ed.), *Rapporto sulle relazioni sindacali in Italia 1982/83*. Rome: Edizioni Lavoro, 407–432

Cella G. P. (1989). "Criteria of Regulation in Italian Industrial Relations: A Case of Weak Institutions." In P. Lange and M. Regini (eds.), *State, Market, and Social Regulation*. New York: Cambridge University Press.

Desario, V. (1995). "La concentrazione del sistema bancario." *Bancaria*, 11: 2–17.

Di Monaco, R. (1993). *Il mito della tecnica e il presidio del potere*. Rome: Ediesse.

Forestieri, G., and M. Onado (eds.) (1989). *Il sistema bancario italiano e l'integrazione dei mercati*. Milan: Egea.

Gasparini, G. (1982). *Banche e bancari*. Milan: Franco Angeli.

Izzi, R. (1991). *Linee storiche della contrattazione collettiva dei bancari*. Rome: Assicredito.

Locke, R. (1995). *Remaking the Italian Economy*. Ithaca, NY: Cornell University Press.

Lombardini, S. (1986). "La Legge bancaria nello sviluppo del sistema creditizio italiano." *Note economiche*, 3/4, 197–218.

Pelaggi, L. (1995). "Procedure europee di informazione e consultazione dei lavoratori fra banca e industria." *Massimario di giurisprudenza del lavoro*, 2: 285–302.

Pietrabissa, E. (1994). "Le banche italiane verso il 2000: orientamenti per una strategia." *Bancaria*, 2: 6–20.

Prosperetti, L., and G. Durante. (1995). *Retribuzioni e costo del lavoro nelle banche italiane ed europee 1995.* Rome: Assicredito.

Prosperetti, L., and G. Durante. (1994). *Retribuzioni e costo del lavoro nelle banche italiane ed europee 1994.* Rome: Assicredito.

Prosperetti, L., and G. Durante. (1993). *Retribuzioni e costo del lavoro nelle banche italiane ed europee 1993.* Rome: Assicredito.

Regalia, I. (1990). *Al posto del conflittto. Le relazioni di lavoro nel terziario.* Bologna: Il Mulino.

Regalia, I., and M. Regini. (1995). "Between Voluntarism and Institutionalization: Industrial Relations and Human Resource Practices in Italy." In R. Locke, T. Kochan, and M. Piore (eds.), *Employment Relations in a Changing World Economy.* Cambridge: MIT Press, 131–196.

Regini, M, (1997). "Social Institutions and Production Structure: The Italian Variety of Capitalism in the 1980s." In C. Crouch and W. Streeck (eds.), *Political Economy of Modern Capitalism.* London: Sage, 102–116.

Scalfi, E. (1995). "L'identikit del bancario." *Banca e Lavoro,* November–December: 44–55.

Storer, F., and M. Mazzini. (1995). "Il processo di liberalizzazione degli sportelli e le politiche distributive delle banche: un'analisi ed alcune evidenze empiriche." *Bancaria,* 3: 52–75.

Trentini, M. (1994). "La formazione nel sistema bancario." *Il Mulino,* 6: 1095–1104.

Vaciago, G. (1987). "Novità e problemi nei rapporti tra industria e finanza." *Economia e politica industriale,* 56: 49–64.

7 French Banks: Between Deregulation and State Control

Marnix Dressen (translation by Edgar Blaustein)

The Context of Employment Relations

Between 1992 and 1994, the bottom line of French banks was in the red. France was trailing the pack in terms of profitability, just ahead of Japan. The crisis of the banking system (which might better be called an adaptation to new market conditions) has had economic as well as legal and technological dimensions. Banks suffered from the difficulties of their business clients in adapting to globalization. Above all, the more they had invested in real estate, the more they were in difficulty when the speculative bubble burst. It is now evident that the state prudential control system left a lot to be desired.

This crisis situation is one of the effects of weakened regulation and of disintermediation. Everything that had proven functional and coherent in the French banking sector—the rules of competition between establishments, client relations employees management, labor relations—was now perceived as maladjusted, obsolete, or counterproductive. Restructuring in response to market pressures is well underway, and its effects are already visible: (a) optimizing sales activity to adapt to the needs and desires of its clientele (needs and desires that banks fashion); and (b) reorganizing back offices and middle offices to react rapidly and economically to the needs of sales activity, transforming the internal labor market as a result.

Change in the Institutional Environment of the Banking Industry

Historically, the state has strongly supervised the banking sector to guarantee the stability and reliability of this key link in the economic system. France, perhaps more than other countries, has used banks as a tool of economic, industrial, and even foreign policy. The state has micromanaged the sector, going well beyond simple regulation of prudential ratios. Since the Popular Front in 1936, through the post war Gaullist period (nationalizations immediately after the war) and the beginning of the Mitterrand period (1981–83), state regulation of banks has been pervasive, according to Andrieu (1990).

In the last fifteen years, a dual tendency has characterized French capitalism: internationalization and privatization. State protection of large groups has gradually disappeared because of European regulations. Nonetheless, French capitalism seems to hesitate, as Morin and Dupuy (1993) show, between Anglo-Saxon capitalism (laissez-faire model privileging the stock markets) and continental capitalism (protectionist, in search of scale economies to ensure external competitiveness). The state is withdrawing from the productive system, and market logic is taking over in the management of public enterprises (French railways, France Télécom, etc.). The Bank of France was the object of a law of independence in 1993.

This evolution toward less regulation can be seen in the Banking Law of 1984, which reorganized the financial system so as to adapt it to public authorities' conception of the role of finance in the economy. It introduced four major reforms:

1. Harmonization of legislation. The law created the notion of "credit establishments," designating all financial intermediaries ranged across nine subsectors. Our study for this chapter focused on commercial banks, a subsector belonging to the Association Française des Banques (AFB). In 1996, the AFB, the main professional organization, represented 387 private banks (French or foreign owned) and a few nationalized banks. Each of the eight other subsectors also has an organization that represents its members before public authorities, holds high-level technical discussions, and is the representative of employers in labor contract negotiations. The law does not cover the Caisse des Dépôts et Consignations (a state institution) and the financial activities of the Post Office.

2. The same rights and constraints for all credit establishments. In fact, the law only partially harmonized the status of banks, leaving some important differences.

3. Wide auto-regulatory power for the banking industry.

4. Measures aimed at helping credit establishments in difficulty through a "solidarity" mechanism (see Moussy 1997: 24–29).

The banking law of 1984 had five objectives:

1. Stimulate economic activity. The state believed that more competition would lower intermediation costs, thus helping industry.

2. Hoist France to the level of American and British markets to attract big investors.

3. Find resources to finance state borrowing.

4. Work to constitute a unified, wide, deep capital market. The idea was to facilitate French banks' activities overseas. France is a net exporter of financial services and is well placed in world competition. Eliminating obstacles to the expansion of French enterprises demands reciprocity. The Economic and Monetary Union Treaty (1991) emphasizes the tendency toward liberalization and integration of the sector. Since 1993, the last protectionist barriers within the European Union have been eliminated. Deregulation has become the rule.

5. Lower entry barriers so as to open banking activities to new actors. Thus large distribution chains (Marks & Spencer, Virgin, etc.), credit organizations, and mail order houses have become "nonbank banks."

At the same time that the banking law partly deregulated banking, disintermediation (a mechanism by which enterprises borrow money directly on capital markets rather than from banks) cut into what was once the main part of banks' incomes. AFB banks were harder hit than cooperative and mutualist banks, whose business is more oriented to consumer credit.

Structures and Relationships between Banks and Industry

Beginning in 1989, the organization of French finance was characterized by the creation of poles within the public sector through crossed share holding between banks, insurance companies, and industrial groups. This recomposition has increased the capital of the financial entities and particularly of banks. The policy has allowed banks (especially Crédit Lyonnais and BNP) to develop a vigorous policy of external growth through increased shareholding in private groups. The state has transferred stock in public enterprises to these banks. These poles began a phase of recomposition of their activities and participated in fusions and takeovers. They thus hoped to reach critical mass in France and then in Europe. But financiers feel that the market is still too small, and hope for the development of pension funds invested in stocks (as in the United Kingdom). "The environment of large French enterprises is gradually approaching

the Anglo-Saxon model" ("Corporate governance et capitalisme à la française," 1995, *Centre d'Information sur l'Epargne et le Crédit*: 183–184).

In 1995–96, the strategic retreat of Crédit Lyonnais, heavily indebted
and constrained to sell its foreign subsidiaries, reduced from three to two
the number of pillars of French capitalism. Each pole has a business bank,
an insurance company, an investment bank, an industrial group, a water
and municipal services company, and a series of alliances and international
holdings. French capitalism has therefore been reorganized into two major
groups:

• the first includes Banque Nationale de Paris (BNP, a bank), Union des
Assurances Parisiennes (UAP, an insurance group), and SUEZ (another
bank);

• the second includes Société Générale (a bank), Assurances Générales de
France (AGF, an insurance group), and ALCATEL-ALSTHOM (an industrial group) (F. Morin 1995b: 18).

The development of "bank assurance" reinforces this bipolarization (see
below). This "circular hard core" model has exhausted its capacity to protect and legitimize management (F. Morin 1995a). Recently, foreign institutional investors (including many British and Americans) have invested
massively in the French stock market. France has become the second most
important country for management of bonds. These new investors seek
short-term profitability and are very exacting with corporate management, which has destabilized the traditional system of crossed ownership
characteristic of French capitalism.

Major Changes in Labor Market Regulation

In France, labor relations are conditioned by a large number of national
laws that constitute the *Code du travail* (labor law code), as well as governmental decrees, national collective bargaigning agreements, individual
employment contracts, and labor law jurisprudence. Laws that guarantee
union rights are better respected in large enterprises than in small ones. In
banks, five unions are a priori considered to be representative and may
negotiate with employers. In decreasing order of importance, they are
CFDT (Democratic French Confederation of Workers, ideologically close
to the Socialist Party), SNB-CGC (National Bank Union-General Confederation of Cadres), FO (Force Ouvrière, considered to be independent),
CGT (Confederation General of Workers, ideologically close to the Com-

munist Party), and CFTC (French Confederation of Christian Workers, considered to be rightist). Other unions exist but are not usually considered to be representative in banks. In particular, since 1988, a new union named SUD (Solidarity, Unity, Democracy) has grown rapidly, particularly in the public sector. Employees are represented and defended by *délégués du personnel* (workers' delegates) chosen through elections and most often members of the representative unions. Contrary to the situation in countries such as the United States, several unions can be present in one enterprise. French labor law mandates the existence of a *Comité d'entreprise* ("Enterprise Committee," referred to as the "CE"), consisting of elected worker representatives and presided over by the employer, in all enterprises with more than forty-nine wage earners. Its powers are limited, but it must be informed of most major decisions affecting the enterprise. Institutional union recognition remains strong.

Under French labor law, every worker benefits from an individual contract with his employer. In the past, these contracts were of unlimited term, that is to say, that the worker benefitted from a weak form of job-for-life protection. Although the great majority of wage earners still have this type of contract, in recent years limited-term contracts have grown in importance: In 1996, 85 percent of new labor contracts were for a limited term.

Classically in France, labor law is based on a pyramidal model, a top-down model in which national norms are applicable in all enterprises (Commaille 1991; M.-L. Morin 1994). Sector or enterprise collective bargaining agreements may adapt or complement national law and regulations but cannot reduce protection of the wage earner (Chalaron 1989; Rotschild-Souriac 1986: 1334–49); Couturier 1993, t. 1: 52). Paradoxically, enterprise agreements, usually the lowest-level source of labor law, are becoming autonomous with respect to higher levels. De facto, the center of gravity of negotiation is shifting from the sector to the enterprise, modifying the conditions of negotiation, for unions are less powerful at the enterprise level than at the national level. Enterprise agreements are becoming vectors of evolution of national labor law. One can say that enterprises have internalized the production of labor law, in particular to externalize redundant employees (Blaustein and Dressen, 1995; Dressen and Roux-Rossi 1997: 96–102).

The 1982 Auroux laws were supposed to change labor relations and union certification in enterprises fundamentally. Under those laws, salaries have to be negotiated at least once per year at the subsector level. In enterprises where a representative union exists, wages and working conditions must be negotiated at least once per year. Likewise, job classifications have to be examined every five years. But results have not lived up to expectations. Apart from the banking sector, the obligation to negotiate has not resulted in real negotiation: A 1993 study showed that 55 percent of enterprises in the private sector with fewer than 100 wage earners were not complying and that four out of five employees are not covered by an enterprise agreement. Nonetheless, enterprise level negotiations increased fourfold between 1982 and 1992, according to the Ministry of Labor. Note that the increase in enterprise agreements does not imply a decline in the number of subsector agreements (Hoang-Ngoc and Lallement 1994).

The government presented the December 1993 five-year labor relations law, which treats job creation, access to employment, working hours, job training, and the coordination between labor and management, as "a real program for society", according to the Ministry of Labor. In theory, an employer can now vary the workweek from zero to forty-four hours, provided that the average week is thirty-nine hours. But very few enterprises have used this regulation. Recourse to limited-term contracts, intermittent unemployment (paid or not), and overtime is the usual manner of meeting fluctuating needs. One observes a certain tendency toward part-time work.

Unemployment has continued to increase in France and now exceeds three million, or 12 percent of the labor force. Government agencies estimate that the unemployed together with those with unstable jobs account for seven million people, out of a total labor force of twenty-five million. The tax structure as well as French managerial culture favor automation: Layoffs are often the first solution when difficulties arise.

The state "continues to play the central role" in the areas of salary and employment policy (Hoang-Ngoc and Lallement 1993: 459). The right to lay off employees is contingent on the existence of an outplacement program, including an evaluation of transferable skills and as much as 300 hours of training.

Changes in the Vocational/Educational Institutions

Education institutions in the banking industry have been subject to multidimensional change due to the high rate of failure and attrition in the course of studies. One of the most important changes over the last few years is that many universities have developed professional diplomas at the undergraduate or master's level that prepare students for work in banks. Today there exists an abundant highly trained work force on the labor market. A large proportion of those under the age of twenty-five are unemployed.

Changes in the Social Security System

In the autumn of 1995, reforms aimed at dealing with budget deficits, in particular of the French social security system, provoked the most important national strike since 1968, affecting the nationalized and public sectors of the economy. Social security in France covers more people than a decade ago because of the "minimum insertion income" (that is, a form of welfare for people who have no other source of income; 900,000 beneficiaries in 1997), but the level of social security *stricto sensu* is no doubt declining: Worker contributions are increasing, whereas the percentage of health expenses reimbursed is declining.

Competitive Pressure from Markets and Technology

Technical progress is the most visible cause of change in the sector in the last ten years. Nearly all bank workers use a computer at least occasionally. Automation has spread to many activities and now touches complex intellectual tasks (for instance, assistance to sales persons) formerly considered typically human.

Increasingly, sales people directly type in client data, often guided by software that assists in the sales process. As a result, face-to-face sales are more rapid, the productivity of salespeople is improved and the rate of data entry errors decreases. The evaluation of client risk for loans is now computer assisted. In France, this type of service is available on the minitel (a simple terminal connected to the telephone system; four million were distributed free of charge by France Télécom. From their first use (1979) until around 1992, at which time they were sold for a modest monthly rental charge (20FF/month)) In general, specialists put France in the first level of follower countries in the banking services area (behind the United States and United Kingdom) (de Boissieu 1992: 62).

Dematerialization of means of payment and their numerization on magnetic supports is spreading rapidly, replacing paper supports and microfilming. This allows reduction of processing time and facilitates centralized management. Sometimes, enterprises outsource their financial management to the bank, limiting their internal workforce to data entry.

From the banks' viewpoint, this improves the quality of service while decreasing operating expenses.

The introduction of ATMs in 1972 is of fundamental practical and symbolic importance. ATMs replace jobs and certainly contribute to bank employees' feeling of insecurity. But experts are divided as to the economic impact and gains in productivity from their implementation. Note that ATMs and home banking have similar side effects, transforming the relationship between sales personnel and clients.

The "Client as King" Imposes Cost Cutting for Growing Profitability

French banks are seeking to institute a new type of relationship with their customers by substituting a service- or results-oriented relationship for the previous rule-based administrative relationship. Bankers are seeking to adapt to the current situation in which clients are less tied to one bank (Courpasson 1995: 162–171).

Banks have restructured and specialized sales services, segmented clients according to income and consumption habits, and personalized relationships between clients and accounts managers. They have increased the number of financial and insurance products, which for instance reached 300 at Société Générale in 1996 (as opposed to about fifteen at the beginning of the 1980s). The evaluation of client risk has become more sophisticated through computerized scoring of credit. The aim is to improve efficiency of the sales effort while decreasing the rate of bad loans.

The Salesperson Dethrones the Administrative Worker

Traditionally, sales people have been overshadowed, numerically and symbolically, by administrative workers in "production departments" that process means of payment. Banking used to be based on impersonal processing, in which discipline and respect for procedures were cardinal virtues. In the beginning of the 1960s, with help from public authorities, banks built paper processing factories employing thousands of workers. At that time, two out of three hires in AFB banks were of administrative personnel. The culture of salespeople in contact with clients was colored by the worldview of their administrative colleagues. This resulted from the configuration of the market at that time: It sufficed to wait for clients looking for consumer credit or standard financial products.

Administrative trades are declining, both in reality and symbolically, as paperwork reduction projects are developed. Administrative tasks have been eliminated, automated, and integrated into the sales process or externalized. In 1992 administrative employees constituted 28 percent of AFB bank staff but less than 17 percent of recruitment. Sales persons made up 37 percent of the workforce but 46 percent of recruitment.

The salesperson has become the new professional model, with redefined work and professional identity (Courpasson 1995: 161). But there is often a gap between the idealized salesperson, portrayed as a responsible and autonomous entrepreneur, and day-to-day reality. The profession of "client account manager" is stressful if one wants to be well judged, according to high individual sales objectives, now controllable instantaneously through on-line data entry programs. Thus, salespeople often feel like pieceworkers.

All banks, seeking activities with high value added, stress financial counsel to clients and other service activities. This evolution of banking activity is judged to be so significant that some observers feel that banks are no longer essentially distributors of credit, but rather financial service companies. Although not all service activities are yet billed to customers, many, such as management of working capital or financing of takeovers, are.

Chasing Waste, Duplication, and Errors

Following in industry's footsteps, banks now worry about the cost of defects and errors. Financial products not being patentable, banks cannot count on the originality of their banking products to assert their competitive advantage: Thus quality of service tends to take on more importance (Lalle 1990). The quest for quality is also a means for encouraging employee participation (Mispelblom 1995). From a management standpoint, the definition and measure of quality poses many problems (CNC: 1990: 22; Barcet and Bonamy 1994: 156; Blaustein and Dressen 1995). Traditionally, workers had an obligation of means. It seems that the evolution under way is towards an obligation of results.

For industrial-type banking activities (check processing, for example), it is easy to find objective measures of the quality of the work (for instance, the error rate in processing means of payment). On the other hand, for commercial and service activities, quality control is more difficult. Different types of indirect measures are used: Surveys of client satisfaction or rate of nonperforming loans accepted (Blaustein and Dressen 1995).

"Have Done" Rather than "Do"

The actual tendency is clearly toward the reduction of the perimeter of the enterprise, including only core activities of a strategic nature and

externalizing the rest. The search for the optimal size of banking enterprises is one of the key factors in the improvement of productivity.
Notions such as streamlining and "mean and lean" suggest that small
units are more efficient than large units. The choice of activities that are
externalized is frequently made according to the following criteria: Low
value-added activities, activities that add nothing to the enterprise's competitiveness, and tasks that others can accomplish better or more cheaply
because they are better qualified. High-skill activities (data processing and
telecommunications) as well as low-skill activities (grounds keeping, office
cleaning, or check processing) are also externalized. In the case of externalization, wage earners of subcontractors benefit neither from union protection nor from the different national collective bargaining agreements
in the banking sector (job security, salaries, and so forth). The cost of
externalization is not always easy to evaluate and is sometimes higher
than anticipated. Paradoxically, some bank directors assert that enterprises
really control certain functions from the moment that they are externalized. Nevertheless, reversibility is a key issue in externalization: If it is not
possible, the enterprise may become prisoner of a service provider.

Determination of the perimeter of the enterprise is blurred. One of our
interviewees joked that everything can be externalized except the client
file and the bank president. We see, as Michael Piore observed during
a seminar at the Conservatoire National des Arts et Métiers in Paris
in 1994, that the "heart" of the trade is like the heart of an artichoke:
Nobody knows where it begins. In fact, an enterprise is more like an
onion than a cherry.

Note that one observes reinternalization of some activities once subcontracted: for instance check printing, formerly subcontracted but now
done internally by BNP and by Crédit Lyonnais. Management made this
decision to reinternalize and approved the necessary investments to find
work for wage earners whose jobs had disappeared but who could not be
laid off.

Is France on the Road to Building Banking Giants?

Several French banks have reached international size. Many mechanisms
contribute to growing concentration in the sector, in particular, provisions
of the 1984 banking legislation dealing with bank failures. In case of
serious difficulties (since 1976, involving some twenty-five small banks),
solvent competitors take over client accounts through AFB "solidarity
mechanisms" (Moussy 1995). The most recent crises were of the Banque

Commerciale Privée and the Pallas-Stern bank. In 1995, the Banque Française du Commerce Extérieur was taken over by Crédit National; in 1997, Société Générale bought out Crédit du Nord. The Indosuez bank (a business bank specializing in Europe-Asia trade) is henceforth controlled by Crédit Agricole (the largest and most profitable French bank and second in the European Union); Banque Hervet and the Marseillaise de Crédit were sold off. The CIC (composed of a dozen regional banks) has been bought by Crédit Mutuel (which is at the same time a cooperative bank and a subsector). Since the end of 1998, French banks seem to favor increasingly the Anglo-Saxon style of restructuring. Since the announcement in 1999 by Société Générale and Paribas, the BNP (which belongs too to the AFB) has made a hostile tender offer on its two competitors. There are many conflicting interests involved, and therefore the case has been brought before the courts. Should BNP win, it would become one of the leading banks in the world. Note that the French government opposes takeovers of the biggest banks by foreigners.

The Development of "Bank Assurance" Contributes to the Emergence of Financial Giants

Traditionally in France, banking and insurance were distinct sectors. One of the adaptive strategies of all French banks has been to combine banking and insurance products and services, creating "bank assurance." The links between banks and insurance companies have grown stronger with the development of financial markets (F. Morin 1997). Interpenetration aims for sales synergies through rationalized product distribution and the suppression of redundancies (wage earners, offices, etc.). Beginning in 1971, Crédit Mutuel Alsace (inspired by the German model) created an injury and life insurance company. In the area of life insurance, they were followed by Crédit Lyonnais and Crédit Agricole. Since 1975 most banks have entered the field of liability insurance. Banks estimate that by the year 2000, they will control 75 percent of annual sales of life insurance and 70 percent of policies in force. Insurance companies lead in the race for size (F. Morin 1997: 10). Banks also count on the growth potential of pension funds, which permit wage earners to compensate for the diminution of state distributive pensions by capitalized pensions based on personal savings. According to the CEO of Fructivie, the expected rate of expansion is approximately 15 percent per year during the next fifteen years (Garsuault and Priami 1995: 430).

The Development of Telebank

A battle is raging in the domain of telebanking, also called direct banking or banking at home. In the last three years, Banque Directe (a subsidiary of Paribas) and other bank-by-telephone services have been created, modeled after First Direct in Great Britain. But until April 1997, the start-up of telephone services necessitated special enterprise labor contracts because of the requirements of the Decree of 1937, with strictly regulates work time in banks (Dressen and Roux-Rossi 1997). Telebanking is aimed at yuppies familiarized with modern communication tools: PCs, Internet, fax, and minitel. Although bankers expect high profits from telebanking with minimal investment, they have put only a small number of employees into these services.

Field Work

Our research is based on three case studies, all belonging to the AFB subsector. The first, CIAL (Crédit Industriel d'Alsace-Lorraine) is a subsidiary of CIC (Crédit Industriel et Commercial); at the time of our Survey (1997), 92 percent of CIAL was controlled by the Groupement des Assurances Nationales, a state insurance company. In the spring of 1998, CIC was bought by the mutualist bank Crédit Mutuel, and a few months later the GAN was bought by Groupama (a subsidiary company of the cooperative bank Crédit Agricole), so the GAN has been privatized. CIAL is a regional bank of medium size (2,350 employees in 1994) whose clientele consists of small and medium-sized businesses, artisans, professionals, and well-off individuals. CIAL was the "jewel" of the CIC. It explains its profitability by the fact that it started restructuring earlier than others and by its geographical position close to the borders with Germany, Switzerland, and Luxembourg.

The second bank in our study, Crédit Lyonnais, is (still) an international bank and is the last nationalized bank of the AFB "Big Three." Its disastrous financial situation has been in the news over the last few years. It employs approximately 36,000 persons, but its restructuring implies drastic staff reductions and cuts in all areas, in particular foreign subsidiaries. Among AFB banks, Crédit Lyonnais has long symbolized traditional French banking.

Crédit Lyonnais and CIAL are similar to many other French banks in that they have significantly reduced and modified their workforce through internal means (retraining and job mobility) as well as external means (incentives for departure). For each of these banks, after inquiry with the human resources department, we conducted field studies of two reconversion operations.

For our third case study, we have in addition analyzed the emergence of a new credit establishment, Banque Directe, a subsidiary of Compagnie Bancaire/Paribas. This led us to investigate rules and negotiations concerning work time.

We therefore did field studies of three banks and of a subsector negotiation about work time. Six monographs, totaling approximately 400 pages, preceded the synthesis published by the French ministry of labor at La Documentation française.

Change and Variation in Employment Relations

The will to break with the past has consequences for all aspects of management of the workforce. Change aims at increasing labor market flexibility, that is to say, optimal adaptation and adaptability to the market. Cost reduction is an important dimension of the adaptation of banks to their new context. Because salaries are 70 percent of expenses, banks reduced employment. Newly hired (and therefore less expensive), younger personnel, better trained for sales work, generally replaced a proportion of those departing. Furthermore, because the AFB banks' collective bargaining convention and the law protect the most senior employees against layoffs, most banks' staff reduction plans are based on voluntary departures. These plans of voluntary departures have targeted certain categories of personnel: administrative employees, older personnel, personnel with low skill levels whose jobs are disappearing, and personnel at some regional sites.

Because of employer-aided departures and the nonreplacement of natural departures between 1984 and 1997, credit establishments have lost nearly 7,500 jobs, that is to say about 1.8 percent of their staff (the banks alone have lost 2.8 percent). The global decline hides contradictory evolution, however. As we see in table 7.1, some establishments lost a significant number of jobs, but others maintained or increased staff.

Interpretation of these statistics is difficult because the perimeter of banking activity changed in the period because of subcontracting, externalization of some tasks, disintermediation, and the entry of new actors into the field of financial services. Thus some of the jobs that appear to have disappeared in the statistics were in reality transferred to other enter-

Table 7.1
Evolution of employment in credit establishments (1981–1997)

	1981	1984	1994	1996	1997*	1984–97 (%)
AFB banks**	243,918	251,498	235,900	227,000	223,300	−11.2
Crédit Agricole***	62,496	69,804	68,838	69,376	72,916	+4.45
Banques populaires	27,000	28,800	26,340	26,937	27,240	−5.4
Crédit Mutuel	15,501	18,830	22,081	22,754	23,309	+23.8
Crédit coopératif	1,472	1,685	1,985	2,098	2,133	+26.6
Caisses d'epargne	21,139	25,700	35,671	36,996	36,233	+41
Total banks	**371,526**	**396,317**	**390,815**	**384,161**	**385,131**	**−2.8**
Crédit Municipal****	NA	NA	1,220	1,069	1,105	
Specialized financial institutions	10,379	11,415	10,018	9,606	7,670	−32.8
Financial societies	13,400	14,570	19,500	20,500	20,900	+43.4
Total: all credit establishments	**395,305**	**422,302**	**421,553**	**415,336**	**414,806**	**−1.8**

Source: Annual report of the committee of credit establishments.
* Previsional data
** Number of people (not converted to full-time-equivalent positions) covered by the collective bargaining agreement in France and foreign countries. AFB has just revised that data for the period after 1993.
*** Salaried workers at the Caisse Nationale du Crédit Agricole.
**** Salaried workers have been counted only since the creation of the Union Centrale des Caisses du Crédit Municipal.

prises. It is difficult, in fact, to get a precise idea of the number of direct and indirect jobs in financial services. Nevertheless it is probable that total employment through 1994 was stable.

The relative weight of financial institution wage earners in the economy has not changed much since 1980, as table 7.2 shows. According to Eurostat in Luxembourg, in 1991 France was one of the countries of the European Union in which bank employment was the smallest proportion of total employment. As for adjustment of working hours, feminization of the sector probably facilitated flexibility of the work force.

The Proportion of Women is Slowly Increasing

Since 1984–85, women have become the majority in AFB banks, as shown in table 7.3. This progressive feminization masks two facts: (a) the variation between banks, from almost 63 percent at the Caisse d'Epargne to less than 48 percent at Société Générale; and (b) variation among job

Table 7.2
Proportion of employment in French financial institutions

	1980	1985	1988	1991	1992	1994
Financial institutions/service employment		3.8	3.6	4.7	4.5	4.4
Financial institutions/total employment	2.3	2.5	2.4	2.4	2.3	2.3

Sources: Statistical office of the European community; national accounts from *La Banque en Chiffres.*

Table 7.3
Percentage of women on AFB banking staff (1985–1996)

Year	1985	1987	1989	1991	1993	1995	1996
Percentage	50.7	51.5	52.1	53	51.9	52.2	52.2

Source: La banque en Chiffres.

classifications: In 1996, 26.2 percent of *gradés* were women, and only 19.6 percent of *cadres* were women (the terms *gradé* and *cadre* are defined below).

Aside from Part-Time Work, Nonstandard Work Arrangements Are Rare

In banks today, part-time work fulfills three objectives among employers:

1. reduce total paid working hours
2. adapt working hours to the employer's needs
3. correct the age pyramid

Jobs involving nonstandard work arrangements are rare in banks in France. Nonetheless, they have developed in other sectors. AFB banks resort rarely, and probably less and less, to temporary work. A 1990 inquiry concluded that banks "do not wish to have a subgroup of personnel that could be seen as precarious" (Dejonghe and Gasnier 1990: 43). Thus between 1994 and 1997, CIAL never employed more than twelve temporary wage earners per month. The average duration of such employment was less than four days in 1994. The most common form of unstable employment is the limited-term work contract. But in the case of CIAL, its use remains marginal at only 6.5 percent of the current contracts in 1994, 1995, and 1996; and Crédit Lyonnais had only twenty-two limited-term contracts in 1995 and eight in 1996 (with a small increase in 1997).

The adjustment of the labor force in French banks is accomplished essentially through incentive plans for voluntary departures and through part-time work (traditionally little used in the subsector). A comparative United Kingdom/France study shows that in France, the law regulates recourse to part-time work, and in general, work schedules are fixed. On the contrary, in the United Kingdom, the law allows employers to vary work schedules according to their needs. One explanatory factor is that this difference is possible because child care in the United Kingdom is usually arranged informally, whereas parents in France resort to a state system that imposes fixed schedules for children (O'Reilly 1992b: 293–313; Boulin, Tallard, and du Tertre 1991: 44).

Nonetheless in the last few years bankers have encouraged workers to adopt part-time work according to many different formulas: in one system, wage earners do not work Wednesdays, when French schools are closed. As well, employers negotiate agreements with unions in which part-time workers are paid more than the hours worked (60 or 70 percent of full-time wages for half-time work). Whatever their form, part-time jobs are almost exclusively held by women.

These incentives have succeeded in increasing part-time work progressively from 5.3 percent of Crédit Lyonnais personnel in 1985 to 7.5 percent in 1990, 14.3 percent in 1995 and 16.7 percent in 1996. At CIAL, 10.5 percent of wage earners were part-time workers in 1996. In AFB banks, part-time work increased from 7.7 percent in 1992 to 12 percent in 1996.

Training, Skill Formation, and Career Development Policies

The AFB collective bargaining agreement classifies personnel in three large categories: *employés*, *gradés*, and *cadres*. *Employés*, in principle, do low-skill jobs, most often administrative. The *gradés*, middle-level wage earners, are usually skilled and are the equivalent of foremen and technical personnel, although given their large number, most command no other workers. The category *cadre*, which has no equivalent in the United States or in Germany, includes high-skill or professional workers as well as middle and upper management. Classifications have sometimes only a distant relationship with real functions: *gradés* sometimes have more hierarchical responsibility than some *cadres*; *employés* sometimes fill functions that call upon more competence than those of the *gradés*.

For at least twenty-five years, management has contested the system of bank job classifications, largely for the following four reasons:

Table 7.4
Distribution of staff by category in AFB banks (1975–1996)

Category	1975	1980	1983	1985	1990	1995	1996	1983–96
Employés	53%	40.3%	35.9%	32.5%	20.5%	7.6%	6.3%	−82.4%
Gradés	36	45.2	49.7	52.7	60.7	66.6	66.8	+34.4
Cadres	11	13.5	14.3	15	18.8	25.7	26.9	+88.1
Total	100	100	100	100	100	100	100	

Sources: "Les clés de la banque," databank of the AFB, and *La Banque en Chiffres*, 1996.

1. It has become of little significance because a disproportionate number of wage earners have de facto climbed the ladder due to seniority. Seniority plays an excessive role, encouraging passivity.

2. It is archaic and too detailed, leaving out new functions.

3. It freezes wage scales and obliges enterprises to remunerate know-how that they no longer need.

4. It has become an obstacle to cooperation between wage earners and management.

Non-AFB banks, with their own collective bargaining agreement, have changed the names of categories. Thus, Crédit Mutuel has redefined the three classes as agents of application, technicians and unit leaders, and management.

In AFB banks, the evolution of the distribution by professional category has evolved considerably over the last twenty years or so. Statistics presented in table 7.4 show a very clear diminution in the number of *employés*, albeit with variations among banks (in 1993, Crédit du Nord (an AFB bank) had only 2.5 percent *employés* whereas the Caisse d'Epargne, which is at the same time a bank and a subsector, had more than 48 percent). This decline in the number of *employés* has resulted from promotions to the category of *gradé*, retirement, voluntary departures, the decrease in recruitment of low-skill wage earners, and subcontracting of repetitive tasks with low competitive advantage.

The large overall increase in the *gradé* category also masks disparities (between 35 percent at Crédit Mutuel (which is at the same time a bank and a subsector) to close to 70 percent at BNP (an AFB bank) in 1993). The growing numerical weight of the *gradé* category has several causes:

1. Most importantly, *employés* are automatically promoted to *gradés* through seniority.

Table 7.5
Evolution of the structure of personnel at Crédit Lyonnais (1950–1996)

	1950	1960	1970	1980	1990	1993	1995	1996
Employés	74.4%	68.2%	59.8%	35.2%	17.1%	9.9%	7.6%	6%
Gradés	17.9	22.1	30.8	52.4	66.4	71.4	73	74.2
Cadres	7.7	9.7	9.4	12.4	16.5	18.6	19.4	19.8
Total	100	100	100	100	100	100	100	100

Source: Crédit Lyonnais France.

2. *Employés* who go to school and acquire a university-level banking diploma are automatically promoted.

3. *Employés* who exercise hierarchical responsibility even temporarily may be promoted.

4. Young, college-educated youths (sometimes from highly regarded business schools) destined to become *cadre* after one or two years are hired as *gradé*.

One also observes from the data a significant increase in the *cadre* category. In 1991, *cadres* became more numerous than *employés* for the first time, again with large disparities between the Caisse d'Epargne (less than 7 percent in 1993) and Crédit du Nord (more than a third of staff in the same year). One gets a good idea of the progression of employment classes by observing the evolution at Crédit Lyonnais as depicted in table 7.5.

The current tendency is toward replacing the traditional notion of qualification, negotiated with unions, with the more individual notion of competence, defined by the employer (Dressen and Roux-Rossi 1997: 109).

The market for job training in banks is now less captive to subsectorial training institutions, such as the Center for Professional Training in Banks. Such institutions now play a more limited role as consultants on training. Crédit Agricole created its own in-house training organism in 1976. In AFB banks, 30 percent of training is now done in-house. CIAL has chosen a mixed formula: Some courses are subcontracted to external organizations according to specifications written by the training department, whereas others are conducted in-house by bank personnel. The internalization of training reduces costs and facilitates adaptation to changing needs.

The 1994 and 1995 interprofessional report on training places banks clearly at the top of the list (with energy and insurance) in terms of the

Table 7.6
Percentage of labor costs devoted to training

	CIAL	Crédit Lyonnais	BNP	Société Générale	Crédit Agricole	AFB	Total*
1989	5.7	5.8	5.3	5.0		4.8	2.9
1990	6.4	6.7	5.3	5.0	5.1	4.8	3.1
1991	6.4	7.1	5.6	4.7	5.1	5.0	3.2
1992	7.1	6.8	5.7	4.5	5.2	4.9	3.3
1993	5.9	6.4	5.5	5.1		4.9	3.3
1994	5.9	6.3	5.9	5.4	5.9	5.1	3.3
1995	5.49	5.8	5.9	5.0	5.6	5.1	3.3
1996	5.98	5.7				5.2	3.3

Sources: Crédit Lyonnais, department of human resources for the group; CIAL, department of human resources; Association Française des Banques, "Les clés de la banque."
* All economic sectors, enterprises with more than ten wage earners.

proportion of workers who benefited from job training. Training budgets vary widely among banks and are correlated with the size of the enterprise (Blin 1993: 32), as table 7.6 suggests.

In the past, one of the banking sector's characteristics was the status and recognition it accorded training. The AFB collective bargaining agreement makes training imperative for employers, and several clauses encourage wage earners to participate. To the extent that banks recruited little in the external labor market, it was necessary to train workers for promotion. All bank employees had the right to ask for training, but only a minority the hierarchy actively encouraged to do so. Field investigation shows that many low-skill employees received little or no training. This is not surprising given the Taylorization of many jobs. Until the end of the 1980s, the beneficiaries of training were most often middle- and upper-level workers. The banking sector is still exceptional in that university-type training still automatically leads to higher wages and often to a higher job classification. In this respect, banks are similar to public sector industries such as railroads and electricity.

Up until a few years ago, banks and insurance companies often used training as recompense, a lubricant for work relationships (Cossalter 1990: 65). The current tendency is toward more precisely targeted, problem-oriented training. Directors of human resources seem to agree with one Shell manager's declaration that "the capacity to learn more rapidly than ones competitors is the only durable competitive advantage" (Meignant 1993: 31.)

Specifically, training in banks aims to achieve the following three objectives:

1. To aid the internal reconversion of workers whose jobs disappear. Thus Crédit Mutuel de Bretagne in 1992 expended 50 percent of its training budget on wage earners with twenty or more years of service. This is a break with the past in that training is now being offered to lower classifications, implying that "learning by doing" no longer suffices even at lower levels of employment. Pedagogical innovations—learning games, field studies—are more often used. Training stresses knowledge and know-how but also includes behavioral training. One of its main objectives is the "intellectual reawakening" necessary to prepare for reconversion. Often called "adaptation to change," such training stresses self-knowledge and "learning to learn."

2. To orient ideologically "high-potential" wage earners, salespersons, and management destined to become key actors in a bank's effort at adaptation to the market.

3. To train salespeople to sell increasingly sophisticated products.

In the case of CIAL, the transformation of training has been very clear. According to the head of the training department of the CIAL, five years ago, training at CIAL was composed "training leading to bank diplomas; maintenance of basic banking knowledge; rewards for meritorious management, that is to say seminars on communication, transactional analysis, etc." According to a section chief: "Before, one relaxed for three or four days, sometimes for no reason...." Two changes mark recent developments at CIAL. The first is that training became, in 1990–91, a strategic tool in restructuring the bank. Henceforth, more people have attended training programs aimed at more precisely targeted objectives. Attendance is according to precise criteria. A computerized census of training was created. The second change is the decreased importance of outsourced classroom training and greater emphasis on in-house, on-the-job training. This led, as Blaustein, Dressen, and Roux-Rossi show (1994a: 102–3), to a paradoxical decrease in the training budget in 1993, even though training increased in terms of trainee days. Training now has to comply with profitability criteria.

One of the difficulties of training programs is what happens after. The best training can be rendered useless if workers return to jobs dominated by the same old organization of work that the training is designed to counter. Not only does this induce skepticism on reforms, but it generates a fatalistic attitude among workers.

Banks are making use of special forms of work contracts ("contracts of qualification," "contracts of adaptation") created by legislation aimed at facilitating hiring of low or unskilled youths from sixteen to twenty-six years old for their first job. These fixed-term contracts, from six months to two years, are organized according to a work-study scheme. They allow below-minimum-wage salaries and reduced social security contributions.

Work Organization

The tendency among French banks is to shorten hierarchical lines of command to render organizations more efficient: The reorganization of the Crédit Lyonnais administrative center that began in 1992 at Bayeux is a good example. For a 300-person work group, the center moved from an organization that used 12 to 15 managers and 30 to 35 group leaders to a new organization that uses 5 to 6 managers and 25 group leaders.

At CIAL, the rationalization of administrative procedures in head office production services and branch back offices has aimed at specialization and proximity to clients ("shortening of decision and processing chains"). Thus checks are now processed in two stops (the branch office and the subcontractor) instead of three (the branch office, a regional administrative center, and the head office). In branch offices, the sales person now directly processes opening of accounts.

One observes among French banks concurrent decentralization and recentralization of administrative tasks. At Crédit Lyonnais as well as at CIAL, current reorganization has resulted from decentralization (from large processing centers to smaller units or to branch offices) as well as from recentralization (from branch offices to commercial support units or to the head office). Banks are also redefining the workload in branch offices, in some cases, by increasing work done at the counter to decrease redundant procedures; in other cases, by transferring work from the counter to the back office to decrease processing time while face to face with the client.

Current evolution gives a key role to "optimal" reorganization of enterprises, which has become a constant area of concern for bank organization departments. Non-AFB banks succeeded in restructuring to reach critical mass between 1989 and 1993. For instance, the Caisses d'Epargne combined 224 regional groups into 35. At the same time, Crédit Agricole closed 20 percent of its regional groups. In these two cases, restructuring did not necessitate layoffs: on the contrary, these banks increased staffing under the restructuring.

Several banks have reorganized their headquarters to regroup dispersed central services. Bank headquarters now specialize to concentrate on their strategic functions but also on new activities such as data processing, international law, telecommunications, marketing, and so forth.

Compensation Levels and Structure and Role of Incentives

Since the 1952 Collective Bargaining Agreement, an individual bank worker's salary (like as those of public service workers) has been based on the product of an index corresponding to his or her classification level and the value of a "salary unit" (*point* in French), which is negotiated yearly at the subsector and enterprise levels. The salary system has been greatly transformed since the beginning of the 1980s, however, and is one of the areas in which structural change has been most visible to wage-earners, argues Martory (1993). Under the new system,

1. labor costs rise less rapidly than inflation.

2. salary gaps between banking and other sectors are diminishing, to the detriment of bank workers, according to two inquiries (Dejonghe and Gasnier 1990: 42; Petit and Vernières 1990: 17). Thus in 1984, average net salaries in banks were 33 percent higher than those in other sectors of activity, but in 1990 only 29 percent higher (Gauthronet, Aslaug, and Lion 1992: 39). According to INSEE (a national statistics agency) the gap has been reduced to only 10 percent (CNC 1989). As a result, despite general unemployment, some young salespeople quit banking, discouraged by low salaries and high sales objectives.

3. subsector level negotiations are decreasing in importance, with governmental action and enterprise level negotiation taking their place;

4. general wage increases are diminishing, with individual merit–based measures taking their place;

5. certain fringe benefits (preferential loan rates, etc.) are being cut.

Beginning in 1976, salary increases determined by the AFB diminished, and since 1982, general wage increases by themselves have been insufficient to maintain purchasing power.

Despite the slow increase in the value of the bank salary unit, a combination of individual and collective increases has generally led labor costs to increase more rapidly than consumer prices. Management, opposed to centralized negotiations, fears the negative effect on employment of identical wage increases applied indistinctly to well-performing and poorly performing banks (Careil 1994).

Table 7.7
Monthly average remuneration by category at CIAL (1994–1996) and Crédit Lyonnais (1995–1996)

Category	1994	1995	1996
Employés	8,879 to 10,459	9,694 to 10,522 (10,623)	9,060 to 10,753 (10,864)
Gradés	11,876 to 16,279	11,984 to 16,306 (14,886)	12,287 to 16,681 (14,170)
Cadres	18,392 to 38,835	18,454 to 39,060 (26,197)	18,646 to 39,208 (27,322)

Source: CIAL, départment of human resource.
Note: All figures are in FF. The figure in parentheses represents the average. The other figures are the interval, dimensionless quotient between two percentile salary levels. These data do not include overtime and bonus pay.

Management would like a system under which sector negotiations fix only minima, leaving the rest of a worker's salary to be determined through enterprise negotiations. For given total labor costs, this would allow them to encourage their "best workers," whereas general measures would satisfy no one. In addition, impersonal salary fixing does not allow sufficient sensitivity to external market conditions for certain rare qualifications. Management would like first of all to decrease its costs so as to lower its break-even point. In 1993 the ratio of labor costs to value added was 47.8 percent at BNP, 48.2 percent at SG, 55 percent at Crédit Lyonnais and 52.8 percent at Crédit du Nord (Force Ouvrière 1994). Second, management wants to encourage departures of certain workers.

The relative diminution of bank salaries hides variations between AFB banks and non-AFB banks as well as variations among AFB banks. (In comparing salaries, variations in monthly wages due to end-of-year bonuses make it necessary to use average monthly wages, equal to one-twelfth of annual remuneration.) On July 1, 1994, minimal hiring salaries were 6787 FF per month for AFB banks, the Banques Populaires and Crédit Mutuel (6872 FF at the end of the trial period; the trial period is when the first person is first hired). On November 1, 1994, they were 8449 FF at the Caisse d'Epargne (Force Ouvrière 1994). Table 7.7 shows pay scales at CIAL and Crédit Lyonnais in the mid 1990s.

It is difficult to examine the totality of salaries and gaps for various reasons:

1. For cultural reasons, in France, individual and collective salaries are taboo in conversation. (The more one climbs in the hierarchy, the more this is true.)

2. Enterprise policies are variable in this area.

Table 7.8
Evolution of salary gap, CIAL (1980–1994) and Crédit Lyonnais (1995–1996) (gap between
10th and 90th percentiles of salaries)

1980	1982	1984	1986	1988	1990	1992	1994	1995	1996
4.90	4.81	4.87	4.81	3.52	3.41	3.35	3.38	3.33	3.30
								(2.32)	(2.41)

Source: Directors of human resources, CIAL and Crédit Lyonnais.
Note: The data in parentheses refer to Crédit Lyonnais.

3. It is difficult to take into account direct as well as deferred elements of remuneration (especially for management and high-level salespeople who benefit from stock options, loans, etc.).

At AFB banks, from 1992 to 1996, salaries of low-skilled women increased more than salaries of high-skilled men (without taking into account non-monetary remuneration of upper management). At CIAL, the gap between the best- and least-paid wage earners decreased between 1980 and 1994, as table 7.8 shows.

The general tendency in French banks is toward personalization of pay increases and the limitation of automatic measures. This is especially true in private establishments, according to a 1990 inquiry (Dejonghe and Gasnier 1990: 40). In other words, the tendency is to increase, according to an AFB expression, "the reversible share of the salary" to the detriment of base salaries.

Generally, Hay-type evaluation (which takes into consideration responsibilities and the contribution of the job to enterprise profitability) is restricted to management. Upper management earn more than the minima determined by the collective bargaining agreement and benefit from indirect salaries in kind (car, apartment, stock options, and so forth).

Individualization of remuneration often implies individual interviews between wage earners and their hierarchy. Remuneration can also take the form of individual or collective bonuses, which constitute, on the average, 7 percent of annual salaries for the sector. Bonuses are more important for high classification levels: 10 percent for those "above classification", 8.4 percent for *cadres*, 6.2 percent for *gradés*, 5.5 percent for *employés*. According to a Ministry of Labor survey, the two forms of individualization can coexist in the same enterprise (Dejonghe and Gasnier 1990: 43).

At CIAL, bonuses in the form of extra salary units are no longer distributed automatically to everyone but are increasingly limited to upper and middle management. The total number of salary units distributed is constant, but the number of wage earners concerned has decreased. Almost everyone agrees on the principle of merit remuneration, even trade unionists. But one often hears that increases are decided for personal reasons rather than according to merit. Practice in this area is perceived as arbitrary, confused and, inequitable.

Examination of professional journals shows great variety in the methods used for determining individualized compensation. In general, salespeople benefit from individual or collective commissions on sales (Grafmeyer 1992: 113–18; Courpasson 1995: 148–152; Dejonghe and Gasnier 1990: 45). In 1994, CIAL distributed approximately 8,000,000 FF to its 1,250 sales persons, an average of 6,400 F per person. When bonuses are collective, they aim to encourage cooperation among sales people and possibly between sales and administration. Bonuses are less expensive than salary increases to the extent that they are directly linked to profitability and productivity. Nevertheless, according to a CIC manager, there is no causal relationship between profit sharing for salespeople and the bank's profitability. The director of human resources of the Caisse Nationale du Crédit Mutuel believes that "people are still at the stage of questions, nobody has found the solution." One of characteristics of a "good" system of commissions, if such is possible, is its clarity. "Sales people have to believe in it. It is necessary to sell it to them and results have to be intelligible."

Changes in Firm Governance and Labor Relations in Banks

The culture of the bank sector is manifested in the collective bargaining agreements. Banks have a tradition of labor relations dialogue (both a condition and a result of the constitution of the internal labor market). Directors of human resources (DRH) are more and more often members of the board of directors, so as to better take into account the personnel factor in decision making. As for heads of training departments, they are usually subordinate to the DRH, but their role has also increased in importance (even if their budgets have decreased because of rationalization of training).

In the banking industry, essential rules cannot be modified without consulting unions. Unions are still capable of mobilizing wage earners on certain delicate questions such as staff reduction plans. Recently, by occupying their workplace, workers succeeded in forcing Société Générale to abandon a plan to eliminate jobs.

Two major changes are observed in labor relations in French banks:

1. The content of the labor relations dialogue has evolved. Management now wants to discuss staff reduction, cost reduction, and flexibility. Unions have rarely been able to refuse this discussion.

2. One observes a tendency for enterprise negotiations to replace stalled sector negotiations. With the exception of three agreements (on retirement in 1993, on professional training in 1993, and on safety conditions in branches offices in 1996), sector negotiations have generally failed. The freeze of national negotiations is a sign of problems in the labor relations system. AFB seeks to negotiate "framework agreements" that give employers wide latitude. Confronted with the difficulty of modifying national rules, employers seek internal solutions to their problems of staffing and work time.

Now that they have succeeded in cutting staff, HR directors often say that geographical mobility has become their number one problem. To overcome resistance to geographical mobility, enterprises negotiate agreements including bonuses for workers who relocate.

The Difficult Renegotiation of the Collective Bargaining Agreement

All nine subsectors of the banking industry (except Banques populaires) have their own collective bargaining agreement. In 1989, AFB banks tried without success to renegotiate their agreement. Management's idea was to "modernize" human resources management after having modernized financial management and legal regulations. Various subjects were discussed: "modernization of work contracts," "personnel management better adapted to the evolution and the diversification of bank trades," "readapting working conditions," and "favoring proactive management, through better knowledge of the evolution of employment and skills," according to AFB expressions.

The 1989 negotiations were soon abandoned. One of the AFB negotiators explained in an interview that "unionization in banks is non-negligible and we are in a sector of activity of hyper-strategic national importance. We therefore have to be very prudent in canceling the convention." In 1997, the AFB tried to restart the negotiations. Then in February 1998, the AFB decided that negotiations were stalled and exercised its right to cancel the agreement unilaterally. Unless a new agreement is negotiated, the old one will still be applicable until December 31,

1999. On February 27, 1998, employees walled off the entrance to the AFB during a massive union protest demonstration against the canceling of the collective bargaining agreement.

Outside of the AFB subsectors, in 1989 and 1990 Crédit Foncier de France (3,500 workers), and the Comptoir des Entrepreneurs (1,800 workers) renegotiated their conventions with unfavorable results for wage earners. It is now permissible, under the renegotiated conventions, for the organizations to recruit at all classification levels. At Crédit Mutuel de Bretagne (3,500 wage earners) a new convention was signed in 1991 by the CFDT and the union of *cadres*, after five years of negotiation. In these three cases, the role of seniority in remunerations was weakened.

Since 1939, banks have tried to obtain abrogation of the decree of 1937, which strictly regulates working hours. They finally managed to do so in April 1997, after several banks had succeeded in circumventing it through enterprise level negotiations.

Within the framework of the June 1998 law, called "Loi Aubry," which brings down the legal length of the work week, subsector bargaining began in spring 1998, at the request of the AFB trade unions. In January 1999, the employers' federation had obtained the signature of only SNB-CGC, the union that especially represents the "cadres." The legality and legitimacy of this agreement have been questioned by the other sector's unions, who appealed to the ministry of labor and are now awaiting the judicial decision.

At Crédit Agricole (which is at the same time a enterprise and a subsector), the hostile negotiation regarding the thirty-five-hour work week has been raging. This is because the base of the main union, the CFDT, announced that they judged the employers' compensation insufficient in terms of jobs creation and effective reduction in working time.

On the other hand, an agreement was signed by Banques Populaires (also a subsector). The agreement was signed by SNB-CGC and CFTC.

Making Sense of Intrasectoral Variations in Employment Relations

Four variables must be taken into account to explain the differences in labor policies among enterprises:

1. The level of the particular enterprise's exposure in real estate.

2. The subsector (AFB, cooperative, or mutual banks) to which the enterprise belongs. This determines fringe benefits, the applicable collective bargaining agreement, and until 1997 whether they were covered by the

decree of 1937. Globally, AFB banks started efforts to gain flexibility in labor relations later and with more difficulty than mutual and cooperative banks. But this may not explain the better earnings of the latter, because non-AFB banks have long benefited from nonnegligible competitive advantages. In addition, non-AFB banks' integration into local economic systems seems to help them.

3. The bank's status (private or nationalized), which changes the nature and level of state intervention. The Crédit Lyonnais crisis would probably have been dealt with differently if the state had not directly controlled the bank.

4. The size of the enterprise. Large and medium banks negotiate more readily than smaller banks. Size is generally correlated with a stronger union presence, particularly in large administrative centers.

Conclusions: Markets, Technology, and Institutions as Factors of Change and Diversity

Because of computerization and subcontracting, part of the administrative workforce in French banks is considered to be useless to the enterprise. Tasks with low value added tend to be subcontracted or handled through telecommunications, computers, or robots (such as ATMs or voice message systems). Some functions have purely and simply disappeared. An increase in the productivity of capital allows a decrease in human work. These changes give rise to a new combination of factors of production. In terms of the professional paradigm, as well as in number of workers, one clearly sees a reorientation of banks toward sales activity.

Have AFB banks achieved the objectives of restructuring that they had in mind when they began in the middle of the 1980s? The answer is complex and has to be finely shaded. By weakening regulations, the state aimed to adapt the economy to the world market. From this viewpoint, enterprises (at least those that survived) are in a better competitive situation, reflected in the French foreign trade surplus of recent years. But at the same time, long-term unemployment rose, and many societal problems worsened (Castel 1995).

Weakening regulation has had very noticeable effects, some beneficial, others less so. Banks have been able to develop their insurance activities spectacularly. Until the Asian crash at the end of 1997, French banks' performance overseas was globally excellent. The AFB wants more deregulation, in the form of the suppression of the "competitive advantages" that benefit mutual and cooperative banks as well as the post and Caisses d'Epargne. From time to time, banks' demands go in the opposite direction, demanding state intervention (e.g., some ask the state to reduce the value-added tax on data processing investments).

In economic terms, between 1992 and 1994 many French banks were in difficulty (particularly those that had invested heavily in real estate), and all suffer from the reduction of intermediation margins and from disintermediation. This leads analysts to believe that bank restructuring is far from over in France. But the state's strategy in the Crédit Lyonnais affair is symptomatic of French contradictions. On the one hand, the state, for various reasons (maintaining employment, fear of a chain reaction in the sector, political considerations), has committed itself to a costly bailout (at least 120 billion FF) despite warnings from the European Commission in Brussels and the anger of the competitors of Crédit Lyonnais. On the other hand, the state continues to weaken regulation to increase competition between banks.

From the management viewpoint, the organizational consequences of restructuring have been positive. They have greatly decreased operating expenses, simplified structures by reducing hierarchical lines of command, shortened processing chains, and in general better adapted procedures to the market. In some cases, entire departments or administrative centers have been eliminated. Between 1995 and the first semester of 1999, the profitability of most French banks has been spectacularly restored. From now on, their aims will be similar to those of the Anglo-Saxon banks.

The future of administrative and other low-skill or low-status workers was at the center of our investigations. What has become of the many men and women who occupied bank administrative posts and are now bearing the brunt of restructuring? Despite alarmist estimates, to this day there have been few economic layoffs in French banks. But thousands of wage earners have been offered bonuses to leave enterprises, usually within the framework of "social agreements on employment" negotiated with unions. To persuade wage earners to leave an enterprise, employers offer bonuses that exceed allowances the collective bargaining agreement guarantees. There were more than thirty such agreements in AFB banks in 1995, according to the SNB-CGC union. At CIAL, for instance, these negotiated agreements have proved very effective, the number of candidates for departure or for part-time work exceeding objectives. However, in a few banks, such projects have failed for want of volunteers for departure. Globally, until now employers have controlled the situation: Banks have reached staff reduction objectives and, with the exception of Crédit Foncier de France, have had little conflict with unions.

By means of enterprise level negotiations, usually at the initiative of employers, unions are associated with management decisions without really becoming administrators, because they have no real power over enterprise strategy. Analysis of union action reveals an evolution from a logic of opposition aimed at qualitative or quantitative gains to a logic of negotiated participation in management decisions to avoid the bankruptcy of enterprises and layoffs. The idea of the best interest of the enterprise, and the maintenance of staffing levels has displaced concerns with gains or losses for wage earners.

To what extent do banks still have an internal labor market, as was clearly the case ten years ago? The answer is mixed. On the one hand, there are many stable elements. A good proportion of wage earners have high seniority, an important fact given that many functions have evolved. This means that employers have sought and found within the enterprise most of the workforce that they need. Management of staffing is oriented toward future needs and functions within the logic of an internal market. An example is the return of apprenticeship. Similarly the all-around rehabilitation of job training used as a tool in reconversions strengthens the internal market. Another example is a clause in the staffing agreement at CIAL that stipulates that only those wage earners whose departure would not entail an external hire can benefit from voluntary departure incentives. In AFB banks, the 1952 collective bargaining convention de facto guarantees workers a job for life: This is also typical of a closed labor market. Short-term contracts remain rare and temporary work almost nonexistent. The increase in part-time work can also be interpreted as a manner of preserving the work contract, thereby respecting the idea of a job for life. Plainly, many elements point toward the conclusion that the traditional bank culture is still alive.

But this reality coexists with contradictory trends. Incentive plans for departures still succeed. In addition, banks have started recruiting at high classification levels. This is not completely new and has been the case for data processing since the middle of the 1960s. But the practice has increased. This is a partial rupture with the traditional culture, because in the past, qualified positions were filled by internal promotions. As observed by G. Vallery (1992), we see recourse to the external market as well as redeployment in the internal market through in-house reconversions. One could speak of a partly open market, compared to what it was fifteen years ago. In fact, this partial opening aims not only at recruiting new blood but also at facilitating departures.

Note also that banks have sought efficiency in all directions but one: Tasks continue to be defined rigorously by the hierarchy. Team work remains exceptional. In other words, banks have until now been loath to seek productivity gains through horizontal coordination.

Acknowledgments

Special thanks to Edgar Blaustein (industrial economist) and Dominique Roux-Rossi (legal expert in industrial labor relations), my colleagues during five years of interdisciplinary research.

List of Interviewees

Olivier Robert de Massy, responsible for social affairs at the Association Française des Banques

Michel Cantegril, member of the Director of Human Resources, Caisse Nationale du Crédit Agricole

Director of Human Resources of the Chambre Syndicale des Banques Populaires

Michel Mayer, Director of Human Resources of the Caisse Nationale du Crédit Mutuel

CIAL (Strasbourg) Jacques Scheer, Director of Human Resources

Jocelyne Loos, head of training

Jean-Marie Notter, responsible for personnel at the head office and for recruitment of *cadres*.

Director of organization

Director of information systems

CFDT union representative

FO union representative

SNB union representative

eleven *employés* and *gradés*

CIAL (Metz) Director of Human Resources of Metz

two *gradés* and eleven *employés*

Crédit Lyonnais (head office in Paris)

Michel Guigal, manager at the Director of Human Resources

Lucile Daher, manager at the Director of Human Resources

M. Gosset, responsible for the "map of trades"

Françoise LeBorgne, responsible for the social audit

CGT national union representative

two CFDT national union representatives

two SNB national union representatives

FO national union representative

Crédit Lyonnais (administrative center at Bayeux)

two CGT union representatives

two CFDT union representatives

two FO union representatives

CFTC union representative

Crédit Lyonnais (administrative center at Rillieux)

CGT union representative

three CFDT union representatives

two FO union representatives

Compagnie Bancaire

two CGT union representatives

Jean-Pierre Nerré, CFDT union representative

Manager of a subsidiary

M. Poli-Simon, responsible for banks and finance at the CGT

Pierre Gendre, responsible for banks at FO

Jean-Pierre Moussy, manager in the training department at BNP, member of the Conseil National du Crédit, and the Conseil Economique et Social, ex-secretary general of the CFDT bank union

M. Lemee, responsible for reconversion of low-skill *employés*, Director of Human Resources of BNP

Michel Watier, comptoir des entrepreneurs, responsible for training

Michel Schwab, comptoir des entrepreneurs, director of the cabinet of the CEO

Pierre LeMaitre, Centre Formation de la Profession Bancaire

Annie Moisson, comptoir des entrepreneurs

Héliette Paris, comptoir des entrepreneurs

Divers

François LaGandre, ex-Director of Human Resources of La Hénin, author of a thesis on work time in banks

Jean-Louis Cressent, consultant at Bernard Bruhnes Consultants

M. Bernard, Director of Human Resources of Crédit Mutuel Centre-Est-Alsace

Mme. Menardi, responsible for reconversions at the Caisse d'Épargne de Bretagne

A branch office director at Société Générale.

Sandrine Gayet, journalist at *Banque Ressources Humaines*

Gilles Lockart, journalist at *La Vie des Agences*

References

Andrieu, C. (1990). *La Banque sous l'occupation: paradoxes de l'histoire d'une profession, 1936–1946*. Paris: Presses de la Fondation Nationale des Sciences Politiques.

Annandale-Massa, D., and H. Bertrand. (1990). *La gestion des ressources humaines dans les banques européennes: quelles stratégies?* Economica (B. Bruhnes consultants).

Barcet, A., and J. Bonamy. (1994). "Qualité et Qualification des services." In J. de Bandt and J. Gadrey (ed.), *Relation de service, marché de services*. CNRS éditions, 153–174.

Blaustein, E., and M. Dressen. (1995). *Recherche de la productivité et rentabilité dans le secteur bancaire: théories, pratiques et conséquences sur la gestion des ressources humaines (France et Etats-Unis)*. Geneva: Bureau International du Travail.

Blaustein, E., and M. Dressen. (1993). *La banque française en mutation: marché, profession, organisation, culture*. Geneva: Bureau International du Travail.

Blaustein, E., M. Dressen, and D. Roux-Rossi. (1995). *Les restructurations au Crédit Lyonnais. Tendances antérieures et mesures récentes en matière de gestion des ressources humaines et de relations professionnelles*. Report CNAM-CNRS/DARES of the Ministry of Labor. September.

Blaustein, E., M. Dressen, and D. Roux-Rossi. (1994a). *Crise et restructuration dans une banque régionale. La reconversion des employés faiblement qualifiés*. Report LERPSO-CNAM/DARES of the Ministry of Labor, October.

Blaustein, E., M., Dressen, and D. Roux-Rossi. (1994b). *Internalisation/externalisation, deux volets d'une même politique de restructuration (Le cas d'une banque régionale en France)*. Communication of the French-Canadian conference on industrial relations research perspectives. Univ. Laval (Québec) and GDR-CNRS 41, June.

Blin, M. (1993). "La formation professionnelle." *Gestion des ressources humaines*. Paris: La Documentation française.

de, Boissieu Ch., and L. Martray. (1992). *Prospective financière: banques, assurances, marchés. Rapport du groupe prospective finacière et bancaire*, La Documentation française (Commissariat général du plan).

Boulin, J.-Y., M. Tallard, and Ch. du Tertre. (1991). *Les nouvelles technologies et négociations en Grande Bretagne*. Editions de l'IRIS (Paris IX-Dauphine).

Cancel, S., and G. Duval. (1998). "La fin du capitalisme à la française." *Alternatives économiques*, 160: 28–31.

Careil, P. (1994). "La convention collective des banques AFB tue l'emploi." *AGEFI*.

Castel, R. (1995). *Les métamorphoses de la question sociale*. Fayard.

Chalaron, Y. (1989). "L'application de la disposition la plus favorable." In *Les transformations du droit du travail. Etudes offertes à G. Lyon-Caen*. Dalloz.

Commaille J. (1991). "Normes juridiques et régulation sociale, retour à la sociologie générale." In F. Chazel and J. Commaille (éd.), *Normes juridiques et régulation sociale*, 13–22. L.G.D.J.

[CNC] Conseil National du Crédit. (1989). *Modernisation et gestion sociale des établissements de crédit*.

"Corporate governance et capitalisme à la française." 1995. *Centre d'Information sur l'Epargne et le Crédit*-n 183–184, September-October.

Cossalter, C. (1990). *Renouvellement des qualifications et de la gestion des ressources humaines dans les banques et les assurances*. CEREQ (Coll. des études-N°53, February).

Courpasson, D. (1995). *La Modernisation bancaire*. (Préface de Paradeise, C.), L'Harmattan.

Couturier, G. (1992). "L'intérêt de l'entreprise." In *Les orientations sociales du droit contemporain*, écrit en l'honneur de J. Savatier. Paris: Presses Universitaires de France.

Dejonghe, V., and V. Gasnier. (1990). "Pratiques salariales et gestion du personnel dans les banques et les assurances." *Travail et Emploi*, 45(3): 40–46.

Dressen, M., and D. Roux-Rossi. (1997). *Restructuration des banques et devenir des salariés*. La Documentation française (coll. Travail et emploi).

Dressen, M., and D. Roux-Rossi. (1996a). *La banque sans face à face ni robot ou la brèche dans le décret de 1937*. Report of the Ministry of Labor/CNAM, October.

Dressen, M., and D. Roux-Rossi. (1996b). "La reconversion des employés de banque faiblement classés." *Travail et Emploi*, 68(3): 3–22.

Dressen, M., and D. Roux-Rossi. (1996c). "Banque Directe ou la brèche dans le décret de 1937." *Travail et Emploi*, 68(3): 23–38.

Favereau, O. (1989). "Marchés internes, marchés externes." *Revue Economique*, 40(2): 275–329.

Force Ouvrière. (1994). Fédération des employés et cadres, *Conférence nationale professionnelle du crédit, Document de réflexion*, October 11–13.

Garsuault, P. and S. Priami. (1995). *La banque, fonctionnement et stratégies*. Economica (CFPB).

Gauthronet, S., J. Aslaug, and J., Lion. (1992). *Evolution de l'emploi et des qualifications dans le secteur des banques et des assurances*. Ed. B. Belloc. Report Dares, Ministry of Labor.

Grafmeyer, Y. (1992). *Les gens de la banque*. PUF (Sociologies).

Hoang-Ngoc, L., and M. Lallement. (1994). "Décentralisation et relations professionnelles et gestion de l'emploi en France." *Relations industrielles*, 49(3): 441–464.

Lalle, B. (1990). *Pour une nouvelle performance de l'agence bancaire*. Paris: Editions comptables Malsherbes.

Martory, B. (1993). "Les rémunérations." *Cahiers français* no. 262 (July–September): 24–31.

Meignant, A. (1993). *Manager la formation*. Editions Liaisons (2d edition).

Mispelblom, F. (1995). *Au delà de la qualité, démarches qualité, conditions de travail et politique du bonheur*. Paris: Syros.

Morin, F. (1995a). "Le coeur financier français: morphogénèse et mutation." *Marchés et techniques financières (AGEFI)* no. 72 (July–August).

Morin, F. (1995b). "Le capitalisme européen resserre les rangs autour de deux grands pôles." Interview by Martine Orange, *Le Monde*, November 7.

Morin, F. (1997). "La finance européenne en ébullition." *Alternatives économiques* no. 155 (January): 10.

Morin, F., and C. Dupuy. (1993). *Le coeur financier européen*. Economica.

Morin, M.-L. (1994). *Le droit des salariés à la négociation collective, principe général du droit*. Librairie Générale de Droit et Jurisprudence.

Moussy, J.-P. (1997). *L'avenir du système bancaire en France dans le contexte de la monnaie unique*. Conseil Economique et Social.

Moussy, J.-P. (1995). *Les banques françaises, bilan et perpectives*. Syndicat CFDT banques et sociétés financières.

O'Reilly, J. (1992a). "Subcontracting in Banking: Some Evidence from Britain and France." *New Technology, Work and Employment*, 7(2): 107–15.

O'Reilly, J. (1992b). "Comparaison des stratégies d'emploi flexible dans le secteur bancaire en Grande-Bretagne et en France." *Sociologie du travail*, 34(3): 293–313.

Petit, P., and M. Vernières. (1990). "La banque et ses emplois, un service en transition." *Travail et Emploi*, 44(2): 7–18.

Rotschild-Souriac, M.-A. (1986). *Les accords collectifs au niveau de l'entreprise*. Thesis, Paris I.

Vallery, G. (1992). *Travail et concertation sociale dans la conduite d'un projet informatique: le cas de la Caisse d'Epargne de Paris*. Anact.

8

Employment Relations in the Spanish Banking Industry: Big Changes

Faustino Miguélez, Carlos Prieto, and Cecilia Castaño
With the collaboration of
C. Llorens, J. Martí, J. M. Verd,
P. Ferrer, and E. Mora

The Context of Employment Relations

Changes in the Institutional Environment of the Banking Industry in Spain

Structure

The Spanish private banking industry has traditionally been favored by protectionist, interventionist mechanisms. Although there were 163 banks in 1996, their unequal size and the disproportionate market power of the largest of them has given rise to an uncompetitive level of performance. Nonetheless, the acceleration of concentration has coincided with a period of liberalization and Spain's entry into the EU. This has stimulated competition in a market that the Spanish private banks must share with savings and loan institutions and foreign banks (Ontiveros and Valero 1994).

The economical crisis in Spain among 1978 and 1985 had a profound effect on the banking sector (Cuervo 1988), favoring concentration, as 58 small and medium-sized banks were taken over by larger ones and incorporated as second trade names. A process of consolidation in the banking sector, encouraged by the economic authorities with the goal of increasing the average size of the banks in the pursuit of greater efficiency and economies of scale, accompanied Spain's entry into the EU (Ontiveros and Valero 1994). Mergers occurred as a consequence of later crises.

Toward the end of 1996, the five largest Spanish banks had accumulated more than 55 percent of the sector's total assets, and the ten largest controlled nearly 70 percent. The foreign banks, after the elimination of the previous restrictions on competition, continued in their orientation toward serving large commercial clients. All of the above has contributed to the introduction of greater levels of innovation and competitiveness in Spanish financial markets.

The importance of savings and loan institutions[1] in the Spanish financial system is noteworthy and distinguishes it from other countries. They compete seriously with the private banks for dominance in the financial system, because they hold nearly 50 percent of total customer deposits. Accordingly, they have acted as true universal banks for the past ten years and compete for the financing of companies. The private banks, on the other hand, compete with them in their traditional markets of mortgages and consumer lending for families. At the end of 1996, there were 50 savings and loan institutions, and they also had gone through a significant concentration process (in 1988 there were 78) for the same reasons as the banks. Currently, the five largest savings and loan institutions hold more than 45 percent of the total assets of the savings and loans in Spain.

Regulation and Deregulation of Banking
The process of liberalization in Spanish banking is very recent. In 1974 the licensing of new banks, the relaxation of rules governing the opening of new branches, making different types of banks legally equivalent, and the consolidation of their operations, including savings and loan institutions, initiated interbank competition. From 1977, restrictions on the expansion of banking networks were increasingly liberalized. In the absence of freedom to set interest rates, such expansion constituted the retail banks' basic competitive strategy, despite its high economic costs. At the same time, the differences between commercial and merchant banking were eliminated, returning the system to mixed banking and a reduction of specialization. From then on, Spanish banking institutions were general or what we call "universal" banks, a feature that differentiates them from banking institutions in some other countries. It is important to note that they all contend for the whole of the market.

In 1978, in return for the setting up of Spanish banks abroad, foreign banks were allowed to enter the market in Spain, with some restrictions regarding the activities they could carry out, the volume of their capital, the number of their branches, and limitations in the total amount of their deposits. Savings and loan institutions formerly had restrictions when expanding outside of the provinces and regions in which they were headquartered. These were loosened in 1979. In 1987 interest rates and banking commissions were deregulated, making increased competition possible. Also in this year, a timetable for the reduction of required investment was put into effect from 1987 to 1992, and the required reserves coefficient was also reduced.

Starting in 1993, the European Common Market increased levels of competition as a consequence of the loosening of restrictions on the movement of capital and the providing of services. This put an end to the restrictions in the 1978 legislation on the entry of foreign financial institutions in Spain. With all the changes, the European regulations for the construction of a unified banking market were not approved until April 1994, and some regulatory problems remain because the savings and loan institutions are answerable not only to the central government but to regional governments as well.

Relations between Banks and Industry

The Spanish banking industry is a good example of what has been described as the continental model[2] of banking, characterized by the banks' being the main providers of corporate financing in the medium and long term. This is due to an insufficient development of capital markets. The Spanish banking industry has traditionally maintained a very close relationship with the manufacturing industry (Torrero 1989), not only as a shareholder with presence on corporate boards, but also in special engagements of lending capital in critical situations, resulting in the taking of an ownership interest.

In recent years, doubts have been expressed as to the appropriateness of banks' maintaining these close links with the manufacturing industry, because this might entail problems of profitability, even damaging the solvency of financial companies, as occurred during the banking crisis. In consequence, banks have to a certain extent retreated with respect to the manufacturing industry, prompted additionally by European regulations that restrict these types of banking activities (Directive 89 646). The Spanish banking industry has a ten-year period that began January 1, 1993, to satisfy these regulations.

The Competitive Pressures from Market and Technology

Market Competition

Currently, one of the defining characteristics of the Spanish banking industry is the increased competitive pressures (see table 8.1) that have come about as a result of the changes effected in their market, both by deregulatory measures and by the actions of economic agents themselves. One element that has intensified competitive pressures has been the process of disintermediation (Ontiveros and Valero 1994) by which economic agents in need of financing have direct recourse to the saver by

Table 8.1
Financial institutions data (1991–1997)

	Private banks							Savings banks						
	1991	1992	1993	1994	1995	1996	1997	1991	1992	1993	1994	1995	1996	1997
1. Net interest income (p. Average assets)	3.5	3.3	2.8	2.6	2.2	2.0	1.9	3.9	4.0	3.8	3.7	3.5	3.3	3.2
2. Operating costs (p. Average assets)	2.5	2.5	2.3	2.1	2.0	1.9	1.8	2.9	2.9	2.8	2.7	2.6	2.5	2.4
3. Productivity														
Net profit/common equity (percentage)	17.2	12.6	−8.5*	9.1	10.2	10.9	12.1	13.3	14.4	13.7	13.1	14.0	14.2	15.4
Net profit/employee (million pesetas)	3.0	2.5	−1.9*	2.0	3.0	3.0	4.0	2.6	2.7	2.7	2.9	3.3	3.8	4.4
Deposits/employee (million pesetas)	168	178	202*	233	271	291	320	268	289	314	341	370	391	404

* Only private banks.
Source: AEB's Statistical Yearbooks, CECA's Statistical Yearbooks, and authors' elaboration.

issuing securities to attract funds (e.g., the public sector, strained by its need for resources because of a growing public debt, has created new financial instruments such as debentures and treasury bills; private companies, to avoid the high interest rates of bank loans, issue company debentures.) Doubtless, the most important changes from the point of view of competitiveness are those that have originated in the formation of the European Common Market and the requirement that there be free circulation of capital and no restrictions on the provision of services and the setting up of businesses. This will probably result in a drop in the prices for financial services, especially in those countries, like Spain, that have the highest tariffs in the European Union.

Nonetheless, idiosyncratic characteristics of Spain's banking business remain that are far removed from what one would define as perfect competition. A market situation akin to price leadership is maintained (when one of the large banks increases the rate of return on its deposits and reduces its rates on mortgage loans, the other companies feel forced to modify their rates as well). Similarly, an extremely obscure policy governs the charging of commissions and service fees (despite legal regulations, all the banks charge different rates to similar clients, a function of factors unrelated to actual banking considerations) and the larger banks still do not take advantage of this state of affairs to develop competitive strategies based on a clearly set out price policy.

As a result, the customer loyalty that is established with banking institutions does not need to be based only on an evaluation of costs and benefits. Although there has been a significant trend toward the opening of accounts in banks that offer better conditions, this has not been accompanied by a mass desertion of other banks that maintain less attractive conditions. Because most of the time, better conditions are theoretical and a marketing tool, the granting of loans and the provision of other financial services depend largely on an element of trust that is built on personal relationships.

Technological Change and Competitiveness

By the mid-1990s, technological modernization was essentially completed in the banking industry, which has been the main consumer of computer hardware and services in Spain. In general, the attitude toward the introduction of computer-based innovations and strategies was too cautious until ten years ago because of the banking industry's secretive and risk-averse character.

The implementation of information technologies (computers and tele-communications) has taken place in tandem with the liberalization of financial markets and the establishment of higher levels of competitiveness. Technology, acting both as an engine and a tool of the changes in progress, has contributed to the stimulation of competition in the Spanish financial sector and at the same time has helped banks modernize to face more intense competition. Technological innovation has played its role in four basic ways (Castaño 1995):

1. It has allowed banks to reduce the time and costs involved in the majority of activities, increase productivity, improve efficiency, and offer better quality, new services, and a more differentiated product.

2. It has contributed to a restructuring in the utilization of human resources and the network of branch offices: Workers are now more concerned with the commercial activity of attracting deposits and acquiring loans and less occupied with the tasks involving the recording and carrying out of transactions.

3. It has led to greater control of the workforce.

4. It has changed the organization of work (see the discussion of centralization and decentralization below).

The role that technology has played has been different for different sorts of banks. For the private banks (whose network of operations was growing at its fastest rate just before the beginning of computerization), technological modernization has been a tool of reconversion. For the savings and loan institutions the situation was completely different: It has been a tool of innovation, because information technologies were applied in an expansive context and the resulting structure grew taking into account the new technology.

The Range and Types of Market Strategies Adopted by Spanish Banks

The main strategy in operation in the Spanish financial sector to deal with widening competition has been a profound concentration process (Cals and Garrido 1995; Valero 1995) supported by the Spanish administration not only for efficiency reasons (in the hopes of reaching an appropriate scale and a rationalization of the operating network) but also to maintain control of a sector considered to be of strategic importance. In particular, the following strategies have been implemented: mergers and acquisitions within the same banking segment, control or takeover of the firms of one segment by those of another, and the restructuring of publicly owned banks that then became the holding Argentaria (1991, Corporación Bancaria de España), which has become completely private in the last four years.

A second strategy (Cals and Garrido 1995) in the face of increased competition is based on gaining market share in certain segments, such as retail banking, that are considered to be protected against foreign banks. The density of branches in the network of Spanish banks represents a barrier to entry that is difficult for newcomers to overcome because of the significant investments needed to reach a customer base that is extremely spread out geographically.

As for cost reduction strategies, the situation is more complex. Up until now, Spanish banks, despite being relatively small and inefficient, have been highly profitable. From the point of view of size, the Spanish banking system is made up of smaller firms than its European counterparts, has a denser network of branch offices (8.9 outlets per 1,000 residents, as compared to 6.3 in Germany, 4.4 in France, and 3.5 in Italy, Holland, and the United Kingdom) and has a higher number of employees per institution, even though the branches are significantly smaller than elsewhere in Europe in the number of employees (eight employees per branch in Spain on average, as opposed to thirty in Germany and the United Kingdom, twenty-two in France, and fifteen in Holland and Italy). This kind of structure makes for higher operating costs.

Better customer service as well as fairly attractive prices and conditions, however, along with the rise in costs such as computing and telecommunications and the training of personnel, has depressed financial margins. A temporary solution to this situation has been the search for nontraditional sources of income such as the sale of assets.

Cost reduction measures in the larger private banks mainly focus on the reduction of employment by nontraumatic means (early retirement, voluntary redundancy) and on the employment of temporary workers, which is also a selection mechanism for the recruitment of new employees. As well, these banks are attempting to reduce their network of branches in those cases in which, as a result of mergers or acquisitions, they are too close together. Nonetheless, total costs are rising over the whole of the private banking system; variable costs especially are growing, in direct relation to the increase in banking activity, while fixed costs are stable or have a downward tendency.

The fundamental change in relationships with customers when compared to those under the Spanish banking practices of ten years ago is
that, instead of waiting for the customer to arrive to deposit savings or
apply for a loan, banks now actively pursue customers, using marketing
techniques (personal, telephone, and mail) and advertising (the financial
sector ranks fourth in the Spanish market in advertising expenditures,
maintaining a level of spending close to that of the food sector and above
that of beauty products). As well, different strategies are being implemented for different segments of banks' clientele (retirees, young people),
though this is still undeveloped.

As for strategies based on internationalization, even though exchange
controls were eliminated from 1992 onward and Spanish banks have
increased their lending operations abroad, such strategies cannot be considered a priority in Spanish banking (Ontiveros and Valero 1994).

Major Changes in Labor Market Regulation and in the Labor Supply in Spain

Increasing Labor Market Flexibility

The Spanish labor market has the highest rate of unemployment of those
in all the countries of the European Union. It also has labor laws that,
since 1984, have significantly liberalized the established forms of hiring.
Therefore, Spanish companies in general have made their hiring policies
(diversification of contractual status) the focal point of their human
resources policies (Prieto 1991).[3] The same cannot be said of the banking
sector.

The workforce hired during the employment boom in Spanish banking
(the second half of the 1970s) had low levels of education and indefinite
full-time contracts. Now that, in the context of massive unemployment
and a liberalized labor market, banks want to reduce their workforce and
take advantage of the potential highly skilled workforce available at a
low salary, they have found that dismissals are problematic and costly,
because voluntary redundancy is close to nonexistent and labor unions
are strong and disputatious. This could be why the unemployment rates
in the Spanish banking industry are not significant.

New hiring is rare in large traditional banks but higher in firms in
expansion, and it is always highly selective. Preference is usually given to
young people, highly trained, preferably with university degrees, who
have considerable potential and absolute adaptability (including geo-

graphical mobility). Although they are usually hired for lower-level jobs,[4] the objective is moving them into positions of higher responsibility after they have been involved in the firm's culture. Career training is especially oriented to them. Their initial labor contract is always temporary, previously *Fomento del Empleo* (promotion of employment), after the 1994 labor reform *de Aprendizaje* (of apprenticeship),[5] but the majority of the new hires end up being permanent (Martín Artiles, Miguélez, and Pastor 1994). This hiring policy means that the percentage of temporary contracts is much lower in the banking sector (around 10 percent, including those hired on a temporary basis for specific needs) than in the private sector as a whole (33.6 percent in 1997).

We can explain this situation by pointing out that Spanish financial firms' hiring policies (policies for differentiating personnel in various contractual situations) are not a key part of their strategy of efficiently allocating labor. This does not mean that the general situation in the Spanish labor market over the past ten years, with its high unemployment rate, is not a framework from which the banks develop their strategies, but rather that banking employers are strengthened by the situation, just as the employees and their unions feel, on the contrary, weakened.

Employment Structure

In the second half of the 1970s, bank employment grew significantly, but from the beginning of the 1980s onward it has been falling. This overall reduction masks two extremely important trends: a process of feminization and a process of rejuvenation of the workforce. The number of women in the workforce is growing while the number of men is falling (see table 8.2), but what is taking place is not simple substitution; women generally move into lower-skill positions that are more poorly paid (Castaño 1986) and more insecure (Carrasquer and Varella 1994) than the ones held by men. Furthermore, as stated above, individuals who have difficulty adapting to the new ways of working that their firm demands are being retired early, and in their place, younger, better trained workers more willing to take on the challenges of flexibility, versatility and ongoing education at a lower salary are being hired. These two characteristics constitute the most radical changes in traditional banking.

Another aspect of great importance is related to shifts in occupational structure (see table 8.3). Although the job classifications for banks and for savings and loan institutions vary, two common features emerge strongly: an increase at higher levels (middle management and specialized workers)

Table 8.2
Evolution of employees and banking offices network (1979–1996)

Year	Number of employees	Growth (1979 = 100)	Percentage female	Number of offices	Growth (1979 = 100)	Employees per office	Growth (1979 = 100)
1979	179,382	100.00	12.56%	12,235	100.00	14.66	100.00
1980	180,274	100.50	12.72%	13,223	108.08	13.63	92.99
1981	177,230	98.80	12.83%	14,290	116.80	12.40	84.59
1982	175,757	97.98	13.02%	15,374	125.66	11.43	77.97
1983	172,580	96.21	12.88%	16,064	131.30	10.74	73.28
1984	168,888	94.15	13.13%	16,399	134.03	10.30	70.24
1985	163,591	91.20	13.44%	16,568	135.41	9.87	67.35
1986	159,342	88.83	14.03%	16,471	134.62	9.67	65.98
1987	156,986	87.51	14.53%	16,449	134.44	9.54	65.09
1988	156,484	87.24	15.22%	16,651	136.09	9.40	64.10
1989	157,056	87.55	16.49%	16,623	135.86	9.45	64.44
1990	158,160	88.17	17.85%	16,835	137.60	9.39	64.08
1991	159,101	88.69	18.90%	17,923	140.93	8.87	62.93
1992	152,025	84.75	19.75%	18,154	142.28	8.37	59.57
1993	153,638	85.65	21.02%	17,713	144.77	8.67	59.14
1994	150,624	83.97	21.89%	17,405	142.25	8.65	59.00
1995	147,452	82.20	22.80%	17,841	145.82	8.26	56.34
1996	141,640	78.96	23.95%	17,657	144.31	8.02	54.70

Source: Anuario Estadístico de la Banca en España.

Table 8.3
Distribution of employees by categories in Spanish banking industry

	1980	1985	1990	1992	1994	1996
Heads/graduates	30.24%	37.55%	45.99%	49.76%	51.16%	55.14%
Clerical staff	55.37	52.45	51.62	48.34	48.53	42.48
Auxiliary and others	14.39	10.00	2.39	1.90	0.31	2.38

Source: Anuario Estadístico de la Banca en España.

of training and responsibility, and a relative drop in both areas in lower levels (clerical work, assistants, etc.) of the workforce. Age differences do not seem so relevant here, because frequently young graduates in economics, management, or law move into the higher segment after a sufficient time in their career within the firm enables them to identify with the objectives of the company, as we were able to confirm in various interviews. On the other hand, however, differences in gender are relevant, for much of the recent hiring of women has been to cover positions in the lower segment, sometimes left vacant by men who have been promoted. Gender differences are not so much a matter of differences in hiring but rather differences in career track (Carrasquer and Varella 1994) in which women encounter specific sociocultural barriers or male chauvinist opposition, as men block certain promotions of women.

Temporary employment, early retirement, and voluntary redundancy have significantly reduced the average level of seniority of bank workers. Seniority was traditionally such a fundamental issue that it was practically the sole basis for promotion along the career track.

In summary, the new trends in bank employment make for three features that differentiate it from what it was like fifteen or twenty years ago: more women, more young people, less security. Doubtless, these factors are the bases for making bank employment less costly and more adaptable to the goals of firms.

Relevant Changes in Skill and Educational Levels
Educational levels of the Spanish population are still low, especially among the middle-aged, because of the low importance placed on education during the Franco era. The political changes during the early 1980s allowed greater educational opportunities, and educational levels have increased substantially in all professional categories and industries.

We have no official statistics on educational levels of those employed in the banking sector. On the basis of various studies as well as bank reports we can deduce that the sector has two distinguishing features (Grup d'Estudis Sociològics sobre la Vida Quotidiana i el Treball 1993): The average levels of education among employees in the banking sector are higher than those of the overall workforce; and over recent years, the proportion of workers entering the banking sector with high levels of education has risen (or, put another way, education is acquired subsequent to employment).

Among the banks we have studied, we can affirm that in the most innovative cases, practically a third of the personnel had some higher education, whereas only 20 percent had just the EGB (general basic education). Considering the high correlation between age and educational level as well as current staff policies, within a few short years, half the workforce in the banking sector can be expected to have some higher studies.

The average level of education in the industry is a sound basis for implementing policies of ongoing education as well as the development of new flexible and multifaceted careers (Villarejo 1990).

Changes in the Regulation of Industrial Relations
The most striking feature of industrial relations in the Spanish banking industry is the lack of equivalence between actors at the sector and the firm level, and consequently between the comprehensiveness of regulation at these two levels. At the industry level, the relationship is between the banking sector's employers' organizations (the Asociación Española de Banca and Asociación Española de Cajas de Ahorro) and the general labor unions. In the case of the former, their representation of the firms is never at issue, since there are no competing employers' organizations. Things are much more complicated in the case of the other party, the unions, whose right to represent is verified every four years via an electoral process that chooses worker delegates, from which the "most representative" unions emerge, that is, those which have bargaining power.

The majority of the unions in the sector are general unions, whether at the state level (CCOO, UGT, USO, CGT) or at the regional level (ELA/STV in Euskadi and CIG in Galicia) (see table 8.4). However, there are also sector-specific unions: CC (which also represents other industries and is oriented toward specialist and professional labor), FITC, and AMI.[6] Because the process through which an organization passes to be part of the collective bargaining is full of territorial filters, CCOO and UGT hold the vast majority of the union members (91 percent in the last general wages agreement in banking and 71 percent in the last collective negotia-

Table 8.4
Elections for workers' representation in the banking industry: Results

Year	CCOO	UGT	FITC	CC	CGT	CIG	ELA	Others
1982	26.8%	31.3%	16.7%	1.9%	0.2%	0.8%	2.3%	20.0%
1986	33.2	27.8	15.7	4.6	4.3	2.3	2.3	9.8
1990	37.8	30.1	8.5	5.8	6.8	2.4	2.1	12.4
1994	38.5	23.6	10.9	6.3	7.1	2.5	2.4	8.8

Source: Ministerio de Trabajo y Seguridad Social.
Legend: CCOO: Comisiones Obreras (Workers' Comissions); UGT: Unión General de Trabajadores (General Workers' Union); FITC: Federación Independiente de Trabajadores de Crédito (Loan Workers' Independent Federation); CC: Confederación de Cuadros (Intermediate Management Confederation); CGT: Confederación General del Trabajo (Work General Confederation); CIG: Confederación Intersindical Gallega (Galician Interunion Confederation); ELA-STV: Sindiato de Trabajadores Vascos (Basque Workers' Union).

tions in the savings and loan institutions), which makes them de facto the only negotiators. This dominance reflects that of collective bargaining in Spain in general (Miguélez and Prieto 1991).

Union strategy in the industry has traditionally followed two basic lines: to achieve wage increases and to reduce and reorganize the workday to obtain a workweek comparable to those in other sectors (i.e., Saturday free). The recent regulatory changes in the job market have pointed out the importance of other union objectives, such as job security and education and training, and also the rejection of geographical mobility and wage flexibility. Both traditional goals and newer ones have been put into practice differently according to the features of various firms and the unions themselves.

At firm level, there is a far greater number of unions and no equivalence or relations with unions at the industrial level, and management has little contact with the employers' organization when it comes to many of the basic issues of collective bargaining and human resources. Individual firms completely control the forms of remuneration or work organization. Firms see human resources issues as strategic, and in that sense, a ground on which to compete. Thus policies are not communicated to competitors through the employers' organization (Miguélez and Llorens 1994). The relationship between unions at the industry level and unions at the firm level may be problematic, since they are not always the same ones. This renders it more difficult to come to an agreement, although in fact efforts are made to reach an agreement that sometimes succeed. The gap between the employers' organization and the individual firms is more difficult to bridge.

Change and Variations in Employment Relations: National Trends and Evidence from Case Studies

Change in the Banks' Employment Practices

In spite of common shifts in the financial sector, as is shown in the study carried out by O. Bertrand and T. Noyello,[7] international differences in human resources policies originate in the existence of social institutions specific to each country, such as "industrial relations, labour market, and educational systems" (OCDE 1990: 21) and even the idiosyncrasies of individual firms.[8]

An Organization for Catching Clients

If products, however innovative they may be, end up in the short run being common to all the banks, and if financial margins are essentially uniform, banking competition can only focus its business strategy on attracting and retaining its customer base. The central role in attracting and retaining clients falls on the employees themselves, but this role is only possible if the prerequisite organizational conditions are met. Over the past few years, Spanish banks have therefore undertaken a profound process of structural reorganization.

In those firms that are currently undergoing rapid quantitative as well as qualitative expansion, as is the case with firms B and C, reorganization has occurred above all to bring the bank closer to its current and potential customers, that is, by expanding its network of branches and outlets. This is in marked contrast to larger, more traditional firms, which expanded their network of outlets by a factor of more than two and a half from the mid-1970s to the mid-1980s, to the point of covering the entire territory.

The second key to reorganization is the clear specialized segmentation of the banking business depending on the different kinds of customers. Thus in addition to the traditional distinction between retail banking, which mainly served individuals and PYMES (small to medium-sized businesses), and commercial banking, which served large enterprises, has been added private money management, which sees to the management of the financial interests of large fortunes, institutional banking, which is oriented toward public and semipublic entities as well as treasury and capital markets (securities transactions, futures, derivatives, and currency trading). Furthermore, traditional banking activity now more clearly distinguishes individuals from PYMES. Sometimes, each one of these business segments is organized and administered in an independent manner, in all its components.

This does not mean that all these differentiated segments receive the same strategic attention on the part of the banks. Institutional and treasury are merely "emerging" businesses, and the main focus is still on the traditional business segments, that is, individuals, PYMES, and large enterprises, the segments with which the banks are most familiar.

The differentiation in banking activity in various segments goes beyond forming them into separate divisions with separate accounting of profits. The common policy in most institutions is to convert all the units that manage loans and deposits into independent profit centers. However, this does not amount to decentralization in the strictest sense, because it is no more than a dispersal of management responsibilities and of the reporting of results. Decision making has probably never been more centralized,[9] a process that is favored by computerization. In fact, headquarters have been reduced and specialized in the design of business and human management strategies and in the setting of criteria and rules.

Some activities are being subcontracted, particularly those not related to finances themselves, such as security, deliveries, cleaning, or gardening. Firm B is leading a deeper decentralization in this sense, subcontracting technical experts such as lawyers, computer programmers, or teachers. In any case, these subcontracted companies are offering services in a centralized way, for the whole of the firm.

The policy of attracting and retaining customers has also led to a profound change in Spanish banks related to the division of labor in the branches: These were previously only of a clerical nature and were quasibureaucracies; now commercial activities and tasks clearly dominate. This dominance means not only that these activities have become relatively more important, to the extent of taking up the largest amount of working hours within each bank branch, but also that they have penetrated into the clerical activities themselves. This penetration takes two forms. In the smaller banks the newer branches tend to be smaller, and all the branches of firm B are small. All the employees (two clerical and two middle management) do practically the same sort of work, although distinct levels of responsibility and a constant concern with commercial activities characterizes the work. The employees are multiskilled and play multiple roles (Rodríguez Fernández 1994). Large branches maintain a clear division of labor between marketing and clerical activities (particularly in firms A_1 and A_2). Nonetheless, sales activity takes place alongside clerical work, as shown by the information offering the firm's various financial products to the customers being attended to.

Computerization plays a central role in the reorganization of the content and the division of work in the branches. Needless to say, computerization via distributed processing has become an omnipresent tool in sales and customer service with a wide installation of expert systems, just as it has in clerical activities, to the point that it has completely modified clerical work.

All in all these changes are leading to the elimination of workers' specialization in certain tasks and is promoting the multiskilling and expansion of role tasks of all the staff, who are expected to understand the full range of financial activities—which grows wider everyday. Furthermore, employers want to eliminate professional categories in the collective agreement.

Changes to Working Time

A new organizational structure designed in terms of its ability to attract and retain customers cannot avoid the problem of work time arrangements. This situates us in a very different dynamic from that of the organization of labor discussed above. The union representatives of bank workers have not made the organization of labor and its content a priority. Thus the management of banks has been able to act in this field as they have seen fit.[10] The same does not hold for working hours, an issue that has been the object of fierce union pressures.

In principle, collective bargaining establishes the length of the workday and its scheduling. However, the way the work of those employees considered technical experts (business agents) and especially branch directors[11] is designed makes it difficult to impose a rigid time structure on their daily activities; they are to achieve, either on their own or as leaders of the unit they run, certain objectives that are previously assessed and set out by the firm (on the basis of which, as we shall see, they are to be paid). Thus within such conditions, the majority of these employees work far more hours than set out in the collective bargaining norms. Directors and specialists are not a minority in the professional structure and hierarchy of the Spanish banking system; they represent more than 50 percent of the total number of employees.

The lower-level employees, as a rule, follow the work schedule established by collective bargaining. On the other hand, in each branch, the workload in principle fills up the employees' entire day, and all the banks both know and apply techniques of measurement and distribution of workload to occupy the entire working day for each employee. As a result, work has become more intensive.

In this framework of rules, when the usual workload increases, the response in most countries is to hire extra workers on a part-time basis (OCDE 1990). In Spain, however, this practice is much less frequent than in the rest of the European countries, and it is even less so in the banking sector, to such an extent that it could be considered nonexistent. (One bank offered us the figure of 0.2 percent.)

With this route closed, there would only seem to be one solution, which is the one Spanish banks use: intensification of work and a slight increase of a quarter or half hour in the usual workday, which is not accounted. If in some extraordinary circumstances, the workday is lengthened by several hours, employees can accumulate these added hours until they can be compensated with entire days off. However, since the entire day is filled up, there is no time left to compensate them, so this uncompensated overtime becomes important for a possible promotion, as it is considered a sign of commitment. Moreover, when branches are small, trade unions have minimal possibilities of control, so most of the time, directors are not the only ones who daily expand their working day, since all of the staff in branches are becoming coresponsible for the daily work in their own units. Moreover, training and quality circles—in recession—are taking place within this already lengthened workday.

In this way, the banks achieve work schedule flexibility among lower-level employees while still officially complying with the established workday schedule. This intensification of work and the lengthening of the workday do, however, create a certain amount of tension among employees whom the branch has no means of compensating for their extra time and effort.

Training, Skill Formation, and Career Development Policies

New skills and knowledge are indispensable, and they are little more than prerequisites for the real task: getting the customers who arrive at the bank to become loyal customers, and getting those who already are to increase their commitment to the firm. This means that the new banking sector employees must above all have a set of interpersonal skills that has as much to do with attitude as aptitude (the "ability to explain, negotiate, and convince," OCDE 1990: 83), in addition to company culture.

If one takes into account the drastic change that these new skill requirements imply when compared with those demanded in the previous situation, as well as the fact that the majority of employees are still the same as ten years ago (although on this point, there is a significant difference between firms A_1 and A_2, on the one hand, and firms B and C on the other), that the professional skills in banking are sector specific, and finally that in Spain there is no public apprenticeship system, one can understand why, according to one manager interviewed, internal training has become the banking industry's basic strategic tool of human resources policy. In a short period, expenditures on training have risen from approximately 1 percent to around 3 percent of the total payroll expenditures of the banks studied.[12]

Training unfolds in various directions with various implications that originate in the relationship of two variables, each of which has two dimensions, as the following table shows:

Types of training

Initiative Objective	From the firm	From the worker
Updating	1	2
For the career	3	4

On its own express and direct initiative, the firm conducts two types of training: that oriented toward all employees, which is offered partly by the demands of the unions, as a path toward job security and promotion and has as its object an updating of knowledge and skills vital to carrying out tasks and duties (area 1 of the table) and that directed toward employees whom the firm believes to have a greater potential to carry out sales and customer service activities or to manage other people (area 3).[13]

Training on the initiative of the employees themselves has a special feature: The bank for which they work both encourages and facilitates such training. For training meant to bring workers' skills up to date (area 2) the employees usually have, on their computer screen, a menu of courses offered by the firm, and this is even the case with the local bank-programmed courses designed to be followed individually on the office computer or even on the worker's own PC. Career training on the initiative of the employees (area 4) is the least common and appears to occur almost exclusively when those demonstrating a high degree of commitment are conscious of belonging to the group of employees in their bank who have real career possibilities (upward mobility).

Compensation Levels and Structure: A Pay Policy in Deep Change
Little more than four or five years ago, except for a few positions with special responsibilities, the industry's collective wage agreement (firms A_1, A_2, and C) or the firm's agreement, which improved on the wages determined by collective bargaining (firm B) controlled the pay policy in financial firms. The basic pay in each one of the approximately twenty job categories was improved by bonuses and benefits of various types in which seniority played a key role. Seniority was based on periods of three years. For a worker with eight such periods (twenty-four years), a fairly common situation in various firms (A_1, A_2), the seniority bonus could represent almost 25 percent of his or her base salary.

Because of both the wages themselves and the additional benefits, the salary average in the financial sector is far higher than the national one. According to the salary poll in 1996, the average salary in the financial sector was 1.62 times higher than the average in the overall economy. Whereas the average level of salaries is already high in the financial sector, it is even higher in savings and loan institutions because of pacts in specific firms. In firm B, it is almost double the rest of the banks studied.

Because labor costs constitute a large portion of any bank's overall transaction costs, all banks have implemented a policy intended to reduce labor costs, specifically by nontraumatic means: negotiating agreements with wage increases that do not keep up with the consumer price index, reducing that part of the workforce with more seniority, because it represents a proportionally high cost and hiring new personnel with temporary labor contracts (mainly on a training basis) at low salaries.

At the same time, banks have introduced performance-based variable compensation with the goal of stimulating work effort using payment levels that are always higher than those established in collective bargaining. At the moment, this new mode of compensation affects only management and certain technical experts in the sales and customer service field; therefore, the wage scale has grown in the last years. Only firm A_1 has generalized it to all the workers in the branches, but even there it still represents only a small percentage of clerical workers' salaries. Nevertheless, as we will see later, it is all showing a new trend toward the individualization of wages.

All the financial firms complement the current pay policy with a set of fringe benefits of various types that originate in old paternalistic practices, which collective bargaining at the firm level has reinforced and given a more modern character. Among these are benefits such as cheap home loans, life insurance, school loans, vacation homes, company stores, and similar offerings.

Change in Firm Governance and in Labor Relations in Banks

Interest Representation and Labor Relations: An Unbalanced Entente

Different objectives guide management and unions in their reciprocal relations. Unions want to maintain, as much as possible, regulations governing both the access to work and changes in work conditions. Further, they want regulation to be set by norms. For them, this is crucial to safeguarding against a management strategy that seeks increasingly to transform the work conditions and the professions of its workers. On the other hand, management, when interviewed, imply that the prevailing hiring codes and industrial relations in general are too rigid. Their goal is to deregulate and diversify as much as possible, so that the firm can decide things according to the changing situation in the industry.

In relation to union activity at the firm level, one highly significant phenomenon differentiates banking from any other industry: the respective roles of the workers' committee and the unions.

In the Spanish system, according to the Estatuto de los Trabajadores (Workers' Charter), workers' committees are the site of workers' representation as a whole in the company. Workers elect their members directly, and they carry the entire responsibility of labor relations within the firm.[14] But in the banking industry, this same role is played directly by the unions as a result of agreements between firms and unions. The reason for this lies in the structure of firms that in each case must have some hundreds and even thousands of establishments represented by committees of different nature (from 20 to 40 committees total). This number of committees makes coordination among them difficult and also, in practice, could break the coherence of the firm's human resources policies.

This has given the unions a leading role at company level that they do not have in other industries, either in collective bargaining or agreements within individual firms, which could be a key reason why unions in banking firms maintain an exceptionally high membership rate (on average, around 50 percent, a bit more in savings banks and a bit less in private banks) as compared to the Spanish average (no more than 20 percent).

However, unions in the banking industry are more capable of establishing a general bargaining agreement favorable in terms of wages or work conditions (work hours, vacations, health and safety, training, promotion) than of influencing the concrete work arrangements in the workplace itself. The reasons lie in the size of branches, which have only between four and eight employees, and in the lack of channels for unions to maintain contact with such a dispersed workforce, which involves great problems in achieving a unionized structure.

The forms of collective participation can be characterized as an interchange, but absolutely not one of joint management, using the terminology of Regini (1991), even though in the savings and loan institutions, via existing rules, unions participate on the board of directors, and in the majority of banking firms they often participate on various joint committees: the health and safety committee (obligatory by law), the training committee, and the committee on company policy. Formally there is very little difference in this as compared to the overall Spanish labor market (Grup d'Estudis Sociològics sobre la Vida Quotidiana i el Treball 1993; Rebollo, Martín, and Miguélez 1991).

If we look into the dynamics of the aforementioned committees, we find that their supposed joint nature hardly exists; rather, the firms unilaterally impose most of their policies. So collective participation can be characterised as nil, or by saying that it simply consists of consent. On the one hand, firms firmly obstruct union participation in work organization, because their goal is restricting decision making on the maximum range of subjects to top management. On the other hand, unions mistrust any participation policy coming from top management. All in all, this leads us to describe labor relations more in terms of cooperation than conflict when referring to the concrete framework of the firms.

Forms of Employee Involvement: Professionalization and Individualization

Prior to the 1980s the basis for the productive mobilization of the workforce was the legitimacy of the rules agreed to through collective bargaining. Membership in a concrete professional category, among the twenty-one such categories defined, implied both certain duties (above all, that of carrying out the exact work stipulated) and certain rights (above all, that of receiving the exact compensation stipulated).

At present the general wages agreement has insufficient stipulations from the management viewpoint, though this does not mean that they have fallen into complete disuse. Banks can attract and keep customers only if the workers are committed to this goal. Firms endeavor to turn productive mobilization of the workforce into self-mobilization individual involvement.

Those first affected by the new type of productive mobilization are employees whose responsibilities are directly commercial (business agents) and those whose responsibilities are managerial. The tool intended to motivate them in their work is performance-based individual compensation, whether based on individual performance, in the case of the former group, or the performance of the branch office, in the case of the latter. Under this compensation system, the general wages agreement plays no more than a secondary role. All the firms studied have already implemented this system of compensation for technical experts and managers. The unions have done nothing or have been able to do nothing to prevent this or even to exercise any control over it.

The new pay policy nevertheless has perverse effects. Those it governs evidently do work harder, and their performance improves. However, the branch personnel who are not subject to variable compensation point out that these results are not obtained without their own effort. Most employees state that their workload has increased, though only the managers stand to gain. Many of those interviewed have expressed unrest over this (Recuero, Ramos, and Carpio 1995), and all the more so when the resulting wage difference is higher.

The firms intend to expand this form of individualized compensation as much as possible, but they must consider the unions' response, as the clerical categories are the unions' turf. One of the three banks in our study has already implemented the system for all its office employees, after an agreement negotiated with the unions. The others intend to implement it in the near future.

Individualized variable compensation has several limitations. The most important is that it will end up significantly increasing labor costs, because the variable part is added to the base salary arrived at by collective bargaining (firms A_1, A_2, and C) or to the even higher established wages arrived at separately at the firm level (firm B).[15] Thus on the one hand, in order for variable compensation to be extended to all the employees, it must be at a very limited cost (as it is in firm A_1), and on the other hand, in working toward their objective of generating worker involvement, the firms should use other methods.

Taking into account that the vast majority of the workforce works in a small workplace (the branch offices), the policy of worker involvement should go through the branch offices. This is possible via a relative decentralization of human resources management and an effort to foster teamwork. A quasi-informal network of personal interchange develops between managers and subordinates that allows the former to request and obtain effort from the latter that goes beyond what is strictly defined. Furthermore, that the unions lack a significant presence at the branch level encourages this type of relationship.

Teamwork extends from the joint responsibility of the branch's entire staff for the results obtained, made possible by the workers' diverse practical skills of the workers (firm B), to what is no more than a spirit of collaboration among employees at the same level (firms A_1, A_2, and C).

Management interviewed tended to take for granted the aforementioned autonomy within the branches, because almost by definition, the work carried out in a small branch is closely interrelated and requires that all its employees be multiskilled; thus workers rotate and switch between tasks a great deal. However, once we look into this analysis of teamwork, we realize that the branch manager strongly monopolizes its direction. There is no real balance between the various members in the decisions made in the branches, and in reality branch managers have no autonomous decision-making power with reference to the policies set by the firm's central administration.

The hierarchical nature of the relationship between the manager and the rest of the branch staff is critical because, as we mentioned above, the manager's evaluations determine promotion, training, and variable compensation. With such a hierarchical relationship, worker commitment, involvement, and participation is necessarily tinged with personal loyalties and impositions.

Another way of trying to involve employees combines what we could call professionalization (especially in sales and marketing activities) and promotion. Professionalization on its own, that is, knowledge alone, is insufficient to trace out an upwardly mobile career path: One must also use this professionalization to show positive results, that one attracts customers or is building customer loyalty. One must also demonstrate that one is not content with the skills acquired but rather wants to improve on them in an ongoing fashion via training.

The importance of new forms of productive mobilization of the workforce described above has granted human resources management policies a much more important place in banks than they have held traditionally, even more important than in other types of firms, as can be deduced from the influential position that human resources managers have acquired in the overall bank management (Carrasquer, Coller, and Miguélez 1991).

Nevertheless, one must not think that new human resources management policies alone can explain the increase in employee involvement. One must always take into consideration that productive bank activity is a service and therefore involves a direct relationship between the worker and a customer. Furthermore, the new human resources policies exist within a general setting of massive unemployment, in which having and keeping a job, especially a good job, is a true privilege worth hanging on to at whatever cost.

Conclusions: Change and Diversity in the Spanish Banking Industry

The changes that have taken place in the Spanish banking industry in recent years, particularly in terms of human resources management and labor relations, have moved quickly, but probably have still not covered enough ground. For these reasons, the slight current differences among banks could increase significantly in the near future. The mechanism for such differentiation may be individualization, which is, as we have seen, already significant in human resources management. But it may also be collective bargaining at the firm level or the combination of both.

Making Sense of Intrasectoral Variations in Employment Relations

As has been stated thoughout the chapter, changes in the banking industry have followed similar patterns in the four institutions that we analyzed. Nevertheless, differences can be found among firms, originating mainly because of their size and trajectory in the market.

One of the points on which firms clearly differ is the composition of the workforce and its organization. In the traditional large institutions (firms A_1 and A_2) we find differences in the size of the branches, which are bigger than those in smaller institutions; and in the profile of the employees, who are older and have lower educational levels and wider seniority. In the innovative large institution (firm B), branches are smaller (from three to six employees) and directors play a certain role in the management of the workforce, which is younger and more highly skilled. The medium-sized financial institution (firm C), where the management is also relatively young, shares this latter characteristic.

Seniority of the workforce can partly explain the presence and strength of trade unions in the traditional large institutions, given that trade union culture is stronger among more experienced workers and that this culture is easier to maintain in big branches as well. In firms A_1 and A_2, trade unions have not only a high membership rate but also strong bargaining power. Cooperation is the trend, because trade unions and management both seem to exert an influence over employees. In firm B, employee representatives in a trade union with a solid institutional presence and high membership rate have considerable power in relation to salary conditions and timetable at the firm level but a very weak influence when it comes to human resources policies. Finally, in firm C, trade unions with a low membership rate play a minimal role, making suggestions rather than bargaining.

The tendency in the banking industry toward a human resources policy differentiated by segments of the workforce has different nuances depending on the firm involved. In firms A_1 and A_2, diversity in terms of salary variations affects both the first and second segments of employment. Employees' commitment is based on a relation between unions and firms that could qualify as cooperation as well as on a broad social policy (education, loans, holidays) tinged with a certain paternalism that is deeper than in other institutions. In firm B, human resources policy is becoming individualized, stressing promotion and, for the first segment of employment, incentive schemes. However, salaries are higher in firm B than the industry average for all job categories. Finally, the most significant feature in this area in firm C is the strong power of intermediate territorial and central structures, which have persuasively spread the enterprise culture. In firm C, the first group of employees has a performance-based salary, whereas the second group has had little compensation for their increased effort or involvement.

This differential treatment of the first and second segments in firms' human resources policy has not as yet created profound cleavages among the workforce, though progressively a group of workers belonging to the second segment—mainly young, female workers hired after the reform of labor contracts—is being hired with significantly poorer conditions than their counterparts of the same segment hired before the reform.

Market and Institutions as Factors of Change

Product Markets: Services Offered

The first step by which banks have sought to improve their competitiveness is in cost reduction. Great organizational changes wrought for this purpose have had significant repercussions on the organization of work itself. But above all, they have emphasized the containment of labor costs, which had increased very significantly in the 1970s. Not only staff reductions but also the ways in which new hiring is done and even variable compensation itself function to reduce these costs.

The adaptation of banking products to customers has become another avenue for greater competitiveness. Differentiation between firms and individuals and differentiated segments within both groups are increasingly consolidated as specific nuclei on which bank policies focus. Campaigns for young people or old people, those relating to small business or farmers, the rapid growth of home-based telephone banking, the offering of a multitude of services for consumption (trading stocks and bonds) and leisure (packaged holidays) are examples. The banking market seems to be heading toward unlimited diversification and in this, human resources play a key role, because they make diversification possible.

The Labor Market: The Type of Human Resources

Greater market penetration and cost reduction have meant overcoming a level of human resources utilization that some years ago was deemed bureaucratic to move to a level that is clearly professional. The goal is for the workforce to take a step toward quality performance, which is much more active, guided by a certain capacity for autonomy at least for a good part of the employees, middle management, and specialized workers in carrying out their work.

However, there are obstacles of various types. Some relate to employees' low educational level, which banks have addressed by hiring employees with higher qualifications and eliminating the older, generally less qualified workforce, and with ongoing training. The results of the first aspect of the policy will be slow in coming and, for now, uncertain, because although the newer employees have more education, they also have little experience in banking.

Other obstacles have to do with upper management, in particular mistrust. Management is fearful of losing authority in the organization of work, which is why direct participation is so undeveloped, and in the general management of its own human resources. This leads managers to maintain strong attitudes of control, at times demanding loyalty above the normal requirements of professional behavior. A third type of obstacle springs from distrust of management on the part of the workers' representatives, in particular the large general unions, which leads them to believe more in regulated agreements than dynamic ones.

These obstacles are probably why certain mechanisms of change in human resources have been emphasized at the expense of others. For example, training, promotion, and motivation via individual compensation have all been emphasized, whereas changes in the organization of work or union participation have been rare.

As to the consequences of human resources policy, it is worth focusing on the employment segmentation taking place. In the overall banking workforce, two large segments are emerging: on the one hand, middle management and specialized workers, and on the other, clerical workers and assistants. The former tend to be better paid, with better possibilities for promotion and greater incentives of both the professional and financial types. In general, they are men, with a growing number of highly educated young people in their ranks. Their bargaining capacity seems to be individual, either unattached to unions or attached to staff associations. The latter group is more poorly paid and less motivated, either by professional or financial rewards. These are individuals at a lower educational level, largely women and middle-aged or older men. In general their bargaining capacity is collective, and they have a high rate of union membership.

Within this perspective, the tendency of the firms may be, as some signs indicate, to concentrate their innovation in human resources policy among the first segment, leaving the second in the traditional framework of labor relations. This would mean that certain issues, especially those affecting the second segment, are negotiated with unions; as for the others, a more individualized approach prevails, with which management seeks to motivate workers while still preserving their authority and control over them.

This two-pronged policy has the potential danger of rendering labor disputes more likely in one part of the workforce, and this would eventually have its effects on the rest, even though disputes have been rare in recent years. It may also make it difficult to generate commitment on the part of the first segment if there is no way for them to achieve greater autonomy in their work. At the moment, high salaries and good working conditions work against the first possibility, but the second is becoming more plausible. Nevertheless, because the banking industry is in a process of deep change, the features discussed could alter significantly in a short period of time.

Appendix: Information about the Financial Institutions Studied

Bank A_1:
Large traditional institution
Ranking position by common equity (1996): 3.
Employment and branch offices*

	1980	1985	1993	1996
$A_1(a)$** employment	18,697	15,675	—	—
$A_1(b)$ employment	19,655	18,956	—	—
Total employment	38,352	34,631	26,231	21,231
Offices***	2,981	3,470	2,780	2,574
Employees per office	12.9	10.0	9.4	8.5

* There was an amalgamation of two banks in 1991.
** (a) and (b) show figures for institutions before their amalgamation.
*** Sum of offices from $A_1(a)$ and $A_1(b)$.

Bank A_2:
Large traditional institution
Ranking position by common equity (1996): 1.
Employment and branch offices*

	1980	1985	1993	1996
$A_2(a)$** employment	17,371	16,169	—	—
$A_2(b)$ employment	10,562	8,992	—	—
Total employment	27,933	25,161	20,468	20,205
Offices***	1,984	2,377	1,934	2,168
Employees per office	14.1	10.6	10.6	9.3

* There was an amalgamation of two banks in 1989.
** (a) and (b) show figures for institutions before their amalgamation.
*** Sum of offices from $A_2(a)$ and $A_2(b)$.

Bank B:
Large innovative institution
Ranking position by common equity (1996): 2.
Employment and branch offices*

	1980	1985	1993	1996
$B(a)$** employment	5,640	6,389	—	—
$B(b)$ employment	2,708	2,936	—	—
Total employment	8,348	9,325	12,079	15,248
Offices***	971	1,419	2,362	3,343
Employees per office	8.6	6.6	5.1	4.6

* There was an amalgamation of two banks in 1990.
** (a) and (b) show figures for institutions before their amalgamation.
*** Sum of offices from $B(a)$ and $B(b)$.

Bank C:
Medium-sized institution
Ranking position by common equity (1996): 10.
Employment and branch offices

	1980	1985	1993	1996
Employees	2,502	2,851	4,611	4,931
Offices	125	193	359	425
Employees per office	20.0	14.8	12.8	11.6

Sources: AEB, Statistical Yearbooks; CECA, Statistical Yearbooks; and authors' elaboration.

Numbers of people interviewed

	Sector level	A₁ Traditional large bank	A₂ Traditional large bank	B Innovative large bank	C Medium bank	Total
Heads of human resources management department	—	5	2	5	3	15
Regional management	—	—	—	1	1	2
Union representatives	1	5	4	6	5	21
Branch offices directors	—	1	—	3	3	7
Workers	—	9	8	5	2	24
Total	1	20	14	20	14	69

Notes

1. Throughout this chapter what we refer to as banks or banking institutions are the private banks and savings banks. At present, the main differences between them are that savings banks lack the pressure of shareholders and in consequence, they may take fewer risks and their profits may be lower.

2. This is in contrast with the Anglo-Saxon model, in which capital markets dominate the financing of companies.

3. In this sense, these policies can therefore be called "human resources management" only euphemistically.

4. One exception to this tendency is the case of specialized personnel hired for emerging business segments with which banks still have little experience.

5. On the changes in the Spanish labor market between the 1970s and 1990s, see Prieto 1994 and Recio 1997.

6. CCOO: Comisiones Obreras (Workers' Comissions); UGT: Unión General de Trabaja-dores (General Workers' Union); USO: Unión Sindical Obrera (Workers' Trade Union); CGT: Confederación General del Trabajo (Work General Confederation); ELA/STV: Sindicato de Trabajadores Vascos (Basque Workers' Union); CIG: Confederación Intersindical Gallega

(Galician Interunion Confederation); CC: Confederación de Cuadros (Intermediate Management Confederation); FITC: Federación Independiente de Trabajadores del Crédito (Loan Workers' Independent Federation); AMI: Asociación de Mandos Intermedios (Intermediate Management Asociation).

7. This study was published in 1990 by the Spanish Ministry of Labor and Social Security along with that of R. Dore, J. Bounine-Cabaló and K. Tapiola, entitled "Japón en Marcha" ("Japan on the Move"), in the volume *Recursos humanos y flexibilidad* (*Human Resources and Flexibility*). From now on this will be cited as OCDE 1990.

8. Four financial firms were studied via a case study methodology: a large and traditional one (A_1), to which was added another complementary case with similar characteristics, though less information was obtained (A_2); a second firm that was large and innovative (B); and a third, medium-sized firm (C). Firms B and C are firms in rapid expansion, particularly geographically. The field work—consisting of structured interviews with managers and worker representatives—was carried out in the first six months of 1995. Seventeen of the interviews with employees were carried out by C. Recuero, I. Ramos, and A. M. Carpio (1995) for a research project on the labor market in the private banking industry that was conducted by the School of Labor Relations at the Universidad Complutense in Madrid.

9. It is interesting to observe how executives always assess the subject of decentralization positively. They all defend it as a necessary business policy that consequently is put into practice in their firm. Very likely their assessment originates in the model, in both senses of the word, of management taught in the university business schools where they have studied or are currently studying. From an analytical viewpoint, therefore, it is best not to put too much trust in what they say, but rather to observe real applications of the idea.

10. They have had such latitude on the condition, of course, that they respect the formal labor categories of employees and their corresponding salaries.

11. The branch director is the person in charge of the management of a branch.

12. Over the past two years, about 10 percent of the total funds expended have been from the amounts granted each bank—on their own request—from FORCEM (the foundation for ongoing education in the firm), a public entity created by the Ministry of Labor and Social Security in 1993 to manage the corporate tax for professional training that is directly administered by representatives of corporations.

13. This is not training for a specific career. Precise career tracks have disappeared from Spanish banking. There are no preset tracks that go more than one or two years into the future.

14. In Spain there are elections in companies about every four years to choose the members who are to make up the Comité de Empresa (Workers' Committee). Officially, this committee has the right to represent and defend the workers' interests. The vast majority of the members elected are union members.

15. The problem especially poses itself in this last firm, because its compensation level is well above that of the other financial firms with which it is competing in the marketplace.

References

Cals, J., and A. Garrido. (1995). "Sistema y mercado financiero," in J. L. García Delgado (ed.) *Lecciones de economía española*. Madrid: Civitas, 277–297.

Carrasquer, P., X. Coller, and F. Miguélez. (1991). *Políticas de Regulación de la Mano de Obra en la Europa de los 90. El Caso de España*, Barcelona: Grup d'Estudis Sociològics sobre la Vida Quotidiana i el Treball, Universitat Autònoma de Barcelona.

Castaño, C. (1995). "Cambio tecnológico y estructura del empleo." *Información Comercial Española*, 743: 45–58.

Castells, M., A. Barrera, P. Casal, C. Castaño, P. Escario, J. Melero, and J. Nadal. (1986). *Nuevas Tecnologías, economía y sociedad en España*. Barcelona: Alianza Editorial.

Cuervo, A. (1988). *La crisis bancaria en España: 1977–1985*. Barcelona: Ariel.

Grup d'Estudis Sociològics sobre la Vida Quotidiana i el Treball. (1993). *Economía, trabajo y empresa. Sobre el impacto económico y laboral de los Juegos Olímpicos de 1992*. Madrid: Consejo Económico y Social.

Martín Artiles, A., F. Miguélez, and I. Pastor. (1994). *La regulación social de los recursos humanos en Catalunya*. Barcelona: Grup d'Estudis Sociològics sobre la Vida Quotidiana i el Treball, Universitat Autònoma de Barcelona.

Miguélez, F., and C. Llorens. (1994). *La posición de los actores sociales ante la participación directa*. Barcelona: Grup d'Estudis Sociològics sobre la Vida Quotidiana i el Treball, Universitat Autònoma de Barcelona.

Miguélez, F., and C. Prieto. (1991). *Las relaciones laborales en España hoy*. Madrid: Siglo XXI.

OECD. (1990). *Recursos humanos y flexibilidad*. Madrid: Ministerio de Trabajo y Seguridad Social.

Ontiveros, E., and F. J. Valero. (1994). *Introducción al sistema financiero Español. Análisis económico y tendencias*. Madrid: Civitas.

Prieto, C. (1994). *Trabajadores y condiciones de trabajo*. Madrid: Ediciones HOAC.

Prieto, C. (1991). "Prácticas empresariales de gestión de fuerza de trabajo." In F. Miguélez and C. Prieto (eds.), *Las relaciones laborales en España hoy*. Madrid: Siglo XXI, 185–210.

Rebollo, O., A. Martín, and F. Miguélez. (1991). *Primera encuesta de Relaciones Laborales en Catalunya*. Barcelona: CERES-CONC.

Recio, A. (1997). *Trabajo, personas, mercados. Manual de economía laboral*. Barcelona: Icaria and Madrid: FUHEM.

Recuero, C., I. Ramos, and A. M. Carpio. (1995). *Mercado de trabajo en la banca privada*. Madrid: Escuela de Relaciones Laborales Universidad Complutense de Madrid.

Regini M. (1992). "Los empresarios frente al problema del consenso." *Sociología del Trabajo*, 16: 53–76.

Rodríguez Fernández, J. M. (1994). "Las entidades financieras en la década de los noventa: nuevos desafíos, otros derroteros." *Papeles de economía española*, 58: 43–61.

Torrero, A. (1989). *Estudios sobre el sistema financiero*. Madrid: Espasa Calpe.

Valero, F. J. (1995). "El sistema bancario español." *Economistas*, 66–67: 118–132.

Villarejo, E. (1990). "La renovación en la aplicación de los recursos humanos en la banca española." *Sociología del Trabajo*, 9: 55–70.

9

Corporate Strategy, Institutions, and Employment Relations in Dutch Banking

Jelle Visser and
Pieter-Jan Jongen

Until long after World War II, Dutch banks were "beyond the horizon of the general public" (van den Brink 1967: 151). They were joint stock companies, providing credit for industry and trading stocks for wealthy clients. Then in the 1960s, they opened their doors to the general public, whose rising salaries and savings could no longer be ignored. Because proximity was a key element in winning customers, banks expanded their branch networks and became part of our everyday landscape. With one office for every four square kilometers, the Netherlands has one of the highest banking densities in the world. This is changing, however. With the advent of electronic "beyond the wall" banking and telebanking, people have less reason to enter a bank. Soon our knowledge of what actually happens in a bank will no longer be supported by the images of staff sitting behind counters or walking between desks with pieces of paper. The mystique of "money creating money" (Galbraith 1975) will probably reach untold heights with new chip technologies. For the average customer the inside of a bank may become as obscure as the inside of a pharmaceutical factory is for most users of makeup.

Banks are in the forefront of change, not just under the influence of information technology, but also because of rapid internationalization. Several truly global markets have developed with the rise of Eurodollars, offshore banking, foreign exchange brokerage, securities, derivatives, and project finance. In spite of their centuries-old presence in foreign markets, at home Dutch banks have been part of a closely knit, local, Amsterdam-based community that kept outsiders at bay and competition to a minimum. Cartelization was the name of the game, both in the pricing and offering of services and in the labor market. In both domains sectoral governance institutions have come under pressure, however.

"If you find a career in insurance too exciting, try banking." Not long ago this joke was still being told. Working in a bank invariably meant (for males) a steady career and a job for life. Banks seemed to be beyond the usual troubles of layoffs, unionization, and industrial unrest. They were revered institutions, led by conservative men, not given to risk taking. Any mishaps that occurred despite this conservative approach would rarely reach the outside world. This has changed as well. Nearly all Dutch banks have been involved in mergers; banks have frantically tried to capture a place in international financial markets in London, Singapore, and Tokyo; aggressive traders and financial whiz kids have introduced new mores; financial scandals have rocked the community and careers have brutally ended; employment in banking has declined after decades of growth; and labor unions and industrial unrest have entered the scene. Banking is among the few sectors in the Netherlands in which unions have strengthened against a receding tide. Employment in banking has feminized, outside the boardrooms that is, without disturbing what Kanter (1977) has dubbed "the homosexual reproduction of management." (Of the 89 top executive positions in the five banks in our study, a woman held only one.)

In short, banks have become "normal," sharing the pathologies of other bureaucratic organizations (Mintzberg 1979). Indeed, one of our themes is the "industrialization" of employment relations in banking under the influences of increased competition, relentless restructuring, and mounting work pressure and anxiety over jobs. Whether this is but a stage in the transition from paternalistic to sophisticated management of human resources, with a balanced division of rights, more reliance on consultation, continuous training, and increased employability, remains to be seen.

In this research project we take a close look at five banks: AbnAmro, Rabo, ING-bank (formerly NMB), ING-Postbank, and MeesPierson. AbnAmro (in full, Algemene Bank Nederland and Amsterdam-Rotterdam Bank), Rabo (short for Raiffeissen Bank Organization) and ING (Internationale Nederlanden Groep), are the "Big Three" in Dutch banking. Our fifth case, MeesPierson, is a medium-sized bank, mainly for wealthy clients and firms, at the time of our research owned by AbnAmro, but with an independent management, and since sold to the Belgian-Dutch Fortis group. Together these five banks employ around 90,000 of the sector's total of 113,000 staff, not counting those that work abroad. AbnAmro, the two ING banks, and MeesPierson were still absorbing the effects of recent mergers at the time of our study. Rabo was involved in a process of rationalization and centralization while retaining its federal character. Each of these banks was internationalizing; ING and AbnAmro, in particular, were involved in a string of cross-national ventures.

Sectoral Organization and Institutions

From Community to Sector

Banking communities throughout the world are characterized by codes of who belongs and who doesn't (Moran 1984). In banking the elite of commercial bankers met in the Dutch Bankers' Association (NBV, Nederlandse Bankiersvereniging) which long retained the character of a social club. In close interaction with the Finance Ministry and De Nederlandsche Bank (DNB, the Dutch Central Bank) this association acted as a formally recognized cartel and as the sector's informal subgovernment. In the 1980s its position came under attack from other banks or near-banks, customers, public policies, and, not least, the anticartel policy of the European Commission.

Savings and cooperative banks had their niches outside this clique but gradually gained recognition. The public Postbank was kept outside but accepted after privatization. Informal exclusion mechanisms, still applied in stock trading at the Amsterdam bourse, foundered in banking under pressure of intensified competition, accompanied by successive rounds of de- and reregulation. Banks have become the target of state policies and in the process, regulators have come to define who the members of the club might be and what they can or cannot do.

What is a bank? Initially, the term applied to commercial banks. In the Netherlands such banks had developed in the second half of the nineteenth century in response to the borrowing needs of industry. Then came banklike organizations with activities geared toward special groups like farmers, shopkeepers, and workers, each operating in distinct and often entirely local settings. In the past few decades, these distinctions have faded. Commercial banks moved into the retail market, and cooperatives and savings took on more functions of a full-service bank. Commercial banks, insurance companies, savings and loans, and stock traders and brokers are now legally empowered to offer the full range of retail banking products. All types of banks converged toward the German form of a universal bank. The regulator gradually sanctioned this practice, though it took until 1989 before the structure of the sector's subgovernment was adapted to the new situation with the formation of the Dutch Association of Banks (NVB Nederlandse Vereniging van Banken). This trade association encompasses all banking types and has a sectorwide mandate to negotiate with the Central Bank, the Finance Ministry, the European Banking Federation, and other interlocutors.

Structural deregulation has led to desegmentation of the market. The crisis of the mortgage banks that followed the collapse of the property market in the early 1980s led to rescue operations in which life insurance companies moved into the banking preserve and banks were allowed to take a substantial share in nonbanking activities. In 1990, DNB lifted the demarcation between banking and insurance. The rule that participation in nonfinancial business requires prior approval is still in force, but in 1989 DNB relaxed its criteria to remove the disadvantage of Dutch banks compared to the competition in Germany and France, where *banques d'affaires* are common. Dutch banks have remained true to their tradition as major providers of loans to industry and usually refrain from a direct role in the management of industrial firms.

Concentration and Internationalization

Staff members of the Ministry of Economic Affairs claim that banking is among the least dynamic sectors of the Dutch economy and suggest that collusion between the major banks is common (van Bergeijk et al. 1995). Banks operated a cartel until fairly recently. As a rule, competition and innovation have come from outside, from the public Postbank, the Rabo, or smaller savings institutions. The industry's response has been neutralization of invaders through co-optation, integration and rationalization of distributive channels through automation, increased interfirm cooperation, and outright integration through consolidated mergers.

The Dutch banking sector is among the most concentrated in Europe (Gardiner and Molyneux 1990). In 1996 there were 148 licensed Dutch banks: 98 general banks, 26 savings banks, 6 mortgage banks, and 18 stock-trading credit houses. The concentration ratio for the three largest banks, reflecting their market share in the home market, stood at 82 percent, up from 30 percent in 1960 and 70 percent in 1985 (DNB figures). Two merger waves, the first in the mid-1960s and the second in the early 1990s, changed the landscape in Dutch banking. The latter wave resulted from intensified international and domestic competition; increased economy of scale; rationalization of branch networks; the fading of traditional distinctions between finance, savings, investment, and insurance markets; the Single European Market; and a bandwagon effect on banks that feared to miss out on opportunities or become the target of international predators (Metze 1995).

In 1990 the two largest universal banks and focal members of the banking community, Abn and Amro, decided to join forces. The previous year, Amro's bid to merge with Belgian Generale Bank had failed. That same year, NMB, the third-largest bank, had merged with the Postbank, the successor of the Post Office Savings Banks and Post Giro. In 1991, the new combination merged with the major insurance firm in the country to become ING. Rabo responded by strengthening its alliances with a major insurance firm and largest Dutch investment fund. Mees, owned by Abn, and Pierson, owned by Amro, followed the example of their parent organizations and merged in 1992.

In the retail market, the two ING banks, combined, are largest, with a share of 42 percent in the home market, followed by Rabo (24 percent) and AbnAmro (16 percent). Rabo is a federation of some 500 member banks that have retained their cooperative format, with an overall membership of 600,000. It is the largest holder of savings deposits and provider of mortgages. AbnAmro is the leading financial intermediary and treasurer for large firms and the most important Dutch bank internationally, with a presence in 80 countries via more than 600 branches. It has strengthened its position through an alliance with Rothschild and various banks in the American Midwest. Its recent takeovers of Barings and Mendes Gans testify to ING's aim to become an international player and gain a stronghold in London. In 1997 ING bought Banque Bruxelles Lambert, the second-largest bank in Belgium. Rabo is particularly active in the international agro-industry, with a strong position in the United States, New Zealand, and Australia.

The concentration trend did not stop with the Big Three. Savings banks combined in a few remaining groups. A group of Dutch and Belgian banks and insurance firms formed the Fortis group, which now owns MeesPierson. Except between Dutch and Belgian banks, there have been no cross-national mergers in retail banking. Presumably, linguistic and cultural barriers are too high and methods of direct banking have not yet developed far enough. The attempt of French Crédit Lyonnais to establish itself through acquisitions failed, and in 1992 its ailing Dutch affiliate was bought by Belgian Generale Bank, which tries to tap the upper segment of the retail market. Other foreign banks, like Deutsche Bank or Barclays, tend to serve specialized functions for international finance, trade, shipping, and expatriates. Their share in the Dutch market had stagnated at around 10 percent at the time of our research.

National and Sectoral Regulation of Labor Relations

Labor markets and labor relations in Dutch banks are embedded in a dense institutional environment. In banking, as in most other sectors, collective agreements are negotiated between the employers' association and trade unions. Multiemployer bargaining has been the norm in banking since the first agreement in 1950. The Employers' Association in the Banking Industry (WGVB, Werkgeversvereniging in het Bankbedrijf) comprises all major and nearly all smaller banks, including foreign-owned banks. Membership, calculated on the basis of employees working in affiliated banks, is near 100 percent. WGVB runs a tight ship; members have to announce their disaffiliation one year in advance. The association is a focal member of the central employers' federation VNO-NCW.

There are five unions in banking, each taking part in collective bargaining. The Service Union (Dienstenbond), an affiliate of the main Dutch Federation of Trade Unions, FNV, organizes about 10,000 staff. A comparable union, affiliated with the minority Protestant Christian Federation, CNV, has some 3,200 members in banking. The Union of Clerical and Commercial Staff (Unie BHLP), which is affiliated with the MHP (Federation for Medium and Higher Employees), also has 10,000 members in banking. Another MHP affiliate organizes about 500 senior staff. An autonomous staff association, BBV, with around 1,600 members, completes the quintet. All of these, with the exception of BBV, also operate in other sectors of the economy. Together they represent 25 percent of all banking staff, up from 10 percent in the mid-1980s. The main factor behind this increase has been the growing anxiety over jobs in the aftermath of the mergers. The arrival of the highly unionized Postbank employees also helped. Finally, in the 1990s, the five unions were able to put their rivalries behind them, using joint membership forms. In the difficult negotiations of the 1994–98 collective agreement, they made common cause in an unusual display of militancy.

Multiunionism in the Netherlands is combined with single-table bargaining, and only one agreement applies *erga omnes*. The banking agreement covers all banks except DNB and all employees except managing directors. In addition to defining salaries, working hours, overtime payment, and holiday entitlements, the agreement defines rights and obligations (peace clause, employer contribution to union training, etc.) for the signing organizations. Unlike many sectoral agreements, for instance, those in metal engineering or insurance, the banking agreement determines standard rather than minimum provisions. Any bank must ask approval if it wants to derogate and offer better or lesser terms. (A 15 percent individual allowance above the standard, however, is built in and offers some flexibility.)

Union-management relations in banking have developed in a highly centralized fashion (Wieringa 1979). At the time of our research there were union committees at the place of work in just two banks, and they were not particularly alive and well; union activities, if manifest, are concentrated at headquarters, among support and technical staff (Wijmans 1992, 1993). However, Dutch employees have representation rights outside the union through mandatory works councils.

This is not the place to describe the changes in Dutch economic policies, industrial relations, and labor markets in recent times (Visser and Hemerijck 1997; Visser 1998). The Netherlands is no exception to the general European trend of a deteriorating labor market, a movement to relax state regulation, and employers' pressure toward decentralization. On an international scale of change in regulatory frameworks, the Netherlands may be placed between Britain and Germany. The country endured a severe job crisis in the early 1980s; unions went through a difficult time, and aggregate union density fell from 37 to 25 percent. However, institutional support was maintained, and with the backing of nationwide corporatist institutions, Dutch trade unions have continued to influence the direction of social and economic policies. In banking, as in the economy at large, attempts at finding joint solutions rather than expressing conflict have characterized union-employer relations.

Pressures from Markets and Technology

From Expansion to Maturation

In the last decade, markets for financial products have become more volatile (Boonstra and de Jong 1993). Historical claims on particular market segments or client groups have disappeared. As an unintended effect of the concentration process, many companies lost their traditional "home" bank and took the opportunity to shop elsewhere. Most companies and many private clients now use more than one bank, and large firms moved some of their financial operations in-house. The traditional banking client of higher social status who established an enduring relation of trust with a bank is disappearing. With this decrease in customer loyalty, pricing and quality of services are of vital importance. The greater the volatility and heterogeneity of customers, the more distribution becomes a critical issue.

In the 1980s the retail market showed signs of maturation. Worried by the fact that firms used the cheaper Post Giro for transferring wages and salaries to their employees, Dutch banks jointly launched the salary account in 1967. To 1980, the number of personal accounts increased fivefold, from two to ten million. In nominal terms deposits also increased fivefold. The strongest impetus behind this rapid growth was undoubtedly the sustained economic growth and increased wealth of large parts of the population (Wilterdink 1984). After 1980 growth continued at a slower pace, to 14 million accounts in 1992, roughly one per inhabitant.

Between 1965 and 1982 the three leading commercial banks doubled the number of their branches; cooperatives and savings banks defended their share with an expansion of 50 percent, and the Post Giro retaliated by modernizing its money services, introducing a greater variety of products, direct marketing, and home banking. The battle for the citizen's savings guilder in the 1970s, when it was believed that proximity of the outlet was essential to marketing, saddled the banks with a cost crisis. A dense branch network has grown more costly to maintain and will continue to do so given the need to upgrade staff. Average labor costs have risen to some 60 percent of total operating costs. The lower margins on retail products, further depressed by falling interest rates on savings and deposits, and increased market volatility have added urgency to finding new marketing solutions. Although the sharp fall in profitability in the early 1980s was first and foremost related to the general recession, the collapse of the property market, and bad loans amid a spate of firm closures and bankruptcies, the banks found it impossible to return afterward to the comfortable levels of the 1960s and 1970s. Only in the 1990s, through rationalization and cost cutting, did 10 percent profit margins again come within reach. In 1996 total profits as a percentage of total assets owned by all licensed banks had risen to 11 percent after taxes (DNB 1996). Traditionally, Dutch banks evaluated performance in terms of market shares rather than in profit ratios or shareholder value, but this is changing. Hidden reserves to cover bad risks add up to 15 percent of total assets but have been written into the books from 1997 on.

Automation and Information Technology

Automation has been the banks' main answer to the growing (labor) costs of retail banking, but this response has proven very expensive and not always effective. Studies of automation in banking conclude that there has been a considerable bias toward technology push, with rather vague objectives, no clear view on users or organizational consequences, and a severe underestimation of development and implementation costs (Buitelaar and Bilderbeek 1991; Tijdens 1991). The main objective of process innovation in retail banking was to create a central, real-time, accessible administration of accounts and balances, and to introduce a data input facility that registers and processes transactions at source without the need of further checks or alterations. It took twenty-five years to realize these contradictory aims. The first steps were taken in the late 1960s when, having standardized their account and checking systems, banks began to purchase central mainframe computers linked with a small number of regional communication stations. Initially the overriding objective was to gain efficiency in the administrative process. The banks established a national interbank clearing system in direct competition with the 1922 Post Giro system; government pressure to create one system failed. Only with the merger, in 1989, of the Postbank was this objective reached (Hulsink 1994).

Today automation supports process innovation based on local area networks and client-server technology, linking front and back office operations. Electronic home banking, voice response telephone services, and the use of ATMs and EFTPOS technology not only cut costs but also have advantages for clients. The chip card, which can be reloaded and used for payments in shops or gas stations, was introduced in 1997. Video conferencing technology in ATM terminals, enabling clients to consult with a wide array of specialists, has not yet reached an operational stage.

The dual processes of expansion and automation have changed work and work organization in the branches. Expansion first affected the front office: More clients now enter a bank, coming from varied and lower social backgrounds and demanding other services than those traditionally offered; cash transactions become the main activity and require more tellers. The strategy of cross selling, by which banks try to make up for the costs, requires front office employees to have a broader skill basis as well as more specialized knowledge and management support in the branch. The greater variety in customers, products, and services creates tensions in the traditional functional structure when counter activities become differentiated by client and product groups. Processing and verifying cash checks, transfers, and withdrawals, the main administrative activity in the back office, has gradually been computerized, moved out of the branch, and centralized in regional data processing centers in areas where cheap (female) labor is available. After a new spell of front office automation, the same work has been relocated to the branch but now integrated in data processing by tellers or clients.

Strategic Responses, Organizational Change, and Retrenchment

Integration of Networks, Product Differentiation, and Customer Segmentation

The choice of an AllFinanz strategy is an attempt to make better use of an increasingly expensive branch network, and this strategy has been implemented through various mergers and alliances between Dutch banks and insurance companies. As a marketing strategy, AllFinanz has major implications for the branch organization as well as for the job makeup in the branches. Branches lose their quasi-independent character and become local outlets in a far more centralized marketing organization. In most larger branches, it is possible to shop for all kinds of financial services, from do-it-yourself services to advice on complicated decisions involving stocks, investment, or life insurance.

Banks have begun to differentiate among products and create a physical demarcation between standardized transactions and high net worth customer services (Smulders 1993). With lower margins as a cause and information technology as a means, the service of standard transactions is deferred to ATMs, forms of electronic banking, and voice response systems. For the selling of *bancassurance* products (financial insurance products—like life insurance—sold by banks), personal contact with customers by skilled employees in well-designed outlets is as yet irreplaceable. Product differentiation is combined with customer segmentation and programs for retaining their loyalty. Some clients accept or prefer do-it-yourself services; others demand elaborate advice and personal attention (Verkoren 1989). For the first group, loyalty programs are developed through new chip technology; for the second group, relationship banking has gained prominence.

Organizational Change

Strategic choices like AllFinanz, customer segmentation, and product differentiation, combined with a new generation of IT, call for a redesign of the branch office. All banks, with the exception of MeesPierson, which does not rely so much on a branch network, are currently making such changes. The reception hall with its occasional grandeur or bad taste is disappearing, and the floor space is cut up into departments servicing specific groups of customers. Less attention is given to the traditional counter, many of whose functions are externalized in beyond-the-wall electronic machines. Some branches have deleted the counter altogether, fragmenting the traditional teller function to small amounts of cash at hand at different desks. A representative at a small reception desk guides customers to different sections and makes connections to specialist staff.

Segmentation tends to increase task specialization. Changes therefore go in two directions: job upgrading and job differentiation. Initial developments in automation had little impact on jobs in banks; they mainly

Table 9.1
Employment in Dutch banks by profession

	1981	1985	1989	1993
Staff	5%	6%	8%	12%
Management	3	4	5	8
Administrative	84	81	76	70
Commercial	2	3	4	5
Support	4	4	4	4

Source: Central Bureau of Statistics.

introduced two new occupations: data typists and computer experts. When automation was applied in the front office and local area networks allowed integration of roles and new applications, all types of jobs were affected. Already in the 1980s there had been a shift toward commercial activities and away from administrative jobs (see table 9.1). Commercial employees and client advisers shifted from the head office to the branches. Our case studies support the conclusion of Tijdens (1989) that bank office automation had led to upgrading and phased out the lower-skilled and narrowly specialized jobs in the back office, and the process extends into the 1990s. The knowledge of a larger variety of financial products and social and communication skills have gained prominence in job requirements (Kamstra and Swiebels 1995).

All banks in our case studies showed a noticeable centralization of planning and product development functions. Within ING and AbnAmro there are direct functional lines between product groups at central office and commercial employees within branches. Within Rabo, with its cooperative structure, such links are defined within an internal market, in which central departments must sell their products or advice, but pressure is put on affiliates to follow national marketing strategies (Diekman 1993). All banks have created a hierarchy of sorts in their branch network, with regional offices as intermediaries between headquarters and local branches. Thus although new commercial strategies require local entrepreneurship and upgrading of branch offices, we find that product development, support activities, and data processing, to the extent that it is not integrated in point of sale procedures, remain centralized.

Mergers and Retrenchment

Interrelated with attempts to rethink the distribution of financial products, banks have embarked on cost reduction through rationalization. In the

1990s this became their leading concern. In each case study, our respondents argued that increased competition had necessitated that banks become leaner, bringing an end to what many described as "overprotective" and "generous" personnel policies of the past. A reversal of employment trends reflects this.

In the early 1990s job growth turned into decline. Employment in the banking sector had increased an average of 10 percent per year in the 1960s, then slowed to 4 percent in the 1970s and 1 percent in the 1980s. In the 1990s, retrenchment affected all types of banks (see table 9.2). Overall employment has fallen by about 10 percent since 1991 but has since stabilized (at around 113,000 in 1997).

Retrenchment is related to three main factors: saturation of the domestic market, automation, and rationalization, this last accelerated by the recent mergers. Automation affects not only the number but also the nature of jobs. The automation of bulk processes in the back office tends to destroy low-skilled jobs. Until well into the 1980s banks' overall expansion masked this effect. By the end of the 1980s a new wave of automation, with a higher IT content, reached and began to transform the front office. At that time, nearly all banks were involved in efficiency drives. The "1/8 operation" at Rabo is a typical example of across-the-board cost cutting. The performance program at ING-bank also had a large cost-cutting component. In their search for lower expenses, most banks have also turned their attention to outsourcing. MeesPierson, in line with its strategic choice to move out of the retail market, has gone farthest and sold its unit dealing with mortgages and externalized what is left of payment processing. AbnAmro externalized catering and brought it under a cheaper collective agreement.

Retrenchment affected especially those merging banks, like AbnAmro, that had overlapping branch networks. AbnAmro's operation "Integration Branches" was run from headquarters in almost military fashion, involved a huge cost reduction process and was not completed until the end of 1994. When the smoke cleared the bank had lost 300 of its 1,400 branches and 4,000 (of 25,000) employees working in its domestic branch network. In all, the Netherlands division employs 32,000 people, of whom 8,000 are in specialized divisions and 3,000 at headquarters, where restructuring has only just begun. In the foreign departments and branches (where the overlap was much smaller) employment has expanded by 5,000 to around 30,000 employees, but these involved different jobs for different people.

The two ING banks did not merge their branch networks because domain overlap was negligible. ING-Bank has its own relatively small

Table 9.2
Employment figures

	1981	1983	1985	1987	1989	1991	1993	1995
Universal banks	75,139	72,646	71,353	73,926	74,705	72,443	68,222	62,987
Cooperative banks	27,938	28,536	30,542	32,026	33,669	37,966	37,086	36,078
Savings and loans	5,015	6,556	6,556	7,188	8,475	8,281	9,010	8,914
Mortgage banks*	1,846	1,776	1,646	±1,000	794	754	491	485
Total**	113,820	114,300	115,000	119,188	122,908	125,079	119,919	113,800

Source: NIBE, various years.

* The decline in mortgage banks is primarily caused by takeovers and consolidations of universal banks.
** The total includes small financial institutions and employment in the Central Bank (1,400 in 1994); hence, totals do not simply add up the different categories included in the table, but depict the total employment in the sector.

network, and ING-Postbank uses the 2,200 or so post offices. In this case
the problems were concentrated at the central level, reflecting different
business cultures and traditions. ING-bank is a major provider of loans
to small and medium-sized business and had engaged in an aggressive
growth strategy in the 1980s. ING-Postbank is the largest holder of
deposit accounts, but was seen as a money processing factory, its staff
being derided as "a bunch of dull civil servants" by the "fast boys" of
ING-bank. However, each had something the other wanted. The Postbank
had access to six million accounts, whereas its partner had the license and
expertise to offer a full range of banking services. Consequently, the
merger has affected the two banks' administrative and support centers
more than their branch network, and overall job losses from the merger
were much smaller than in AbnAmro. Currently ING-Postbank employs
4,200 people in its processing and 2,700 in its direct mail divisions; ING-
bank employs 8,300 staff in its domestic operations.

    Rabo has also reduced the number of staff in the main office and central
service units. Local banks and branches are persuaded to form a hierarchy
with some larger ones serving as regional support centers for others, but
cooperation is not always secured. A concentration process has taken
place, and the number of local banks has fallen from around 1,000 in 1980
to 851 in 1990 and a little more than 500 in 1996. The number of
branches, still 3,000 in 1980, has been halved. Until 1991 these developments were paralleled by a steady expansion, but between 1992 and 1995
employment in the branches decreased from 41,000 to 38,000. The central
Rabo organization employs 9,000 people, of whom 2,000 work abroad.

    Our fifth case, MeesPierson, has four main offices in Amsterdam and six
local branches. In 1994 the bank employed 2,526 staff in the Netherlands,
down from 2,786 in 1992. Prior to the merger, Mees had completed a
painful reorganization and cost-cutting operation, reducing its staff from
2,600 to 1,400. The merger caused a further 450 redundancies, and that
may not be the end of it. MeesPierson's foreign department and offices
are expanding and give work to 1,446 employees, up from 880 in 1992.

    Our case studies suggest that we are in for further changes. AbnAmro
has floated new ideas about its branch network, to be restructured into
about 300 full-service branches with regional market responsibility and
700 small outlets with mostly electronic banking facilities. ING-bank is
working on a new layout for its 400 branches, refining its already existing
segmentation of services. ING-Postbank has recently revised its contract
with PTT Post and undertaken to restyle a number of post offices to
enhance a "shopping atmosphere." (The staff handling banking services

is recruited by PTT Post, which is reimbursed for each transaction performed.) Rabo has implemented a new strategy, introducing a segmentation of "clusters of needs," a redesign of the branch layout, new staff training schemes, and a remake of its corporate image.

Human Resources Policies in Dutch Banks

Destaffing Policies and Social Plans

Under Dutch law, mergers, takeovers, and major changes in investment, work organization, or staffing require consultation with the works council (Visser 1995). The collective agreement for the banking sector stipulates that prior agreement must be reached over procedures for the reduction or transfer of staff. In case of major layoffs, involving twenty or more staff, the employer must ask a permit from the director of the Regional Employment Office, who nearly always delays the decision at least one month to create time to negotiate a socially acceptable solution.

Typically in these cases the unions are called in to negotiate a "social plan." These plans made their entry into banking with the privatization, in 1986, of the Postbank, whose incumbent staff lost civil servant status but were guaranteed the same favorable terms of employment (state pensions and a "no redundancies" pledge until 1991). These promises were widely seen as a key factor in allowing a smooth restructuring process and became the model for later years. As a matter of fact, social plans applied to all the banks in our study. They invariably contain a "no forced dismissals" clause, spell out procedures for relocating staff, and often guarantee the retention of salary levels. Negotiations are always conducted at the highest possible level between executive directors with HR/IR responsibility and high-ranking union officials. Although works councils in the banks are not union controlled, management attempts at ING and AbnAmro to cut a deal with the council and sideline the unions have failed. Retail banks depend on their goodwill among the general public and are (perceived as) highly profitable; at least in the Netherlands, they cannot afford to throw redundant staff on the open labor market against their will. In this sense, unions in banking, despite their lower membership, have an advantage over unions in manufacturing.

Negotiated Mobility

Given these constraints, destaffing has to take place by voluntary means, through natural wastage, early retirement, and voluntary outplacement sugared with severance payments. Recruitment bans have been another widely used instrument. During our research, AbnAmro ordered a ban on hiring domestic staff, except for management trainees. ING and Rabo also applied restrictions to hiring. MeesPierson has avoided this crude measure for all but some months at the end of 1994. All banks in our study have hitherto managed to avoid breaking the "no forced layoffs" rule, but with growing strains.

With their back door locked and the front door ajar, mobilizing the internal labour market is crucial to banks. Until recently, fixed-duration contracts have been rare, except for female data typists. Employment in banking in the Netherlands was traditionally characterized by long and secure career tracks over many hierarchical levels. Banks offered the image if not the reality of lifetime employment. Together with above-average wages and fringe benefits, this has created what some in the industry have dubbed a "golden cage" for employees. (In 1994, hourly earnings in banking ranked third out of a total of 48 sectors.) Sector-specific skill profiles and training programs did not prepare people to take up jobs outside banking, and in the three major banks the average tenure of male employees had risen by several years to 15 years. The average length of service of women was half that of males but showed the same upward trend (Tijdens 1991).

The current no-hiring measures reinforce the aging of the workforce. The effects of hiring policies in the past is now clearly felt, and the age groups of 35–44 and 45–55 are by far the largest in banks' demographic makeup (van Klaveren and Tijdens 1995). This bubble tends to obstruct vertical job mobility and makes horizontal mobility ever more important. Banks have tried to find a way out by lowering the preretirement age to 60 (instead of statutory retirement at age 65). This escape route is becoming more costly, however, and is met with increased resistance from the government. Moreover, highly valuable staff will also choose to leave, if offered the choice, along with those the banks would like to entice.

After the AbnAmro merger, almost one-third of its domestic staff had to be relocated within the new entity. These changes came on top of the so-called five-year rule for (branch) directors and specialists, which requires them to move to new positions within regular intervals. Clearly, AbnAmro's internal labor market has been stretched to the limit. Automation and rationalization have rendered obsolete those very jobs into which redundant employees have been transferred only recently and for which they have been retrained with such effort. Another round of upgrading toward the new customer service jobs might be too much for these formerly administrative employees, who have meanwhile grown older as a group. Hence in late 1995, within a year of concluding a new social plan, central management, under pressure of branch directors who wanted more room to maneuver, announced that it could no longer avoid forced dismissals. This led to an angry outcry by the unions, causing management to back down. Currently AbnAmro is establishing a new mobility center and trying to implement a new HR philosophy, emphasizing that employees must take responsibility for maintaining their own employability within or outside the bank.

Mobility is also an issue in ING. Its unique problem concerns the differences in the sectoral collective agreements covering its 20,000 banking and 10,000 insurance staff in the Netherlands. The banking agreement covers nearly everybody and determines collective pay standards which, legally, translate into individual contracts. The agreement for clerical staff in insurance determines only minimum levels of pay; the agreement for sales staff is procedural only and leaves full scope for individual pay determination. The salary of lower-graded insurance staff is relatively high, whereas the banking agreement assures middle- and higher-level staff a comparative advantage. Mobility in ING is therefore hindered in three ways: not enough at the lower end from insurance to banks; not enough at he upper end from banks to insurance; and too much at the upper end from insurance to banks. ING has floated the idea of negotiating a company agreement, but this would precipitate the end of sectoral bargaining in banking.

In Rabo the federal structure poses additional problems, not least in creating one internal labor market. Recall that Rabo's affiliates are autonomous within the limits of the supervisory powers of central office, mandated by the Central Bank, the obligations created by the (sectoral) collective agreement and the social plan. Rabo did not go through a recent merger but many of its affiliates did. It has eased the doubling of positions, especially at (branch) management level, through voluntary retirement and costly severance payments. Like AbnAmro, Rabo is trying to establish a mobility center. Unlike our other cases, Rabo's central HR department cannot rule by managerial fiat, at least not outside departments and units located at headquarters. Instead, it has to sell its mobility policies to sometimes reluctant followers.

Even before its merger, MeesPierson had a surplus and mismatch in its internal labor market. Its approach to job mobility deviates from that of the other banks in our study. At the time of the merger, management declared many staff members, far in excess of redundancies, fit for

mobility. This was intended to increase overall mobility, remove the redundancy stigma, enhance the career orientation of staff that the bank
wanted to retain but whose jobs had disappeared, and vacate positions to
which they might move. These policies worked as intended, but the repo-
sitioning of this bank requires more change still. Compared to other
banks, its problems seem larger, because of the smaller size of its internal
labor market and its decision to leave the retail market.

Working-Time Reduction

The difficulty of managing job decline and job mobility within the limit of
a "no forced layoffs" rule may explain why banking employers were
ready to accept a collective reduction of working time. In fact, WGVB
was the first to move when VNO-NCW finally lifted its ban on working-
time reduction and accepted that each sector should stand by itself, in
accordance with the New Course accord with the unions of December
1993 (Visser 1998). It took WGVB only a few more months to negotiate
a new collective agreement, breaking a stalemate that had lasted a year
and prevented the renewal of the agreement that had expired in early
1993. The new agreement, concluded for the unusual length of four years,
introduced a flexible thirty-six-hour workweek, to be negotiated on an
individual or workshop basis before the end of 1996. The unions conceded a standstill on real hourly wages.

Dutch trade unions had unearthed their working-time reduction strategy in 1991–92, when the economy moved into a recession and unemployment figures went up again. In 1982–85, like many European unions,
they had chosen a similar response to the jobs crisis and achieved a reduction from 40 to 38 hours. However, after 1985 employers had blocked
further reduction, and amidst strong job growth the unions shifted their
attention to making up for years of wage moderation. In the 1990s the
unions returned to their original strategy. Unlike ten years earlier, they
were now prepared to accept a larger degree of negotiated flexibility, as
the employers demanded. Applied to banking, this choice reflected two
things: gloomy forecasts of a possible 20–30 percent job decline in banking and a newly discovered conviction that people should decide for
themselves whether they wanted to share work and give up money for
extra days off. At the time, a union survey of 9,461 banking staff conveyed a deep sense of pessimism over job security and career development, especially among lower-graded staff (Noten and Warnink 1991).

The 1994–98 banking agreement was in many ways a breakthrough, and not only because it took so long and required a radical change of heart among employers and unions and a huge wage concession. The implementation of the thirty-six-hour workweek was traded off against longer opening hours and a reduction, in some cases a renunciation, of overtime rates for nonstandard hours and Saturdays. Individual employees, departments, branches, or units are, within limits, free to choose their own time schedules. Management is allowed to set aside a small number of jobs and exclude staff in these jobs from taking shorter hours, but such an action has to be justified. Consultation is to take place on an individual or shop basis under procedural rules spelled out in the agreement.

Apart from its novel character—offering a "menu" for choice—the agreement was the unions' attempt to halt job retrenchment. In this objective they seem to have succeeded; employment has stabilized since 1996. A survey of banking staff, with nearly 30,000 returned interviews distributed via the works councils (Tijdens 1997a), shows that 82 percent of all employees have converted to a thirty-six-hour week. This percentage varies among the banks: 89 percent in Rabo, 84 percent in ING, 79 percent in MeesPierson and 70 percent in AbnAmro, the only bank that explicitly excluded a large group of commercial staff from choosing a shorter week, against the protests of the unions. AbnAmro employees who were allowed a choice thereby indirectly discovered that their supervisors had deemed them of lesser value. The other banks have avoided such demoralizing conflicts or used more subtle methods; supervisory and specialist staff in all banks have made less use of shorter hours. With the exception of those at AbnAmro, most employees appeared satisfied with the way they were given a choice, but a majority in all banks complained about an increased workload and mounting stress.

Both employees and banks have gained flexibility from the new arrangement. Various workweek schedules can now be found: the unchanged 5×8 hours week, 4×9 hours with a fixed or variable day off, a two-week $8 + 4 \times 9$ regime (whereby an employee works eight nine-hour days plus one eight-hour day in each two-week period, for an average of forty hours per week); and a flexible, individually negotiated working time regime that changes over the year, the choice of a large group (one-third) of employees. Employers have clearly gained flexibility and can better adapt employee working time to changes in business peak hours or seasonal changes, for instance, at seaside resorts. Banks tend to follow the longer opening hours of department stores and shopping centers, where an increasing number of their outlets are now located.

Women and Part-Time Jobs

In 1994, 45 percent of banking employees were female; this is above the national average but lower than in banks elsewhere in Europe (Rubery 1995). The history of women's work in banking is described in Tijdens 1997b and can be summarized as follows. For a long time, employment in banking was a male preserve. Women worked mainly as typists and were encouraged to leave after marriage. In the 1960s and 1970s, when banks expanded and labor markets were tight, employers needed married women and encouraged them to stay or reenter on a part-time basis. In the 1980s, when labor markets slackened and unemployment among women rose, employers saw part-time jobs as a flexible response to union demands for a collective reduction of the workweek. Women, whose educational attainments had increased, wanted to retain their jobs after childbearing, because they were apprehensive about unemployment and the chances of reentering later. In the 1990s most banks have started to help pay for private child care facilities. Tax, social insurance, and legal disadvantages for part-timers have been lifted, and the full-time/part-time wage differential has narrowed.

The share of women in banking working part-time rose from 22 percent in 1982 to 40 percent in 1995. This is lower than the national average (67 percent), but that figure is strongly influenced by the high incidence of part-time jobs in cleaning, catering, retail, health care, and education. The low percentage (5 percent) of male part-time staff is striking (compared with 17 percent in the entire economy) and indicates job segregation and aging of male banking staff. Statistics on working hours by salary scale or department reveal that part-time jobs are more often found at the lower end, in branch offices and among support staff. At corporate headquarters, among specialists and managers, part-time and female staff are vastly underrepresented.

Training and Skill Formation

Training and skill formation in Dutch banks has traditionally been sector and job specific. For training purposes, banks work together in the Dutch Institute of Banking and Investment (Nederlands Instituut voor het Bank-en Effectenbedrijf, NIBE), which is cofinanced by all banks, organizes training courses, undertakes research and development, and serves as the sector's publishing house. Training used to be based on uniform standards for teaching curricula throughout the sector.

Table 9.3
Education in banking and in national economy

	Banking sector				Economy
	1981	1985	1991	1993	1993
Lower level	6%	5%	4%	4%	10%
Medium-level general	20	13	12	10	7
Medium-level vocational	12	11	9	8	16
Higher-level general	13	13	12	12	5
Higher-level vocational	36	42	43	43	38
Professional (bachelor)	8	10	12	18	17
Academic	3	5	8	8	7

Source: Central Bureau of Statistics.

As in other sectors, the depressed state of the labor market during the 1980s and the rise in general education levels encouraged a substitution process of lower with medium, and of medium with higher education. Employers raised standards and used education as a screening device. Secondly, there was a shift toward economic and administrative education, both in regular professional schools, before entry, and in the NIBE courses after or upon entry. In the 1990s the continuing rise in the level of education among employees has resulted from the demand for new specialist skills, job upgrading in the branches, and the phasing out of low-skilled work. Table 9.3 gives the relevant statistics and shows a pronounced rise in educational attainment.

In the 1980s banks tried to incorporate professional training courses into the public education system along with government programs aimed at improving school-to-work transfers. New industry-specific programs and schooling institutions were created. Employers have taken active roles in these new programs, for instance through the development of course descriptions and participation in school boards. Trade unions are involved in a new, middle-level vocational education program. As a result and a likely rationale for this shift to preentry training systems, part of the costs are transferred to the public system. Another rationale is the increased demand for general commercial skills that can be used in a larger variety of jobs. In addition, about one in five employees takes part in postentry training provided by NIBE, often on a voluntary basis and in evening or weekend hours (van den Hoven and Tijdens 1990).

In addition to these general and sectoral training efforts, large banks have developed firm-specific training courses, in some cases together with specialist schools or universities. We observe a tendency toward training tailored to special needs and on-the-job training, supporting (horizontal) job mobility (Donkersloot 1994). Each of the banks spends between 3 and 4 percent of gross revenue on training (Keetels 1994).

Job Classification

In the Dutch tradition of central wage determination, established after 1945, sectoral job classification systems played an important role. These systems were intended to provide a strong measure of equity and trans-parency in remuneration, suppress jealousy and wage drift in the work-place, and prevent poaching among employers. Job classification systems entered the service sectors in the 1970s. Under pressure from the govern-ment, WGVB started in 1976 to negotiate a classification system with the unions. It took five years to design a new system, and another five years to agree on a corresponding salary system. The new system increased the number of job groups from five to fifteen and raised coverage from 70 to 100 percent (excluding managing directors), which is exceptional for any collective agreement.

In the past decade the classification system has grown large and unwieldy in an attempt to catch up with new job developments. All our respondents on the management side complained about red tape; some clearly wanted the system to be abandoned, arguing that the method used and the jobs it described were out of date. AbnAmro has started to cut down on the total number of job descriptions but has refrained from a complete overhaul. Rabo did begin a revision in response to its new strategy, as a basis for training, but not for remuneration, where it is still bound by the sectoral agreement. ING has clustered job descriptions into job families in such ways that individual ranking can still be achieved, but job rotation and redeployment of staff is easier.

Remuneration and Incentives

Remuneration is another area where the tradition of sectorwide regulation is apparent. Table 9.4, which depicts the distribution of staff across wage scales, shows that the lower scales (levels 1 and 2), covering standard clerical jobs in the back office, have almost disappeared. New jobs with greater emphasis on commercial skills (levels 4/5 and higher) have increased. The slope with which the wage level rises across the scales is

Table 9.4
Employment by salary scales

	1983	1987	1991	1995
1	2.0%	2.2%	1.1%	0.5%
2	19.4	15.9	10.6	5.0
3	31.3	27.1	27.1	22.5
4/5	15.4	21.4	24.7	27.8
Higher than 5	31.9	33.3	36.6	44.2

Source: WGVB.

quite flat, and the ratio among the scales has remained constant since 1986. At first glance earnings differentials do not seem large and are similar across banks. However, in all banks in our study there was a noticeable pressure toward individual assessment. In nearly all interviews, general and HR managers expressed a desire to create stronger links between performance and pay.

The collective agreement stipulates three criteria for pay determination: job description, seniority, and a bonus, maximized at 15% of the contractual wage and depending on "the way the job is executed." Performance and appraisal systems used for determining annual contingent pay were fairly similar across our cases. They evolve around annual interviews between an employee and manager. A fairly rigid set of predetermined criteria on which behavior or performance can be rated underlies these talks. The bonus is usually awarded in steps of 3 or 4 percent, and in some instances a normal distribution of sorts governs the outcome. These performance and appraisal systems are increasingly used for other HR purposes as well. Mobility and career planning have been added in the ING-group and gained more weight in AbnAmro; in all banks there is some relationship with the assessment of training needs.

The "variability" or contingent pay is, however, limited. Most add-ons have sunk into the contractual salary through agreements negotiated with the works councils. Only higher management (in MeesPierson, everybody) starts from scratch each year. Other rewards, such as the profit-related end-of-year bonus, which parallels dividend payment on stocks or options, and the annual 13th month, have become a tradition. Management in all banks attempt to recapture some pay flexibility. Most of these attempts depart from behavior rating as a basis for evaluation and move instead toward output-related measures.

Firm Governance and Human Resources Management

Works Councils and Employee Participation

Statutory rules on firm governance and employee consultation, as determined under the 1972 Company Act and the 1979 Works Council Act or its later changes, provide for a fairly uniform system. Dutch firms are managed by a board of directors that is supervised by a board of supervisors representing the shareholders. Unlike in Germany, there is no legal requirement to allocate seats to employee representatives, but the central works council must give its consent to appointments to the Board of Supervisors and may propose alternative candidates. In establishments with thirty-five or more employees, works councils are mandatory. Members of these councils are elected from and by the employees. Unions usually participate in these elections with lists of their own, but non-members can stand as well. Management must meet with the council six times per year and provide the council with information. On strategic matters (mergers, takeovers, investments, and the like) the council must be consulted; on social matters (job restructuring, contingent pay, job assessment, working schedules, and so forth) the councils have codecision rights. Works councils cannot renegotiate pay or issues determined by collective agreement and cannot call strikes. These arrangements make for a strong (legal) regime, comparable with that of Germany (Rogers and Streeck 1995).

All the banks in our study have works councils. The council structure tends to mimic the structure of the corporation; usually, the large divisions have their directly elected council, which in turn elect members for a central council for the bank's domestic operations. (For the purpose of representing employees working abroad, ING and AbnAmro have started to implement the EU directive on European works councils). Rabo, because of its cooperative status, operates a somewhat different form of consultation, with management representation and without codecision rights. In none of the banks, according to our interviews with managers and council representatives, does consultation go much beyond the extent of the law, and in banks one does not find the type of strong works councils that one finds in industry (Visser 1995).

Workplace consultation (werkoverleg) within the hierarchical relationship between supervisor and his group is common in Dutch banks. It has both a collective and individual dimension. The unions have no place in such consultations. Other forms of employee involvement, for instance through quality circles, are not used in Dutch banks, except some scattered experiments with TQM. AbnAmro has the most elaborate procedures; group meetings typically take place once every two weeks. The two ING-banks and Rabo do not have company-wide rules, but many cycles of group meetings at the level of smaller units are held as a channel for employee involvement. MeesPierson, in particular, stresses individual consultation between supervisor and employee.

The Organization of the Human Resources Function

At first sight, the organization of the HR function varies from bank to bank, reflecting the banks' diverse histories as well as personal idiosyncrasies (Sijbrands and Jansen 1995); there are strong functional parallels, however. In most banks, personnel management has traditionally operated in a fairly centralized, predictable, and hierarchical environment. There has been an effort to fit in with policies designed at the sector level, such as the job classification system, the 15 percent bonus system, or the NIBE training criteria. This has created coercive and professional isomorphism in HR policy (DiMaggio and Powell 1991).

Many HR departments and policies were in a state of change during our research. These changes were twofold. Structurally, the HR function moved closer to line management. In AbnAmro, the idea is that HR consultants should become professional "sparring partners" for line managers. This presupposes that HR people are near but not under the wings of these managers as they are now. In this bank HR used to operate its own vertical structure, with HR departments under the command of central office. In ING the evolving business unit structure influenced the buildup of stronger HR departments under unit management's control, a solution duplicated in the branches. A corporate social policy statement is issued to set group objectives. Indicators on mobility, salary and training costs, productivity, age, and affirmative action encourage an output-oriented and detached form of central guidance, although most decision-making takes place locally. Rabo has always had different HR policy structures. The autonomy of local banks limits the scope for top-down steering, and local banks can buy services from internal HR specialists competing with external agencies.

The IR function is invariably centrally placed and functionally differentiated. Traditionally, banks have a special department dealing specifically with IR issues and contacts with the unions and the central works council. Its head is an executive director. Although boardroom decision making is collegial, it is unusual for CEOs or other directors to intervene in this policy domain. In ING, the IR function has been centralized, in contrast to the bank's business unit structure, but appears unable to prevent wage drift through locally negotiated pay awards (with works councilors mailing their successes through the company electronic mail system). Within Rabo, there is a mandate to negotiate centrally on IR issues, and this function is one of those few not subject to the internal market model.

Conclusions

Employment relations in Dutch banks have evolved within a strong sectoral framework. Whether or not causally linked, this went hand in hand with fairly homogenous social policies across banks. In trade policies, many examples demonstrate the overriding importance of interfirm cooperation, over and above competition. In addition to a joint training board and publishing house, the banks run jointly a credit registration office and interbank clearing system. The Schumpeterian idea of new entrants who successfully introduce new products and revolutionize business relations hardly applies. Instead, most new banking products are carefully planned and introduced by all banks together. Sectoral cooperation is especially important in the case of process innovation. Most steps in the rationalization and automation of the administrative processing of transactions have the character of collective goods and bear more fruit when taken by all participants together.

However, in the social domain the regulatory power of sectoral institutions appears to be fading. The NIBE training curricula no longer provide the only standard nor does the industry's job classification system. The parallel with product market developments is evident. Banks have trouble maintaining their united stance in the development of electronic banking products, and competitive drives in booming markets have undermined the traditional cozy relationships. All our respondents talked about increased competition, not just from the outside, but among banks.

A heterogeneous picture emerges. The path through history for most large Dutch banks has saddled them with extended branch networks that involve large sunk costs. Although all banks have rationalized these networks, they still seek new ways to improve operating results. AllFinanz, maximizing the synergy with insurance services, has been the dominant response. This homogeneity in strategy has instigated parallel approaches to restructuring, for instance, hierarchical ordering between and segmentation within branch offices and upgrading the social and commercial skills of staff. However, heightened awareness of differences in product markets and sales strategies may easily trigger a differentiation process in employment relations.

Strategic changes create pressure on the organizational structure (Chandler 1961). The structure of Dutch banks has long been stable and straightforward. Natural bureaucratic tendencies in administrative organizations, where continuity, reliability and accountability tend to be all-important, lead to tall hierarchies. In banks, formal control procedures, a conservative ("sound finance") culture, and a paternalistic style of personnel management reinforced these tendencies). In Mintzberg's (1979) typology, banks were a full bureaucracy but are now pushed to become more entrepreneurial. The large conglomerates that have emerged as a result of mergers are trying to adapt their organizational structures to match both change and diversity in environment and activities. Currently, one can detect a hybrid of three forms (Buitelaar and Bilderbeek 1992): around the main "machine-bureaucracy" for batch processing of financial data, we find a "professional bureaucracy" for complex products (mortgages, financial management, *bancassurance*) and an "adhocracy" for special projects, the latter most specifically in the international domain.

In a traditionally highly centralized bureaucracy like AbnAmro, the greater diversity of clients and markets pull the organization in different directions. Staff functions like IT and HR are restructuring their departments, moving their staff closer to line managers. Among the banks in our study, true delayering was only found, as expected, in (international) divisions that dealt with truly turbulent markets like investment banking. Here, as in MeesPierson, the pressure is also coming from the increasingly tight labor market for financial and IT specialists. AbnAmro had to relax its five-year rotation rule in the case of international finance specialists for the first time in 1993.

Employment conditions in and across banks will probably become more diverse. The overarching strategic dichotomy that we have described has led AbnAmro to hire temporary workers in its twenty-four-hour call center whom the collective agreement does not cover. Increased specialization in the front office leads to different types of career paths. The branch director, traditionally on a career path toward the profession of "banker," has become a manager, executing and selling central policies in local markets, not dissimilar from the *chef* in a supermarket chain. Recruitment of bankers is increasingly assured through specialized (university) training. Sociologically, the loss of the "banker career" prospect for branch directors helps explain the considerable resistance to change among this still powerful group.

In our interviews, MeesPierson's executives expressed a wish to decentralize sectoral bargaining. ING executives clearly consider the advantages of company bargaining a way of integrating conditions in banking and insurance. Rabo and AbnAmro seem to put their weight still behind sectoral bargaining. But all want more differentiation in the sectoral agreement and more scope for pay flexibility and individual, performance-related remuneration. Both ING and AbnAmro have tried to put pressure on the unions by courting the relationship with the central works council, but neith r sees the council as an alternative to the unions. Only Mees-Pierson executives argued that the sectoral agreement should be reduced to a framework for company bargaining with the works council. This view reflects the bank's different strategic position in that it is the only one to move out of the retail market. It may also reflect resistance to the dominance of the Big Three. (Like other medium-sized banks, Mees-Pierson is still part of WGVB's inner circle of ten HR/IR directors who meet monthly to discuss social policy developments, however). In the other banks of our study, council members and managers expressed reluctance to involve works councils in pay bargaining. Many managers had good things to say about union professionalism and responsibility, a view often found among Dutch managers (Visser 1995). Works council members realize that they are too weak without union backing. We repeat that banking ranks high on the scale of sectoral corporatism and that social plans negotiated with the unions have helped to manage the hard times following mergers.

How sectoral arrangements will develop under these pressures is impossible to predict with any confidence. The 1994 agreement was an unanticipated and surprising outcome with innovative aspects. At the time, many believed that there would be no sectoral agreement, and both Rabo and ING had indicated that they might go it alone. The agreement, with its emphasis on individual and group consultation, was a proposal of Rabo, whose management style it reflected. At the time all banks saw the benefit of a deal with the unions to relax the pressure on their strained internal labor markets. Four years later it turns out to be extremely difficult to find a formula for a new contract. For the time being, unions and employers have renewed, only for 1998, the pay section of the expired agreement, allowing a 3 percent raise. Employers have disclosed plans to differentiate the agreement in three groups, moving ancillary staff to a substandard agreement and allowing more scope for individual and flexible pay awards for highly valued staff. For the unions this is unacceptable, but it is unclear whether they can maintain the common front of four years ago, let alone mobilize banking staff.

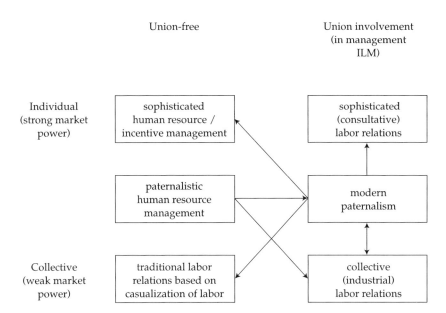

Figure 9.1
Trajectories of HR policies in Dutch banking

With the help of the model of Kessler and Purcell (1995), we project developments in different directions (figure 9.1). Banks have moved away from the paternalist model, in which trade unions were included but played no significant role. Confronted with an increase in union density, a shift to "modern paternalism" occurred, underscored by a regained "logic of influence" and proven capacity of unions to mobilize in hard times. For clerical staff for whom there is no longer a place, bargaining becomes harder, as employer attempts to renege on the social plans reveal. Cost-cutting operations and outsourcing in call centers or data processing firms tend to exclude this group from the lofty employment conditions of the standard banking agreement. We classify this as a move toward "traditional" labor relations. At the other end of the strategic dichotomy a different development is possible, one based not so much on cost-effectiveness but on commitment and involvement. In the case of extra bonuses for specific financial specialists, this resembles the "sophisticated human relations" arrangements in which unions have no place. But in instances such as increased working time flexibility, unions and collective bargaining may continue to play a role in providing the safeguards and trust for "sophisticated (consultative)" labor relations.

Appendix

Most of the interviews for the sector study preceded the case studies and were held throughout 1995. They included the vice-chairman and chief negotiator of the employer's association WGVB; four union representatives and chief negotiators for three of the unions and the main architect of the 1994–98 agreement; one representative of the foundation that monitors the job classification system; NIBE staff and a representative of one of the training institutions.

The AbnAmro interviews took place in autumn 1995 and included five central HR/IR executives, three divisional HR directors, two high-ranking managers in the investment banking division, three in the Netherlands division, one manager and one consultant in the IT division, and one member of the central works council. Interviews in the ING-group started in autumn 1995 and continued into 1996 and included six executives at the central HR/IR departments, one HR executive for ING-bank and one for ING-Postbank, and one member of the central works council. Interviews in Rabo were conducted in early 1996 and included five executives from central HR/IR departments, one regional director, and two branch managers. In MeesPierson the interviews took place in the last months of 1995 through early 1996 and included four executives at the central HR/IR department, including its director, one manager at the IT business unit, and one representative of the works council.

We express our gratitude to all respondents for spending their valuable time with us and sharing their insights with us. We also thank the librarian of NIBE, where we consulted annual and social reports of these banks and many other documents. We thank the FNV Service Union for permission to consult and access to two employee surveys and are particularly grateful to Kea Tijdens. Not least we thank sociology students Jos Diekman, Ilse Donkersloot, Jan Kamstra, Aart Swiebels, Sabine Keetels, and Patrick Smulders, who wrote detailed studies on aspects of HR policies in banks (see references).

References

van Bergeijk, P. A. G., C. van Gent, R. C. G. Haffner, and A. J. M. Kleiweg. (1995). "Mobiliteit en concurrentie op de kapitaalmarkt." *Economisch-Statistische Berichten*, 6 September, 780–84.

Boonstra, W. W., and J. de Jong. (1993). "The Future of European Banking." In S. C. W. Eijffinger and J. L. Gerards (eds.), *European Monetary Integration and the Financial Sector*. Amsterdam: NIBE, 85–115.

van den Brink, J. R. M. (1968). "De plaats van het bankwezen in het girale betalingsverkeer." In H. Reinoud (ed.), *Een halve eeuw Postcheque- en Girodienst*, 149–62. Utrecht, the Netherlands, and Antwerp, Belgium: Het Spectrum.

Buitelaar, W., and R. Bilderbeek. (1992). "Technology, Organisation and Human Resources in Dutch Banking." *P+, European Participation Monitor*, 4: 4–7.

Buitelaar, W., and R. Bilderbeek. (1991). "Bankinformatisering en organisatieverandering." In N. van de Heuvel (ed.), *Informatietechnologie en arbeidorganisatie in de dienstensector*, Amsterdam: Siswo, 35–51.

Chandler, A. D. (1961). *Strategy and Structure*. Cambridge, MA: MIT Press.

Diekman, J. (1993). "Autonomie bij de Rabo-bank, vrijheid in gebondenheid." Unpublished master's thesis, Department of Sociology, University of Amsterdam.

DiMaggio, P. J., and W. W. Powell. (1991). "The Iron Cage Revisited: Institutional Isomorphism and Collective Rationality in Organizational Fields." In W. W. Powell and P. J. DiMaggio, *The New Institutionalism in Organizational Analysis*, Chicago: University of Chicago Press, 63–82.

DNB. (1996). Jaarverslag 1996 (annual report). Amsterdam: De Nederlandsche Bank.

Donkersloot, I. (1994). "Functiemobiliteit binnen de Ing-bank." Unpublished master's thesis, Department of Sociology, University of Amsterdam.

Galbraith, J. K. (1975). *Money: Whence It Came, Where It Went*. Boston: Houghton Mifflin.

Gardiner, P. M., and P. Molyneux. (1990). *Changes in Western European Banking: An International Banker's Guide*. London: Routledge.

van den Hoven, T., and K. Tijdens. (1990). "Opleiden binnen het gezichtsveld van de banken." *Vernieuwing, Tijdschrift voor Onderwijs en Opvoeding*, 49(10): 15–17.

Hulsink, W. (1994). "Monopolised, Privatised, Diversified and Incorporated: An Institutional Analysis of the Evolution of the Dutch Postbank (1945–1994)." Paper presented at the WESWA Research Conference on Labor and Organization Studies at Twente University, Enschede, 25 November 1994.

Kamstra, J., and A. Swiebels. (1995). "Van Bankbediende tot adviseur: Een onderzoek naar de factoren die van invloed zijn op de selectiecriteria voor baliemedewerkers en accountmanagers bij de ABN Amro, ING-bank en Rabobank." Unpublished master's thesis, Department of Sociology, University of Amsterdam.

Kanter, R. M. (1977). *Men and Women of the Corporation*. New York: Basic Books.

Keetels, S. (1994). "De vorming van opleidingsbeleid in het bankwezen." Unpublished master's thesis, Department of Sociology, University of Amsterdam.

Kessler, I., and J. Purcell. (1995). "Individualism and Collectivism in Theory and Practice: Management Style and the Design of Pay Systems." In P. Edwards (ed.), *Industrial Relations: Theory and Practice in Britain*. Oxford: Blackwell, 337–367.

van Klaveren, M. and K. Tijdens. (1995). "Kwalificatie-ontwikkeling en interne arbeidsmarkten in het Nederlandse bankwezen." In J. J. J. van Dijck (ed.), *Liber Amoricum voor Albert Mok*. Lauret.

Metze, M. (1995). *De geur van geld*. 2d ed. Nijmegen, the Netherlands: Sun.

Mintzberg, H. (1979). *The Structuring of Organizations*. Englewood Cliffs, NJ: Prentice Hall.

Moran, M. (1984). *The Politics of Banking*. London: Macmillan.

Noten, H., and J. Warnink. (1991). "Zo zit u op de bank. Onderzoeksverslag van een enquête." Mimeographed. Dienstenbond FNV, Woerden, the Netherlands.

Rogers, J., and W. Streeck (eds.). (1995). *Works Councils: Consultation, Representation, and Cooperation in Industrial Relations*. Chicago and London: University of Chicago Press.

Rubery, J. (1995). "Internal Labour Markets and Equal Opportunities: Women's Position in Banks in European Countries." *European Journal of Industrial Relations*, 1(2): 203–28.

Sijbrands, S., and P. G. W. Jansen. (1995). "Personeelsmanagement & HRM in de financiële sector." *M&O Tijdschrift voor organisatiekunde en sociaal beleid*, 49(1): 4–21.

Smulders, P. (1993). "Verdwijnt het bankkantoor? De veranderingen in de distributiestructuur binnen het Nederlandse bankwezen." Unpublished master's thesis, Department of Sociology, University of Amsterdam.

Tijdens, K. (1997a). "De 36-urige werkweek bij de banken. Een analyse van verschillen tussen banken." Mimeographed. Faculty of Economics, University of Amsterdam.

Tijdens, K. (1997b). "Job Allocation: Personnel Policies and Women's Working Hours in the Banking Sector." In K. Tijdens, A. van Doorne-Huiskes, and T. Willemsen (eds.), *Time Allocation and Gender: The Relationship between Paid Labour and Household Work*, Tilburg, the Netherlands: Tilburg University Press, 189–212.

Tijdens, K. (1991). "25 jaar automatisering in het betalingsverkeer." In N. van de Heuvel (ed.), *Informatietechnologie en arbeidorganisatie in de dienstensector*, Amsterdam: Siswo, 127–156.

Tijdens, K. (1989) *Automatisering en vrouwenarbeid. Een studie over beroepssegregatie op de arbeidsmarkt, in administratieve beroepen en in het bankwezen*. Utrecht, the Netherlands: van Arkel.

Verkoren, H. K. (1989). "Retailbanking in Nederland: van bediening naar zelfbediening." In H. K. Verkoren (ed.), *Retailbanking*, Amsterdam: NIBE, 5–66.

Visser, J. (1998). "Two Cheers for Corporatism, One for the Market." *British Journal of Industrial Relations*, 36: 269–293.

Visser, J. (1995). "The Netherlands: From Paternalism to Representation." In J. Rogers and W. Streeck (eds.), *Works Councils: Consultation, Representation, and Cooperation in Industrial Relations*, Chicago and London: University of Chicago Press. 79–115.

Visser, J., and A. C. Hemerijck. (1997). "*A Dutch Miracle*": *Job Growth, Welfare Reform and Corporatism in the Netherlands*. Amsterdam: University of Amsterdam Press.

Wieringa, H. (1979). *Arbeidsverhoudingen in het bankwezen*. Nijmegen, the Netherlands: SUN.

Wijmans, L. (ed.). (1993). "Vakbonden, namens wie eigenlijk. Een onderzoek naar de representativiteit van vakbonden in het bankwezen." Mimeographed. University of Amsterdam, Department of Sociology.

Wijmans, L. (ed.). (1992). "Bankpersoneel en vakorganisatie. Een onderzoek onder leden en ex-leden van de FNV Dienstenbond binnen de AbnAmro bank." Mimeographed. University of Amsterdam, Department of Sociology.

Wilterdink, N. (1984). *Vermogensverhoudingen in Nederland*. Amsterdam: Synopsis.

10 The End of Institutional Stability? The German Banking Industry in Transition

Martin Baethge,
Nestor D'Alessio, and
Herbert Oberbeck

In contrast to that of many other OECD countries, the German banking industry has during the last fifteen years been a model of enduring stability. The crisis of the savings banks in the United States, the liquidity problems of the Japanese banks, the deregulation shocks in several countries, and the collapse of the mortgage market in Great Britain and Sweden have no comparable counterparts in Germany.

In our opinion two factors have contributed to this stability. First, the strong presence of universal banks capable of reacting flexibly to swings in the interest cycles and changes in demand made gradual market adjustments possible. Second, the gradual abolition of the administrative controls on the deposit and credit markets combined with a strict prudential regulation prevented financial shocks and speculative bubbles. These two factors, resulting from institutional arrangements and regulations, contributed to the long-term stability of the German banking industry. Moreover, they permitted the banks to develop long-term strategies of diversification that prevented competitors from entering their core markets. Consequently, they were able to stabilize their business, steer the changes in the national financial market, and preserve their dominant position. In addition, highly institutionalized systems of training and industrial relations facilitated a smooth adjustment of the workforce to the firms' new competitive strategies and rationalization policies.

Nevertheless, the German banking industry is currently in a phase of transition. Growing competition in the changing national and international markets is modifying the industry's business parameters. In addition, requirements of foreign investors and the exigencies of the EU, if accepted, could lead to the abolition of some business practices and weaken the stabilizing effects resulting from the current framework of regulation.

Confronted with a new business environment and many uncertainties, the banks are currently developing new competitive strategies, with the aim of improving their cost/output ratios. New criteria of market segmentation and advising intensity have been introduced, and delivery channels are being restructured. This process has begun to erode some of the institutional arrangements of the past and is affecting employment practices and industrial relations.

The Institutional and Business Environment of the German Banking Industry

Universal Banks as a Basis of Business Flexibility

In Germany there are three basic bank groups: the commercial banks, the savings banks (*Sparkassen*) and the cooperative banks (*Volks- und Raiffeisenbanken*) as well as a small number of specialized banks. All the banks in the three bank groups are universal banks authorized by the German Banking Act to conduct the whole range of banking business, and they are active with differing intensities not only in the deposit and credit markets but in the securities and investment business as well. Additionally, subsidiaries of the banks dominate the home mortgage market.

This broad spectrum of activities enables the banks to react flexibly to changes in consumer demand as well as to the swings of the interest cycle. In periods of decreasing intermediation margins, the banks can compensate for falling profitability in the credit business by expanding the securities business. This practice of internal resource allocation leads to relatively stable returns throughout the interest cycles (D'Alessio and Oberbeck 1995).

The conventional wisdom on the German banking industry emphasizes the existence of large universal banks that not only have equity in big companies but also exercise control through proxy rights and representation on those companies' supervisory boards. Apart from the fact that this theory of control is not undisputed (Edwards and Fischer 1993), the approach dismisses other important structural aspects of the industry, such as the fact that most of the banks have a relatively small business volume and are locally oriented, so that the five largest banks controlled only 17 percent of the total assets in 1995. Although important mergers that have taken place in 1997 and 1998 indicate an increasing concentration, one can suppose that in the near future the degree of concentration in the German banking industry will remain relatively low in international terms.

In 1996, there were 332 commercial banks which controlled 28 percent of the total deposits and 38 percent of the credit volume. Additionally, there were 607 public savings banks (*Sparkassen*), with a 43 percent share of the total deposits and 41 percent of the credit volume, as well as 2,510 credit cooperatives which controlled 20 percent of the total deposits and 14 percent of the credit volume (see tables 10.1, 10.2, and 10.3). In contrast to that of the deposit and credit shares, the distribution of the sum of the nominal value of shares deposited with banks shows a higher degree of concentration. The commercial banks controlled 77 percent of the total in year 1995, whereas the share of the three big banks amounted to 39 percent (Deutsche Bundesbank 1996).

The savings banks, which are public institutes owned by the municipalities, are authorized to conduct their banking activities only within the borders of their communities. However, they constitute only the first tier of the *Sparkassen* system. The giro institutions (*Landesbanken-Girozentralen*), which are state banks owned by the government of the respective states, and the associated *Sparkassen* represent the second tier of the system. These *Landesbanken-Girozentralen* manage the financial service requirements of their own federal states (*Länder*) and the regional and international business activities of the local savings banks. With only a narrow deposit base, the *Landesbanken-Girozentralen* meet their need for funds by borrowing from other banks, predominantly savings banks. Finally, the Deutsche Girozentrale (DGZ) constitutes a sort of central bank of the *Sparkassen* system; it conducts clearing activities and holds the liquid reserves of the *Landesbanken-Girozentralen*.

The system also includes an integrated ensemble of specialized firms that support the business of the local savings banks in areas such as mortgages, insurance, investment funds, and securities and offer marketing and technological support. This means that the relatively small local savings banks are actually part of a highly developed business system, which allows them to provide the whole range of universal bank activities. Because of their local embeddedness, they are able to carry out a business strategy finely tuned to the requirements of local markets. They can evaluate risks and chances more efficiently because the proximity of their clients makes it easier to gather relevant business information (Quack and Hildebrandt 1995).

Finally, the cooperative banks are also local banks integrated in a business system similar to the *Sparkassen* system. The cooperative bank sector has, like the savings banks, not only a three-tier system but also an ensemble of specialized firms that support the local banks in their universal banking activities.

Table 10.1
German banking industry: Number of categories of banks and of their branches, 1990–1996

Bank groups	1990[1] No. of banks	1990[1] No. of branches	1990[2] No. of banks	1990[2] No. of branches	1992 No. of banks	1992 No. of branches	1994 No. of banks	1994 No. of branches	1996 No. of banks	1996 No. of branches
Commercial banks	**332**	**6,289**	**338**	**6,552**	**334**	**7,302**	**331**	**7,348**	**326**	**7,277**
Big banks	6	3,105	6	3,224	4	3,553	3	3,621	3	3,579
Regional and other commercial banks	185	2,847	191	2,976	197	3,485	196	3,466	190	3,423
Private bankers	81	303	81	308	77	224	69	216	59	233
Savings bank sector	**586**	**17,521**	**781**	**19,347**	**730**	**20,008**	**656**	**19,704**	**620**	**19,331**
Regional Giro institutes	12	309	12	311	13	432	13	433	13	436
Savings banks	574	17,212	769	19,036	717	19,576	643	19,271	607	18,895
Credit cooperative sector	**3,046**	**15,800**	**3,384**	**17,435**	**2,915**	**17,872**	**2,664**	**17,449**	**2,510**	**17,019**
Regional institutes	4	31	4	33	4	47	4	46	4	42
Credit cooperatives	3,042	15,769	3,380	17,402	2,911	17,825	2,660	17,384	2,506	16,977
Mortage banks	36	49	36	58	34	258	33	283	34	305
Specialized banks	16	82	18	98	17	144	17	155	17	79
Building societies	23	61	23	63	25	3,047	35	3,788	34	3,712
Other credit institutions	131	5	131	6	136	14	136	14	133	18
Total without Deutsche Postbank AG	4,053	39,284	4,711	43,559	4,061	47,606	3,872	48,721	3,674	47,741
Deutsche Postbank AG	—	—	—	—	—	—	—	—	1	18,922
Total	**4,053**	**39,294**	**4,711**	**43,559**	**4,061**	**47,606**	**3,872**	**4,872**	**3,675**	**66,663**

Source: German Bundesbank.
Notes:
1. Only West Germany.
2. West and East Germany.

Table 10.2
German banking industry: Bank deposits by bank type, 1990–1996

Year	Total (MRD DM)	Commercial banks[1]	Savings banks[2]	Cooperative banks[3]	Others[4]
1990	2,418	29%	43%	20%	8%
1991	2,556	28	42	21	8
1992	2,694	29	42	21	8
1993	2,952	29	42	21	8
1994	3,057	28	42	21	9
1995	3,246	28	42	21	9
1996	3,515	28	43	20	9

Sources: Bundesverband deutscher Banken.
Notes:
1. Big banks, regional banks, private bankers, branches of foreign banks, private mortgage banks.
2. Regional giro institutes, savings banks, public mortgage banks.
3. Regional banks, cooperative banks.
4. Specialized banks, Postgirobank and Post savings bank.

Table 10.3
German banking industry: Bank lending to nonbanks by bank type, 1990–1996

Year	Total (MRD DM)	Commercial banks[1]	Savings banks[2]	Cooperative banks[3]	Others[4]
1990	3,043	41%	38%	14%	7%
1991	3,336	40	38	14	8
1992	3,693	39	38	15	8
1993	4,089	38	39	14	9
1994	4,395	37	40	15	8
1995	4,726	39	40	15	6
1996	5,125	38	41	14	7

Source: Bundesverband deutscher Banken.
Notes:
1. Big banks, regional banks, private bankers, branches of foreign banks, private mortage banks.
2. Regional giro institutes, savings banks, public + B21 mortgage banks.
3. Regional banks, cooperative banks.
4. Specialized banks, Postgirobank and Post savings bank.

The institutional networks developed by the savings banks and cooperative institutes have enabled them to provide the local markets with a wide range of banking and investment products at acceptable prices. The small and middle-sized commercial customers have predominantly benefited from this system. Its competitive advantage lies in the combination of local presence, flexibility, and business efficiency. In this sense, the case of the German savings and cooperative banks shows that a relatively low degree of concentration in the banking industry does not constitute a constraint on developing economies of scale and scope.

German Banking Regulations

Early deregulation of product markets and the abolition of administrative controls on interest rates in combination with strict prudential rules characterize the regulation framework of the German banking industry. This is the basis of the relatively conservative risk management and long-term business approach within the industry.

In contrast to some of the other OECD countries, Germany had already begun to liberalize its financial system during the 1950s. This facilitated smooth adjustments to new developments in the international financial markets. The Bundesbank Act of 1957 stipulates that the Bundesbank is independent of the federal government and responsible for ensuring consumer price stability. The Bundesbank has, until now, attempted to accomplish its task by using instruments that influence interest rate levels and access to the money market without distorting competition in the economy's financial sector. In the early 1960s, it abandoned direct control of bank interest rates and, beginning in 1958, abolished capital movement controls.

In the 1960s and the 1970s the Bundesbank also removed the administrative rules that segmented the markets through differentiated reserve requirements. Today the only functions of the minimum-reserve instrument relate to the management of liquidity and the demand for money. Rediscount and Lombard policies as well as open-market activities—purchases, sales, and repurchases of securities—are the contemporary instruments with which the Bundesbank carries out its monetary policy and interacts with the banks (Issing 1994).

The early and gradual deregulation of the financial system along with the Banking Act (1961), which allowed the banks to conduct universal bank activities, made a liberalization at the microlevel unnecessary and gave rise to a stable business environment. However, widespread, unregulated bank competition coexists with strict prudential regulation that stipulates minimum capital requirements, liquidity standards, and risk diversification to minimize bank default risks and stabilize the banking business in the long run. The regulations now in force stipulate the following:

• Long-term investments (four years or more) must be fully covered by long-term funds.

• Investment in property and shares cannot exceed the value of the firm's capital resources.

• A single large credit (credit exceeding 15 percent of capital) cannot be greater than 50 percent of the capital resources.

• The total volume of large credits is limited to 8 times the capital.

• Mortgage loans are not to exceed 60 percent of the worth of the collateral.

These regulations not only have led to a relatively conservative approach to risk management but also have reduced market volatility by imposing strict constraints on the transformation of maturities: Short-term funds cannot be used to fund long-term credits. Both of these factors have reinforced the stability of the German financial market without hindering a competitive environment (Vitols 1995).

Highly Qualified Staff as the Basis for Product and Service Diversification

The performance of universal banks depends on the effective management of a wide range of deposits, credits, securities, and other investment products, and this requires a highly skilled workforce. The basic and advanced vocational training systems in Germany supply the banks with the highly qualified employees they require.

In Germany employers, unions, and the government cooperatively organize vocational training. They determine together the syllabus of the training programs (*Berufsordnung*) and the requirements of the final examinations. Organized as a dual system, vocational training combines elements of on-the-job training with theoretical instruction at vocational schools. Although employers and the state share the costs of the training, the banks bear the larger part of the investment.

In the banking industry apprenticeships last two and a half to three years and offer trainees a broad vocational training that includes subjects such as account management, payments system, deposit products, credit evaluation, and the rudiments of the securities business. If the apprentice successfully completes the program, he or she is awarded the official title of Bank- or Sparkassenkaufmann. Although the banks are not bound by law to hire the apprentices after the examination, so far a large proportion of them have been incorporated as full employees. In this sense, vocational training continues to be the most important entrance to the banks. At the end of the 1980s almost 90 percent of bank employees had passed an examination as Bank- or Sparkassenkaufmann.

In addition, the majority of the banks send their personnel for further training to external regional institutes organized by the employers' associations. Commercial banks run the Bankakademie and the savings banks manage the Sparkassenakademie. The certificates these institutes award are considered a prerequisite for a managerial career at the banks. About 25 percent of the *Sparkassen* employees had, as of 1994, been awarded the title of Sparkassenfachwirt, whereas around 33 percent of the commercial bank employees were in possession of the Bankfachwirt certificate (Backhaus and Wagner 1996).

The importance of training is reflected in the fact that it constitutes 5–6 percent of the banks' total personnel costs. Cooperation among the state, firms, and unions makes training into a public good within the industry. Everyone pays, and poaching practices are not widespread. The banks benefit from a well-trained workforce, the small firms meet their training needs cost-effectively, and the unions use training achievements as criteria for job reclassification and higher wages.

The System of Industrial Relations

In the German banking industry, the organization of industrial relations corresponds to the dual system of interest representation prevalent in almost all German industries. This includes autonomous collective bargaining at the industry level and codetermination at the firm level. The levels are separated both legally and institutionally. The unions conduct the industry-wide negotiations for the collective wage agreements, whereas the works councils have, at the firm level, the right of codetermination on social concerns and personnel issues such as in-house training, reassignments, dismissals, and working time.

Within this institutional framework, three unions are active in the German banking industry. Whereas the Public Employees Union (ÖTV) represents the employees at the public *Sparkassen*, the Union of the Employees in Commerce, Banks, and Insurance (HBV) is active at the commercial and cooperative banks, and the Union of the German Employees (DAG) at the commercial banks and the *Sparkassen*. Only the first two are members of the Confederation of German Unions (DGB). According to unofficial estimates, combined union membership has never exceeded 15 percent of the bank industry workforce.

Skill level, which is the basis for wage group classification, and additionally seniority determine individual compensation. Consequently, the collective negotiations concentrate predominantly on wage group specifications and salary increases, thus management-union relations are not adversarial.

The collective salary agreement is binding only for banks that are members of the bank associations, and all the employees of these banks enjoy the collective agreement benefits irrespective of whether they are members of the unions. The collective salary agreement covered 65 percent of the employees in 1994. Executives, managers, and professionals in specialized areas (*Außertarifliche Angestellte*) are excluded from the collective wage agreement and are compensated on an individual basis.

Despite the relatively low level of union membership, unions and works councils, because of the prosperity of the industry in the past, have had little problem representing the employees' interests. In this sense, figures on salary differences among industries show that bank employees are among the best-paid workers in the German economy. Comparing the annual basic incomes of the middle wage groups in 1995, only employees in the energy industry with 55,900 DM, surpassed bank employees, with 47,200 DM, whereas the employees in the retail trade received 36,700 DM, and the income of the public employees amounted to 41,000 DM (WSI-Tarifarchiv 1996). Moreover, although control of technological and organizational changes has remained in the hands of the firms, the unions and the works councils have been able to influence some of the consequences. In 1983, the unions and the employee associations came to a collective agreement on rationalization that regulates not only requalification and internal reassignments of the affected employees but also severance pay in case of dismissals. The agreement also created the legal conditions for the intervention of the works councils at the firm level in matters of rationalization and facilitated a flexible adjustment of the workforce to technological changes.

Dynamics of Market and Employment

In the last two decades the expansion of services and bank products for private households has essentially determined, both quantitatively and qualitatively, the development of work and employment in German banking.

By the end of the 1980s the degree of market penetration in retail banking was relatively high. The overwhelming majority of private households (90 percent) had a checking and a savings account and made use of a comprehensive system of payment transfers that includes all regular payments by standing order or direct debit. By the end of 1987, automatic transfers and direct debiting represented 90 percent of the number of cashless payments and 81 percent of the volume of cashless payments (BIZ 1989). As of 1989, more than 50 percent of the people between ages thirty and fifty-nine and 43 percent of those between twenty and twenty-nine had at least one so-called *Bausparvertrag* (agreement under which a loan toward the acquisition of property is financed; DEKA 1990).

The creation of the German electronic payment system was the principal motor of market expansion for German banks. After lengthy and complicated negotiations on technological standards among representatives of the three bank groups, the German banking industry began at the end of the 1960s to set up the technological foundation for a homogeneous nationwide electronic payment system used by all the banks. Through a discriminatory fees policy—fees for traditional forms of money transfer for wage and salary payments were higher than fees for direct account payment—German firms were forced gradually to adopt the new method of payment introduced by the banks, whereas their employees had to open non–interest bearing checking accounts at a bank of their choice. Originally called "wage and salary accounts," these were the lever to integrate private households into a dense net of bank products and services. The transformation of the payment system contributed to greater consumer demand and strong expansion of retail banking activities (Baethge and Oberbeck 1986).

The high degree of market penetration at the end of the 1980s shows the success of a strategy of market control that combines technological cooperation with competition in the product and service markets. The forced integration of firms as well as households into the payment system facilitated cross-selling strategies, which increased the universal banks' marketing flexibility and reinforced their position at the center of the financial system.

To illustrate, 40.6 percent of the outstanding personal assets in 1990 were in the form of bank deposits, the life insurers had a share of 26.4 percent, and 16.6 percent were invested in bonds. Although the life insurers' share of the annual increases in personal assets grew from 15.2 percent in 1980 to 20.1 percent in 1989, while in the same period the bank deposit share dropped from 42.8 percent to 26 percent, the growth of investment in bonds best illustrates the changes in consumer demand. Their share of the growth in personal assets increased from 19.9 percent to 32.9 percent between 1980 and 1989 (Schulemburg 1991).

Although at first glance this looks like a weakening of the banks' market position, it is actually a product of their diversification strategy. The banks sell their own bonds directly and also control 72 percent of the growing investment fund business, whereas the insurance companies' market share is only 10 percent and that of the independent financial consultants 13 percent (BBE–Report Geldanlage 1993). Moreover, in spite of the growing competition with the insurance companies for personal assets, the banks still administer the insurance firms' asset management through special investment funds.

From the mid-1980s, the limitations of the expansion model of the preceding one and a half decades have become clear. As will be discussed in the second part of this chapter, market saturation in the segment of the basic bank products and services, falling profitability of the retail banking business, increasing operating costs, changes in the savings and investment behavior of private clients, and growing uncertainty on the corporate side of the business are indicators of a new business environment that have transformed the banks' business parameters and are forcing them again to revise their marketing strategies, rationalization concepts, and personnel policies.

As consequence of the strong business expansion described above, banking employment in West Germany increased from 543,850 employees in 1980 to 697,500 in 1989. The strongest growth within the bank groups occurred at the cooperative banks, followed by the savings banks and the commercial banks. However, with 761,150 employees in West and East Germany, the German banking industry reached its peak in 1994. Since then, employment has decreased slightly, to 753,750 employees in 1996. At the same time, the number of apprentices, which increased after reunification, started to fall in 1993 (tables 10.4 and 10.5).

Even though the increase in the number of jobs lost some of its momentum in the 1980s, this did not cause any change in the general picture dominating the postwar decades: The banking industry increasingly stood for stable and attractive jobs; employment was secure, and dismissals did not take place in this sector of the economy. In addition, employment in banks gained in attractiveness because the occupational structure had clearly shifted toward the highly qualified segment. Highly qualified staff

Table 10.4
German banking industry: Employment by bank type, 1980–1996

Year	Commercial banks and private building societies	Savings banks	Regional giro institutes and public building societies	Cooperative banks and Sparda banks	Total
1980	193,550	194,200	36,300	119,800	543,850
1985	200,700	213,650	38,000	146,550	598,900
1989	208,600	233,600	38,750	149,850	630,800
1990[1]	228,100	266,500	40,100	162,800	697,500
1991	233,150	281,350	38,600	170,450	723,550
1992	238,000	284,150	47,150	175,100	744,400
1993	238,400	287,750	49,450	178,600	754,200
1994	238,250	291,150	48,950	182,800	761,150
1995	235,400	290,050	49,650	185,850	760,950
1996	229,950	288,450	51,100	184,250	753,750

Source: Bundesverband deutscher Banken.
Notes: Does not include Bundesbank and Postbank.
1. 1990/1996: West and East Germany.

Table 10.5
Numbers of apprentices in the German banking industry, 1977–1994

Jahr	*Sparkassen/ Landesbanken*	Private banks and cooperative banks	Total
1977	16,501	11,065	27,566
1980	21,302	13,383	34,685
1985	25,264	15,718	40,982
1987	26,182	17,018	43,200
1989	26,378	15,842	42,220
1990	26,815	16,718	43,533
1991	30,730	18,451	49,181
1992	32,236	18,992	51,228
1993	31,740	17,793	49,533
1994	29,448	16,143	45,591

Source: Backhaus and Wagner, *Ausbilder-Taschenbuch,* 1996.

Table 10.6
German banking industry: Basic monthly salaries, 1996

Length of service	Salary groups								
	1	2	3	4	5	6	7	8	9
1–2 years	2,829	2,929	3,076	3,208	3,337				
3–4 years	2,986	3,108	3,226	3,370	3,516	3,705			
5–6 years	3,144	3,285	3,375	3,530	3,698	3,932	4,201		
7–8 years	3,337	3,499	3,525	3,692	3,882	4,160	4,481	4,843	
9 years			3,710	3,852	4,064	3,494	4,755	5,155	5,552
10 years				4,010	4,247	4,628	5,033	5,464	5,900
11 years					4,439	4,865	5,312	5,778	6,246

Source: Gewerkschaft HBV 1996.
Note: All figures in deutschemarks.

showed proportionally higher rates of growth, whereas the number of employees with less-challenging activities feel markedly.

The share of employees classified in the upper groups (7, 8, and 9) of the salary and classification scale (which include highly qualified financial advisers; specialists with demanding tasks in credit, deposits and investment; foreign business experts; human resources and computer specialists; as well as branch managers) grew from 19 percent of the employees in 1975 to 42 percent in 1994.

These figures also indicate that during the 1970s and 1980s positions in the back office were eliminated as a consequence of the automation of the payment system. The share of employees classified in the bottom groups (1, 2, 3) of the classification scale, which include clearing personnel, employees with simple tasks in back offices, and support employees in data processing and accounts departments, decreased from 22 percent in 1975 to 5 percent in 1994.

Finally, the share of employees classified in the salary groups 4, 5, and 6, which embrace counter staff involved in service and advice tasks as well as employees in credit, deposit, investments, foreign business and human resources, decreased from 59 percent in 1975 to 53 percent in 1994. Figures in table 10.6 show the basic monthly salaries in 1996 according to the salary groups included in the collective contract. The West German banking industry is dominated by female employees. In 1996, 54 percent of the employees in the private sector and 63 percent in the savings banks were women. For a long time the enterprises profited from this fact. Because of the high ratio of women, the level of turnover among bank employees was relatively high. Thus the enterprises had scope for flexible staffing practices and recruitment of new personnel. Furthermore, early retirement schemes have facilitated the numerical stabilization of staff.

Recently this relatively stable and attractive world of work and employment seems to be getting into more troubled waters. In the past, commercial and savings banks were synonymous with attractive work and a guaranteed future. Today, not only is the thesis of a necessary reduction of employment gaining force but a concrete decrease has taken place in the last three years.

The question of how far the process of bank restructuring has actually developed and which problems for work, employment, and industrial relations are connected with it is presented in the second part of this chapter by means of case studies of individual firms. Our four case studies are a large bank with a nationwide branch network (bank A); a large savings bank located in an important big city's affluent surrounding area (bank B); a wholesale bank without branches, which concentrates its retail banking activities on wealthy clients (bank C); and finally, the subsidiary of an international financial conglomerate with nationwide presence through a relatively small branch network, which runs only retail banking activities (bank D).

Bank Responses to the New Business Environment

Starting in the 1990s, all German banks introduced new criteria of market segmentation and client selection in their retail banking. These criteria arose from an observation of current market trends, which necessitate new competitive strategies, as well as from a more sophisticated analysis of the business relationships between clients and banks, developed with the help of new computer programs. This new strategy explicitly aims to achieve cost reductions through the standardization of administrative work and a more efficient use of technology.

In retail banking, both the savings and investment potential of the various client segments and the cost/output ratios of the specific products have been evaluated, with a twofold result. On the one hand, the differentiation between "nor-mal" clients, with little savings potential, and wealthy clients has become more pronounced. On the other hand, changes in advising practices have taken place. Wealthy clients are defined as advice-intensive clients with higher levels of demand for financial advising. In contrast, the advising services for standard clients are being reduced. Simultaneously, the range of products and services are changed.

Three of the banks investigated (A, B, and C) conducted a profit analysis of the products and services offered. In the past, products were usually developed separately. They were considered as packages when marketed, but in terms of product standardization and technological support, the label was not justified. Currently not only a redefinition of the range of products and services but also the creation of genuine "product packages" based on standardized work procedures and technological support is taking place. For example, credits in retail banking with maturities and repayment forms suited to clients' individual demands are no longer available at bank A. This indicates that the current rationalization process is dealing with standardized products and service packages, rather than with isolated products and services.

In addition to redefining and standardizing the spectrum of products and services, firms are restructuring their branch networks. Three groups of branches are distinguished in general: automated branches without employees, where clients handle standard bank transactions through multifunctional machines; branches in which self-service coexists with a minimum of personal service and advice; and branches in which the full range of products and services are offered (Terrahe 1992). At the same time, the number of ATMs increased from 8,775 in 1990 to 37,650 in 1996.

Among the firms we investigated, only bank B (*Sparkasse*) intends, within the next three or four years, to transform a part of its network into fully automated branches without personnel. These restructuring plans will affect, above all, branches in small villages, where business has decreased notably. In contrast to bank B, which aims to transform normal branches into full automated outlets, bank D has set up six new fully automated branches in selected locations in large cities. Bank A, as distinct from Banks B and D, has a dense, nationwide network of branches located in urban areas, does not intend to introduce full automated branches.

The cases investigated show that cost and marketing considerations play a considerable role in the selection of technology. Whereas bank B's strategy aims to reduce the costs of a dense regional branch network without abandoning the market, that of bank D, which has a relatively small branch network, aims at penetrating the market through fully automated branches, which represent a cost-effective alternative to the normal branches with personnel. On the other hand, bank A, which is exposed to fierce competition with the savings banks and cooperative banks in urban areas, does not intend to give up direct contact with its clients. Fully automated branches are not part of its delivery strategy. Finally, banks A,

B, and D all offer PC banking services, and banks A and D have set up subsidiaries, which as direct banks sell bank and investment products by phone.

Even if one can identify cost and marketing considerations as the forces behind the new technological patterns, the actual consequences are unpredictable. For example, in the eyes of several managers, phone banking does not appear to be a profitable innovation for the long run. Because it is often considered nothing more than a temporary first step in the transition to PC banking, many firms offer it only to prevent the loss of clients to banks that already offer phone banking. Competitive pressures can apparently force firms to institute business practices that have uncertain profit prospects.

New Organizational Structures

Corresponding to the new marketing and delivery strategies, a growing functional differentiation within the bank organization has modified not only the branches' structure and function but also the way retail banking activities are performed. Competencies and spheres of responsibilities no longer strictly correspond to the traditional hierarchical lines, and new forms of management and control are being introduced.

Both banks A and B have implemented an internal reorganization of their branches according to new criteria of client segmentation. With a range of sixty different highly standardized products and services, which includes not only transaction services and savings products but also securities in the form of investment funds, the branches of bank A offer service and advice only to less-affluent clients.

On the other hand, wealthy private clients with higher income levels are served in special centers, which are being created in selected branches. Teams consisting of two advisers, one specializing in securities business and the other in lending and real estate, are responsible for the personal service of a given number of clients. In contrast to the past, when the advisers worked independently, the bank intends to create better conditions for a more fluid processing of *AllFinanz* business strategies in retail banking through the constitution of teams.

The centers for wealthy clients report not to the branches in which they are located but to the retail banking division. The same form of supervision is being practiced in commercial banking. These activities are being consolidated at the regional headquarters level but are supervised by the bank's business division. Only the business of less-affluent clients and basic payment transactions of wealthy clients and firms remain under the jurisdiction of the branches, which the regional headquarters still directly supervises. But this is only a temporary solution. In the future, the branches will also be integrated into the retail banking division, whereas the regional headquarters will do no more than coordinate the different divisions' activities at the regional level.

Bank B is also involved in the internal restructuring of its branches according to the new criteria of client segmentation. However, in contrast to bank A, it does not intend to divisionalize its business activities. The creation of centers for wealthy private clients in selected branches took place within the organizational framework of the traditional structure, and the regional headquarters retained jurisdiction over the centers.

The situation at bank D is different. As part of the retail banking division of an international financial conglomerate, the bank is organized as an autonomous subsidiary, and its business activities are restricted to retail banking. Bank D offers a narrow range of standardized products. Consumer credit, for customers with average or low incomes, is handled as a "bulk good." Applications for credit are accepted in the branches, where automated evaluation systems make it possible for employees to give preliminary approval immediately. Afterward the documents are sent to a central office where final approval is granted and repayment is supervised. The branches are highly automated sales outlets integrated into a traditional hierarchical structure.

Bank C represents a special case within the general trend of the organizational restructuring processes we described above. The bank has concluded the divisionalization of its organizational structure and is implementing a program of client segmentation. However, as a wholesale bank without a branch network, the firm is not confronted with the problems arising from the reorganization of branch networks based on new client segmentation schemes. The main element of its reorganization is an advanced training program for its existing advisers.

Summing up, the banks we investigated are involved in programs of restructuring their organizations to adapt to new criteria of client segmentation based on financial means and the profits the business generates. Along with the transformation of the business and service units into profit or cost centers, the restructuring allows a new form of directing and controlling the banks' business affairs.

The introduction of centers for wealthy clients in the branches, the divisionalization of specific businesses (retail, corporate, investment), and the establishment of subsidiaries to manage direct banking services (we return to this point later) are examples of organizational reactions to current market trends and the higher level of business segmentation. One can speak of "banks within the banks" that have their own specific business and marketing strategies and profitability criteria.

The banking business has become more specialized and centralized. Whereas branch activities are being restricted through product standardization and the abolition of negotiable conditions for individual clients, the business of the divisions, subsidiaries, and centers has become more autonomous. Simultaneously, the headquarters now audits the performance of the various business units more strictly than in the past. This control takes the form of fixed budgets, highly differentiated risk limits, and strict profit goals.

Changes in Work and Employment Practices

The innovations in the business, marketing, and delivery policies described above are causing changes in employment practices. Even if the changes have, until now, not had a disruptive impact on the institutionalized framework represented by the collective salary agreement and the vocational training system, they will notably affect the ways that banking staff perform their work.

Changes in Work Organization and Occupational Structure

The most serious changes will affect bank employees in the branches. Client segmentation in retail banking, with its sharp differentiation between advisers for standard products and less-affluent clients, and *All-Finanz* advisers for clients with greater financial potential, will transform the structures of branch staff. New lines of differentiation within the staff in the next few years will lead to greater variations in bank employees' professional status.

Advisers for less-affluent clients, who will be responsible for payment transactions to all types of clients but provide service and advice only to the less-affluent clients (overdraft, consumer credit, credit cards, investment funds, and life insurance), will perform the administrative work connected with the products sold. As result of the new work organization that joins front and back office functions in one person, these employees will be confronted not only with downgrading of their work but also with the spread of self-service in the form of telephone banking or automated branches, which will threaten their jobs in the mid-term. In this sense, they will find themselves in a situation similar to that of the back office employees in the past.

Furthermore, the advisers for less-affluent clients will have to sell products according to computer-based qualitative and quantitative targets set in the head office. This will reduce individual advice to short talks oriented toward the sale of standardized products. Thus the work of well-trained employees will be downgraded not only in terms of tasks but also in terms of status: They will do no more than sell standardized products.

In contrast to the advisers for less-affluent clients, the advisers for wealthy clients and credit officials for small and midsized firms will experience a professional upgrading. Further training programs in insurance, real estate, and taxes will reinforce their know-how in the area of *All-Finanzstrategien*. In the internal labor market, this group of employees will constitute a source of recruitment for some of the leading management positions of the future.

The managements of both banks A and B have conceded that they do not at the moment have enough qualified employees to implement their new marketing strategy. It is difficult to overcome the old separation between the securities and lending departments, and to train employees to handle and sell both forms of service. Although conceived as a transitional solution for the integration problems, the creation of adviser teams, as in bank A, might become the prevailing form of organizing advising activities in the near future.

The work autonomy of the advisers for wealthy clients will probably be greater than that of the advisers for less-affluent clients. However, headquarters will also set their sales targets, and their professional success will strongly depend on the achievement of these sales and turnover targets. The professional role of branch managers has already changed in bank A. Having lost the responsibility for wealthy clients and small and midsized firms, the branches have become sales outlets, where the managers' tasks are limited to staff deployment, work coordination, the achievement of sales goals, and the observation of the local market. Traditional tasks of branch managers, such as the cultivation of the small and midsized firms, have disappeared.

Working Time
Although the legal workweek is 48 hours from Monday to Saturday, the collectively agreed weekly working time varies among different industries. In the case of the commercial banks, the weekly working time amounts to 39 hours per week averaged over three months, within which

45 hours in any given week is the maximum permitted. Both provisions define the framework within which work councils can negotiate flexible working-time schemes. Saturday is not a normal working day, and the contract establishes the compensation to be paid when employees work on Saturday. Work conditions and compensation of part-time employees are also regulated through the collective contract.

In contrast to commercial banks, working time in the savings banks amounts to 38.5 hours weekly. One year, as a maximum, instead of three months, is the basis for the calculation of the weekly working time. Saturday is not a working day.

Part-time employment in commercial banks grew from 9.0 percent in 1980 to 12.0 percent in 1996; women represented 95 percent of the part-time employment pool. On the other hand, part-time work in savings banks grew from 14 percent in 1986 to 19 percent in 1996. The increase in part-time work has allowed the implementation of new flexible working-time schemes in banks A and B, so that they have extended their banking hours.

In spite of the increase of part-time work in the last years, banks A, B, and C have started an offensive to increase further the amount of part-time work as an instrument to cope with a surplus of employees without dismissals. Plans for new part-time schemes at bank B include innovative variants of job sharing, such as the possibility of working full time for three months and not at all for the following three. As mentioned, systems of flexible banking hours are being introduced to optimize workforce deployment. For example, at bank C, the new system permits deviations up to a total of forty hours—whether more or less than the norm—to be accumulated and equalized almost without exceptions at employee's will.

Recruitment, Training, and Career Patterns

In the 1970s and 1980s, the majority of German banks supported their territorial expansion and market penetration by increasing their number of apprentices and expanding the internal advanced training programs. However, changes in recruitment practices and the organization of further training are apparent. The firms expect a further decrease in employment in the back office and in advising for less-affluent customers as a consequence of technological rationalization and the redefinition of delivery channels. Accordingly, the number of apprentices (see table 10.5) as well as expenditures for advanced training within the institutionalized system (Bankakademie and Sparkassenakademie) are decreasing.

Simultaneously, the firms are reorganizing their internal training programs and have recently increased their recruitment of university graduates. The four banks investigated justify the new recruitment practices with the argument that only university graduates possess the skills required for the commercial and securities business. The positions in headquarters will also increasingly be filled by employees with a university education.

In the mid-term, the recruitment of university graduates will restrict the promotion prospects for advisers of both the less-affluent and the wealthy clients. Whereas in the past the Bankkaufmann and the Sparkassenkaufmann (titles obtained after completing apprenticeship) had to overcome at most two main training barriers to move up, today they face more obstacles. In both banks A and B the human resources department have developed more-differentiated career and promotion schemes that include additional training requirements.

In contrast to the 1970s and 1980s, the selection criteria for employees destined for the Bankakademie or Sparkassenakademie have become stricter in the 1990s, and the number of participants will probably decrease. On the other hand, the number of internal advanced training programs that train employees exclusively for specific tasks is growing. Internal advanced training is being reorganized into a set of modules based on specific tasks. Each module constitutes a barrier in the career path of the upwardly mobile Bankkaufmann/Sparkassenkaufmann. Earlier training was more likely to be external and based on standardized programs, so the employees could change firms relatively easily.

A consequence of these developments is an erosion of the German training system in the banking industry. However, banks do not intend to abandon the institutionalized framework of the basic and advanced training system in the next few years, although managers in banks A and B concede that advisers for less-affluent clients, the first job after completing the apprenticeship, could be trained internally in one year rather than through the typical two-and-a-half-year apprenticeship. Additionally, the increasing recruitment of university graduates will make access to leading positions more difficult for employees trained exclusively within the institutionalized training system.

Bank business has to do with money collection and money allocation. However, the increasing differentiation in performing these functions means that the old bank organization no longer exists. Actually, a bank now consists of distinct business areas each with its own internal complexity, work practices, and professional mentalities. All this casts doubts on the future of an institutionalized training system well adapted to the relative homogeneity of the German banking world of the past. Adjustments will be necessary if the training system is to survive.

Classifications and Compensation

The collective wage agreement is still the central instrument of regulation for bank employees' job classifications and levels of compensation. However, despite the stability of the institutionalized framework, plans to rearrange the wage groups, which also entail modifying the job task spectrums and skill requirements, and the gradual introduction of new, performance-oriented compensation schemes will alter the prevalent employment practices. They will not negate the traditional payment system, but they will make it considerably more complicated.

At banks A and B, task spectrums and skill levels of the advisers for less-affluent clients are being redefined in a way that will allow them to be classified one or two wage groups lower than the advisers currently working in the branches. Considering the employers' practices up to now, it is difficult to imagine that they will reclassify the advisers currently employed. For the newly hired, however, the works councils probably will not be able to hinder the change, because if their work activities are limited to the business intended for less-affluent clients, their assignment spectrum is thus reduced, and in such cases the wage agreement stipulates a lower salary classification.

Apart from a few exceptional cases, until the mid-1990s there were no compensation schemes linked to employee performance in the German banking industry. The few exceptions were executives at the *Sparkassen* and cooperative banks as well as at the commercial banks and credit officials in the field of corporate finance at the big banks. The compensation of employees occupied in retail banking was regulated solely by the collective salary agreement, which as indicated above distinguishes between classifications on the basis of the tasks performed, the level of qualification, and seniority.

The issue of performance-related salaries will be emphasized in the next years, though it is not yet clear which of the concepts currently being discussed will be agreed upon. The banks investigated have not yet introduced new forms of compensation, but they do not exclude the possibility of doing this in the near future. Currently, one can observe in other German banks new compensation and incentive schemes linked to employees' performance:

• collective performance premiums for work teams or branch staff that have reached or surpassed sales goals

• individual performance premiums for employees who have reached or surpassed the sales goals for specific products particularly important to the firms' marketing strategy

• allowances that the firms grant voluntarily, at times linked to firm profitability or individual performance

The unions do not necessarily reject the new criteria of performance evaluation and compensation schemes, though in several cases where commercial banks are attempting to personalize performance evaluations and bonus payments, some fractions of the works councils, supported by one of the unions (HBV), are resisting. They suspect that the new scheme will lead to work intensification and growing competition among the employees. These functionaries propose the introduction of bonus payments on a collective basis, such as at the branch level. They also want to make sales goals an object of negotiation to prevent the intensification of competition within the workforce. The increasing significance of sales targets for employees stems from its linkage with performance evaluations, which determine the employees' opportunities for advanced training and promotion.

In the next years, the works councils will increasingly have to negotiate such new forms of performance-oriented payment at company level. However, no serious conflicts with employers are likely to arise in this field. Any serious conflicts are much more likely to be expected in matters of security of employment and the settlement of working hours. The most recent pay agreements of June 1996 show that both employers and unions expect a progressively larger reduction in the number of employees in the next few years. It was agreed, however, that if the need for a reduction in the number of employees should arise, it should be achieved primarily through the shortening of working hours for all employees (without pay compensation) and not through dismissals. Currently, the reduction practices of recent years are continued: increasing part-time work, natural turnover, and the use of early retirement regulations to stabilize employment levels and still modify staff structures. Whether all these instruments will suffice to guarantee flexible adjustments of the number of employees to new operational structures and a varying amount of work, only the coming months and years will show.

Direct Banks: A Provocation for Industrial Relations

Although the world of the industrial relations in the German banks seems to be largely in good order, the employers and unions are confronting each other irreconcilably over the question of the conditions of work and employment in the newly founded direct banks. The conflicts arise over foundations outside the institutionalized practices.

In the past two or three years several banks have started to offer bank products and services by phone. They have organized the new direct banks as subsidiaries not affiliated with the bankers' associations, so the collective wage agreement does not cover the employees. Although some of the direct banks are subsidiaries of firms that were not members of the bank associations, association members are setting up most of the new direct banks. Through the creation of subsidiaries, these banks evade the regulations concerning job classification, compensation, and wage premiums contained in the collective wage agreement. Because the unions cannot negotiate with banks not affiliated with the banking association, they have no way of influencing the developments at the direct banks. To win influence, the unions must convince the employees of the direct banks to organize works councils and to demand the negotiation of a salary agreement at the firm. This is a difficult task in a time of high unemployment.

The work and employment relationships in the direct banks deviate in almost all central points from those typical of the banking business:

• Work is carried out in shifts, twenty-four hours a day and seven days a week.

• A sophisticated computer program for the analysis of the frequency and nature of calls permits flexible deployment of the workforce based on the specialized skills required (information, bank products, investment products) at specific times.

• The compensation of the employees, converted into hourly rates, is lower than the wages the collective agreement fixes for the same tasks in normal branches, and there are no premiums for night or weekend work.

• Most of these banks are located in regions where the structure of the labor market allows the banks to easily hire the necessary workforce.

• A commercial clerk certificate (graduates of a basic sales training program not specifically oriented to the financial business) is a prerequisite for being hired, and after a nine-to-ten-week training course, the employees are fully integrated into the work process. Only the applicants to be employed as specialists for investment products need the Bankkaufmann certificate.

We do not expect these new strategies of the employers to become a precedent for the banking business as a whole. Even in the next years, the direct banks will serve only a certain, restricted segment of the market for financial services, and their employees will correspondingly represent only a relatively small minority in relation to the number of the typical bank employees. Nevertheless, a certain symbolic effect arises from this completely new practice: It will become obvious to everybody that employees who have no special training are satisfying at least a part of the needs of customers in the financial services sector. Perhaps just this will have an explosive effect for the commercial banks and savings banks, for it might in future be increasingly asked whether highly paid, qualified employees are still necessary, at least for dealing with less-affluent clients. The emergence of the direct banks and their recruiting and training practices makes it, all in all, more difficult for both those in the employers' camp and those on the side of the unions, who do not wish to see the basic principle shaken that a two-and-a-half-year basic training is necessary for the qualification as Bank- and Sparkassenkaufmann.

Conclusions

After a relatively long phase of business expansion in the field of retail banking, increasing cost/output ratios at the end of the 1980s forced the German commercial and savings banks to reconsider their business policy in retail banking. Thus a business policy that had been successful for more than two decades, sustained by the expansion of the branch network, automation of back office tasks, and computer-aided service and advice in the front office areas, was called into question. In this respect, the credo in retail banking up to the end of the 1980s was to assign customer advising to qualified bank employees only, and mostly to get by without self-service technologies and standardized advising. This credo was abandoned in the first half of the 1990s.

Today most German commercial and savings banks are profoundly restructuring their retail banking businesses. In contrast to other industrial countries, where the restructuring of the capital- and labor-intensive retail banking involved a drastic reduction of the number of branches as well as mass dismissals, the strategy of the German banks, at least for the time being, aims at a strong reduction neither of their territorial presence nor of their staff. Rather, the banks are attempting to establish a new balance between operating costs and market presence by reorganizing the hierarchy of branches according to customer segmentation, using technology (automated branches, PC banking, and direct banks), introducing new schemes of job classification, working time, banking hours, and performance-linked payment, and redefining further training substantially. In this respect, as banks are confronted with decreasing interest margins, increasing competition (in terms of business volume rather than price competition), convenience, and cost-cutting policies seem to be the central elements of the new business strategy of German banks.

However, against the background of the general tendencies that characterize the restructuring process, our empirical research shows that differences exist relating to the use of technology, organizational structures, and the degree of centralization. As indicated in the chapter, market position, size, and business policies are determinant in explaining the different strategies banks A, B, and D are pursuing. In contrast, the differences in work organization at the branch level are less pronounced.

Even if the changes affecting job classification, working time, banking hours, and payment are notable, the three central institutions of the German labor market—collective bargaining at the industry level, codetermination at the firm level, and the vocational training system—as well as the legislation on early retirement continue to frame the human resources policies of banks and their industrial relations. For this reason, in matters of HR/IR the banks investigated bear a great resemblance. The force of the institutional framework homogenizes the changes in work and employment practices. Only in the case of the direct banks can we observe a departure from the institutionalized practices; its consequences are hardly to be forecast.

Of course, this restructuring has not been concluded anywhere, that is, management, works councils, and unions as well as the employees themselves are gathering experience with the new forms of organization and evaluating them. Thus all those involved in the implementation of this restructuring are acting in an environment where uncertainty concerning the results of these strategic options and restructuring efforts has increased.

The management of one of the big private banks, for example, has conceded that, among other things, customers have not fully accepted the division of providing advice in accordance with the income level and the financial position of private households. Consequently, in the course of this restructuring the bank had to accept the loss of some 150,000 private customers whom it would have liked to keep because of their income levels.

Management often expresses such uncertainties concerning customer reactions. This has had consequences, for example, in the field of savings banks, where the implementation of new concepts for customer selection and the quality of advising is not as radical as conceived at the beginning of the 1990s (for instance, the three-class hierarchy of branches; cf. for details D'Alessio and Oberbeck 1994).

At the firm level, the long-term consequences resulting from a stricter distinction between advisers for routine business and advisers for wealthy clients are also open. From today's view, we cannot exclude a trend for the advisers for routine business to become the losers in restructuring in retail banking: financial devaluation of their work, a very restricted range of tasks, high performance requirements, and loss of status and image because they seldom come into contact with economically interesting bank customers. This newly created division of tasks might result in an impasse for some staff, unless the chances of in-house mobility into other fields of work are arranged in a sufficiently flexible way and are at the same time promoted by the firms.

Whereas management faces the challenge of creating and stabilizing organizational and incentive structures, which enable a relatively smooth reorganization of staff structures without any loss of market shares, new constellations of interest demanding innovative answers also confront the unions and works councils. Job reclassifications, increasing part-time employment, and performance-oriented payment systems will lead in the next few years to greater variations in salaries and professional status among different categories of employees. And since issues such as job reclassification or changes in working hours require consultations with the works councils, the firms will become an important arena for conflicts and negotiations. Thus the developments for industrial relations observed in German banking show similarities to those in manufacturing (cf. Dörre and Neubert 1995).

However, a considerable difference between banking and manufacturing is evident. For the employees themselves, the restructuring processes in retail banking hardly offer any new chances of participation in organizing work processes: More than ever, the management of the company, particularly the heads of the newly created divisions, is defining the way private customers of different level are to be advised, the standards for the duration of consultations, and the definition and control of bonus payments. The scope of action has been restricted here, even for middle management. Thus in contrast to observations concerning German manufacturing (cf. Wolf 1994; Dörre and Neubert 1995), no new quality of participation for employees in banking is emerging. Rather a development in the opposite direction is evident: Central planning and control on the enterprise level is increasingly enforced.

Despite all the tensions that accompany the restructuring processes in banks, there are, no serious indications that banks aim to carry out the business and organizational transformation outside the institutional terrain of industrial relations. As indicated above, the only exception is the direct banks. Unions and works councils realize that in the face of a structural change that cannot be prevented, the institutional system with its representative boards is still the best instrument to prevent the negative consequences of a painful adaptation process being carried exclusively by the employees concerned. The forces of the market push restructuring in retail banking forward in Germany, but the social partners still appear careful and flexible enough to want to adjust without destroying the institutional framework. However, to what extent the changes in the work and employment practices will transform the substance of the institutional framework in the long run is a question that remains open.

The Interviews

In the four banks, A, B, C, and D, thirty-four interviews with top managers, division heads, and works councils were carried out. In addition, discussions with four leading union officials took place. The inteviews in the four banks were performed in the following organizational areas:

	A	B	C	D
Personnel/Works council	4	4	3	6
Organization	1	1	–	1
Sales	3	–	2	1
Controlling/quality Management	–	1	1	1
District management/Direct bank	1	–	–	4

References

Backhaus, J., and R. Wagner. (1996). *Ausbilder—Taschenbuch.* Stuttgart: Deutscher Sparkassen Verlag.

Baethge, M., and H. Oberbeck. (1986). *Zukunft der Angestellten.* Frankfurt am Main and New York: Campus.

BBE-Report Geldanlage. 1993. In *"Handelsblatt."* Düsseldorf, December 9.

[BTZ] Bank für Internationales Zahlungsausgleich. (1996). *66, Jahresbericht.* Frankfurt: BIZ.

[BTZ] Bank für Internationales Zahlungsausgleich. (1989). *Zahlungsverkehrssystem in elf entwickleten Ländern.* Frankfurt: Fritz Knapp Verlag.

D'Alessio, N., and H. Oberbeck. (1995). "Strukturveränderungen im Wettbewerb der Finanz-dienstleistungsunternehmen." In *Konzepte zur Reorganisation von Finanzdienstleistungen,* 13–26. Düsseldorf: Hans-Böckler-Stiftung.

D'Alessio, N., and H. Oberbeck. (1994). "Lean Banking: Klassische Rationalisierung im neuen Gewand oder Methaper für eine komplexe Neuorientierung von Finanzdienstleistern?" *SOFI-Mitteilungen,* 21 (February): 53–64.

[DEKA] (1990). "Investmentgesellschaft der Sparkassen" In U. Perina (ed.), *Kurzbuch Geld* 25–27. Frankfurt am Main: Fischer.

Deutsche Bundesbank. (1996). *Statistische Sonderveröffentlichung* 9. August.

Deutsche Bundesbank. (1994). *Monatsbericht.* October.

Dörre, K., and J. Neubert. (1995). "Neue Managementkonzepte und industrielle Beziehungen: Aushandlungsbedarf statt Sachzwang Reorganisation." In G. Schreyögg and J. Sydow (eds.), *Managementforschung* (5), 167–213. Berlin/New York: de Gruyter.

Edwards, J., and K. Fishcer. (1993). *Banks, Finance and Investment in Germany.* Cambridge: Cambridge University Press.

Issing, M. (1994). "Experiences Gained with Monetary Policy Instruments in Germany." Paper presented at the Seventeenth Symposium of the Institute of Bank Historical Research, Frankfurt am Main.

Oberbeck, H., and N. D'Alessio. (1997). "The End of the German Model? Developmental Tendencies in the German Banking Industry." In G. Morgan and D. Knights (eds.), *Dereg-ulation and European Financial Services,* 86–104. London: MacMillan.

Quack, S., and S. Hildebrandt. (1995). "*Hausbank* or *Fournisseur:* Bank Services for Small and Medium Sized Enterprises in Germany and France." Discussion paper, Wissenschaftszentrum, Berlin.

Schulemburg, Graf von, J. M. (1991). "Organisations- und Steuerungsfragen aus der Sicht eines Versicherungsunternehmens." *Beihefte zu Kredit und Kapital,* 11: 221–36.

Terrahe, J. (1992). "Das Rationalisierungsmotiv der Banken its längst dem Kundenwunsch gewichen." *Banken International, Handelsblatt Beilage* 91 (May), 38.

Vitols, S. (1995). "Are German Banks Different?" Discussion paper, Wissenschaftszentrum, Berlin.

Wolf, H. (1994). "Rationalisierung und Partizipation." *Leviathan,* 22(2): 243–59.

WSI-Tarifarchiv. (1996). In *Handelsblatt,* March 4. Düsseldorf.

III

Conclusions

11

Comparing Banks in Advanced Economies: The Role of Markets, Technology, and Institutions in Employment Relations

Marino Regini

The country studies presented in the previous chapters have shown how and to what extent work practices and labor relations in the banking sector have changed during the last ten to fifteen years. They have also shown how they differ across countries—as well as across enterprises in the same country—and especially, the extent to which new practices are differently implemented. The following key analytical questions emerge from these country studies (not surprisingly, since these questions oriented the fieldwork in each country): Why is there such a wide variation among banks in work practices and labor relations? And why have they changed or not changed? What factors account for the variation and change (or lack of it)?

Change and Variation in Employment Relations: The Available Interpretive Frameworks

In addition to describing the work practices and labor relations prevailing in the banks studied, each national chapter has analyzed their context: the structure of the banking industry, the different business strategies pursued by banks, changes in technology, the regulatory regime, and, more generally, the public policies that affect the way the banking business is conducted. In fact, most available interpretations of change and differences in employment relations in the advanced economies stress precisely one or more of these elements.

Quite often, scholars set two groups of factors against each other as potential independent variables or combine them into slightly more complex explanations. Some of them stress the role of market competition and of technological innovation as the main driving force. They view differences in the rate of change as stemming from the different intensity of market competition and technological innovation (as perceived by economic actors). Other scholars see institutions and processes of institutional regulation or deregulation as the main factors (or culprits) of change (or of retarded adjustment).

The simplest explanation of why employment relations change at different rates, and in some cases even in different directions, across countries and firms is based on a combination of these two groups of factors. The need to respond to increased market competition and to the challenges and opportunities offered by technological innovation, it is maintained, is translated into strong pressures to change. These pressures, however, are filtered through existing institutions (operating economy-wide or specific to the sector), which often retard or cushion their effects on employment relations, whereas in some cases they may be accompanied by processes of institutional transformation that reinforce these effects.

The framework that guided this comparative study of the banking sector (as well as the companion studies of the automobile, steel and telecommunications industries; see the preface to this volume) is an elaboration on that rather simple, and quite widespread, explanation. First, company level employment relations are conceptualized as clusters of HR/IR practices. These clusters vary over time, across nations and across companies of the same country, along a continuum from "traditional" to "new." To test this variance empirically, HR/IR practices have been operationalized into a series of indicators that may be analyzed in each bank in a comparative dimension: most important among them are such practices as the organization of work and working time, training and skill development, compensation and incentives, staffing arrangements, and forms of employee involvement and of interaction with trade unions. The idea was to map the range of diversity in these practices through company-based case studies to discern where and when new employment relations take the place of more traditional ones. Also, we hoped to gain some insights on the actual outcomes of different HR/IR practices, namely, on whether company performance is significantly associated with the adoption of one or another of these practices.

Second, the factors that are given a preeminent role in accounting for change and variation in HR/IR practices are basically the same in our framework as those in the traditional explanations, that is, market competition, technological change, and institutions. However, the way they are supposed to work is different. Market competition and technological innovation are not seen in a deterministic way in the studies presented here. In fact, the pressures coming from these powerful and universal factors are not directly translated into a common managerial policy of change in HR/ IR practices; even without taking into account the role of institutions, there is ample room for "strategic choices" by management. The two basic strategies in this regard are those that base competition on either cost reduction or product quality. The choice made between these alternative business strategies is mainly responsible for how HR/IR practices are transformed and for which clusters of practices come to characterize a company or even an entire industry.

Institutions are not seen in the studies here as necessarily retarding change or simply cushioning the otherwise disruptive effects of markets and technology. Rather, they are an intervening variable that articulates with business strategies in determining the type of transformation that takes place in employment relations. In this regard, we must consider not only the public policies specifically targeted at the sector under study (in our case, banking) but also labor market regulation, industrial relations institutions at the national and industry level, the educational and vocational training system, and the social security system. Thus broadly defined, institutions are not the initiator of change but a factor that helps shape the "strategic choices" made by companies with regard to their HR/ IR practices.

The results of the fieldwork conducted in the banking sector of nine countries, as presented in the national chapters above, have shown this initial framework to be a very useful list of the relevant explanatory variables, but to have clear limitations as an overall hypothesis. We will discuss this crucial point after briefly recapitulating some of the main lines of change and of variation our research has brought to light.

Common Trends versus Cross-Country and Intrasectoral Differences

The introduction to this volume has already discussed the common trends that emerge in the banking sector in a comparative perspective as well as the major differences among the countries studied and even among banks within the same country. It is therefore possible to concentrate here on a few major aspects while referring the reader to the introductory chapter for a comprehensive overview.

It should come as no surprise that in all countries, the actors in the banking sector show an extremely high awareness of the relevance of recent changes in employment relations and tend to emphasize their extent and import even beyond their actual manifestations. In fact, highly traditional work practices have characterized banking everywhere for so long and so uninterruptedly that rapid transformations are now often regarded as a revolution. Major transformations are indeed taking place, but only a few are industry specific; most others represent just accelerated processes of what has taken place in export-oriented manufacturing industries over a longer time span and with (at least so far) more profound consequences.

Two such processes stand out among the latter: an increase in labor flexibility and a decentralization of industrial relations and human resources management. The pressure for greater labor flexibility has been a general trend in all advanced economies since the 1980s (Piore and Sabel 1984; Boyer 1986). It still had a great symbolic impact when it started to extend to the banking sector several years later because employment relations in banks had traditionally been characterized by de facto lifetime employment, structured careers, seniority-based pay, and paternalistic personnel policies. All this has come to an end in the current decade. Furthermore industrial relations, which in most countries reflected the bureaucratized, semipublic character of this industry, inevitably entered a process of diversification and decentralization (Regini 1995).

More interesting, of course, are the industry-specific transformations in HR/IR practices that have occurred in all the countries studied. The previous chapters have highlighted quite a few, but for the purposes of this discussion it may be useful to focus on three that seem to play a crucial role in both the actual processes of change in the organization of work in banks and the actors' perceptions of it.

The first of these transformations is the growing distinction between front office and back office employees. The first wave of technological innovation (electronic data processing) and work reorganization has overwhelmingly hit the back office employees by reducing dramatically the demand for their skills and often concentrating them in large information processing centers organized according to pure Taylorist principles. By contrast, front office employees have for some time enjoyed growing employment, further training, functional flexibility in the forms of job rotation and job enlargement, and requests for greater cooperation. In several countries, the second wave of technological innovation (ATMs, home banking, telephone banking, and the like) is now eroding these privileges, whereas in others the distinction remains sharp. But both the timing of these processes of technological innovation and work reorganization and the ways they affect the two groups of employees have converged in drawing a clear division within a bank's human resources practices.

A second general, though industry-specific, transformation has been the introduction of a sales culture into previously hierarchically based, bureaucratic organizations. Banks are increasingly transformed into market- and customer-oriented companies. The studies presented in the preceding chapters make it rather clear what this involves for human resources management: a change in the role of managers, a demand for social and relational—even more than technical—skills, an encouragement to experiment with job rotation and multiskilling, and the introduction of performance-related incentives. Again, this applies much more to front office employees than to back office staff.

Finally, banking products and services, and hence clients, are increasingly being segmented, overshadowing the relevance of the older distinction between the front and back office. As all the chapters on the various countries show (perhaps with a special emphasis in the German, Dutch, British, and U.S. cases), more and more banks are reorganizing work according to the type of customer their employees have to deal with. In some cases, the relevant distinction seems to be between the corporate sector on the one hand and individuals or small businesses on the other; in others, it is conceptualized as a differentiation between high net worth and standardized mass sectors; in others still, a distinction is simply made between wealthy clients and those less so. The common implication, however, is that work in banks is increasingly reorganized along two opposite lines. The first group of customers, which requires high-level services, personal attention, and elaborate advice, is served either in special branches and centers or by teams of well-trained consultants that emphasize a style of work aptly defined as "relationship banking" (see chapter 2). The second group is increasingly referred to do-it-yourself services or to outlets organized as points of sale of standardized products and advice, requiring only a few lesser-skilled employees whose jobs are constantly under threat from automation.

In addition to common trends, our case studies have revealed wide variations in HR/IR practices among countries and even among banks in the same country. The introductory chapter analyzes these differences, and the reader is referred there. One such difference should be mentioned here, however, because it is relevant to the following discussion of institutions' role in changing employment relations: the varying extent to which banks' growing need to respond to increasing competition and to deregulation of the banking sector has eroded traditionally high levels of employment security. Although downsizing and recourse to nontraditional contracts have not so far been as dramatic in banking as in most manufacturing industries, employment reduction has clearly become an objective of primary importance for management. Only in some countries, however, have employment levels sharply decreased. In others, the combined effects of greater union resistance and an expansion of the outlet network (and perhaps of less emphasis on cost reduction by bank management) have to a large extent offset the consequences of the generalized reorganization of branches and headquarters along principles of "lean service."

Making Sense of Change and Variation in Employment Relations in Banks

The common trends and the differences highlighted by our comparative study and selectively summarized above show how the initial interpretive framework should be reformulated to make sense of change and variation in employment relations in banks.

From Traditional to New HR/IR Practices?

The conceptualization of our dependent variable—the different clusters of HR/IR practices—as a continuum from traditional to new practices, as well as the underlying issue of the differential diffusion of the latter, have proven largely misleading. Of course, "new" was not intended to mean, in this perspective, merely "different from the previous pattern"; if it had, one could indeed offer the empirically grounded but trivial observation that a lot has changed in employment relations in banks, though unevenly and perhaps less than their actors maintain. What it meant instead was a pattern of HR/IR practices described as consistent with the reorganization of production and services along "post-Fordist" lines. This pattern involves, among other things, a high degree of labor flexibility but secure employment for core workers, an emphasis on training and human resources development, the use of teamwork or other innovative methods of work organization, and some forms of employee involvement (Kochan, Katz, and McKersie 1986).

Our findings, however, have shown that change in employment relations in banks has taken place in a more complex and contradictory way. Not only has it often produced mixes of traditional and new patterns—as was probably to be expected—but it has also shown that traditional work practices may sometimes perform innovative functions, whereas apparently new practices may produce old consequences. Even more important, transformations in employment relations may follow directions that, when seen from the perspective of our analytical models, appear contradictory.

This is the case, for instance, for one crucial trend discussed above, namely the polarization between front office and back office employees. In some cases, banks have responded to market competition and technological innovation by transforming HR/IR practices for the former in ways that correspond in many respects to the paradigm of employment relations in post-Fordist settings. This applies more generally to employees in the high net worth segment of the market. But they have at the same time reorganized work for back office employees in ways that produce the opposite effects, namely a Taylorization of their jobs, a concentration in hierarchically organized workplaces, and an overall downgrading.

On the other hand, the persistence of traditional practices sometimes obscures their use as functional substitutes of newer ones. For instance, not all the banks studied have responded in the same ways to the common need to inject a sales culture into their employees to become more customer-oriented organizations. Whereas some have attached great importance to new training programs that teach social and relational skills, others have simply changed their recruitment criteria and reorganized traditional on-the-job training to meet this objective. Hence further research should aim at building typologies of HR/IR practices, rather than categorizing them simply as more or less new/traditional and placing them along a continuum.

Market and Technology as Determinants of Change, and Institutions as an Intervening Variable?

As we saw above, the pressures stemming from market competition and technological innovation are generally regarded as the main factors in the transformation of HR/IR practices. In the interpretive framework that we initially adopted, these pressures are filtered through the "strategic choices" employers make, which give rise to different business strategies, but they retain their role as the engine of change. Institutions and institutional processes are an intervening variable, in that they provide management with a given set of resources and constraints that are often taken into consideration when choosing among different clusters of HR/IR practices; hence they help shape this choice.

However, our comparative study does not fully confirm this hierarchy of explanatory factors. Almost everywhere, processes of institutional deregulation of the banking sector, often accompanied by a trend toward privatization and by a redefinition of relationships between banks and industry, have spurred initial change in HR/IR practices. These processes have only in part been a response to changing markets and technologies. As our cases show, they have more often been stimulated by other factors, and have in turn contributed to create increased market competition and new technological opportunities.

Once such competition and technological innovation have become powerful enough to force banks to attempt further change in employment relations, other institutions have entered the scene, either constraining or fostering these attempts. Labor market legislation in particular, and the type of labor regulation more generally, as well as trade unions and industrial relations institutions have played a key role in shaping the widely different solutions in terms of HR/IR practices that our study has brought to light.

This is not to deny that markets and technology have also contributed independently to producing the same outcomes. The growing volatility of markets for financial products, stemming from customers' greater attention to interest rates and to pricing and quality of service, has increased competition among banks, which as a result can rely less on traditional client loyalty. Also, as some of our country studies show, banks often used automation initially with rather vague objectives, no clear views on users or organizational consequences, and a severe underestimation of costs: in other words, a "technology push" occurred in the banking sector as a very tentative answer to growing costs.

The analysis above implies that markets, technology, and institutions should be seen in an interactive way. Not only is the question of which is the engine of transformation in employment relations misplaced; more importantly, the impact of each of these factors is compounded by its interaction with the others, so that their overall effect varies greatly from country to country.

Two Alternative Business Strategies?

The interpretive framework initially adopted to guide our study relied on a sharp distinction between two alternative business strategies, namely, on the assumption that companies can, by and large, base competition on either product quality or cost reduction. The pursuit of one or the other strategy was expected to be a primary factor in explaining why different companies adopt different clusters of HR/IR practices.

Though admittedly oversimplifying reality, this distinction is very widespread not just in industrial relations studies but also in the broader political economy literature. Hence, it requires some elaboration here before we discuss why it may be misleading in interpreting our evidence. The basic idea is that a firm's choice among different patterns of HR/IR practices depends primarily on its product market strategy, namely, on the specific manner in which the firm chooses to compete. Although the range of organizational and market strategies cannot be reduced to a simple dichotomy, most literature focuses on the two strategies suggested above (product quality versus cost reduction) for the purpose of simplification.

Firms that set out to compete on the quality of their products, rather than solely on their price, generally adopt the former strategy. They aim to avoid competition from companies in low-wage areas by targeting higher market segments, by responding to the greater sophistication and volatility of demand through product customization, and so on. Various factors, such as significant organizational and coordination capacities make quality, thus defined, possible, but the high and broad skilling of all occupational groups in the labor force, workers' ability to integrate several tasks in the performance of work as well as to learn new tasks rapidly, and employees' involvement in corporate objectives of constant improvement and incremental innovation all play a crucial role. To this corresponds a pattern of human resources development based on a large proportion of the labor force receiving extensive vocational training—both basic and company specific—and being encouraged to develop such social skills as initiative, a problem-solving attitude, and ability to work with others, as well as a high degree of identification with the company. Also required of the workforce is high functional flexibility, which is matched by low levels of the other types of labor flexibility: numerical, wage, and working-time flexibility (Atkinson 1987; Piore 1986).

A cost reduction strategy is based instead on holding prices down by mass producing a variety of goods and by containing labor costs. Automation enables companies to reduce drastically the demand for medium- skilled personnel, as well as emphasizing adaptability to change and cooperation rather than technical abilities. On the other hand, demand for high-level skills is concentrated in a few key occupational groups: middle management, technicians, and personnel in the commercial area (sales, marketing, customer relations). The pattern of human resources management deriving from these features involves a polarization between highly skilled personnel belonging to these occupational groups, on one end, and the low-skilled, as well as workers whose skills have become obsolete, on the other. The entire labor force is employed in a context of high flexibility: mainly functional (polyvalence) and wage flexibility (incentives) for the core occupational groups, and mainly numerical (temporary work, training and work contracts, vulnerability to lay off) for the low-skilled groups.

However, the chapters in this volume suggest that management rarely conceives (and pursues) these two analytically distinct business strategies as actual alternatives. The available evidence points instead to their coexistence and tension, often as a result of management uncertainty, dilemmas, and processes of trial and error, rather than of strategic choices.

Two examples serve to illustrate this conclusion. In several countries, an expansion of the branch networks has partly offset the reduction of employment levels taking place in recent years in the banking sector as a result of increased competition and technological innovation. This expansion has allowed many banks to deploy a large part of their workforce to newly opened outlets rather than laying them off. We may clearly interpret this outcome as stemming from a tension between cost-cutting and quality-enhancing business strategies. The former would require downsizing and layoffs to save on labor costs, generally very high in the banking sector. The latter suggests that competition for many banks is not based solely on the prices of their products, which cost reduction can keep low, but also on quality of services, which for many customers implies proximity to their place of residence or business.

Whereas the coexistence of employment reduction and outlet expansion characterizes the banking sector of only a few countries, this is not so for client segmentation, which as we have seen throughout the previous chapters is a universal trend among the banks studied. The growing reliance on do-it-yourself services and standard products sold by poorly trained employees as the main market strategy for lower-end customers does not prevent—and actually goes hand in hand with—the development of close personal relationships and integrated service offered by highly skilled consultants as a way to attract corporate and higher-end clients. Of course, some banks tend to specialize in either segment, but most try to combine the two types of strategies—the cost-cutting and the quality-based ones. With regard to the large number of customers in between (especially small businesses and individuals of moderate wealth), this combination easily turns into tension and uncertainty, as it is not clear which strategy yields better results for banks.

The Outcome of HR/IR Practices: One Best Way or Alternative Solutions?

This last point leads us to the final issue. Our study did not find any significant association between the adoption of one or the other HR/IR practice and the observable indicators of company performance (although it should be noted that we made no rigorous attempts to measure bank performance, given the difficulty of agreeing on objective indicators in this sector). This suggests that banking is not an industry where "one best way" to manage human resources and to organize labor relations can be detected, let alone agreed upon. In fact, several of the chapters note the diffusion of a phenomenon that characterized the industrial sector in the transitional years of the 1980s, aptly defined as "the uncertainties of management in the management of uncertainty" (Streeck 1987). In some cases, performance-related pay has been introduced and then abandoned. In others, branch staff are trained for narrow roles but are afterwards exposed to intensive job rotation to increase their polyvalence.

Several other examples of this uncertainty could be offered. Perhaps the best illustration of the trade-off inherent in decisions concerning the HR/IR practices to adopt in the banking sector, and hence of the dilemmas involving how to calculate the costs-to-benefits ratio, is, however, the debate on whether and how to proceed further in the trend toward client segmentation discussed above. As we saw, a large majority of banks have chosen a cost-cutting strategy for dealing with the lower-end customers. However, should this policy be taken to the extreme consequences of replacing all personal contacts between staff and clients with do-it-yourself operations to save further on labor costs? Or should a bank, against this background of generalized cost reduction, try to differentiate itself for its ability to customize service? Or more radically, should it encourage the lower-end customers to visit its branches even when buying standardized products sold by poorly trained employees to expose these customers to its other product packages and to increase its chances to sell them?

Seen in this light, it comes as no surprise that banking today resembles the industrial sector of the 1980s. As was the case then in industry, the old pattern of employment relations is everywhere being abandoned. However, the widespread variations among countries—and to some extent among banks in the same country—that our study brought to light do not simply reflect different stages in a uniform process of change. They are the outcome of trial-and-error processes, led more by uncertainty than strategy. Whether these will eventually become learning processes, leading to the final emergence of a new hegemonic pattern of employment relations in banks, we are not in a position to predict with any certainty.

References

Atkinson, J. (1987). "Flexibility or fragmentation? The United Kingdom Labour Market in the Eighties." *Labour and Society*, 12: 87–105.

Boyer, R. (ed.). (1986). *La flexibilité du travail en Europe*. Paris: La Dècouverte.

Kochan, T., H. Katz, and R. McKersie. (1986). *The Transformation of American Industrial Relations*. New York: Basic Books.

Piore, M. (1986). "Perspectives on Labor Market Flexibility." *Industrial Relations*, 25: 146–66.

Piore, M., and C. Sabel. (1984). *The Second Industrial Divide*. New York: Basic Books.

Regini, M. (1995). *Uncertain Boundaries: The Social and Political Construction of European Economies*. New York: Cambridge University Press.

Streeck, W. (1987). "The Uncertainties of Management in the Management of Uncertainty." *International Journal of Political Economy*, 17(3): 57–87.

Index

AA Insurance, 35
ABA. *See* Australian Bankers' Association
Abbey National Bank, 137(table), 138(table), 144, 145, 151, 154
ABI. *See* Associazione Bancaria Italiana
AbnAmro, 256, 258–259, 265, 266, 270–271, 273, 276, 277, 278, 279, 281, 282, 284
Acquisitions: customer, 43, 55–56
Acri, 161, 171, 172
ACTU. *See* Australian Council of Trade Unions
Administration, 194–195, 206–207. *See also* Management
Advance Bank (New South Wales), 69
AFB. *See* Association Française des Banques
AGF. *See* Assurances Générales de France, 190
AIRC. *See* Australian Industrial Relations Commission
ALCATEL-ALSTHOM, 190
Algemene Bank Netherland (Abn), 256. *See also* AbnAmro
AllFinanz, 263–264, 304, 305
American Express, 35
AMI. *See* Asociación de Mandos Intermedios
AMP insurance company, 102
Amsterdam-Rotterdam Bank (Amro), 256, 258. *See also* AbnAmro
ANZ Banking Group, 64, 70, 87, 88, 102, 116
Apprenticeships, 15–16, 231, 293–294, 306
Arbitration system, 98–99, 100
Argentaria, 229
ASB, 102, 123n.5

Asociación de Mandos Intermedios (AMI), 234, 251–252n.6
Asociación Española de Banca, 233
Asociación Española de Cajas de Ahorro, 233
Assicredito, 161, 165–166, 171
Association Française des Banques (AFB), 188, 194, 196, 198, 199, 204, 214
  collective bargaining, 212, 215, 216
  job classifications, 202, 203
  labor negotiations and, 211, 213
  salary structure in, 209, 210
Associazione Bancaria Italiana (ABI), 161, 171, 172
Assurances Générales de France (AGF), 190
AT&T, 35
ATMs, 7, 8, 13, 60n.6, 132, 194, 301
  in Australia, 68, 72, 75, 90
  in the Netherlands, 263, 264
  in New Zealand, 102–103, 111
  in the United States, 40, 41, 55
Auckland, 102, 113
Auroux laws, 191–192
Australia, 4, 5, 7, 14, 18, 63, 96, 259
  branch banking in, 8, 13
  career paths in, 17, 78–80, 87–88
  compensation in, 20, 23
  competitive pressures in, 67–72
  deregulation in, 64–65
  employment in, 9, 80–81
  enterprise governance, 84–87
  industrial relations in, 27, 65–67
  labor market in, 72–74
  market forces in, 89–90
  operating hours in, 12–13
  salary structure in, 82–84
  staff reduction in, 90–91

Australia (cont.)
  technological changes in, 68–69
  training, 15, 16, 81–82
  work organization in, 74–77
Australia & New Zealand Banking Group.
  See ANZ Banking Group
Australian Bankers' Association (ABA), 86
Australian Bureau of Statistics, 73
Australian Council of Trade Unions
  (ACTU), 66
Australian Industrial Relations Commission
  (AIRC), 66
Automation, 39–40, 193, 213, 262–263,
  266, 270, 299

Back office, 104, 105, 120, 167–168, 169,
  187, 263, 299
Bailouts, 3, 5, 7
Bankakademie, 294, 306, 307
Bank assurance, 190, 197, 264
Bankers' Institute, 111
Bankers' Trust, 35
Bankfachwirt, 294
Banking Act (Germany), 292
Banking Insurance and Finance Union
  (BIFU), 140, 146, 148, 150, 151, 152
Banking Law (1984) (France), 188–189
Bankkaufmann, 294, 307, 311
Bank of America, 35
Bank Officers' Union, 100–101
Bank of France, 188
Bank of Italy, 159
Bank of New Zealand (BNZ), 96, 102, 103,
  107
Bank of South Australia, 69
Banque Bruxelles Lambert, 259
Banque Commerciale Privée, 196
Banque Directe, 199
Banque Française du Commerce Extérieur,
  196–197
Banque Hervet, 197
Banque Nationale de Paris (BNP), 190, 196,
  208, 218
Banques Populaires, 209, 216
Barclays Bank, 130, 142, 154, 259
Barings, 259
Bausparvertrag, 296
BBV, 260
Belgian Generale Bank, 258, 259
Belgium, 259
Bernard, M., 218
Bertrand, O., 236

Berufsordnung, 293
BIFU. See Banking Insurance and Finance
  Union
Blaustein, Edgar, 206
BNP. See Banque Nationale de Paris
BNZ. See Bank of New Zealand
Bonds, 190, 297
Bonuses, 52. See also Compensation;
  Incentives
Bossards, 197
Branch banking, 8, 13, 35, 40, 45, 87, 164,
  229, 266
  in Australia, 68, 75–77, 82, 90
  in Germany, 302–304, 313
  and information technology, 132, 133
  managers and, 50, 78–79, 168
  in the Netherlands, 262, 263–264, 268–
  269
  in New Zealand, 102, 118
  processing systems and, 11, 12
  reorganization of, 134–135, 141–142,
  237–238, 302–304
  services and, 46–47, 60n.7
  skill development in, 50, 82
  in Spain, 237–238, 244–245
  in United Kingdom, 130–131, 155
  in United States, 41, 43(table)
  work organization in, 74–75, 207
Bretton Woods system, 5
Brokerage houses, 4, 34, 35
Building societies, 77, 86, 131
Bundesbank Act, 292
Business banking, 76, 104, 106
Businesses, 33, 42, 54, 236–237, 303–304
Business units: bank operations as, 142–143

Caisse d'Epargne, 201, 203, 207, 209, 214
Caisse des Dépôts et Consignations, 188
Caisse Nationale du Crédit Agricole, 216
Caisse Nationale du Crédit Mutuel, 211, 216
CAL. See Computer-assisted learning
California, 37(table)
Canada, 68
Cantegril, Michel, 216
Career paths, 15, 17–18, 45–46, 77, 110
  in Australia, 78–80, 83, 87–88
  in Italy, 169–170, 181–182
  in the Netherlands, 255–256, 277
  in Spain, 231, 252n.13
  in the United Kingdom, 129, 142, 146,
  152–153
Cartels, 257, 258

Case managers, 42
Cash cards, 164
CBT. *See* Computer-based training
CC. *See* Confederación de Cuadros
CCOO. *See* Comisiones Obreras
CE. *See* Comités d'entreprise
Central Bank (Netherlands), 257, 271
Centralization, 142, 207, 265
  of back office activities, 167–168
  of branch banking services, 302–304
  of labor relations, 260–261
  of processing functions, 11, 75, 87, 105
CEWU. *See* Communication and Energy
  Workers Union
CFDT. *See* Democratic French
  Confederation of Workers
CFTC. *See* French Confederation of
  Christian Workers
CGT. *See* Confederación General del
  Trabajo; Confederation General of
  Workers
Chartered Institute of Banking, 145
CIAL. *See* Crédit Industriel d'Alsace-Lorraine
CIC. *See* Crédit Industriel et Commercial
CIG. *See* Confederación Intersindical Gallega
Citibank, 67
Clearing banks, 130
Clerical Workers Union, 100, 101
Client segmentation: and work organization,
  302–305, 313, 323
CNV. *See* Protestant Christian Federation
Collective bargaining, 24, 37, 86, 260, 282,
  295
  company-level, 173–174, 176, 282
  and employee training, 16–17, 204
  in France, 190–192, 199, 211–213, 215–
  216
  in Italy, 162, 171, 181–182
  in New Zealand, 98, 100–101, 115–116,
  120
  and personnel surpluses, 174–175
  salary system and, 207, 208, 295
  in Spain, 238–239, 241, 242–243
  in the United Kingdom, 151, 155–156
Collective Bargaining Agreement (France),
  208, 210
Collective employment contracts, 99, 100–
  101
Colonial Mutual Insurance Company, 65
Comisiones Obreras (CCOO), 234, 251n.6
Comité de Empresa, 25, 252n.14
Comités d'entreprise (CE), 27, 191

Commercial banking industry, 36
Commercial banks, 34, 35, 38(table), 41, 47,
  52, 130, 184nn.1, 2, 257, 262
  in Germany, 288–289, 294, 295, 311–312
  skill development in, 48–50
  in the United States, 44, 58–59
Commissions, 21, 52, 54
Committees: employee representative, 175
Commoditization, 55
Commonwealth Bank of Australia, 64, 65,
  72, 85, 86, 87, 88
Communication and Energy Workers Union
  (CEWU), 101
Communist Party, 190–191
Compagnie Bancaire/Paribas, 199, 217–218
Company Act (Netherlands), 278
Company-level bargaining, 162, 173–174
Company training schools, 168
Compensation, 20
  in Australia, 82–84, 92n.9
  in Germany, 295, 308–309
  in Italy, 170–171, 182
  in the Netherlands, 276–277
  in New Zealand, 113–114
  in Spain, 241–242
  in the United Kingdom, 147–149, 154
  in the United States, 51–54
Competition, 3, 28, 35, 206, 258
  in Australia, 63, 67–72
  for customers, 105–106, 230
  and deregulation, 5, 10, 34
  determining, 209–211
  in France, 196–197
  in Germany, 287–288
  in Italy, 162–163, 181
  in New Zealand, 99, 101–102, 104
  in Spain, 225, 227, 229
  and technology, 296–297, 319–321
  in the United Kingdom, 129, 131
  in the United States, 33, 40–41
Comptoir des Entrepreneurs, 213
Computer-assisted learning (CAL), 145
Computer-based training (CBT), 144
Computers, computerization, 10, 15, 39, 69,
  75, 193, 213, 238. *See also* PC banking;
  Technology
Concentration, 3, 7, 28, 164, 223, 261
Conciliation and arbitration model, 98
Confederación de Cuadros (CC), 234, 251–
  252n.6
Confederación General del Trabajo (CGT),
  234, 251n.6

Confederación Intersindical Gallega (CIG), 234, 251n.6
Confederation General of Workers (CGT), 190–191
Conservative government (Australia), 66–67
Contingent pay mechanisms, 21–22, 52, 53
Contracts, 166–167, 171
"Convergence" hypothesis, 4
Cooperative banks, 4, 288, 289, 292, 295
Cooperative (Coop) Bank, 137(table), 138(table) 140, 141, 144, 146, 148, 151, 154
Corporación Bancaria de España, 229
Corporate banking, 10, 16, 42
Cost reduction, 7, 10, 19, 74, 199, 229, 327–328
  market pressures and, 89–90
  in the Netherlands, 265–266, 268
  in New Zealand, 99, 104–105, 120
  in Spain, 247–248
Countrywide Bank, 102
Credit, 36, 39, 47, 188, 189, 198, 293, 303
Crédit Agricole, 197, 207
Credit cards, 5, 134
Crédit du Nord, 197, 203, 208
Crédit Foncier de France, 213, 215
Crédit Industriel d'Alsace-Lorraine (CIAL), 198, 201, 202, 206, 207, 209, 210–211, 215, 217
Crédit Industriel et Commercial (CIC), 198, 212
Crédit Lyonnais, 190, 196, 198, 201, 202, 203–204, 206–207, 208, 209, 213, 214, 217, 259
Credit market, 160, 287
Crédit Mutuel Alsace, 197, 198, 202, 203, 209
Crédit Mutuel de Bretagne, 206, 213
Crédit National, 197
Cressent, Jen-Louis, 218
Crocker's Bank, 135
Customers, 89, 132, 194, 230
  acquisition of, 55–56
  and bank restructuring, 236–238
  competition of, 105–106, 230
  and employees, 243–244
  relationship management of, 56–57
Customer service, 76, 194, 229, 248
Customization: mass, 42–43

DAG. See Union of the German Employees
Daher, Lucile, 217

Databank, 103–104
Debit cards, 132
Decentralization, 24, 66, 90, 120, 149, 183, 207, 244–245, 252n.9, 282
Dematerialization, 193
Democratic French Confederation of Workers (CFDT), 190, 212, 217, 218
De Nederlandsche Bank (DNB), 257, 258
Depository Institutions Acts (1980, 1982), 34–35
Deregulation, 3, 4, 5, 7, 10, 28, 79, 131, 258, 325–326
  in Australia, 64–67
  in France, 224–225
  in Italy, 159–160, 180, 183
  of labor market, 96–98
  in New Zealand, 95, 119–120
  in the United States, 33, 34–35
Deskilling, 14
Destaffing, 269–271
Deutsche Bank, 259
Deutsche Girozentrale (DGZ), 289
DFC Finance, 96
DGZ. See Deutsche Girozentrale
Dienstenbond (Service Union), 260
Direct banking services, 303–304
Direct banks, 13–14, 197, 310–311
Direct deposit services, 40
Directors of human resources (DRH), 211
Disintermediation, 189
Distribution chains, 189
DNB. See De Nederlandsche Bank
Downsizing, 18, 72, 80, 88, 137, 140, 323–324
Dressen, M., 206
DRH. See Directors of human resources
Dutch Association of Banks. See Nederlandse Vereniging van Banken
Dutch Banker's Association (NBV), 257
Dutch Central Bank. See De Nederlandsche Bank
Dutch Federation of Trade Unions (FNV), 260, 284
Dutch Institute of Banking and Investment. See Nederlands Instituut voor het Bank-en Effectenbedrijf

EBA. See Enterprise bargaining agreement
ECA. See Employment Contracts Act
Economic and Monetary Union Treaty, 189
Economic growth, 96–97
Education, 38, 74, 97, 233, 252n.12, 275. See also Training

EFTPOS, 13, 68, 75, 104, 105, 111, 132, 134, 263
ELA/STV. *See* Sindicato de Trabajadores Vascos
Electronic banking, 102, 264, 296. *See also* ATMS; EFTPOS; Telephone banking services
Employees, 13, 29, 38, 40, 54, 105, 133, 199
  branch banking and, 229, 238–239
  branch reorganization and, 141–142
  career paths and, 78–80, 87–88, 169–170
  classification of, 202–204
  client segmentation and, 304–305
  collective bargaining and, 242–243
  company-level bargaining and, 173–174
  compensation levels for, 19–21, 51–54, 147–149, 170–171
  contingent pay mechanisms and, 21–22
  employer relationships, 54–57, 80–81
  industrial relations and, 26–28, 175–176
  involvement of, 243–246, 252n.14, 278–279
  Italian labor market, 160–161, 181
  and job security, 17–18, 45–46, 60n.8, 63, 150, 214–215
  management of, 25–26, 135–136, 178–179
  in New Zealand, 99, 118–119
  participation by, 313–314
  performance and remuneration for, 113–114
  recruitment of, 165–166, 182–183
  reduction of, 90–91, 269–272, 323–324
  relocation and, 270–271
  salary structure, 208–209
  skills of, 14, 230–231
  surpluses, 174–175
  training of, 15–17, 60n.10, 81–82, 143–145, 161–162, 168–169, 204–206
  trust and commitment of, 116–118
  in the United Kingdom, 136–140
  unions and, 114–115, 261
  U.S. treatment of, 57–58
  work organization and, 74–77, 271–273, 321–324
Employers' Association in the Banking Industry. *See* Werkgeversvereniging in het Bankbedrijf
Employers' associations, organizations, 171–172, 233–234, 259–260
Employment, 10(table), 24, 106, 120, 321–322, 324–325

  and direct banks, 310–311
  in Germany, 297–300
  levels of, 9, 17–18, 72–74, 96–97, 123nn.3, 6, 165–166, 185n.12, 199–201, 202–204, 274
  in the Netherlands, 256, 265(table), 266, 267(table), 270
  in New Zealand, 96–97, 98–99, 107–109, 121–122(tables), 123nn.3, 6, 7
  rates of, 230–231
  security of, 45–46, 54–55, 57, 109–110
  and services, 295–296
  skill development and, 48–50
  in Spain, 231–233
  in the United Kingdom, 129, 136–140, 153–154
  work intensification and, 14–15
Employment Contracts Act (ECA), 98, 99, 100, 101, 111, 114, 115, 123n.4
England, 69. *See also* United Kingdom
Enterprise bargaining agreement (EBA), 86
Enterprise governance: and unions, 84–87
Equal Opportunities Commission, 145
Ergo, 102
Ethnicity, 105
EU. *See* European Union
Europe, 68, 69. *See also* European Common Market; European Union; *various countries*
European Banking Federation, 257
European Commission, 214
European Common Market, 225, 227
European Community, 96
European Union (EU), 163, 173, 183, 184n.1, 189, 197, 223, 278
Eurostat, 199
Euskadi, 234
Externalization, 195–196

FABI, 172
FALCRI, 172
Family services, 164
Federación Independiente de Trabajadores del Crédito (FITC), 234, 251–252n.6
Federal Reserve, 34
Federation for Medium and Higher Employees (MHP), 260
Federcasse, 161, 171, 172
Fiba-Cisl, 172
Filiali capogruppo, 167–168
Finance Ministry (Netherlands), 257
Finance Sector Union (FSU), 67, 73, 74, 83, 88, 89, 90, 91
  enterprise governance and, 84–87

Finance Sector Union (FSU) (Australia), 63, 80
and enterprise governance, 84–87
Financial Sector Union (Finsec) (New Zealand), 100, 101, 111, 113, 115–116, 120
First Chicago, 60n. 7
First Direct, 131, 141, 143–144, 197
FISAC-CGIL, 172
FITC. See Federación Independiente de Trabajadores del Crédito
Fleet Financial Group, 35
FNV. See Dutch Federation of Trade Unions
FO. See Force Ouvrière
Fomento del Empleo, 231
Force Ouvrière (FO), 190, 217
Ford Motor Company, 35
Foreign-owned banks, 4, 45, 67, 96, 123n.2, 130, 224
Fortis group, 256, 259
Fourth Labor Government (New Zealand), 99
France, 4, 5, 11, 13, 18, 21, 27, 259
branch banking, 8, 229
competition and takeovers in, 196–197
economic recomposition in, 189–190
education in, 192–193
employment in, 9, 199–201
externalization in, 195–196
government management in, 187–188
job classifications, 202–204
labor law in, 190–191
labor relations in, 211–213
restructuring, 214–215
salary structure in, 207–211
sales culture in, 194–195
technology in, 193–194
telephone banking in, 197–198
training, 15, 16–17, 204–206
unions in, 25, 190–192
work organization in, 201–202
France Télécom, 193
French Confederation of Christian Workers (CFTC), 191, 217
Fringe benefits, 23
Front office, 39–40, 104, 105, 110–111, 120, 169, 263
FSU. See Finance Sector Union

Galicia, 234
GAN. See Groupement des Assurances Nationales

Gaullist period, 188
Gender: employment and, 105, 109, 136–137, 139(table), 143, 145. See also Women
Gendre, Pierre, 218
General Motors, 134
Geographic mobility, 212, 230–231
Germany, 4, 5, 7, 18, 20
banking regulations in, 292–293
branch banking, 8, 13, 229, 302–304
compensation policies, 21, 22, 308–309
competitive strategies, 287–288
direct banks in, 14, 310–311
employee participation in, 313–314
employment, 9, 17, 295–296, 297–300
industrial relations in, 28, 294–295
operating hours, 305–306
recruitment and training in, 306–308
retail banking, 300–302
services, 296–297
training in, 15–16, 293–294
unionism in, 24–25
universal banks in, 288–292
work organization in, 304–305
Giro institutions, 289
Glass-Steagal Act, 34
Gosset, M., 217
Great Britain. See United Kingdom
Groupement des Assurances Nationales (GAN), 198
Guigal, Michel, 217

Hay job evaluation, Hay Points, 113, 147, 210
HBV. See Union of the Employees in Commerce, Banks, and Insurance
Home banking services, 7, 75, 131, 132, 134, 164, 197, 263
Human resources, 25–26, 85, 112, 211, 279, 320–321, 324–325, 329–330
management of, 55–57, 108–109, 114, 118, 119, 138(table)
marketing strategies and, 327–328
unions and, 115–116, 283

IBIS. See Integrated Banking Information System
ICTs. See Information and communications technologies
Incentive pay, 53–54, 171
Incentives, 170–171, 308–309. See also Compensation

Indosuez bank, 197
Industrial Conciliation and Arbitration Act,
  98
Industrial groups, 189, 190
Industrial relations (IR), 4, 24, 320–321,
  324–325, 329–330. *See also* Collective
  bargaining; Unions
  in Australia, 85, 90
  deregulation and, 65–67
  and employees, 26–28
  in Germany, 294–295
  in Italy, 162, 175–176
  in the Netherlands, 279–280
  in Spain, 25, 233–234
  in the United Kingdom, 149–152
  in the United States, 9, 37
Industry Training Act, 97
Industry training organizations (ITOs), 97,
  112
Information and communications
  technologies (ICTs), 132
Information technology (IT), 39–40, 44,
  132–134, 154–155. *See also* Technology
ING-bank, ING-postbank. *See* Internationale
  Nederlanden Groep
INSEE, 208
Insurance, insurance companies, 4, 5, 35, 65,
  102, 258, 264
  in France, 189, 190, 197, 198
  in Germany, 296–297
  in the Netherlands, 259, 264
Insurance Union, 101
Integrated Banking Information System
  (IBIS), 104
Interest rates, 4, 34, 102
Internationale Nederlanden Groep (ING),
  256, 259, 265, 266, 268, 269, 271, 273,
  276, 277, 280, 282, 284
  works councils and, 278, 279
Internationalization, 69, 120, 162–163, 188,
  259
Internet services, 105, 155
Interstate banking, 34–35, 39
IT. *See* Information technology
Italy, 4, 5, 18, 22, 184n.2
  branch banking in, 8, 13, 229
  competition in, 162–163
  deregulation in, 159–160
  employment in, 9, 14–15, 17, 166–167,
    185n.12
  labor market in, 160–161, 184n.4
  labor relations in, 27, 171–176

management practices in, 177–179, 180–
  181
pay and incentives in, 170–171
profitability, 163–164
recruitment and job security in, 165–166,
  182–183
training in, 15, 161–162, 168–169, 181–
  182
unionism in, 24–25
wage setting in, 20, 175
work organization in, 167–168
ITOs. *See* Industry training organizations

Japan, 45, 60n.6, 187
JCNC. *See* Joint Consultative and
  Negotiating Committee
Jobs, 83, 274
  changes in, 14, 194–195, 213, 266, 297,
    299–300
  classification of, 192, 202–204, 206, 232,
    276, 280, 308–309, 310
  promotion and, 51–52
  security of, 17, 18, 45–46, 57, 63, 150, 161,
    182–183, 214–215
  skills and, 37, 111
Joint Consultative and Negotiating
  Committee (JCNC), 151

Labor costs, 19–21, 241
Labor government (Australia), 65
Labor law code, 190–191
Labor markets, 21, 53, 95, 190–192
  Australian, 72–74
  and career paths, 78–80
  deregulation of, 96–98
  Dutch, 259–261
  internal, 78–80
  in Italy, 160–161, 180, 184n.4
  in Spain, 230–231
  in the United States, 36–37, 58
Labor regulations, 10, 19, 36–37, 211, 213
Labour Relations Act, 99
Landesbanken-Girozentralen, 289
Layoffs, 18. *See also* Downsizing; Employees,
  reduction of
LeBorgne, Françoise, 217
LaGandre, Françoise, 218
Legislation, 95, 98, 99, 159, 180, 188, 292
LeMaitre, Pierre, 218
Lemee, M., 218
Liberalization, 223, 224
Licensing, 101, 102

Life insurance, 197
Lloyds Bank, 133, 137(table), 138(table),
    140, 143, 144, 146
  employment structure in, 153–154
  performance-related pay and, 147, 148–
    149
Lloyds Group Union, 149, 151
Lloyds/TSB, 130, 140, 141–142, 143, 151
Loans, 33, 34, 39, 46–47, 67–68, 76, 134,
    193
Lockart, Gilles, 218
Lombard policies, 292
Loos, Jocelyne, 217
Loyalty, 80–81
Luxembourg, 199

Mail order houses, 189
Management, 29, 123n.8, 143, 150, 155,
    156, 177–179, 180–181, 277, 313
  branch, 78–79, 245
  employment relationships and, 114–115
  government, 187–188
  human resources, 108, 109, 118, 119
  personnel, 135–136, 168
  and salary structure, 208, 210
  in Spain, 248–249
  structure and function of, 25–26
  unions and, 115–116, 142, 282
Management-by-objectives systems, 168
Manufacturing, 225
Marks and Spencer, 134
Marseillaise de Crédit, 197
Massy, Olivier Robert de, 216
Mayer, Michel, 216
MBAs, 49
MeesPierson, 256, 259, 268, 271–272, 273,
    279, 281, 282, 284
Men, 81, 82–83. See also Gender
Mendes Gans, 259
Mergers, 5, 7, 35, 43–44, 69, 102, 118, 256,
    258–259, 264
MHP. See Federation for Medium and
    Higher Employees
Middle offices, 187
Midland Bank, 130, 135, 142, 146, 148
  employment patterns at, 137(table),
    138(table), 140, 153–154
  telephone banking at, 141, 143
  unions, 150, 151
Ministry of Economic Affairs (Netherlands),
    258
Ministry of Labor (France), 192, 210

Ministry of Labor (Italy), 174
Mintzberg, H., 281
Mitterrand period, 188
Mobility: employment, 16, 270, 271–272,
    277
Moisson, Annie, 218
Money markets, 130
Mortgage banks, 258
Mortgage lenders, loans, 54, 67–68, 293
Moussy, Jean-Pierre, 218
Muldoon, Robert, 96

National Australia Bank, 64, 69, 70, 87, 88,
    96
National Bank Union-General Confederation
    of Cadres (SNB-CGC), 190, 215, 217
Nationalization, 188
National Mutual Bank, 102
National Mutual Life Association, 102
National Westminster (Nat West), 130,
    142–143, 145, 147, 150, 154
Nationsbank, 35
Nederlandse Bankiersvereniging (NBV), 257
Nederlandse Vereniging van Banken (NVB),
    257
Nederlands Instituut voor het Bank-en
    Effectenbedrijf (NIBE), 274, 275, 280, 283
Nerré, Jean-Pierre, 218
Netherlands, 5, 7, 8, 18, 21, 257, 281
  automation in, 262–263
  branch banking, 229, 263–264, 268–269
  careers in, 255–256
  compensation in, 20, 22, 276–277
  cost reduction in, 265–266
  employee participation in, 278–279
  human resources and industrial relations,
    279–280
  labor relations, 259–261
  mergers in, 258–259
  personal accounts in, 261–262
  segmentation, 264–265
  staff reductions in, 269–272
  training, 15, 16, 274–276
  unionism in, 24–25
  unions in, 282–283
  work-time reduction in, 272–273
Network Incentive Scheme, 147
New Zealand, 4, 5, 17, 20, 21, 23, 24, 26, 27,
    69, 259
  competition in, 101–102, 104–106
  deregulation and legislative reform in, 95–
    96, 119–120

employment in, 107–110, 121–122(tables), 123n.3
employment relations in, 98–99, 106–107, 114–115, 118–119
labor market deregulation in, 96–98
operating hours in, 12–13
technology in, 102–104
training, 15, 111–112
unions in, 22, 115–116, 123n.9
work organization in, 110–111
New Zealand Qualifications Authority (NZQA), 97
NIBE. See Nederlands Instituut voor het Bank-en Effectenbedrijf
NMB, 159. See also ING-bank
Northern Ireland, 69
Notter, Jean-Marie, 217
Noyello, T., 236
NZI Bank, 102
NZQA. See New Zealand Qualifications Authority

Occupational overuse syndrome (OOS), 105
Oil crises, 5, 96
OOS. See Occupational overuse syndrome
Operating costs, 154
Operating hours, 12–13, 77, 89, 111, 150, 197–198, 213, 305–306
ÖTV. See Public Employees Union
Outsourcing, 168, 185nn.8, 9

Pallas-Stern bank, 196
Paribas, 197, 198
Paris, Héliette, 218
Paternalism, 104, 106, 129
Pay. See Compensation
PC banking, 302
Pensions, 97
Performance, 22–23, 70, 71(table), 147, 148–149, 277, 308–309
Performance management approach (PMA), 148
Performance-related pay (PRP), 148
"Persistence" hypothesis, 4
Personal accounts, 261–262
Personal contact, 8
Personnel. See Employees; Management
Personnel departments, 118–119
Personnel costs, 9, 10(table)
Piore, Michael, 196
PMA. See Performance management approach

Poaching, 16, 21–22, 58, 79
Point of sale (POS) terminals, 40, 41
Poli-Simon, M., 218
Popular Front, 188
POS. See Point of sale terminals
Postbank (New Zealand), 101
Postbank (Netherlands), 257, 258, 260, 263, 269
Post Giro (Netherlands), 259, 261, 262, 263
Post office (France), 188
Post Office Bank (New Zealand), 95, 96
Post Office Savings Banks (Netherlands), 259
Post Office Union (New Zealand), 100, 101
Prices: competition in, 40–42, 70
Prices Surveillance Authority, 72
Privatization, 3, 5, 96, 188, 269, 326
in Australia, 64, 65
in Italy, 160, 177–178, 180
Processing centers, 132, 133, 141
Processing functions, 11, 75, 87, 105, 238
Productive mobilization, 244–245
Productivity, 39, 165
Profitability, 7, 10, 69, 163–164, 187, 302
Profit sharing, 147, 148
Promotion, 17, 18, 79
Protestant Christian Federation (CNV), 260
PRP. See Performance-related pay
PTT Post, 268–269
Public banks, 4–5
Public Employees Union (ÖTV), 294
PYMES, 236, 237

Rabo (Raiffeissen Bank Organization), 256, 258, 259, 268, 271, 273, 278, 279, 282
Recession, 73, 86, 100
Record keeping, 11
Recruitment, 17, 18, 60n.11, 80, 123n.7
in Germany, 306–308
in Italy, 161, 164–165, 168–169
in the Netherlands, 269, 270, 281
in the United Kingdom, 140, 145–146
in the United States, 49, 51, 56
Rediscount policies, 292
Registered banks, 102
Relationship banking, 264
Relationship-management strategy, 56–57
Remuneration. See Compensation
Reserve Bank (Australia), 65
Retail banking, 11, 13, 27, 39, 104, 140, 236
in Australia, 64, 67
in Germany, 296, 300–302, 311–312

Retail banking (cont.)
  in Italy, 177–178
  in the Netherlands, 261–262
  in New Zealand, 100, 106
Retail outlets, 12, 133, 134–135
Retrenchment, 265–266
Rothschild, 259
Roux-Rossi, Dominique, 206
Rural Bank, 96

St. George Bank, 69
Salaries, salary structure, 22, 175
  in Australia, 82–84, 89
  determination of, 19, 20, 147, 148, 209–211
  in Germany, 295, 308–309
  negotiation, 191–192
  structuring of, 207–208
Sales culture, 10, 12, 14, 15, 76, 87, 117, 146, 187, 193, 323
  bonuses and, 210–211
  client segmentation and, 304–305
  in France, 194–195
  in New Zealand, 103, 104, 105–106, 111
Salomon Brothers Inc., 35
Savings banks, 4, 5, 165, 251n.1, 258, 259
  in Germany, 288, 289, 292, 294, 311–312
Savings and loans, 34, 44, 46, 47, 49, 51, 59, 224, 228
SBV. See State Bank of Victoria
Scheer, Jacques, 217
Schwab, Michel, 218
Scotland, 69
Sears, 35
Securities, 4, 5, 34
Securities and Exchange Commission, 34
Segmentation, 264–265
Seniority, 17–18, 170, 232, 241, 246–247
Service(s), 8, 10, 60n.7, 142, 164, 323
  access and quality of, 43, 89, 90, 193–194, 229
  competition and, 70, 72, 106
  delivery of, 46–47, 76, 132, 146, 248
  and employment, 295–296
SG. See Société Générale
Shareholders, 70, 89–90
Shell, 205
Shopping malls, 12
Shop Trading Hours Act, 111
Sindicato de Trabajadores Vascos (ELA/STV), 234, 251n.6
Single European Market, 258

Skills, skill formation, 14, 16, 37, 97, 133, 295
  employer-driven, 97–98
  and human resources management, 327–328
  training and, 48–50, 111–112, 144, 239–241, 274–276
Smart cards, 132
SNB-CGC. See National Bank Union-General Confederation of Cadres
Socialist Party, 190
Social security, 193
Société Générale (SG), 190, 194, 197, 201, 208, 211
Solidarity, Unity, Democracy (SUD), 191
Spain, 5, 12, 18, 223, 226(table)
  branch banking, 8, 13
  compensation in, 20, 22, 23, 241–242
  cost reduction, 247–248
  deregulation in, 224–225
  employee involvement in, 243–246
  employment in, 9, 17, 231–233
  industrial relations in, 25, 27–28, 233–234
  labor market in, 230–231
  management in, 248–249
  restructuring, 228–230, 236–237
  technological change in, 227–228
  training and skill development, 15, 239–241
  unions in, 242–243, 246–247
Sparkassen, 288, 289, 294, 295
Sparkassenakademie, 294, 306, 307
Sparkassenfachwirt, 294
Sparkassenkaufmann, 294, 307, 311
Specialized banks, 288, 289
Staffing strategies, 18, 77, 90–91, 143, 153–154, 174, 214–215
  reduction, 199, 269–272
State Bank of New South Wales, 65
State Bank of Victoria (SBV), 65, 70, 88
State banks, 289
Stock market, 190
Strikes, 116
Students, 38
Subsidiaries, 45
SUD. See Solidarity, Unity, Democracy
SUEZ, 190
Superannuation, 97
Supermarkets, 12, 111, 134

Takeovers, 104, 118, 196–197
Taranaki Savings Bank (TSB), 96, 102

Taylorization, 14, 75, 141, 325
Teamwork, 148, 245
Technical services, 143
Technology, 3, 7–8, 13
  in Australia, 64, 68–69
  and competition, 296–297, 319–321
  in France, 193–194, 198
  information, 39–40, 132–134, 154–155
  in the Netherlands, 262–263
  in New Zealand, 102–104
  in Spain, 227–228
  in the United Kingdom, 129, 153
  in the United States, 33, 39–40
  and work organization, 14, 75, 110–111
Telebanking, 198
Telecommunication, 10
Telephone banking services, 7, 41, 68, 75,
  102, 105, 111, 164, 263, 302
  in France, 197–198
  in United Kingdom, 131, 141, 143–144
Telephone centers, 13
Tijdens, Ken, 265, 274, 284
Total quality management (TQM), 279
Trade Practices Commission (Australia), 65
Trading banks, 95, 123n.1, 130
Training, 38, 58, 60n.10, 231
  contracts for, 166–167
  and direct banks, 310–311
  employee, 15–17, 57, 81–82, 88–89, 91,
    143–145, 204–206
  in Germany, 293–294, 306–308
  in Italy, 161–162, 168–169, 181–182
  and job security, 109–110
  in the Netherlands, 274–276
  in New Zealand, 97, 111–112
  opportunities for, 27, 87–88
  and skill formation, 239–241
Training user groups (TUGs), 144
Transaction-based banking, 55
Travelers' Group, 35
Trust Bank (New Zealand) Limited, 100,
  101, 102
TSB, 142, 150. See also Taranaki Savings
  Bank
TUGs. See Training user groups

UAP. See Union des Assurances Parisiennes
UGT. See Unión General de Trabajadores
UIB-UAL, 172
Understaffing, 14
Unemployment, 96–97, 192
Unie BHLP. See Union of Clerical and

Commerical Staff
Union des Assurances Parisiennes (UAP),
  190
Unión General de Trabajadores (UGT), 234,
  251n.6
Unionism, 24–25, 63, 66–67, 260
Union of Clerical and Commercial Staff
  (Unie BHLP), 260
Union of the Employees in Commerce,
  Banks, and Insurance (HBV), 294–295,
  309
Union of the German Employees (DAG),
  295
Unionization, 172
Unions, 21–22, 24, 29, 77, 134, 142
  in Australia, 66–67, 91n.1
  and direct banks, 310–311
  and enterprise governance, 84–87, 88
  in France, 190–191, 202, 212
  in Germany, 294–295, 309
  in Italy, 162, 171, 172–173, 185n.12
  job classifications and, 202, 309
  in the Netherlands, 260–261, 269, 275,
    282–283
  in New Zealand, 99, 100–101, 115–116,
    123n.9
  and seniority, 246–247
  in Spain, 233, 234, 242–243, 246–247
  in the United Kingdom, 140, 149, 150–152
  and work-time reduction, 272–273
Unión Sindical Obrera (USO), 234, 251n.6
United Kingdom, 5, 8, 14, 17, 19, 26, 96,
  129
  branch banking in, 68, 130–131, 229
  career structure in, 152–153
  compensation in, 20, 21, 22–23, 147–149
  employment in, 9, 18, 24
  industrial relations in, 27, 149–152
  information technology in, 132–134
  marketing strategies, 134–135
  and the Netherlands, 259, 282
  processing systems in, 11–12
  staffing in, 136–140, 153–154
  training and recruitment in, 15, 143–146
  work organization in, 141–143
United States, 5, 7, 14, 27, 29n.2, 33, 38,
  60n.6, 69, 259
  branch banking, 8, 68
  compensation in, 23, 51–54
  competition in, 40–42
  deregulation in, 34–35
  employee compensation in, 20–21, 22

United States (cont.)
  employment in, 9, 18, 24
  employment relations in, 44–48
  information technology in, 39–40
  labor market, 36–37
  management structure and function in, 25–
    26
  mergers and acquisitions in, 43–44
  mass customization in, 42–43
  recruitment and promotion in, 18, 51
  training, 15, 48–50
  work organization in, 46–47, 201
Universal banks, 287, 288–292
Universities, 192–193, 204–205, 230–231,
    276, 307
USO. *See* Unión Sindical Obrera

Vallery, G., 216
VNO-NCW, 260
Volk- und Raiffeisenbanken, 288

Wages. *See* Compensation; Salaries, salary
    structure
Water, Michel, 218
Werkgeversvereniging in het Bankbedrijf
    (WGVB), 260, 276, 282, 284
Westpac Banking Corporation, 64, 69, 70,
    83, 87, 88, 102
WGVB. *See* Werkgeversvereniging in het
    Bankbedrijf
Wholesale banking, 41, 44–45, 51, 60, 100
Women, 16, 81, 82, 105
  benefits for, 145–146
  as branch managers, 78–79
  employment levels of, 18, 73–74, 109,
    136–137, 143, 167, 199, 200, 201(table),
    202, 231–232, 256, 274, 299
Work, 38(table), 39
  contracts for, 166, 167
  in direct banks, 310–311
  hours and, 197–198, 272–273
  intensification of, 14–15
  reorganization of, 9–10, 11–12, 46–47,
    74–77, 110–111, 141–143, 154, 167–
    168, 194–195, 201–202, 206–207, 213,
    238, 304–305, 321–324
Workers' Charter, 242
Works Council Act (Netherlands), 278
Works councils, 25, 278–279, 282